GAME WORN

BASEBALL TREASURES

from the Game's Greatest Heroes and Moments

WORN

STEPHEN WONG and **DAVE GROB**

Foreword by John Thorn

PHOTOGRAPHY BY FRANCESCO SAPIENZA

SMITHSONIAN BOOKS
WASHINGTON, DC

CONTENTS

"I'D HAVE PLAYED FOR NOTHING JUST TO GET TO WEAR THE UNIFORM,"

a young Babe Ruth said in 1914 after signing with Jack Dunn's Baltimore Orioles of the International League. Sure, he was the star of the St. Mary's Industrial Home team and knew that he now might have to work his way up from the bottom...but the raiment of the top club was what drove him, and countless other kids in scruffy baseball gear, to dream big. Not long ago, a Ruth jersey from 1920, the Babe's first year with the Yankees—the biggest club—sold for $4.4 million.

Yet such sales are not what account for the booming business of "authentic replica" jerseys and caps; the point of that is to keep the dream alive long past the point of truly believing it could be you down there, on the field. Fantasy baseball is not only a game played with stats online; fantasy is the very essence of being a fan, the idea that the strength of your belief will somehow tilt the game's outcome.

This is why game-worn uniforms have ascended to the pinnacle of the memorabilia hobby. Some vestige of an idol's heroism and personality—authenticity, if you will—attaches to the garment and its new possessor. Would Dr. Freud call this attraction fetishism? Yes, in the sense that the part stands in for the whole and offers some of the gratification provided by a larger relationship. But it is not "mere" fetishism of the sort one might easily scorn; there is a mystic chord of memory that arises from the ceremonial garment.

At the Baseball Hall of Fame, stop at Ruth's locker, forever open to display the Yankee uniform he last wore, and a shiver of unforeseen emotion comes over you.

This splendid book traces the story of game-worn uniforms from roughly 1900 onward, choosing that start date in large part because so few specimens from the 1800s have survived. Of course, baseball was played long before anyone thought that uniforms might be a good idea. Our first record of consistent team garb is from the Knickerbocker Base Ball Club, whose members adopted in 1849 an ensemble consisting of blue woolen pantaloons, white flannel shirt, and chip (straw) hat. Oddly, the Knickerbockers always wore pants, never knickerbockers (also known as knickers or knee breeches), even after Cincinnati innovated its calf-exposing, lady-thrilling red stockings in 1867. A Cincinnati paper noted:

> *Now, be it known that knickerbockers, today so common—the showing of the manly leg in varied colored hose—was unheard of, and when Harry Wright occasionally appeared with the scarlet stockings, young ladies' faces blushed as red as its hue, and many high-toned members of the club denounced the innovation as immoral and indecent.*

Hall of Fame pioneer George Wright, shortstop of the undefeated Cincinnati Red Stockings of 1869, recalled that in the 1860s, "the regularly organized clubs of the time wore uniforms which would seem exceedingly strange and grotesque at the present day. In those days players wore long pants of various colors, either of grey, white, dark blue, or of a mixed check material. Extending down the side of the leg on the seam was sewed a broad white or red stripe, which gave, as you may imagine, a decidedly military air to the garment, in marked contrast to that worn today."

If sport is sublimated warfare, one may understand the appeal of differentiating clubs by the styles and colors of their uniforms. Baseball uniforms of the 1870s and

EXPOSITION PARK

Photo Copyright
1904 by
The Geo. R. LAWRENCE Co.
Chicago

PITTSBURG-NEW-YORK-BASEBALL-GAME

1880s erupted into a rainbow that owed nothing to national aspiration or military tradition but much to the theater: skullcaps of different colors assigned by position played (Chicago, 1876), striped silk jerseys (all teams, 1882), and blood-red flannel uniforms, top and bottom (Chicago, 1883; Louisville, 1888).

Jerry Seinfeld said in one of his routines, "Loyalty to any one sports team is pretty hard to justify, because the players are always changing; the team could move to another city. You're actually rooting for the clothes when you get right down to it....Laundry. We're rooting, we're screaming, about laundry here." Unknowingly,

Seinfeld was echoing an observation offered by Pliny the Younger in the context of chariot races in 109 CE: "If indeed it were the swiftness of the horses, or the skill of the men that attracted them, there might be some pretense for it [the passion of the crowd]. But it is the dress they like; it is the dress that takes their fancy. And if, in the midst of the course and the contest, the different parties were to change colors, their different partisans would change sides and instantly desert the very same men and horses whom just before they were eagerly following....Such mighty charms, such wondrous power reside in the color of a paltry tunic!"

Panoramic photograph by George R. Lawrence of a game between the Pittsburgh Pirates and the New York Giants, Exposition Park, August 23, 1904

BEFORE TURNING A SINGLE PAGE OF

this book, before pouring over the visual feast of twentieth-century game-worn major league baseball uniforms shown on these pages, and before digesting the facts and figures we present about them, we want you to understand that this book is about work garments and their connection to the players who wore them. While always prized and admired, baseball uniforms were long considered to be consumable business expenses for major league clubs. Only during the latter part of the twentieth century did they begin to capture the attention of collectors.

We've been accustomed to saving cards, autographs, programs, ticket stubs, and the occasional game-used bat or glove gifted from players. But the work clothing of the players has become another valuable connection between fans and those who graced the field of America's pastime, and a rarer one than other ephemera of the game. For example, while more than 3,900 professionally graded examples of a 1955 Topps Roberto Clemente rookie baseball card exist, there are likely only a dozen surviving examples of Clemente's game-worn uniforms (in any condition and spanning his entire career) in private hands. A baseball card provides us with a player's likeness and a connection to our youthful passions. A ticket or scorecard reminds us of the happiness of days spent in the sunshine at the ballpark. An autographed ball, a bat, or a glove may elicit excitement because of the connection to a ballplayer who touched the item. But game-worn uniforms—jerseys, trousers, caps, and jackets—provide the closest connection of all. They personify ballplayers, especially famous ones. A number 42 Brooklyn Dodgers jersey, for example, is connected to only one name in all of baseball: Jackie Robinson.

In addition to the team logo, name, or home city, game-worn uniforms were frequently personalized for inventory purposes, with the ballplayer's name stitched into the collar or tail of the jersey. Uniform numbers became more common after 1931, and by the mid-1930s, every major league player had his number attached to his jersey. Many players wore the same number throughout their careers: number 3 for Babe Ruth, 4 for Lou Gehrig, and 5 for Johnny Bench. Other players may be iconically linked to specific numbers, but they began their careers wearing numbers known today only to the most rabid fans. These include 9 for Joe DiMaggio in 1936, 14 for Willie Mays in 1951, and 5 for Hank Aaron in 1953. In the early 1960s, some major league teams began placing players' names in large letters above or, in the case of the Cincinnati Reds, below the numbers on the backs of jerseys. Tracing the history of such details connects us to the larger history of the game itself.

For generations, ballplayers' identities have been inextricably tied to their uniforms. It would be difficult, for example, to envision Ted Williams in anything but a Boston Red Sox uniform, or to separate Joe DiMaggio from Yankee pinstripes or Stan Musial from the St. Louis Cardinals colors. An entire season's worth of wear and tear, of blood, sweat, and tears, shows up on a game-worn uniform, imbuing its fabric with unique personal history. It's not surprising, then, that uniforms hold an evocative power for most players. Stan Hack, third baseman for the Chicago Cubs from 1932 to 1947, remembered the first time he pulled on the Chicago colors. "My first day with the team was unforgettable—not because of my performance, but because I got to put on that uniform. I'll never forget it, the sun hitting me as I emerged from the dugout for the first time, feeling immortal in a garment so glorious. After the game, even though [it was] sweaty and soiled, I felt obliged to hang it with the same care as I found it. As I left the locker room that day, I turned to look at it once more, feeling as if I was leaving a bit of myself there."

Uniforms are also treasured because, as collectors often find, examples from specific clubs or time periods in baseball's early years might no longer exist, in any condition. Even when such artifacts can be found, it is common to discover that they were patched, altered, or issued to another player. Some might have been given

New York Giants slugger Mel Ott choosing his bat in the dugout steps, 1936

a new number, name, or organizational identification when they were passed to minor league teams or spring-training hopefuls. The uniforms that do survive provide invaluable insight into the history of the game, and they reveal what American life looked like before the advent of color photography. Their fascinating kaleidoscope of styles, fabrics, and colors exudes life and suggests the character of both bygone eras and the players who wore these relics. Like the programs sold at games and the advertising signs in ballpark outfields, game-worn uniforms were a vital part of the viewing experience for fans, a delight that can't be fully appreciated by viewing historical black-and-white photos. Take the New York Giants road jersey shown opposite, which was worn by Hall of Famer Mel Ott throughout the 1938 season. Its aesthetic appeal is much more apparent when you can see the actual object than it is when you view old photos of the uniform, such as one of Ott choosing his Louisville Slugger (page 8).

Uniforms also reveal the evolution of textiles and fashion, as well as revolutions in how famous (and not-so-famous) players and clubs chose to publicly express themselves. Linda Baumgarten, textile and costume curator at the Colonial Williamsburg Foundation in Virginia, had this to say about the power of collectible clothing: "An eighteenth-century suit or an heirloom dress is far more than a tangible survivor. It is an event in history that continues to happen. Wrinkled by years of use, stretched and shaped by the body that wore it, clothing is the most intimately human of the surviving decorative arts. In some ways, old clothing brings the original wearers back to life." Baumgarten's observations certainly apply to game-worn baseball uniforms, too, which have become the focal point of many collections of baseball artifacts. The objects you'll see in this book, each among the treasures of its collector, were gathered by individuals and organizations including Thomas Tull, the Bill DeWitt family, the St. Louis Cardinals Hall of Fame and Museum, Gary Cypres, Dan Scheinman, and the National Baseball Hall of Fame and Museum. They generously provided us with access to countless uniforms, many of which have never before been seen by the public. These uniforms were breathtakingly captured, in whole and in microscopic part, through the creative and technical genius of photographer Francesco Sapienza.

You will see uniforms worn by big league luminaries such as Christy Mathewson, Walter Johnson, Babe Ruth, Lou Gehrig, Ted Williams, Stan Musial, Jackie Robinson, Willie Mays, Hank Aaron, Roberto Clemente, Sandy Koufax, Johnny Bench, Lou Brock, Dave Winfield, Fernando Valenzuela, and Randy Johnson. Some were worn during baseball's

"To develop a complete mind: Study the science of art. Study the art of science. Learn how to see. Realize that everything connects to everything else."

—Leonardo da Vinci

most famous moments, such as the flannel Pittsburgh Pirates home uniform that Bill Mazeroski wore in Game 7 of the 1960 World Series, when he hit one of the most incredible home runs in baseball history. And maybe you first saw David Cone's knit New York Yankees home jersey on television or at Yankee Stadium when he pitched his perfect game on July 18, 1999. You'll also appreciate the allure of rare-style uniforms donned by lesser-known men of the diamond and, we hope, deepen your admiration of the players who wore these extraordinary garments. Finally, we will walk you through some uniform details and history—such as buttons, zippers, stripes, patches, and aspects of manufacturing, use, and care—that until now you've perhaps noted only in the background of games and photos.

We have long felt that game-worn baseball uniforms are something special, so, several years ago, we committed ourselves to telling their story. Our book was shaped by Stephen's demonstrated passion for the history of the game and its players and by his lifelong desire to collect, preserve, research, and share its most significant artifacts. Our effort was equally influenced and enhanced by Dave's many decades of intense historical and scientific study of major league baseball uniforms. Like many things in life, baseball is a combination of art and science. And that's also true of the story we have set out to tell.

Mel Ott's game-worn 1938 New York Giants road jersey. The orange patch on the left sleeve, which was applied to all New York-based teams' jerseys in 1938, commemorates the New York World's Fair, which started in 1939.

Photograph of the American League All-Star Team before the Addie Joss Benefit Game, taken by Louis Van Oeyen, League Park, July 24, 1911

THE DEADBALL ERA

1900–1919

Professional baseball was organized into two major leagues in the first year of the twentieth century, and by that time the game was governed by a rulebook and agreed-upon conventions. Spalding's Professional Deadball, as the rubber-center ball used during the period was called, lent its name to a time when the game moved quickly and scores were low, since it was difficult for batters to hit that ball into the stands of large, open ballparks. The batter's job was further complicated by pitchers' liberal use of the spitball, legal at the time, and other trickery by moundsmen who worked to keep the ball in play as long as possible, and often for an entire game.

Batters used heavy bats and did not attack pitches aggressively. Teams relied on strategy, including pitching, the hit-and-run, singles, bunts, and stolen bases to win games. Grown men and boys alike devoured the sports pages and dime novels, eager to follow the exploits and chart the accomplishments of John McGraw, Christy Mathewson, Ty Cobb, Honus Wagner, and "Shoeless" Joe Jackson. While these accounts were long on prose, they were nearly void of photographs or illustrations. What the players looked like and what they wore were often mysteries to those who had yet to see them play.

Spalding dominated uniform manufacture and production of equipment, and players wore loose-fitting, heavy wool flannel garments that must have been uncomfortable in the heat of summer. Players typically were issued one set of home and road uniforms, and surviving examples are extremely rare. They are distinguished by a variety of collar styles, lack of player numbers, sleeve lengths that frequently reach the wrist, and player attribution either sewn into the garments or handwritten on laundry tags.

Coombs   Th

MR. COLLEGE BASEBALL

JACK COOMBS 1906 Philadelphia Athletics Rookie Home Jersey

John Wesley Coombs entered Colby College in Maine in 1902 and majored in chemistry. An excellent student, he became the first Colby student to earn a bachelor of science degree. Coombs was accepted to graduate school at MIT and intended to become a chemist—until Tom Mack (brother of Philadelphia Athletics manager Connie Mack) intervened. As a pitcher who also played every other position, including catcher, in emergencies, Coombs had led Colby to several Maine collegiate championships and in summers played for area semiprofessional teams. Mack, who lived in Worcester, Massachusetts, followed Coombs's college and semipro career, and in 1906, he convinced his brother to make a trip to Maine to meet the Colby senior.

"Chemistry is a hard and tiresome road to independence," Connie Mack told Coombs. "It will take years for you to acquire anything near the competence that a few short seasons on the diamond will promise you. Take my advice and join the Athletics, and you will never regret the move." Coombs heeded Mack's advice and immediately after graduation boarded a train to Philadelphia to join the big-league team.

Coombs shared mound rotation in the 1906 season with three veterans who had been the catalysts of the Athletics' 1905 American League (AL) pennant: Rube Waddell, who led the AL in wins (27), strikeouts (287), and ERA (1.48); Eddie Plank, who won 24 games; and Charles Albert "Chief" Bender, who chalked up 18 victories. All three were well on their way to Cooperstown, but Coombs pulled his own weight. He debuted on July 5 with a seven-hit shutout to defeat the Washington Senators, 3–0. On September 1, he struck out 18 batters, a major league record at the time, in an epic 24-inning victory over Joe Harris and the Boston Americans. "That performance," according to the *Sporting News*, "has made the name of Coombs a household word, and no matter what he does from now out, the fact will never be forgotten that Coombs, just out of Colby College, pitched and won the longest complete-game ever played." Although several major league games have since exceeded 24 innings, Coombs still holds the record for the longest complete-game victory, a record unlikely ever to be broken given today's convention of using relief pitchers.

Detail of Philadelphia Athletics team showing Jack Coombs, 1911

"I have never said a word as to whether this player or that player should be in the Hall of Fame. I have confidence in the men who are selected to make the judgment. However, I think I ought to break the rule to put in a few words for the late Jack Coombs. Coombs was a great pitcher, who could strike out Joe Jackson, one of the game's greatest hitters when he was with the Chicago White Sox, on three curveballs. He was as fine a fielding pitcher as you will see, a switch hitter who could deliver the run, and a man who never let down the team in a hard game."

—Frank "Home Run" Baker, following his own election to the Hall of Fame in 1955

Jack Coombs with his
Philadelphia Athletics
teammates, 1911

Coombs wore this off-white wool flannel jersey
(page 15) featuring a negligee collar (see page 289 in the
Compendium) during 1906 games at Columbia Park,
home of the Athletics until they moved to Shibe Park
in 1909. The A's, as sportswriters referred to them, were
the only team in the early twentieth century, with the
exception of the Washington Nationals in 1905 and
1906, to use the team nickname on uniforms. The Boston
Red Sox and Chicago Cubs came close by using pictorial
references to their nicknames—the Red Sox uniforms
featured a slanted red stocking and the Cubs used a bear
cub symbol. But other clubs in both leagues, including
the Cleveland Naps, Detroit Tigers, and Chicago White
Sox, decorated their flannels with athletic felt lettering
(see page 269 in the Compendium) of the city name
or its first letter applied to the chest area. Philadelphia,
on the other hand, applied an *A* team logo (the first

letter of Athletics) in royal-blue script. The *A* on
Coombs's flannel has faded to lavender over the course
of the century.

The style of the A's uniform remained essentially
the same from 1906 to 1910. Coombs's performance,
however, reached new heights. In 1910, he rediscovered
his overhand drop curve and recorded one of the most
dominant pitching seasons in baseball history, posting
a 31–9 record, 1.30 ERA, and 13 shutouts (still an
American League record) to vault the Athletics to the
pennant by 14½ games. He capped off the season with
three complete-game victories in the best-of-seven
World Series against the Chicago Cubs, becoming the
second player in the majors to accomplish that feat (the
first was Christy Mathewson, whose New York Giants
beat the Athletics in the 1905 World Series). Years later,
when sportswriter Fred Lieb asked Connie Mack about

Derrick   Morgan   Plank   Danforth   Murphy   Barry   Lord   McInnis   Hartsel   Van zelt

mpions 1911

Coombs's performance in 1910, the A's skipper replied, "Jack was magnificent that season. No pitcher ever did more for a manager."

After two more Fall Classic victories, in 1911 and 1913, the Athletics' fortunes began to fade. The "Miracle" Braves swept the A's in the 1914 World Series, and financial issues forced Mack to dismantle the team. Following his release from the A's, Coombs signed with the Brooklyn Robins and in 1915 was 15–10 with a 2.58 ERA. On July 2 of that year, he pitched against—and defeated—the Giants' Christy Mathewson for the first time since the 1911 World Series. He repeated the result on August 17, keeping his perfect record against the Giants legend intact. In 1916, Coombs posted a 13–8 record with a 2.66 ERA and helped Brooklyn to its first World Series appearance. Although the Dodgers lost the Series to the Boston Red Sox in five games, Coombs

started and won Game 3, 4–3, against Carl Mays, giving Brooklyn its only victory. The win boosted Coombs's World Series record to 5–0.

Toward the end of the 1918 season, Coombs announced his retirement from the majors. Later he became a college coach at Williams (head coach, 1921–24), Princeton (pitching coach, 1925–28), and Duke (head coach, 1929–52). While at Duke, he authored the leading instructional book of the era, *Baseball—Individual Play and Team Strategy*, in 1938, which eventually was used at 187 colleges and universities and hundreds of high schools across the country. His accomplishments would earn him the title "Mr. College Baseball."

Coombs died on April 15, 1957. The baseball fields at Colby College and Duke University are named in his honor.

THE HUMAN CRAB

JOHNNY EVERS 1909 Chicago Cubs Road Jersey

An excellent bunter, accomplished base stealer, and reliable second baseman who often earned the best strikeout/walk ratio in the National League, Johnny Joseph Evers was considered one of the most cerebral and best all-around players of the Deadball Era. In the famed "Merkle's Boner" play, Giants baserunner Fred Merkle failed to touch second base, a gaffe that ultimately cost the Giants the pennant in 1908. Not only did Evers notice Merkle's mistake, he also made sure that the umpire was aware of it. "All there is to Evers is a bundle of nerves, a lot of woven wire muscles, and the quickest brain in baseball," said Chicago sportswriter Hugh Fullerton. "He has invented and thought out more plays than any man of recent years."

Evers's nickname, the "Human Crab," was originally conferred due to his unorthodox manner of sliding over to ground balls before guzzling them up, but most considered it better suited to his contentious disposition. Evers, who weighed only 125 pounds, was an argumentative, high-strung screamer best known for his fearlessness and nervous energy. "They claim he is a crab, and perhaps they are right," said Cleveland Indians manager Joe Birmingham. "But I would like to have 25 such crabs playing for me. If I did, I would have no doubts over the pennant. They would win hands down."

Birmingham had foresight. Evers helped lead the Cubs to four National League pennants and two World Series championships, in 1907 and 1908 (the latter being the last ever won by the Cubs). In 1909, the club would commemorate the franchise's Fall Classic reign with a new uniform style for road games—the one shown opposite was worn by Evers—that featured the city name "Chicago" vertically along the front placket (see page 293 in the Compendium). This was the first occasion when the full team name (city and nickname) appeared on a major league baseball uniform. The style was a hit with tobacco and caramel candy companies, which issued baseball cards depicting Cubs players wearing their 1909 Cubs road uniforms.

Although the Cubs would not repeat their 1908 World Series triumph, Franklin Pierce Adams's famous verse, "Baseball's Sad Lexicon"—which first appeared in the *New York Evening Mail* on July 12, 1910—represents a quaint souvenir from a bygone era, when the Human Crab roamed the infield with shortstop Joe Tinker and first baseman Frank Chance and Cubs fans had their last taste of autumn glory.

These are the saddest of possible words:
"Tinker to Evers to Chance."
Trio of Bear Cubs and
fleeter than birds,
"Tinker to Evers to Chance."
Ruthlessly pricking our gonfalon bubble,
Making a Giant hit into a double,
Words that are weighty with
nothing but trouble:
"Tinker to Evers to Chance."

Johnny Evers at the Polo Grounds before a game against the Giants, 1909

Glove and official National League baseball from ca. 1909 atop Evers's jersey

MANAGING IN THE BIG LEAGUES

FRED LAKE 1909 Boston Red Sox Road Uniform

"I n order to become a big-league manager," Leo Durocher once said, "you have to be in the right place at the right time. That's rule number one." This counsel from Leo the Lip, one of the game's most prolific managers, couldn't be more appropriate to Fred Lovett Lake. In 1887, the 20-year-old Lake began his lifelong career in baseball, with the Salem (Massachusetts) Baseball Club. He then played for teams in Dover, New Hampshire, and Hingham, Massachusetts. Following the 1890 season with the Moncton team in the New Brunswick Provincial League, where he was captain and manager, Lake spent a season with the Boston Beaneaters of the National League before embarking on a two-year minor league tour with Milwaukee and Wilkes-Barre. Next up was the Louisville Colonels in 1894, a two-year stint in the minors with Toronto and Kansas City, and a brief stop with the Pittsburgh Pirates in 1898. Lake then wound up back in Massachusetts with teams in Lowell, New Bedford, and Lawrence.

Manager Fred Lake leaping in the air, 1909

> "And this is good old Boston / The home of the bean and the cod / Where the Lowells talk only to Cabots / And the Cabots talk only to God."
>
> —Toast given at Holy Cross alumni dinner, Boston, 1910

On August 28, 1908, the 41-year-old Lake—nicknamed the "Baseball Tourist"—was finally in the right place at the right time. Boston Red Sox owner John L. Taylor hired him to manage his struggling team, which had dropped below .500 under James "Deacon" McGuire's watch. With Lake at the helm, the Red Sox went 22–17 in their last 39 games, finishing 75–79 and at fifth place in the league.

In 1909, the year in which Lake wore this gray flannel Boston Red Sox road uniform (opposite), the team improved to 88–63, advancing to third place. Despite Tris Speaker's poor batting performance (.224 average) in 1908, Lake made Speaker his full-time center fielder in 1909. Speaker would bat .309 that year en route to a Cooperstown career. Lake put rookie and future Hall of Famer Harry Hooper in right field and Smoky Joe Wood (who went 11–7 that year) on the mound. The Red Sox had turned things around, and hopes were high for a pennant in 1910. But following the 1909

season, Lake asked Taylor for a raise. Taylor claimed that it wasn't Lake's managing that had led to the team's improvement and denied his request. Both men refused to compromise. Lake left to manage the Boston Doves of the National League in 1910, and Taylor hired Patsy Donovan to run the Red Sox.

Lake's tenure with the Red Sox may have been brief, but his uniform featured here is timeless. One of the few known surviving examples of a Red Sox uniform from the Deadball Era, this extraordinary relic represents a milestone in the Boston Americans' Red Sox identity. In 1907, the Boston Doves had opened their season with all-white uniforms to complement their nickname. They eliminated red trimmings, especially in the stockings. Most clubs in the American League were using blue or navy blue on their flannels, so red became an attractive option for the Boston Americans after their crosstown neighbor had abandoned the color.

The new home and road uniforms for the 1908 season, which featured a slanted red stocking symbol with "Boston" in white capital letters on the chest area, along with solid red stockings, made it clear that the Boston Americans were now officially the Red Stockings, or Red Sox. The following year, the team continued to wear red stockings but reverted to the city name alone on the jersey, featured in red, as shown on Lake's flannel. This was the first time in Red Sox franchise history that the city name was represented in red on team uniforms.

THE PEERLESS LEADER

FRANK CHANCE 1909–10 Chicago Cubs home uniform

I don't think any player in the game, with the exception of Ty Cobb, did more brilliant work for his team than Frank Chance," wrote teammate Johnny Evers. "He was a great batter, a great fielder, and a great base runner." Frank Leroy Chance was discovered by Cubs outfielder Bill Lange while playing summer league games in California in 1897. Chance was studying to be a dentist at the time, and he joined the Cubs in spring 1898 as a back-up catcher and outfielder. He found his calling at first base and on the basepaths in 1903, when he stole a National League record 67 bases.

Chance became the Cubs manager in 1905 and achieved a .644 winning percentage in seven and a half seasons. He was known for his fighting spirit and as an inspiration to teammates. Chicago sportswriter Charles Dryden dubbed him the "Peerless Leader" in 1906, when the Cubs won 116 games en route to their first World Series appearance. "He is the personification of affability off the field and his Cubs like nothing better than to be invited to smoke, eat, or drink with him or to listen when he is in a conversational mood," wrote *Baseball Magazine*'s Richard Lardner, "but not even his best friend could say that he is a pleasant party to have around when a close game is in progress."

"If [Frank Chance] has to choose between accepting a pair of spikes in a vital part of his anatomy and getting a put-out, or dodging the spikes and losing the put-out, he always takes the put-out."

—Christy Mathewson, *Pitching in a Pinch*, 1912

Chance was hardnosed and tough, with a relentless will to win. He threw beer bottles at fans in Brooklyn, assaulted Giants pitcher Joe McGinnity during a game, and was called "the greatest amateur brawler of all time" by boxing legends Jim Corbett and John L. Sullivan. When the Cubs lost, not even his wife could appease him. After a particularly difficult defeat, he arrived home in a foul mood, refusing to talk or eat. "Don't worry, dear. You still have me," his wife murmured. "I know that," Chance snarled, "but many a time this afternoon, I'd have traded you for a base hit."

The team underwent a number of name changes following its founding in 1876: White Stockings, Orphans, Remnants, and Rainmakers. The nickname "Cubs" surfaced around 1902, and Chance told sportswriters that he liked being a Cub. In 1908, new uniforms featured the team emblem, as seen on this white flannel jersey (opposite), of a lackadaisical bear holding a bat enclosed within a *C*, for Chicago. Chance wore this flannel during games in 1909 and 1910 at West Side Park—home of the Cubs until 1916, when they moved to Weeghman Park, known today as Wrigley Field. In 1909, the Cubs switched to a cadet-style collar (see page 272 in Compendium) from the negligee collar featured on the 1906 Jack Coombs Philadelphia Athletics jersey.

Frank Chance and his Cubs with their polar bear mascot before a game, 1908

THE "$11,000 BEAUTY"

RUBE MARQUARD 1911 New York Giants Home Uniform

Rube Marquard by photographer Charles M. Conlon, 1912

> "A ballplayer? What do you mean? How can you make a living being a ballplayer? I don't understand why a grown man would wear those funny-looking suits in the first place."
>
> —Fred Marquard, father of Rube Marquard

Sheet music featuring Marquard and his future wife Blossom Seeley on the cover atop his 1911 New York Giants home uniform

Richard William "Rube" Marquard was born in Cleveland on October 9, 1886, to Fred and Lena Marquard. Fred, the chief engineer for the city of Cleveland, insisted that his son get an education, but all Rube wanted to do was play baseball. As a teenager, he joined the Telling Ice Cream Company, which paid him $15 per week to deliver ice cream and $10 to pitch for the company team on Sunday afternoons. Marquard also worked as a batboy for the Cleveland Naps, where he befriended future Hall of Famer Napoleon Lajoie, third baseman Bill Bradley, and others. "So by the time I was only fifteen or sixteen, I knew a lot of ballplayers, and I had my heart set on becoming a Big Leaguer myself," Marquard told author Lawrence Ritter.

In June 1906, Marquard traveled from Cleveland to Waterloo, Iowa, by hopping freight trains, sleeping in open fields, and hitching rides, all for a tryout with a team in the Iowa State League. Despite pitching two solid games, he was not offered a contract. Dejected but not defeated, Marquard returned home and played in the Cleveland semipro leagues until he signed with Canton of the Central League. For two years, Marquard dominated the minor leagues, winning 23 games at Canton in 1907 and 28 the following year for Indianapolis in the American Association.

In 1908, the Giants purchased Marquard's contract from Indianapolis for $11,000, by far the most ever paid for a ballplayer. New York headlines called him the "$11,000 Beauty." But after Marquard hit the first batter he faced, then gave up triples to Hans Lobert and Bob Bescher of the Cincinnati Reds, sportswriters dubbed him the "$11,000 Lemon." "I was so badly rattled I didn't get over it all winter," Marquard recalled. "I lost confidence in myself completely and those calls, 'take him out,' '$11,000 lemon,' and so on, they ring in my ears yet."

Marquard's luck changed in 1911, the year he donned this pinstriped flannel New York Giants home uniform, which misspells his name as "Marquardt," stitched in white thread in the collar to the left of the Spalding manufacturers' tag. From 1904 to 1907, the Giants applied a block NY monogram made of athletic felt to the front of the jerseys. Starting in 1908, the club created a new symbol by merging the *N* and the *Y*. This rendition can be seen on the left sleeve of Marquard's flannel, and it became a traditional element on New York Giants uniforms until 1958, when the franchise moved to San Francisco.

From 1911 to 1913, Marquard, who earned his nickname because he reminded fans of pitching great Rube Waddell, helped the Giants secure three National

League pennants by winning 73 games, including a 19-game winning streak in 1912 (20, according to modern scoring methods), which remains a major league record. In 1911, he led the league in strikeouts (237), and the following year he led the league with 26 wins. In 1913, Marquard finished 23–10, with only 49 walks in 288 innings.

Marquard became an overnight celebrity. He starred in a silent movie, *Rube Marquard Wins,* in 1912, and he sang, danced, and joked on vaudeville stages across the country with leggy Broadway dame Blossom Seeley. The act was popular, and each of them earned $1,000 a week. The two had a steamy affair that included Marquard using the fire escape of an Atlantic City hotel to flee Blossom's husband. Blossom, who is featured on the red sheet music "Those Ragtime Melodies," situated on top of the jersey on the previous page, divorced

her husband and, three months' pregnant, married Marquard in March 1913. "We're a great battery, this little girl and I," Marquard told a reporter.

Back on the diamond, Marquard would spend the balance of his career with the Brooklyn Robins (later renamed the Dodgers), Cincinnati Reds, and Boston Braves. He won 13 games with a career-best 1.58 ERA for the pennant-winning Robins in 1916, was 19–12 the following year, and went 17–14 in 1921 for the Reds. Marquard retired in 1925 after four mediocre years with the Boston Braves.

Marquard's relationship with Seeley faded, and the couple divorced in 1920. Just before the start of the 1921 season, Marquard married Naomi Malone. After the 1925 season, Marquard managed in the minor leagues for a few seasons and then settled into a quiet life with Naomi in Baltimore and, in the winter, Coral

Marquard (front row, fourth from right) in a New York Giants team photograph, 1912

Gables, Florida. He took on a new interest: betting on horse races at tracks such as Pimlico and Belmont. Naomi died on July 21, 1954, and Marquard, not one to handle loneliness, remarried in October 1955, this time to the wealthy widow Jane Hecht Guggenheimer, whom he had met on a cruise three weeks before their marriage. Jane shared Marquard's passion for sports, including tennis, golf, and bowling, and the couple even took up ballroom dancing. It seemed that the Marquard story was coming to an end.

In 1966, however, Lawrence Ritter, a New York University economics and finance professor, traveled across the United States and Canada looking for old-time baseball players who could tell him about their lives in the big leagues in the 1890s and the early years of the twentieth century. Ritter recorded conversations with 22 ballplayers, including Marquard. He compiled his interviews in *The Glory of Their Times: The Story of the Early Days of Baseball Told by the Men Who Played It*, which became one of baseball's literary masterpieces. Marquard took some fictional liberty with his past—he romanticized his hobo-style train trip to Iowa and downplayed his scandalous affair with Blossom Seeley. But his story captured the essence of the game during the Deadball Era, and it was featured as the first chapter in Ritter's book. A new awareness of Marquard and his exploits surfaced, and Cooperstown took notice. "I had a lot of fun playing ball and made pretty good money, too," Marquard recalled long after his playing days. "The only regret I have in baseball is that never in my life did I get to see Ty Cobb play." Although he never saw the Georgia Peach, Marquard joined him in Cooperstown when the Veterans Committee elected him, Satchel Paige, and Harry Hooper into the Hall of Fame in 1971.

HARRY AND HIS STRIKING RED BLAZER

HARRY HOOPER 1912 World Series Boston Red Sox Mackinaw Coat

On September 16, 1903, Barney Dreyfuss (owner of the National League's Pittsburgh Pirates) and Henry Killilea (owner of the American League's Boston Pilgrims, later renamed the Red Sox) agreed to play a best-of-nine postseason competition. Boston won, five games to three, and that event is considered the first modern World Series. Generations of baseball followers have embraced the event, nicknamed the Fall Classic, as the sport's sacred crucible, in which legends, dynasties, and even tragedies have been immortalized.

The Boston Red Sox returned to the World Series in 1912, this time to play John McGraw, Christy Mathewson, Rube Marquard, and the New York Giants. Author Mike Vaccaro maintains that the 1912 event "would elevate the World Series from a regional October novelty to a national obsession....And they would deliver what remains, nearly a century later, the greatest World Series ever played—so great, in fact, that in all future years, both words would be permanently capitalized.... The World Series was really born in 1912."

Game 1 of the Series was played on October 8, 1912, a sunny, cool, and breezy day at the Polo Grounds in New York. Dignitaries in attendance included Massachusetts governor Eugene Foss, Boston mayor Honey Fitzgerald, and his New York counterpart, William Gaynor. Ty Cobb, Walter Johnson, and Detroit manager Hughie Jennings were also in the stands, along with "well-known actors, actresses, Wall Street speculators, sporting men, pretty girls, their good looking mothers and clergymen," according to the *New York Times*.

Vaccaro describes what happened next in his book, *The First Fall Classic: The Red Sox, the Giants, and the Cast of Players, Pugs, and Politicos Who Reinvented the World Series in 1912:*

> At exactly 12:45, with the bleachers and most of the grandstand already packed to the gills, the long gate at the bottom of the right-field fence creaked loudly and began to open, parting the Baltimore Whiskey and Peter Doelger ads in half....But when McGraw strode purposefully out of the darkness a few seconds later, the solemnity was replaced by a roar that rattled the year-old yard to its brand-new foundation. Mathewson came next, of course, followed by Rube Marquard and Jeff Tesreau, then Snodgrass and Merkle and Doyle the captain, who was the only one who waved at the adoration. The Giants wore brand-new uniforms, but they were of the exact same design as the ones they wore during the season, more gray than white, with pinstripes and the team's distinctive "NY" logo prominently stamped on the front....Immediately behind the Giants came the Red Sox, and they were an irresistible sight, walking slowly with gray uniforms and red stockings, each of them wearing striking red blazers.

The Red Sox team mackinaw coat, or "striking red blazer," shown opposite, was worn by right-fielder Harry Hooper when he walked onto the Polo Grounds with his

RED SOX COMING ON FIELD

teammates before the start of Game 1. These coats were made by Spalding for the 1912 Series, and this is the only example known to exist.

Harry Bartholomew Hooper was born on August 24, 1887, in a then-rural part of California called Silicon Valley. Harry showed such promise as a student, especially in mathematics, that his elementary school principal convinced his parents to send him to Catholic boarding high school in Oakland. He graduated from Saint Mary's College of California in nearby Moraga, where he acquired a passion for baseball. He had pitched for the 1907 Saint Mary's team, but he moved to the field when he signed with Oakland's minor league club.

He racked up a .347 batting average in 1908, when he moved to the Sacramento Senators. He was signed by the Red Sox for a then-handsome salary of $2,800, and he made his major league debut on April 16, 1909. Affable and modest, Hooper cut a contrast to the players he played with, particularly Tris Speaker, who had come to the Red Sox two years earlier and was not above throwing a punch to make a point. The two became fast friends. Hooper was a decent hitter, but he made his mark as a member of what was known as the

Golden Outfield. Hooper, along with Speaker in center and Duffy Lewis in left, dominated every ballpark they played in from 1910 to 1915. Sportswriter Grantland Rice observed that the three coordinated their movements as if by some sixth sense. "They could move into another country, if the ball happened to fall there," he marveled. Both Ty Cobb and Babe Ruth said that the threesome made up the best outfield they had ever seen.

The rest of the team was not bad, either, and they had a chance to show their power in the 1912 World Series. Fireballer Smoky Joe Wood kept Boston's hopes alive against a New York team that may have been a shade better. What really fanned the Red Sox flames, though, was an extraordinary catch that Hooper made in Game 8, when Giant Larry Doyle ripped a ball to right and Hooper caught it on the run, back to the plate and barehanded, bowling over a couple of rows of temporary seats in the bargain. The Red Sox won the Series, while an awed Tris Speaker called Hooper's game-saving catch "the greatest, I believe, that I ever saw."

The Golden Outfield broke up before the 1916 season following a salary dispute between Speaker and Red Sox owner Joseph Lannin. Speaker went to the

Cleveland Indians, while Hooper remained in Boston. He guided the team through the years of World War I, when many players, Christy Mathewson among them, were sent off to Europe to train and fight. Under Hooper's de facto captaincy in 1918, the Red Sox took the last World Series they would win for 86 years.

In 1919, Hooper, now the team's official captain, convinced management to move five-year veteran Babe Ruth from the pitcher's mound to the outfield, allowing Ruth to put his strength toward hitting. Yet despite his contributions to the team—to this day Hooper holds the team records for triples and stolen bases—Boston traded Hooper to the White Sox in 1921. He had his revenge by posting the best offensive numbers of his career in the five years he played for Chicago. He played his last game on October 4, 1925, and then went home to California.

Had they worn numbers back in Harry Hooper's day, the Red Sox would surely have retired his. He and shortstop Heinie Wagner were the only players to take part in the Red Sox World Series championships of 1912, 1915, 1916, and 1918. Even so, it was not until 1971, three years before his death, that Hooper was admitted to the Hall of Fame, and then only after intense lobbying by a devoted son.

Hooper was the oldest living member of the Hall of Fame when he died at the age of 87 in 1974. Babe Ruth paid him the highest of compliments, writing in *Babe Ruth's Own Book of Baseball*, "There's one man in my experience who was even better than [Ty] Cobb or [Tris] Speaker. He comes about as near to being the perfect outfielder as any man I ever saw. And that was Harry Hooper."

"The advance fanfare is over. The English language has been plucked of its final consonants, and the last of all figures extant has been twisted out of shape in the maelstrom of a million arguments. And now, at the end of it, there is nothing left. Nothing left but the charge of the Night Brigade against the gates at dawn to-morrow—and after that the first boding hush as Harry Hooper flies out from the Red Sox coop and stands face to face with Mathewson, the veteran, or Tesreau, the debutante...."

—Grantland Rice, *New York Evening Mail*, October 7, 1912

"AS WITH ROME, SO WITH BROOKLYN"

EARL YINGLING 1913 Brooklyn Superbas Home and Road Jerseys

On March 4, 1912, Dodgers owner Charles Hercules Ebbets drove a shovel into icy dirt to break ground for a new ballpark in a Brooklyn neighborhood called Pigtown. The plan was to name it Washington Park, after the team's old wooden stadium closer to downtown. But Len Wooster of the *Brooklyn Daily Times* spoke up. "Washington Park, hell," he said. "That name wouldn't mean anything out here. Why don't you call it Ebbets Field? It was your idea and nobody else's....It's going to be your monument." And so the storied ballpark was baptized.

Ebbets Field opened its gates on Saturday, April 5, 1913, for a Dodgers exhibition game against the Yankees. More than 25,000 fans poured in to the music of Shannon's 23rd Regiment Band, a fixture of Brooklyn opening day ceremonies since 1898. To the roar of the crowd, the Brooklyn "Superbas"—a nickname coined by New York sportswriters based on a circus act—took the field. The players wore new oatmeal-gray uniforms with thick, wide-spaced navy blue and black pinstripes, which were in vogue at the time; navy blue trim down the front placket (opposite); and the team's crest—the letter *B* enclosed in a baseball diamond—on the left sleeve. The road version was even more striking, with "Brooklyn" applied vertically along the placket, a style first adopted by the Chicago Cubs in 1909.

Brooklyn ace Nap Rucker threw the first pitch to Bert Daniels, a fadeaway for a called strike. Later, young Dodgers outfielder Casey Stengel, who would one day manage the Dodgers and Yankees, hit Ebbets Field's first

home run, an inside-the-park dinger off Ray Caldwell. First baseman Jake Daubert followed with a deep line-drive homer to give Brooklyn a 2–0 lead. As the *Brooklyn Daily Eagle* reported, the two home runs "brought in thunders of applause that rattled over the valley and dell like the roar of artillery." After the Yankees tied the game in the top of the ninth on a throwing error by reliever Frank Allen, and with future Hall of Famer Zach Wheat on third base, Brooklyn third baseman Red Smith hit a line drive to center field, scoring Wheat and giving the Dodgers the 3–2 victory.

Brooklyn pitcher Earl Yingling wore the home version of the jersey during that fabled game, and he wore the home and road versions (opposite) throughout the 1913 season. Also pictured in a wooden presentation box is the April 9 game ball, as well as dirt taken from the field that day. Yingling posted an 8–8 record for Brooklyn that season, and his 2.58 ERA was well below the league average of 3.20. Manager Bill Dahlen also used him as a pinch-hitter, and Yingling's .383 average (23 for 60) topped the league.

"As with Rome, so with Brooklyn," the *Brooklyn Daily Standard Union* wrote of the new stadium:

> The words "Ebbets Field" are lettered
> on the tiled floor of the Rotunda, at the top
> and bottom of the outline of a baseball. There
> is no apostrophe after Ebbets' name, because
> the huge amphitheater, though named after
> the man who built it, is really dedicated to
> baseball, the fans, and the Brooklyn team....
> It is calculated to outlive by far even those
> veterans of the diamond to whom life seems
> to be eternal. Barring accident, the building
> may last 200 years.

Yet Ebbets Field would last only 47 years. In 1958, owner Walter O'Malley moved the Dodgers from Brooklyn to Los Angeles in search of greater profits. On February 23, 1960, 200 mournful fans and several former Dodgers stars gathered at Ebbets Field for the last time. While a brass band played "Auld Lang Syne," a two-ton iron ball, crassly painted to resemble a baseball, demolished the park, and part of the soul of Brooklyn went with it.

Charles H. Ebbets's daughter Genevieve throwing out the first ball of the exhibition game, April 5, 1913

Yingling's 1913 Brooklyn Superbas home and road jerseys on a wooden presentation box that holds both original dirt taken from the Ebbets Field infield on Opening Day, April 9, 1913, and the first ball thrown out at the game, by Brooklyn Borough President Alfred E. Steers

DEDICATION
EBBETS FIELD BASEBALL PARK
Opening day ceremony
Wednesday April 9th, 1913

This case contains infield soil
ceremonial broken bottle
and first ball thrown out by
Borough President Alfred E. Steers
Brooklyn to Philadelphia

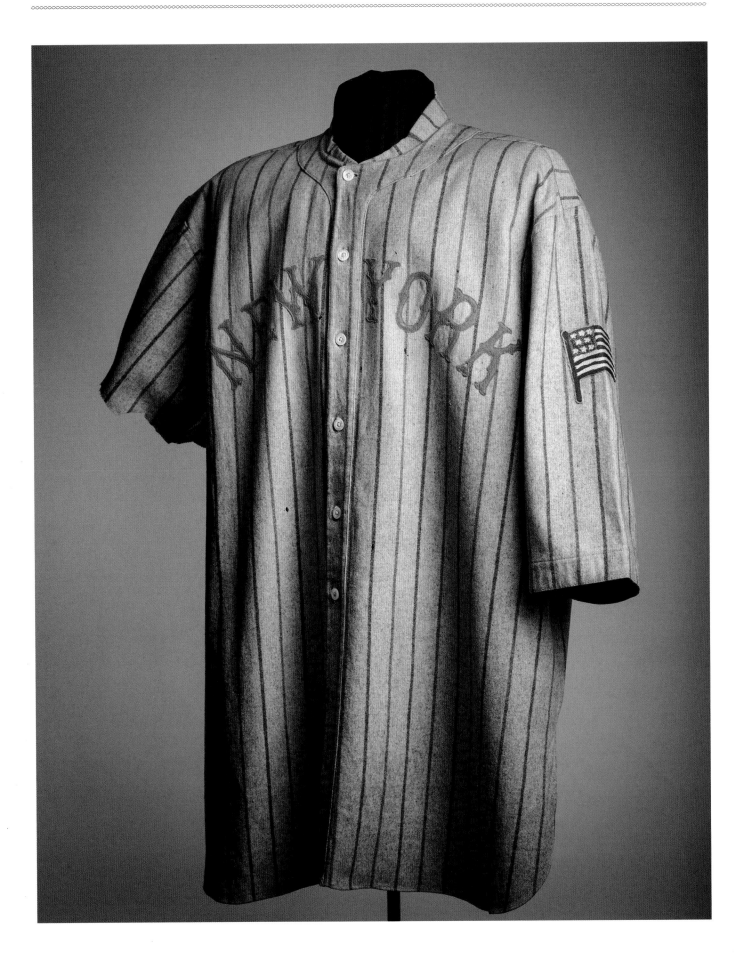

"He gripped the imagination of a country that held a hundred million people and held this grip with a firmer hold than any man of his day or time."

—Grantland Rice

THE BIG SIX

CHRISTY MATHEWSON 1913 World Tour Jersey

In the time when the Giants walked the earth and ruled baseball in New York, no player was more revered than pitcher Christy Mathewson. Chicago Cubs ace pitcher Mordecai Brown recalled Mathewson's "lordly entrance. He'd always wait until about ten minutes before game time, then he'd come from the clubhouse across the field in a long linen duster like auto drivers wore in those days, and at every step the crowd would yell louder and louder." All four pitches in his arsenal, including his celebrated fadeaway (now called the screwball), were delivered with pinpoint control and an easy, fluid motion. "He could throw a ball into a tin cup at pitching range," said Cubs second baseman Johnny Evers. Mathewson's 2.13 ERA over 17 seasons and National League records for wins in a season (37), wins in a career (373), and consecutive 20-win seasons (12) made him unquestionably the greatest pitcher of the Deadball Era's second decade. "He was the greatest pitcher I ever saw," John Kieran of the *New York Times* wrote. "He was the greatest anybody ever saw. Let them name all the others. I don't care how good they were. Matty was better."

Born on August 12, 1880, in Factoryville, Pennsylvania, Christopher Mathewson was the eldest of six children born to Minerva (Capwell) and Gilbert Mathewson, a Civil War veteran who had become a farmer. Christy's childhood playmates called him "Husk" because of his height and frame, which eventually reached six feet one and one-half inches

and 195 pounds. He pitched for the Factoryville town team as a 14-year-old and later for area semipro teams while attending Keystone Academy, a Factoryville preparatory school founded by his grandmother. He learned to throw the fadeaway the summer after graduating from Keystone while playing for a team in Honesdale, Pennsylvania. His teacher was teammate Dave Williams, who pitched three games for the Boston Americans in 1902.

Mathewson enrolled at Bucknell University in September 1898. He served as class president, pitched for the baseball team, played center on the basketball team, and was the football team's fullback, punter, and drop kicker. During the summer of 1899, he signed his first professional baseball contract, with Taunton of the New England League, but the team disbanded in the fall. Former major league pitcher John Francis Phenomenal Smith signed Mathewson to a contract with Norfolk of the Virginia League for the following summer, and Mathewson was 20–2 by mid-July. Smith offered Christy the choice of being sold to Philadelphia or New York of the National League. Christy chose New York because he felt they needed more help on the mound, and he made his major league debut as a 19-year-old pitcher on July 17, 1900.

Mathewson had his work cut out for him. The New York Giants finished seventh in 1901, Mathewson's first full season in the majors, but he pitched a no-hitter against the St. Louis Cardinals on July 15 and finished 20–17 with a 2.41 ERA. Giants fans started calling their new star the "Big Six." At first Mathewson thought it was because of his height, but the sobriquet likely originated when sportswriter Sam Crane compared him to New York City's Big Six Fire Company, "the fastest to put out the fire." Following a dismal 1902 season, when he went 14–17 and the Giants finished in the National League cellar, Mathewson recorded three consecutive 30-win seasons. In 1903, Mathewson was 30–13 with a 2.26 ERA and a career high 267 strikeouts, which stood as the NL record until Sandy Koufax struck out 269 in 1961. Two seasons later, in 1905, Mathewson was 31–9 with a 1.28 ERA, and he finished the year with one of the greatest pitching performances in World Series history. In a span of six days, Mathewson pitched three shutouts against the Philadelphia Athletics to lead the Giants to their first-ever Fall Classic victory.

In addition to his pitching achievements, the "Christian Gentleman," as he was also nicknamed, was the most respected all-around hero of the time, a tall, handsome, college-educated man who helped transform the rough and rowdy world of baseball into a chivalrous sport. "Christy Mathewson brought something to baseball no one else had ever given the game," said sportswriter Grantland Rice. "He handed the game a certain touch of class, an indefinable lift in culture, brains, and personality." Mathewson was the country's first All-American-boy athlete, his life seemingly modeled after the exploits of the popular dime-novel character Frank Merriwell.

His teammates adored him as well. Giants outfielder Fred Snodgrass called Mathewson the greatest pitcher who ever lived, and Chief Meyers, Matty's primary batterymate from 1909 to 1915, told author Lawrence Ritter:

What a pitcher he was! The greatest that ever lived. He had almost perfect control. Really almost perfect. In 1913 he pitched 68 consecutive innings without walking a man. That season he pitched over 300 innings and I doubt if he walked 25 men the whole year. Same thing in 1914. I don't think he ever walked a man in his life because of wildness. The only time he might walk a man was because he was pitching too fine to him, not letting him get a good ball to hit. But there was never a time he couldn't throw that ball over the plate if he wanted to. How we loved to play for him! We'd break our necks for that guy. If you made an error behind him, or anything of that sort, he'd never get mad or sulk. He'd come over and pat you on the back. He had the sweetest, most gentle nature. Gentle in every way.

Mathewson also helped the Giants win NL pennants in 1911, 1912, and 1913, and he led the NL in ERA in 1911 (1.99) and 1913 (2.06). Following the 1913 season, Giants manager John McGraw and Chicago White Sox owner Charles Comiskey led an ambitious international barnstorming tour that included Europe and Asia. Teams on the tour wore pinstriped uniforms that featured an ornamental "New York" in athletic felt across the chest and an American flag emblem on the left sleeve. Mathewson wore the flannel shown on page 34 during the U.S. portion of the tour, though he opted to spend the winter with his family in Pasadena, California, and did not participate in the overseas leg.

The tour marked major league baseball's first visit to Shanghai and Manila and included the first baseball game played in Hong Kong. In addition, the tour brought big-league stars such as Tris Speaker, "Wahoo" Sam Crawford, and Buck Weaver to play in Japan for the first time. Sportswriter Ring Lardner was among the notables who documented the voyage. After Manila, the group sailed to Australia, Ceylon, and Egypt, where the ballplayers were photographed at the feet of the Sphinx. Then they crossed the Mediterranean to Naples and continued on to Rome and Paris, with a brief stop along the Riviera. Before leaving Europe, they played one last exhibition game for England's King George V and an enormous crowd at Stamford Bridge, home of the Chelsea Football Club.

Program for the gala banquet honoring the World Tourists, March 7, 1914

Baseball's World Tours typically included visits to the Sphinx in Egypt. This shot is from the 1888-89 World Tour.

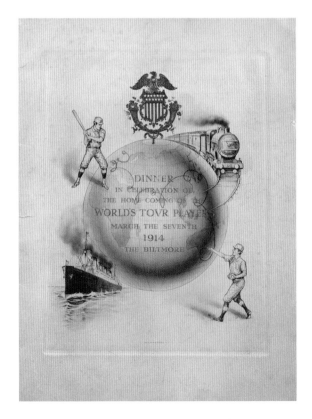

LITTLE NAPOLEON

JOHN McGRAW 1919–22 New York Giants Home Jersey

Tribute to John
McGraw at the
Polo Grounds,
July 19, 1927

> "In Mr. McGraw I at last discovered the real and most authentic Most Remarkable Man in America."
>
> —George Bernard Shaw

n July 19, 1927, 25,000 fans gathered at the Polo Grounds in New York to pay tribute to John Joseph McGraw, the fabled manager of the Giants since 1902 (above). He was being honored with a mammoth silver loving cup at a celebration commemorating his 25 years of service. It was an afternoon of fond reminiscences and a reminder of bygone days when Christy Mathewson, Iron Man McGinnity, Roger Bresnahan, Fred Merkle, and Fred Snodgrass—all members of the Giants' World Series championship or National League pennant–winning teams–had dominated New York's baseball headlines. Many fans in the stands had been present 25 years earlier, on July 19, 1902, when McGraw, then black-haired and small, walked onto the old Polo Grounds to take command of the disorganized team that would finish the season in the National League cellar.

On this silver anniversary day, the crowd witnessed the same man—now portly, gray-haired, and a managerial marvel—saunter out to receive honors from the mayor of New York, the commissioner of baseball, National League club owners, and numerous dignitaries. "In a speech that could not be heard in the stands but was generously applauded nevertheless," wrote James R. Harrison of the *New York Times*, "Mayor Walker presented to McGraw the silver jubilee cup on behalf of the mayor's McGraw Jubilee Committee. After that, Bresnahan gave his chief a silver service—the gift of the Giant players. Then came two other presents—a silver platter from the Lamb's Club, presented by Gene Buck (president of the American Society of Composers, Authors, and Publishers), and a silver cane from the ushers of the Polo Grounds....The rain, which was coming down rather briskly now, drenched the gay flags and bunting and sent the spectators to cover, but it failed to dampen the spirit and enthusiasm of a spontaneous tribute to New York's greatest baseball figure."

Baseball's obsession with statistics compels us to compare players from recent eras with those of the past. For example, the greatness of Pete Rose, Derek

Jeter, Clayton Kershaw, and Ichiro Suzuki is partially predicated upon the achievements of Ty Cobb, Lou Gehrig, Cy Young, and George Sisler. But rarely do we consider what lies behind those statistics. "If you look at pictures of, say, the 1915 Pirates, you're gonna see a very different kind of face than you see today," said journalist George F. Will in Ken Burns's documentary *Baseball*. "Hard men. Baseball at that point was a way out of the mines. This was a way for immigrant Americans to make a career, and they were tough men; hungry young men coming after the established older men. Baseball was played with a ferocity—a kind of life and death, which in a sense it was for these kind of players." Perhaps nobody in major league baseball history personified Will's observation more than John McGraw, who wore the New York Giants home jersey (previous page) from 1919 to 1922. The garment features loops in the lower area of the jersey that attach to the pants to prevent it from riding up above the trousers, and it is a glorious tribute to one of baseball's hardest men—whom Giants coach Arlie Latham described as a man who "eats gunpowder every morning for breakfast and washes it down with warm blood."

The son of an Irish immigrant railroad worker who fought in the Civil War, McGraw was born into working-class poverty on April 7, 1873, in the upstate New York village of Truxton. He lost his mother and three siblings to Truxton's diphtheria epidemic of 1884–85, and his father took out his grief and anger on his son, beating him senselessly and often. McGraw fled home when he was 12 and supported himself by performing chores at the nearby Truxton House Inn and doing other odd jobs. Five years later, in 1890, he landed a third-baseman position on the Oleon baseball team in the New York–Penn League. After a stint with Wellsville of the Western New York League and a winter tour with the "American All-Stars" in Cuba, McGraw joined Cedar Rapids of the Illinois–Iowa League in spring 1891. He played shortstop and batted .276 in 85 games, and the Baltimore Orioles of the American Association were so impressed that they signed him in August 1891.

Winning meant everything to those Baltimore Orioles. They fought hard for every run and every out, often deploying intimidation and violence to achieve victory. "They were mean, vicious, ready at any time to maim a rival player or an umpire if it helped their cause," said John Heydler, who was an umpire in the 1890s before becoming the National League president in 1918. "The things they would say to an umpire were unbelievably vile, and they broke the spirits of some very fine men." The ringleader of this rowdy bunch was McGraw. He was small—he weighed only 121 pounds when he joined the Orioles—but his tenacity was large. "Just get me out there and watch my smoke," sneered McGraw on his first day with the team to the startled

Orioles manager, who was expecting a bigger package. One sportswriter called McGraw "the toughest of the toughs and an abomination of the diamond...a rough unruly man. He uses every low and contemptible method that his erratic brain can conceive to win a play by a dirty trick." Another reporter noted, "I've seen umpires bathe their feet by the hour after John McGraw...spiked them through their shoes." When opposing players spiked him back, McGraw rarely complained. "We'd spit tobacco juice on a spike wound, rub dirt in it, and get out there and play," he said.

In 1902, Giants president Andrew Freedman felt McGraw's ferocity would resurrect his ailing club, and he offered McGraw $11,000 and full autonomy to become a player-manager. In return, McGraw brought him success, but on his own terms: "With my team I am an 'absolute czar,'" McGraw used to say. "My men know it. I order plays and they obey. If they don't, I fine them." The player Sammy Strang once hit a game-winning home run, yet McGraw fined him $25 because he missed a bunt sign. Sportswriters dubbed McGraw the "Little Napoleon."

The Little Napoleon would eventually turn the Giants around and lead them to 10 National League pennants and 3 World Series championships. He did it with tactful strategy and emphasis on base hits, guile, good pitching, sound defense, and aggressive base running, all characteristics of "inside baseball," which was pioneered by the Boston Beaneaters but perfected in the 1890s by McGraw and the Orioles.

"In playing or managing," McGraw once said, "the game of ball is only fun for me when I'm out in front and winning. I don't give a hill of beans for the rest of the game. The man who loses gracefully loses easily. Sportsmanship and easygoing methods are all right, but...once a team of mine is on the diamond, I want it to fight. Namby-pamby methods don't get much in results." At the same time, McGraw was a compassionate man who befriended his players: "On the field," said Mathewson, "he is the captain-general and everybody knows it. Off the field, he is a member of the team and personal friend of every man. Therein lies the difference between other managers and McGraw." Most important, McGraw's men were never complacent. He kept each of them hungry for survival, like the way he felt the day he fled home as a kid. "He kept you liking the game," said Casey Stengel. "If he couldn't, he'd get rid of you so quick you wouldn't have time to notify the post office of your change of address."

McGraw retired in 1932 with 2,763 managerial victories, second only to Connie Mack's 3,731. But even the legendary Mack recognized McGraw's brilliance: "There has been only one manager," he said, "and his name is McGraw."

Elaborate dedication given to John McGraw from the Citizens Committee of New York, 1911

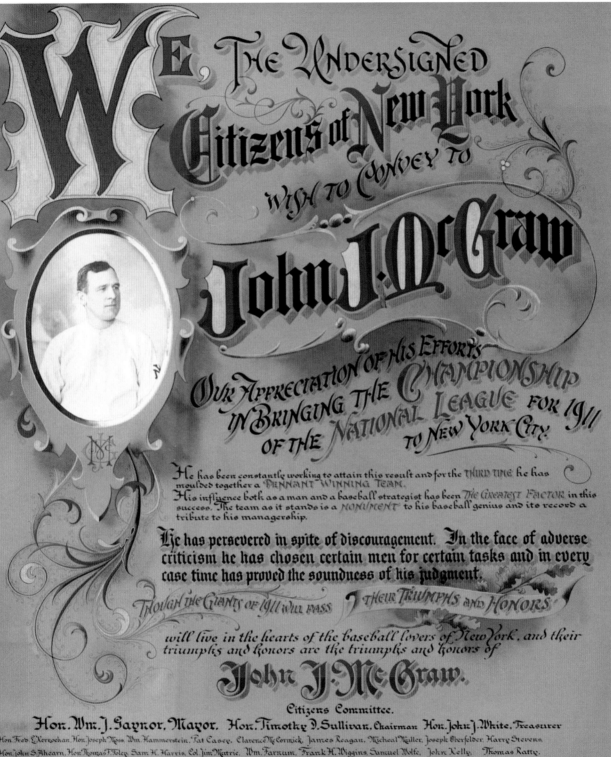

WE, THE UNDERSIGNED Citizens of New York WISH TO CONVEY TO John J. McGraw

OUR APPRECIATION OF HIS EFFORTS IN BRINGING THE CHAMPIONSHIP OF THE NATIONAL LEAGUE FOR 1911 TO NEW YORK CITY

He has been constantly working to attain this result and for the THIRD TIME he has moulded together a PENNANT WINNING TEAM.

His influence both as a man and a baseball strategist has been The GREATEST FACTOR in this success. The team as it stands is a MONUMENT to his baseball genius and its record a tribute to his managership.

He has persevered in spite of discouragement. In the face of adverse criticism he has chosen certain men for certain tasks and in every case time has proved the soundness of his judgment.

THOUGH THE GIANTS OF 1911 WILL PASS THEIR TRIUMPHS AND HONORS

will live in the hearts of the baseball lovers of New York, and their triumphs and honors are the triumphs and honors of

John J. McGraw.

Citizens Committee.

Hon. Wm. J. Gaynor, Mayor. Hon. Timothy D. Sullivan, Chairman. Hon. John J. White, Treasurer.

Hon. Fred C Kernochan, Hon. Joseph Moss, Wm. Hammerstein, Pat Casey, Clarence McCormick, James Reagan, Micheal Muller, Joseph Oberfelder, Harry Stevens,

Hon. John S. Ahearn, Hon. Thomas F. Foley, Sam H. Harris, Col. Jim Mettrie, Wm. Farnum, Frank H. Wiggins, Samuel Wolfe, John Kelly, Thomas Ratty,

Hon. John E Fitzgerald, Hon. Ed F. McCall, Paul Armstrong, E.E. Smatkers, James J. Corbett, Willis McCormick, Chas. Flenn, Wm. Fleischmann, Ernes Haskell,

Hon. A. Gruber, Hon. Christopher Sullivan, Louis Marx, Larry Mulligan, Vic Williams, Henry J. Goldsmith, Max Blumenthal, Jack Gleason, Niles K. Becker,

Hon. Ed. Lauterbach, Hon. James G. Jaffney, George Boldt, A. Erlanger, George Considine, Jack McKean, Ed. Downing, Doctor Herman L Reiss, Wm Fray,

Hon. Chas. F. Murphy, Hon. Dan J. Reardon, George Rector, Ed. F. Albee, Wm. B. Ellison, Harry J. Everall, Joseph Gordon, Henry Tobin, Benjamin Larson,

Hon. Francis X. McQuade, Hon. James J. Smith, John Whalen, Geo. M. Cohen, Wm. Long, Ed. Burke, Lawrence Auterbarg, Leo Mayer, Jacob Field,

Hon. John J. Freschi, Max Klaw, Hale Hamilton, De Wolff Hopper, Sam Meyers, Harry Haggerty, John Zanft, Vernie Barton, Eddie Leonard, The Minstrel

Hon. Alf. E. Smith, Percy G. Williams, Dustin Farnum, Felix Isman, Fred Perry, Harry Sparrow, John Foster, E. A. Higgins,

Hon. Francis S. Dowling, William Fox, James G. Rackett, Digby Bell, George Ehret, Jr., Jacob Josephs, Julian Kaufman, Harry Barry,

Joe Humphreys, Chairman Committee of Arrangements.

SOMETHING LIKE A WAR

TY COBB 1920 Detroit Tigers Team Sweater

If baseball is akin to war, its most ferocious warrior must have been Ty Cobb. Here we present Cobb's armor—his heavy wool Detroit Tigers sweater from the 1920 season—along with his weapons: his bat and spikes. Team sweaters are among the most elusive and coveted parts of major league baseball uniforms from the 1910s and 1920s. Made of thick wool, such sweaters kept players warm during chilly afternoon games in the spring and autumn. By the 1930s, sweaters had given way to shorter wool jackets with stretch waistband and wrists. Jackets are still used today but are made of newer fabrics such as nylon.

In 1909, baseball's consummate photographer, Charles Martin Conlon (1868–1945), snapped a shot of Ty Cobb in combat. The image, captured at a game between the New York Highlanders and Cobb's Detroit Tigers, turned out to be arguably the greatest baseball action photo ever taken (right). Cobb was on second base with one out, and a Tigers batter was attempting to bunt him to third. Conlon was standing off third base, near New York third baseman Jimmy Austin. In anticipation of the sacrifice bunt, Austin had taken several steps toward home plate and was standing in the base path. Suddenly, Cobb broke for third, catching Austin and the Highlanders off guard. "As Jimmy stood there, Cobb started," Conlon later recalled. "The fans shouted. Jimmy turned, backed into the base, and was greeted by a storm of dirt, spikes, shoes, uniforms—and Ty Cobb. My first thought was that my friend, Austin,

had been injured. When Cobb stole, he *stole*. Spikes flew and he did not worry where. I saw Ty's clenched teeth, his determined look. The catcher's peg went right by Jimmy as he was thrown on his face."

At that moment, Conlon's only concern was for his friend. Only after making sure that Austin was unhurt did Conlon wonder if he had captured the moment with his camera. Though he doubted that he had, Conlon removed the glass plate just in case, replacing it with a new one. The next day, when he developed the plates, Conlon discovered that he had snapped the shutter instinctively. The result is an indelible image of perhaps baseball's most irascible, feared, and accomplished player. In a single frame, Conlon distilled the essence of the man who regarded every game as a war. "In legend I am a sadistic, slashing, swashbuckling despot who waged war in the guise of sport," Cobb wrote shortly before his death. "Sure, I fought. I had to fight all my life to survive. They were all against me...tried every dirty trick to cut me down. But I beat the bastards and left them in the ditch."

Born on December 18, 1886, in The Narrows, Georgia, Cobb had been named after the Phoenician city of Tyre, which stubbornly resisted the onslaught of Alexander the Great. The name proved prophetic, as Cobb grew up to become the most stubborn and fierce competitor the game has known. Cobb's father, William, a respected schoolmaster, disapproved of his choice of vocation and sent him off to the big leagues with the words "Don't come home a failure." Two years later,

Ty Cobb sliding into third base, as captured by photographer Charles M. Conlon, 1909

Cobb's game-used bat and spikes from the early 1920s atop his 1920 Detroit Tigers team sweater

"Baseball is something like a war....Baseball is a red-blooded sport for red-blooded men. It's not pink tea, and mollycoddles had better stay out of it. It's... a struggle for supremacy, a survival of the fittest."

—Ty Cobb

Cobb's mother, Amanda, shot his father dead. William had suspected Amanda was having an affair, so he snuck past their bedroom window to see if she was with another man. When Amanda saw a shadow of someone she thought was an intruder, she inadvertently shot and killed her husband. She was later acquitted of voluntary manslaughter. "My father had his head blown off when I was eighteen years old—by a member of my own family," Cobb recalled toward the end of his life. "I didn't get over that. I've *never* gotten over it."

Consumed with a passion to excel and to prove his mettle to his father, even after the man's death, Cobb treated every game as a blood feud. His aggressive style of play was described by the *Detroit Free Press* as "daring to the point of dementia." Sportswriter Jimmy Cannon wrote, "The cruelty of Cobb's style fascinated the multitudes, but it also alienated them. He played in a climate of hostility, friendless by choice in a violent world he populated with enemies....But not even his disagreeable character could destroy the image of his greatness as a ballplayer. Ty Cobb was the best. That seemed to be all he wanted."

At the plate, Cobb had no peer. He hit .400 or better in three seasons, led the American League in batting every year from 1907 to 1915 (as well as from 1917 to 1919), and still holds the highest career batting average (.367) in major league history. The Georgia Peach, as writers called him, held his bat with his hands wide apart, which made it easier to adjust to breaking balls and other trick pitches. For an easy pitch, he would slide his top hand down and swing away; for difficult pitches, he would punch or slap the ball where he wanted it to go. Cobb's objective was to get on base so he could conquer opponents with psychological warfare. Tigers teammate Wahoo Sam Crawford marveled at Cobb's command of mental gamesmanship:

> Talk about strategy and playing with your head, that was Cobb all the way. It wasn't that he was so fast on his feet, although he was fast enough. There were others who were faster, though, like Clyde Milan, for instance. It was that Cobb was so fast in his thinking. He didn't outhit the opposition and he didn't outrun them. He outthought them!

> A lot of times Cobb would be on third base and I'd draw a base on balls, and as I started to go down to first I'd sort of half glance at Cobb, at third. He'd make a slight move that told me he wanted me to keep going—not to stop at first, but to keep on going to second. Well, I'd trot two-thirds of the way to first and then suddenly, without warning, I'd speed up and go across first as fast as I could and tear out for second. He's on third, see. They're watching him, and suddenly there I go, and they don't know what the devil to do.

> If they try to stop me, Cobb'll take off for home. Sometimes they'd catch him, and sometimes they'd catch me, and sometimes they wouldn't get either of us. But most of the time they were too paralyzed to do anything, and I'd wind up at second on a base on balls. Boy, did that ever create excitement. For the crowd, you know; the fans were always wondering what might happen next.

In 1911, when Cobb led the American League in virtually every offensive category, including batting average (.420), hits (248), runs scored (147), RBI (127), stolen bases (83), doubles (47), triples (24), and slugging percentage (.621), he moved to Woodbridge, a historic Detroit neighborhood of primarily Victorian homes. Cobb often walked with his dogs from Woodbridge to the ballpark prior to games. His Victorian duplex still stands there, and his spike marks remain on its wooden floors and stairways.

A few years after Cobb hung up his spikes and uniform, he reminisced about his exploits on the basepaths. "Yes," he admitted, "I guess I may have been a trifle rough. But take a look at this." Cobb rolled up his trousers and revealed what the *New York Times* sportswriter John Drebinger described as "a pair of shins crisscrossed with myriads of scars from ankles to knees." "I didn't get those playing tiddlywinks," said Cobb. "They gave it to me as hard as I gave it to them. The only difference was I never gave them the satisfaction of hearing me squawk. I'd sooner let them cut out my tongue than let them know I was hurt."

Ron Stark, *Ty Cobb*, 2016, oil on canvas

"Walter had such blinding speed that he was the only pitcher I ever saw who made me instinctively shut my eyes. I tried hard to keep peering at the ball but I couldn't help myself."

—Billy Evans, American League umpire (1906–27)

THE BIG TRAIN

WALTER JOHNSON 1919–22 Washington Senators Road Jersey

Walter Johnson with President Calvin Coolidge after being presented with an award commemorating the Senators' 1924 American League win, June 18, 1925

Johnson's 1919-22 Washington Senators road jersey, shown with an oil painting of the player by Ron Stark and a Draper & Maynard baseball glove from the early 1920s

Walter Perry Johnson was born on November 6, 1887, on a 160-acre farm in Allen County, Kansas, to Frank and Minnie Johnson. As a child, he helped his parents with chores and found time to hunt and fish, which became lifelong passions. At the turn of the century, Frank Johnson was forced to relinquish his farm as a result of persistent droughts. The family moved to the town of Humboldt, where Frank found various jobs to support the family. Meanwhile, the parents and siblings of Walter's mother moved to the oil fields of Southern California, attracted by the pleasant weather and abundant employment opportunities. In April 1902, after years of poverty in Kansas, Walter's family moved to Olinda, California, where Frank worked for the Santa Fe Oil Company as a teamster.

Although Johnson played only occasional schoolyard pick-up games as a youth, pitching came naturally when he began playing baseball regularly as a teenager, in part because of his anatomy—gangly-armed Johnson had developed a muscular six-foot-one frame working on the Kansas farm and in the oil fields. "The first time I held a ball," he once explained, "it settled in the palm of my right hand as though it belonged there and, when I threw it, ball, hand and wrist, and arm and shoulder and back seemed to all work together." At 16, Johnson joined a sandlot team and soon began pitching for a semipro team sponsored by a local oil company, honing his skills against town teams, company teams, and barnstorming teams throughout Southern California. In 1906, a former teammate landed him a job playing for the Weiser (Idaho) team in the semipro

Southern Idaho League. He was paid $90 a week to work for the local telephone company and play baseball on weekends.

In 1907, Washington Senators manager Joe Cantillon received a scouting report about Johnson: "This boy throws so fast you can't see 'em," reported the scout, "and he knows where he is throwing, because if he didn't there would be dead bodies all over Idaho." Johnson pitched with a short windmill-style windup followed by a sweeping sidearm delivery, and Ty Cobb said his fastball "looked about the size of a watermelon seed and it hissed at you as it passed." Cobb, the most dominant batsman of his time, was known to be discerning about the pitchers he faced. But when he saw Johnson pitch for the first time, the Georgia Peach seemed to echo the scout's report to Cantillon:

> On August 2, 1907, I encountered the most threatening sight I ever saw in the ball field. He was a rookie, and we licked our lips as we warmed up for the first game of a doubleheader in Washington. Evidently, manager Pongo Joe Cantillon of the Nats had picked a rube out of the cornfields of the deepest bushes to pitch against us. He was a tall, shambling galoot of about twenty, with arms so long they hung far out of his sleeves, and with a sidearm delivery that looked unimpressive at first glance. One of the Tigers imitated a cow mooing, and we hollered at Cantillon: "Get the pitchfork ready, Joe—your hayseed's on his way back to the barn." The first time I faced him, I watched him take that easy windup. And then something went past me that made me flinch. The thing just hissed with danger. We couldn't touch him...every one of us knew we'd met the most powerful arm ever turned loose in a ball park.

During the first part of his career, Johnson relied almost exclusively on his fastball (he wouldn't have a good curve until around 1913), which inspired Ring Lardner to say, "He's got a gun concealed on his person. They can't tell me he throws them balls with his arm." In 1917, a Bridgeport, Connecticut, munitions laboratory recorded Johnson's fastball at 134 feet per second, which is equal to 91.36 miles per hour. Such velocity was virtually unheard of in Johnson's day, with the possible exception of Smoky Joe Wood. The sidearm motion of the Big Train, so nicknamed by sportswriters because he pitched with the speed of a locomotive, made it difficult for right-handed batters to follow because the ball seemed to come from third base. Johnson's strikeout totals demonstrate the dominance and power of his fastball. In his career, he struck out 3,508 batters,

a record that stood until 1983, when Nolan Ryan, Steve Carlton, and Gaylord Perry surpassed it. Johnson also notched 417 career victories (second all-time to Cy Young's 511), and his 110 shutouts still stand as the major league record.

But as legendary as Johnson's fastball was, so too was the longevity of his prowess. He led the league in strikeouts 12 out of 15 seasons, starting in 1910, when he was 22, and concluding in 1924, when he was 36. (Nolan Ryan led baseball in strikeouts for 11 seasons.) He also compiled 12 20-win seasons, the last in 1925, and finished 531 of 666 starts. Sixteen years after his first encounter with Cobb, Johnson's fastball was still hissing. "People always asked me who was the fastest pitcher I ever saw," said New York Yankees pitcher George Pipgras:

> Well, I saw Grove and Feller in their prime, and you can't believe anybody could be quicker than those two fellows. But I'll tell you something. When I broke into the league, I batted against Walter Johnson. He'd been around a long time at that point, seventeen years or so. Well, I stepped into the batter's box, took two called strikes, and stepped out of the batter's box. I turned around and looked at Muddy Ruel, who was catching. I could see he had a little smile on his face, behind his mask. He knew what I was going to say. "Muddy," I said, "I never saw those pitches."
>
> "Don't let it worry you," he said. "He's thrown a few that Cobb and Speaker are still looking for."

The Big Train played his first 17 seasons with the Senators and never reached the postseason. But he decided to give it one last go in 1924. He posted a 23–7 record; led the American League in wins, ERA, strikeouts, and shutouts; and helped the Senators win their first AL pennant. In the team's first World Series, the Senators faced John McGraw's New York Giants. Johnson lost Games 1 and 5. In Game 7, with the Giants leading 3–1 in the sixth inning, a loud cheer echoed across Griffith Stadium when Johnson headed to the bullpen. In the top of the ninth, with the score tied 3–3, Senators manager Bucky Harris called the Big Train in to pitch. Harris handed Johnson the ball and said, "You're the best we've got, Walter. We've got to win or lose with you." Johnson held the Giants scoreless for four innings. Twice, after giving intentional walks to Ross Youngs, he struck out major league RBI champ George Kelly. Finally, in the bottom of the 12th inning, the Senators' Earl McNeely hit a ground ball that struck a pebble and bounced over

WALTER JOHNSON   3820-1

the head of Giants third baseman Fred Lindstrom, scoring Muddy Ruel. Johnson, at last, got what he had always deserved—a Fall Classic title.

After retiring from the majors at the end of the 1927 season, Johnson managed for a year at Newark in the International League before returning to Washington to manage the Senators for four seasons. After three years as skipper of the Cleveland Indians (1933–35), the Big Train left the dugout to work on his farm, serve as a commissioner in Montgomery County, and, in 1939, broadcast games on the radio for the Senators. He also ran for (and lost) a Republican seat in the U.S. Congress. On June 12, 1939, he was inducted into the newly created Baseball Hall of Fame, along with Babe Ruth, Ty Cobb, Honus Wagner, and Christy Mathewson, who had died in 1925.

The Big Train wore this gray pinstriped flannel Washington Senators road jersey (page 47) between 1919 and 1922. It was during this period that he met his teammate and friend Eric "Swat" Erickson. Born in

Vargarda, Sweden, Erickson was the second Swedish player to reach the majors (Charlie Hallstrom of the Providence Grays of the National League was the first). After a poor debut with the Giants in 1914, where he pitched only a single game after giving up seven runs in five innings, and shaky partial seasons with the Tigers, Erickson's fortunes seemed to turn after he was traded to the Washington Senators in 1919. That year he led the American League in strikeouts per nine innings. Two years later, in 1921, he was among the league leaders in ERA, strikeouts per nine innings, and shutouts. His performance kept him on the Senators' roster and in the rotation with Walter Johnson. By 1922, Erickson had stepped out of the big-league limelight in favor of life on a farm with his family in Jamestown, New York. Erickson kept this Walter Johnson jersey tucked away in his farmhouse until his death in 1965.

Besides the example in the National Baseball Hall of Fame, this is the only known Walter Johnson uniform in existence.

Walter Johnson, by photographer George Grantham Bain, ca. 1913

A MAN FOR ALL SEASONS

BRANCH RICKEY 1919 St. Louis Cardinals Road Jersey

Robert Bolt's celebrated play *A Man for All Seasons* is based on the true story of Sir Thomas More, the sixteenth-century chancellor of England. More refused to endorse King Henry VIII's wish to divorce his wife, who could not bear him a son, and marry the sister of his former mistress. Bolt depicts More as a man of unyielding principle, one who remains true to himself and his beliefs despite monumental external pressures—the consummate man for all seasons.

If Bolt had adapted his literary masterpiece to baseball, Wesley Branch Rickey might well have been the playwright's choice for the game's Sir Thomas More. Born to a deeply religious family on December 20,

1881, on a farm in Scioto County in south central Ohio, Rickey was named after John Wesley, the founder of the family's Methodist faith. His middle name, Branch, was indicative of the Christian values by which he would live his life. According to biographer Lee Lowenfish, "One Rickey family Bible contained a handwritten note in which the word *branch* was capitalized in a passage from the Old Testament book of Isaiah, 11:1: 'And there shall come forth a rod out of the stem of Jesse, and a Branch shall grow out of the roots.'"

Branch Rickey's parents, Frank and Emily, imbued their son with a strong sense of social responsibility and the belief that there was no limit to what he could achieve for himself and his community. Rickey strived to embody the sacred principles of John Wesley's precept: "Having, first, gained all you can, and, secondly, saved all you can, then give all you can." Rickey went to elementary school in a one-room schoolhouse and then read all he could to educate himself when school ended. He earned a teaching certificate and landed a job at a local grade school, where he taught to earn money for college. On his own, he learned Greek, Latin, and algebra, but above all he was crazy about baseball. He played on his family's farm with a ball stitched by his mother, caught in local games for his older brother, Orla, and avidly followed his favorite team, the Cincinnati Reds. In 1901, Rickey entered Ohio Wesleyan University. Despite meager finances, he refused to accept the dollar bill his mother sent him every month and instead stoked furnaces and waited tables to make ends

Branch Rickey (right) and Brooklyn manager Leo Durocher (to Rickey's right) with the press, spring 1947

Official National League baseball signed by the 1926 World Series-winning St. Louis Cardinals team, shown with a 1920s Holy Bible and Rickey's 1919 St. Louis Cardinals Road Jersey

meet. He played baseball and football at Ohio Wesleyan and augmented his earnings by playing in baseball's semipro summer circuit in 1902. In spring 1903, he began coaching the Ohio Wesleyan baseball team.

During the 1904 season, Rickey was involved in an incident that demonstrated his character and foreshadowed his move, more than 40 years later, to bring Jackie Robinson to the Brooklyn Dodgers and integrate baseball. When the Ohio Wesleyan team traveled to South Bend, Indiana, to play Notre Dame University, Rickey and his team gathered in the lobby of the Oliver Hotel to check in. But the hotel clerk would not allow team captain and catcher Charles "Tommy" Thomas to register because he was black. Humiliated, Thomas told Rickey that he would return to Ohio Wesleyan and not play. Rickey wouldn't hear of it. He demanded that the hotel manager place a cot in his room where Thomas could sleep. When the manager refused, Rickey threatened to take his team elsewhere. Eventually the manager backed down and allowed Thomas to sleep in Rickey's room. Years later, Rickey recalled what had happened when the team captain came to his room to discuss tactics and strategy for the game against Notre Dame:

> Tommy stood in the corner, tense and brooding and in silence. I asked him to sit in a chair and relax. Instead, he sat on the end of the cot, his huge shoulders hunched and his large hands clasped between his knees. I tried to talk to the captain, but I couldn't take my gaze from Tommy. Tears...spilled down his black face and splashed to the floor. Then his shoulders heaved convulsively and he rubbed one great hand over the other with all the power of his body, muttering, 'Black skin...black skin. If I could only make 'em white.' He kept rubbing and rubbing as though he would remove the blackness by sheer friction.

"I never felt so helpless in my life," Rickey recalled later. "Whatever mark that incident left on [Thomas], it was no more indelible than the impressions made on me." Rickey would become the most innovative and revolutionary figure in major league baseball history, implementing dramatic changes not once but three times against what seemed to be insurmountable obstacles.

Farm System

For the following decade, Rickey's life included a variety of pursuits in academics, sports, and coaching. He was appointed athletic director at Ohio Wesleyan and coached football and basketball as well as baseball. In 1911, Rickey graduated from law school and established his law practice in Boise, Idaho. That

summer, he scouted for Robert Hedges, owner of the St. Louis Browns, who had been impressed with Rickey's skill as a player. When his law practice ran into business problems in 1912, Rickey accepted Hedges's offer of a full-time job with the Browns. He was named the team's field manager in 1913.

In 1915, Hedges first granted Rickey a long-term contract and then sold the Browns to Phil Ball. The new owner was derisive of Rickey's religious beliefs and management style, and in 1917 he agreed to release Rickey so he could become president and general manager of the St. Louis Cardinals. Because St. Louis had scant finances and could not compete with other clubs in purchasing talent from independent minor league teams, Rickey decided to grow his own talent by developing a team-owned farm system. He envisioned a network of minor leagues that would produce talented players who could help the Cardinals and who could be sold to other clubs at a profit. This idea offered the Cardinals a competitive advantage, but it was also a colossal undertaking that involved tracking and evaluating players in every organization, hiring a network of scouts, building and operating minor league tryout camps, and developing a systematic method of training players.

In the summer of 1919, Rickey wore this gray pinstriped road jersey (page 50) featuring the team nickname, "Cardinals," across the chest, predating the well-known "two birds on a bat" logo created by Rickey and first used by the club in 1923. Also in 1919, according to Lowenfish, Rickey opened "the doors of Cardinal Field for the team's first tryout camp. Hundreds of eager amateurs came at their own expense from all over the Midwest and South to work out under the keen eyes of Rickey and his staff."

By the early 1920s, the Cardinals' farm-club system was flourishing, with 800 players under contract on 32 teams. The results were extraordinary: from 1919 to 1942, under Rickey's stewardship, the Cardinals won six National League pennants and four World Series titles. The rest of the league eventually followed Rickey's lead, and today farm clubs are standard, though each major league organization operates only five or six minor league teams.

Integration of Major League Baseball

By late 1942, Rickey's relationship with Cardinals owner Sam Breadon had become strained. The two were fighting over Rickey's bonus payments and Breadon's dismissal of Rickey protégés in the farm system. Brooklyn Dodgers board member James Mulvey had first approached Rickey in 1937 to switch to the Dodgers, but Rickey wasn't ready. But in late 1942, Rickey joined Brooklyn as general manager. In 1945, in one of the most monumental moves in baseball history, Rickey signed Jackie Robinson to a minor league contract with the Dodgers. Two years later, Rickey promoted him to the Dodgers' major league roster. Robinson stepped onto the grass at Ebbets Field for the first time on April 15, 1947, to open the season against the Boston Braves, and with that step Rickey and Robinson demolished the so-called gentleman's agreement that had barred American ballplayers of color from major league baseball and its affiliated minor leagues since the 1880s. The move is considered Rickey's most profound contribution to baseball, and it would play an important role in the national Civil Rights Movement in the decades ahead. In a 1961 *Reader's Digest* article, Robinson described his first meeting with Rickey:

> He was taking off his coat, rolling up his sleeves. His mobile face had suddenly taken on a droll, cunning look.
>
> "Let's say I'm a hotel clerk. You come in with the rest of your team. I look up from the register and snarl, 'We don't let niggers sleep here.' What do you do then?"
>
> Again, before I could answer, the smudgy cigar shot toward my chin, and he was an umpire waving his huge fist too close under my nose, banishing me from the game. As a race-baiting fan he hurled pop bottles and insults. When the performance was over his shirt was soggy with sweat, his hair matted.
>
> His curtain line explained everything. It was the most dramatic I have ever heard, before or since:
>
> "I want you to be the first Negro player in the major leagues. I've been trying to give you some idea of the kind of punishment you'll have to absorb. Can you take it?"

Expansion of the Leagues

Rickey left the Dodgers in 1950 to become general manager of the Pittsburgh Pirates. But his third baseball revolution would not take place until several years after he left the Pirates in 1955. Following the 1957 departures of the Dodgers from Brooklyn and the Giants from New York, a committee was formed to explore ways to bring baseball back to the city. Two years later, the Continental League was formed, baseball's third major league, and Branch Rickey was named its president. The league expected to begin play in 1961 with teams in eight cities: New York, Buffalo, Toronto, Minneapolis–St. Paul, Houston, Dallas–Fort Worth, Atlanta, and Denver. Although the league was disbanded on August 2, 1960, before ever playing a game, its creation had a critical role in the expansion

of the American and National Leagues. At the end of the 1960 season, the American League issued franchises to the California Angels (now the Los Angeles Angels) and a new Washington Senators club (which eventually became the Minnesota Twins). The National League would grow to 10 teams in 1962 with the admission of the New York Mets and the Houston Colt .45s (now the Astros).

"Baseball people are generally allergic to new ideas," Rickey once said. "It took years to persuade them to put numbers on uniforms....It is the hardest thing in the world to get big league baseball to change anything— even spikes on a new pair of shoes. But they will... eventually. They are bound to." Over the course of American history, certain individuals have served as invaluable catalysts for change, including the Founding Fathers of the Declaration of Independence and the Constitution, Duke Ellington in jazz music, and Dr. Martin Luther King Jr. in the civil rights movement. In baseball, we have Branch Rickey, represented here by a uniform that he wore in the early days of his genius.

The African American press eagerly following Jackie Robinson's career, as seen on the front page of the *Washington Afro American*, May 13, 1947

THE FAITH OF 50 MILLION PEOPLE

RED FABER 1919 World Series and 1920 Season Chicago White Sox Home Uniform

Chicago White Sox manager Kid Gleason (wearing his home uniform) and Cincinnati Reds manager Pat Moran shaking hands before the start of Game 1 of the 1919 World Series, Redland Field

he 1919 White Sox were one of the strongest teams in baseball history. After clinching the American League pennant, the club was favored five to one to win the World Series against the Cincinnati Reds. "They were the best," recalled Chicago second baseman and future Hall of Famer Eddie Collins. "There never was a ball club like that one."

Despite the club's success, the White Sox players were unhappy and disillusioned. They were paid poorly by owner Charles A. Comiskey, who showed nothing but disdain for players bound to him by the reserve clause. Eddie Collins, who had been paid handsomely by Connie Mack while with the Philadelphia Athletics, made sure his $14,500 salary was guaranteed before jumping to the White Sox, which paid Shoeless Joe Jackson—arguably, along with Ty Cobb, among the era's greatest hitters— a paltry $6,000 a year. Comiskey, known as the "Old Roman," also failed to honor bonus agreements. Pitcher Eddie Cicotte, for example, was promised $10,000 if he won 30 games in a season. After Cicotte secured his

29th victory in 1919, Comiskey benched him so he wouldn't have to pay. The Old Roman even refused to have uniforms laundered, prompting players in 1918 to wear increasingly soiled uniforms in protest and to rename themselves the Black Sox. Many White Sox players were fed up and thus vulnerable to corruption. The circumstances were ideal for gamblers, but they needed a ringleader. Their man would be first baseman Chick Gandil, who had turned 32 and was looking for one last shot at big money.

On September 18, 13 days before the World Series opener, Gandil met an old acquaintance, Joseph J. "Sport" Sullivan, in a hotel room in Boston. Sullivan was a small-time gambler who, over the years, had profited from Gandil's pregame tips on various players' health and condition. Such a relationship between ballplayer and gambler was common in those days. Although single games had been thrown before, Gandil's proposition to Sullivan was on a new level: For $100,000, Gandil and some of his teammates would throw the 1919 World Series.

Sullivan needed to raise the money, while Gandil went to work on teammates. "The proposition to throw the World Series...was first brought to me in New York City in front of the Ansonia Hotel," White Sox pitcher Claude "Lefty" Williams recalled. "Gandil...asked me if anybody had approached me on the 1919 World's Series with the purpose of fixing [it]....I told him not yet. He asked me what I thought of it. I told [him] I had nothing to say. He asked me if it was fixed, would I be willing to get in and go through with it?" Williams eventually agreed to cooperate with Gandil, as did six other teammates: Cicotte, center fielder Oscar "Happy" Felsch, third baseman Buck Weaver, shortstop Swede Risberg, reserve infielder Fred McMullin, and outfielder Shoeless Joe Jackson.

The only thing missing was the cash. The name of the man who actually fronted money for the fix remains subject to speculation. A cast of underworld characters befitting a B-grade Hollywood mob film was certainly in the mix: Sport Sullivan; Bill Maharg, whose real surname may have been Graham (Maharg spelled backward); former featherweight boxing champion Abe Attell; and "Sleepy" Bill Burns, who likely operated on behalf of New York's most notorious gambler and crime kingpin, Arnold Rothstein. Burns apparently relayed messages among the eight players and a person whose initials were A.R.

Rothstein, upon whom the character Meyer Wolfsheim in *The Great Gatsby* is based, "was said to have been willing to bet on anything except the weather because there was no way he could fix that." He would not confirm his participation until there was a sign that the fix was in, so he told intermediaries that Cicotte should hit the first batter with a pitch as the signal.

"The day before the series was to open in Cincinnati, with Eddie Cicotte slated to pitch for the White Sox, rumors of wrongdoing were everywhere," wrote historians Geoffrey C. Ward and Ken Burns. "For no apparent reason, the odds were steadily shifting away from Chicago. 'You couldn't miss it,' one New York gambler remembered. 'The thing had an odor. I saw smart guys take even money on the Sox who should have been asking five-to-one.' When Cicotte got back to his hotel room that evening, he found the $10,000 he'd demanded under his pillow. He sat up into the night sewing the crisp green bills into the lining of his coat."

A program (opposite) and ticket (below) to Game 1 of the 1919 World Series, played at Cincinnati's Redland Field, signifies the start of one of baseball's darkest chapters. In the bottom of the first inning of Game 1, Cicotte plunked the Reds' first batter (second baseman Morrie Rath), signaling to Rothstein and the gamblers that the fix was in. Claude Williams went on to lose three games, a Series record. Dickie Kerr, who was not part of the fix, won both of his starts. The gamblers, however, started reneging on promised payments, claiming that all the money was in the hands of bookies. Cicotte became angry and turned on the gamblers, winning Game 7 of the best-of-nine Series. Sport Sullivan then took matters into his own hands to save the fix. He supposedly paid a gangster known as Harry F. to threaten to hurt Williams and his family if he did not lose Game 8. Williams was clearly shaken—in the first inning, he threw nothing but mediocre fastballs, giving up four straight one-out hits for three runs before Sox manager Kid Gleason relieved him. The White Sox went on to lose Game 8, 10–5, ending the Series.

Journalist Hugh Fullerton of the *Chicago Herald and Examiner*, disgusted by the ineptitude with which the White Sox had "thrown" the Series, wrote that no World Series should ever be played again. In September 1920, a grand jury was convened to investigate the Series. Eddie Cicotte and Shoeless Joe Jackson confessed their participation in the fix, which undoubtedly influenced the grand jury's verdict to implicate eight players and five gamblers on nine counts of conspiracy to defraud. The case went to trial on June 27, 1921. But before it started, key evidence went missing from the Cook County courthouse, including the signed confessions of Cicotte and Jackson, who subsequently recanted their confessions. Frustrated

Game 1 World Series ticket stub, 1919

Cincinnati National League
BASE BALL CLUB
World's **1919** Redland
Series Field

Pavilion | GAME | ADMIT ONE
Seat | **1** | Pavilion Seat $2.00
| | War Tax Paid .20
| | Cost of Ticket $2.20

RAIN CHECK
If legal game is not played on scheduled date, this coupon is good for admission and same seat for game whenever it is played.
ROESSLER BROS., CINCINNATI

ENTRANCES: Findlay Street, near Western Avenue, and Findlay Street next to main entrance.
Gates at the Park will be opened each day during the series at 10:00 a. m. The holder of this ticket will be given choice of Pavilion seat or standing room in Pavilion or on Field, according to time of arrival.
5305

GOLDEN JUBILEE
CINCINNATI REDS
Champions 1869-1919
OFFICIAL SOUVENIR SCORE CARD.

WORLD'S SERIES
GAMES

REDLAND FIELD
1919

Price, 25 Cents

"The idea staggered me. I remembered, of course, that the World Series had been fixed in 1919, but if I had thought of it at all I would have thought of it as a thing that merely happened, the end of some inevitable chain. It never occurred to me that one man could start to play with the faith of fifty million people—with the single-mindedness of a burglar blowing a safe."

—F. Scott Fitzgerald, *The Great Gatsby,* 1925

Game 1 official
World Series
program, 1919

by delays in the trial, new commissioner Kenesaw Mountain Landis, who was also a federal judge, suspended the eight players from baseball. On August 2, the jury returned verdicts of not guilty on all charges for all of the accused players. The following day, Landis upheld his ban, ruling that the players had broken the rules of baseball and destroyed public trust. "Birds of a feather flock together," he said in a press release. "Men associating with gamblers and crooks could expect no leniency."

The Chicago White Sox home uniform (page 55) was worn by pitcher Urban Clarence "Red" Faber during Game 1 (yes, the White Sox wore their home uniforms at Redland Field that day) and in the subsequent games of the 1919 World Series. Faber, who was inducted into the Hall of Fame in 1964 and is one of the last pitchers permitted to throw the spitball, witnessed the events from the dugout but did not pitch in the Series due to a bout with influenza. Teammate Ray Schalk believed that if Faber had been healthy, the Black Sox scandal would not have happened because the conspirators wouldn't have had enough pitching to succeed. "If he'd been able to [pitch]," said Schalk, "we'd have beaten the Reds despite the gamblers."

This uniform is the only known surviving example that was worn in that infamous World Series.

THE GREATEST GENERATION

1920–1945

The Deadball Era ended with the crooked World Series of 1919, the so-called Black Sox scandal. The era of the pitcher gave way to the period of the hitter, largely because of a 1920 rule change that outlawed tampering with the ball. Pitchers no longer were allowed to throw spitballs, shine balls, and other trick pitches that sent balls flying in unnatural arcs through the air. The dawning Live Ball Era had its chief protagonists with Babe Ruth at the beginning and Joe DiMaggio and Ted Williams at the end, when the conclusion of World War II brought a close to the period and many players who served in the war overseas returned to the diamond. Baseball by now had night games, a 154-game schedule, iconic diamonds such as Ebbets Field and Comiskey Park, and legendary players such as Lefty Grove and Stan Musial. The major league game was still confined to 16 teams playing in 10 cities in the Midwest and Northeast, but fans across the country followed their favorite teams and players on sports-based news features at the movies and in a rising national press. Players were now identifiable across the field thanks to the 1929 introduction of numbers on the backs of uniforms.

The jerseys of the time enabled greater freedom of movement with more comfort, and teams routinely ordered multiple sets of home and road uniforms. Heavy wool flannel gave way to lighter blend fabric, innovations such as zippers and vests were introduced, and sleeve patches began to commemorate anniversaries, civic events, and patriotism. The A.and G. Spalding Company retained its hold on uniform manufacture, but other firms began to provide gear in local markets: Wilson in Chicago, Goldsmith in Cincinnati, Rawlings in St. Louis. Surviving uniforms from this era are more abundant than those from the previous two decades, though they still are not common.

Photograph taken at the Polo Grounds during the 1936 World Series between the New York Giants and New York Yankees. Lou Gehrig has just made a hit to right field as Joe DiMaggio dashes towards second base.

OUR NATIONAL HEIRLOOM

BABE RUTH 1920 New York Yankees Road Jersey

I t is the fall of 1919, and the Chicago White Sox are facing the Cincinnati Reds in a much-anticipated World Series showdown. Chicago is better by almost every measure. Even so, White Sox pitcher Claude "Lefty" Williams loses three times and Cincinnati takes the Series in eight games. So egregious are the errors and bad plays committed by Chicago players that word quickly spreads that something is rotten in the Series. In an ensuing investigation, it is discovered that the White Sox—its 1919 lineup known forever afterward as the Black Sox—were on the take, paid to lose.

In revulsion, audiences stayed away from ballparks around the country the following season, disdaining the game as crooked and those who played it as untrustworthy goons. It was a sad fall for a sport that had been proclaimed America's pastime.

Enter George Herman Ruth. Big, gawky, and decidedly proletarian, he made no secret of his origins. Born on February 6, 1895, into poverty to German immigrants in Baltimore, Maryland, he was tarred as incorrigible when he was seven and locked up in an industrial school for boys. He learned to sew, dig ditches, build cabinets, make shoes, and cook.

He also learned to play baseball, and he was permitted to favor his left hand and play every position on the field. Ruth eventually became a pitcher for the school, and he compiled a record so sterling that he was allowed to pitch for various amateur and semi-pro squads in Baltimore in the summer of 1913, when he was 18. Impressed by Ruth's performances, Jack Dunn, owner and manager of the Orioles, the city's minor league team, signed Ruth to a contract. Orioles players called the tough rookie "Babe." The following spring, the Orioles played several major league teams. In two contests against the Phillies, Ruth faced 29 batters and allowed only six hits and two unearned runs. One week later, he threw a

complete-game victory over the Philadelphia Athletics, champions of three of the past four World Series. Dunn ran into financial difficulties that summer and sold Ruth to the Boston Red Sox.

The Babe debuted for the Red Sox on July 11, 1914, and beat the Cleveland Naps, 4–3, in his first game. But after the Detroit Tigers hit him hard in his second start, Ruth was sent to the minor leagues, where he helped the Providence Grays capture the International League pennant. Ruth returned to Boston for good in the final week of the 1914 season. On October 2, he pitched a complete-game victory over the Yankees and doubled for his first major league hit. After a slow start in 1915, he won three complete games in a span of nine days in June and finished the season with an 18–8 record. In 1916, Ruth posted a league-leading 1.75 ERA and won

Babe Ruth with six-year-old Paul Harrington at Comiskey Park, June 6, 1922

Ruth's game-used bat from the early 1920s and his 1920 New York Yankees road jersey

23 games, including nine by shutout, still an American League record for left-handed pitchers (it was tied in 1978 by the Yankees' Ron Guidry).

During the 1918 season, Ruth's versatility on the diamond became unprecedented—from mid-July to early September, he pitched every fourth day and played left field, center field, or first base on the other days. During one 10-game stretch at Fenway Park, Ruth batted .469 (15 for 32) and slugged .969 with four singles, six doubles, and five triples. On the mound, he allowed more than two runs only once in 10 starts. In three games spanning the 1916 and 1918 World Series, Ruth pitched 29⅔ consecutive scoreless innings, a Series record that stood until Whitey Ford broke it in 1961.

But Ruth's talent as a pitcher would start to be overshadowed by his feats as a hitter. By late June 1919, the Red Sox were clearly out of the pennant race and manager Ed Barrow had no objection to Ruth

concentrating on hitting, if only because it drew people to the ballpark. The season was not a brilliant one for the Red Sox, but it was for Ruth. During the regular season, he hit 29 home runs, breaking the major league single-season record of 25 set in 1899 by Buck Freeman of the Washington Senators.

It remains a mystery why Boston's management sold Ruth's contract, but the Red Sox sent him to the New York Yankees at the end of the 1919 season. Because of the Black Sox scandal, baseball was in disarray. Ruth, a careful student of power politics, realized it was not enough for him to be a great athlete—he had to be a showman as well. Ruth cooked up all manner of razzle-dazzle, developing a scowl calculated to terrorize pitchers as well as a bright, toothy grin just right for the front page.

Boston fans were not happy to lose Ruth, and the Red Sox would not win another World Series for nearly

The Babe Bows Out, by photographer Nat Fein, Yankee Stadium, June 13, 1948

a century, giving rise to the notion that the deal cast a curse on Fenway Park. One of Ruth's first games as a Yankee was against the Red Sox, and he hit a home run. He hit 11 home runs in May 1920 and 13 more in June, and he ended the season with 54. No other player hit more than 19 that season, and Ruth alone hit more homers than the total accumulated by 14 of the other 15 major league teams.

Ruth was emerging as the most charismatic and famous player in baseball history, a Bunyanesque figure who transcended the game. In the early 1920s, when Ruth wore this gray flannel New York Yankees road jersey (page 61)—the earliest Ruth jersey known in existence—he helped lure fans back to the ballparks after the Black Sox scandal. Throughout the 1920s, he gained renown as a pitcher's nightmare and a nation's dream. Not that Ruth was entirely free of scandal himself; while still in his 20s, he developed a girth and a propensity toward gout owing to his appetite for beer, whiskey, rich food, and cigars. "How did a man drink so much and never get drunk?" a young teammate wondered. Although he drank beer by the crate and ate hot dogs by the dozen, Ruth worked magic in whatever ballpark he appeared, drawing huge crowds wherever he traveled.

Ruth was voted the most popular American of the Roaring Twenties in magazine polls, and he helped average Americans forget their troubles during the Great Depression. His round belly, spindly legs, twinkling eyes, and impish grin gave him an almost cartoonlike appearance. But he was serious on the field, and his performances showed his devotion to winning. "It is impossible to watch him at bat without experiencing an emotion," wrote Paul Gallico, a *New York Daily News* sportswriter who followed Ruth's development over the years. "I have seen hundreds of ballplayers at the plate, and none of them managed to convey the message of impending doom to the pitcher that Babe Ruth did with the cock of his head, the position of his legs, and the little gentle waving of the bat, feathered in his two big paws."

In 1926, Ruth was the de facto leader of a Yankees lineup that sportswriters called Murderers' Row, so intimidating was its batting power. The lineup annihilated every team it faced so handily that audiences became slightly bored. Ruth, with his show-business instincts honed to a fine sharpness—and most famously displayed when he pointed to the center-field bleachers and then hit a home run there during Game 3 of the 1932 World Series—determined that he needed to start amazing audiences with his skill at the plate. During the off-season in 1927 and 1928, Ruth and teammate Lou Gehrig toured the country to play exhibition games against teams composed of local amateur players, giving fans who lived in remote areas of the country the

> "He was a parade all by himself, a burst of dazzle and jingle, Santa Clause [*sic*] drinking his whiskey straight and groaning with a bellyache caused by gluttony. Babe Ruth made the music that his joyous years danced to in a continuous party."
>
> —Jimmy Cannon, sports journalist

chance to see the stars in action. Known as the "Bustin' Babes and Larrupin' Lou's" barnstorming tour, the campaign also included entertainment such as the hijinks of Ruth hamming it up for a crowd in Brooklyn while touting a rodeo at Madison Square Garden.

Ruth had by now acquired a host of nicknames: the Colossus of Clout. The Sultan of Swat. The Wizard of Wham. The Potentate of Pow. The Bambino. The Babe. And he delivered: By the time he retired in 1935, he had racked up more home runs (714) than any other hitter in baseball history, a record that would stand until 1974, when Hank Aaron hit number 715. In 1927 alone, he hit 60 homers, and his career slugging percentage of .690 still stands unbeaten. He also had winning pitching records in 10 seasons, though he took the mound sparingly after the 1919 season.

On the rainy afternoon of Sunday, June 13, 1948, at Yankee Stadium, Ruth—terminally ill with throat cancer—made his last public appearance, to commemorate the stadium's silver anniversary. While in the locker room, the frail Babe put on his old uniform—its number 3 would be retired that year— and went out to the plate, using a bat that belonged to ace Cleveland Indians pitcher Bob Feller for support. Nat Fein, a staff photographer at the *New York Herald Tribune*, captured the moment in a photograph entitled *The Babe Bows Out* (opposite), which won the 1949 Pulitzer Prize, the first sports photo ever to earn the honor.

Ruth died two months later, on August 16, 1948. More than six decades after his death, we still revel in Ruth's uncompromising power at the plate, his gregarious demeanor, his cheerful grin, his penchant for shenanigans and carousing, his bellyaches, and his lifelong affection for children, especially children down on their luck in hospitals or reformatories. From one generation to the next, our national heirloom has proven an inspirational metaphor for the human spirit. As Ruth himself put it: "I swing big, with everything I've got. I hit big or I miss big. I like to live as big as I can." And so he did.

"If it weren't for Babe Ruth, we wouldn't be sitting here now."

—Don Pruett, son of Hub Pruett, 2014

DR. PRUETT

HUB PRUETT 1924 St. Louis Browns Road Jersey

Although St. Louis Browns pitcher Hub Pruett had only a seven-year major league career, with an anemic record of 29 wins and 48 losses (.377), his record against Babe Ruth was nothing short of spectacular. In 1922, the rookie southpaw struck out the Bambino 10 of the first 13 times he faced him. Pruett's uncanny fadeaway pitch, a version of the screwball popularized by Christy Mathewson over the previous two decades, was the secret to his success against Ruth. Pruett threw his fadeaway from three different angles: top, sidearm, and underarm. "All I did was swing at his motion," recalled Ruth. "He was an octopus pitcher, one of those guys who throws everything at you except the ball." While Ruth was known to swing for the fences, his career strikeout average versus plate appearances was just under 13 percent. The Bambino's lifetime batting average was .345, but only .190 against Pruett.

Pruett loved pitching in the majors, but his real dream was to follow in his father's footsteps by becoming a doctor. He received his Doctor of Medicine degree in obstetrics and gynecology from St. Louis University School of Medicine in 1932. New York Giants manager John McGraw offered Pruett a salary raise and contract to pitch in 1933, but Pruett, who had been suffering from a sore arm, decided to

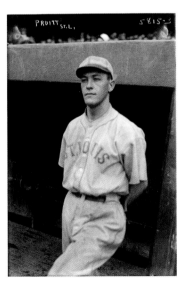

pursue a career in medicine. "After I hurt the arm, pitching became drudgery," said Pruett. "The arm would hurt so much I'd have to tie a pillow to it in order to get some sleep—but I never could have made it through medical school without my baseball earnings."

Dr. Pruett got a chance to thank the Bambino just before Ruth's death in 1948: "I went up and introduced myself and said, 'Thanks, Babe, for putting me through medical school. If it hadn't been for you, nobody would ever have heard of me.' The Babe remembered me and replied, 'That's all right, kid, but I'm glad there weren't many more like you, or no one would have heard of *me*.'"

Pruett wore this rare wool flannel St. Louis Browns jersey during road games in 1924, his last season with the team. At the end of the season, he gave the jersey to teammate and fellow pitcher Walter "Boom Boom" Beck, who kept it for most of his life. Although Pruett played with the St. Louis Browns from 1922 to 1924, the jersey can be dated to 1924 by the size and font style of the athletic felt lettering (see page 269 in the Compendium), with special emphasis on the size of the letter *O* that is centered on the placket. St. Louis Browns road uniforms from the 1922 and 1923 seasons appear to have a much more elongated cut, with the letter *O* covering most of the space between the second and third buttons.

Hub Pruett outside of dugout, c. 1922

DIVINE INTERVENTION

MUDDY RUEL 1924 Washington Senators Home Jersey

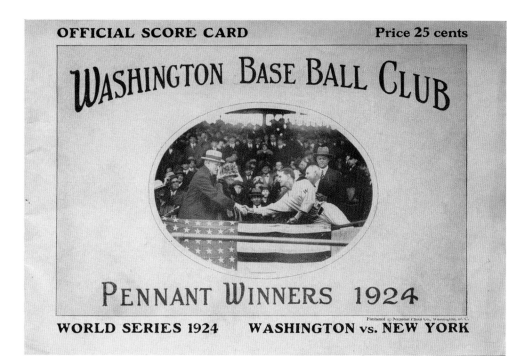

OFFICIAL SCORE CARD — Price 25 cents

WASHINGTON BASE BALL CLUB

PENNANT WINNERS 1924

WORLD SERIES 1924   WASHINGTON vs. NEW YORK

Washington Senators official World Series program, 1924

The Washington Senators had a lousy start to the twentieth century. In 1901 and 1902, they finished in sixth place. The following nine seasons, they landed in the American League cellar or just above it. The abyss was 1904, when the club finished 38–113, the team's worst record and the AL's second-worst Deadball Era record. Following their dead-last 1909 season, Chicago sportswriter Charles Dryden coined a maxim: "Washington: First in war, first in peace, and last in the American League." The franchise redeemed itself with second-place finishes behind Walter Johnson's epic pitching in 1912 and 1913 but couldn't hold onto the magic. After a third-place finish in 1914, they slid back into mediocrity for the next nine years.

The Senators finally broke the spell in 1924, when they won the AL pennant and faced John McGraw's New York Giants in the World Series. As *Washington Post* columnist Shirley Povich wrote in 1994: "The like of it had never been known before....The Washington Senators vs. the New York Giants of John McGraw, in the seven games of the Fall Classic. In America's mindset, it ranked as one of the great improbables....It was never thought that the Washington Senators, long scoffed at as the American League's patsies, would ever win a pennant, much less a World Series."

Yet the Senators defeated the mighty Giants with a dramatic 12-inning victory in Game 7, giving Washington its first—and only—Fall Classic title. The unlikely hero was Senators catcher Herold Dominic "Muddy" Ruel (given his moniker, it's said, by childhood friends for playing catch with a mudball). He had played his first season with the Senators in 1923, and in 136 games he batted .316 with 54 RBI and 24 doubles. His fielding percentage was .980 in 133 games behind the plate. "Ruel is the best catcher in either major league this year," said Philadelphia Athletics manager Connie Mack in 1923. "He has handled his pitchers in fine style and has been a terror at the bat....He is tireless, the type of catcher that makes every player on his club perk up." Walter Johnson later echoed the sentiment: "Muddy made a pitcher out of me. He was the smartest catcher baseball ever had, and certainly the greatest handler of pitchers. When I worked with Muddy, it was like sitting in a rocking chair. I never disputed his choice of pitches."

Ruel's 1924 Washington Senators home jersey with an early 1920s professional-model catcher's mitt, face mask, and chest padding

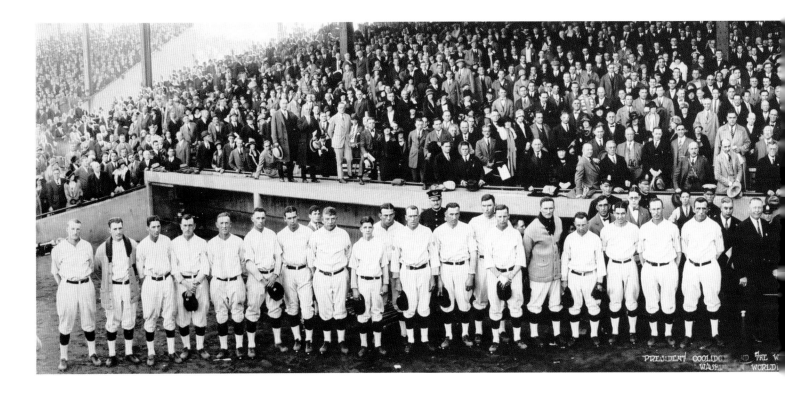

PRESIDENT COOLIDGE AND THE W
WASH   WORLD

Panoramic photograph of the Giants and Senators taken before start of Game 7 of the World Series, 1924. Muddy Ruel stands 17th from the left.

In the 1924 Series, Ruel was hitless through the first six games, though he was behind the plate for every inning. In Game 7, the Giants led, 3–1, in the eighth inning. With bases loaded and two outs, Senators player-manager Bucky Harris hit a "bad-hop" ground ball that Giants third baseman Fred Lindstrom failed to catch. Two runs scored to tie the game, 3–3. Walter Johnson took the mound in the ninth for the Senators and pitched four scoreless innings, with Ruel calling signs behind the plate. In the bottom of the 12th, Giants catcher Hank Gowdy stepped on his own discarded mask while trying to catch Ruel's foul pop-up and dropped the ball. With a second chance, Ruel doubled. After Johnson reached first on another error, Earl McNeely hit a sharp ground ball toward third, and again the ball took a bad hop past Lindstrom and bounced into the outfield for a single. Ruel scored from second with the winning run, and, as Povich wrote, "the crowd catapulted out of the stands to thrash onto the field and to dance on the dugout roofs, refusing to leave the park until long after nightfall. The cup of joys spills its intoxicating bubbles over the Monument, the Capitol, the White House, the Griffith Stadium, and all

over the town. Washington has found something that is more heady than wine, more exhilarating than strong drink. It is victory! Triumph!"

Ruel wore this jersey (page 66) during that remarkable 1924 season. The Senators wore this style of jersey from 1923 to 1925, but evidence dates this jersey dates to 1924 specifically even though jerseys of the period did not feature supplemental tagging that identified their year of use. First, the garment features a standard manufactured collar instead of the sun collar (see page 303 in the Compendium) that was common in the era. Photographs from 1923 show Ruel in a home uniform with the sun collar cut away, and the standard manufactured collar appears in shots of Ruel from both the 1924 and 1925 seasons, so 1923 can be excluded.

A second factor enabling attribution to the 1924 season is the name. Uniforms produced in the same year by the same manufacturer share common characteristics, including the way players' names appear. Ruel's 1924 jersey shows only his last name embroidered in the collar area. But a 1925 Bucky Harris Senators jersey features a first initial and a last name: "B. Harris." In 1923 and 1924, the team had only one

W YORK, N. L. WORLD'S SERIES BASE BALL TEAMS.
OCTOBER 10, 1924.

player named Harris: Bucky. But the 1925 club had two: Bucky and utility infielder Joe Harris. However, the Senators did not acquire Joe Harris until April 29—well after the 1925 uniforms would have been ordered and even after Opening Day on April 14. Thus it's clear the Senators ordered the 1925 jersey tagged "B. Harris" because the first initial was standard that year, not because they had acquired a second player with the same last name. Further research demonstrates that every 1925 Senators jersey featured the first initial and last name of the player. Therefore, the way the name appears on the Harris jersey versus the way Ruel's name is displayed indicates that they were manufactured in different years: the Ruel jersey is from 1924, not 1923 or 1925.

A final clue dates the jersey to 1924: the position of the *W* team logo embroidered onto the left and right sleeves. In period images, the location and alignment of logos in relation to the pinstripes on home uniforms differ slightly from uniform to uniform. A 1924 photo of Ruel tagging out Babe Ruth at home plate shows an alignment of the *W* on the right sleeve that matches the alignment on the jersey pictured here.

"Don't tell me the breaks of the game don't either make you or break you. If Gowdy had caught my foul—an easy one—in the twelfth, I'd never have gotten a chance to double and later bring in the winning run. But he did, and I did, and that's why we're champs. Hot doggie."

—Muddy Ruel, 1924

BASEBALL ABROAD

FRANKIE FRISCH 1924 World Tour Jersey

In 1874, George Wright (legendary shortstop for the 1869 Cincinnati Red Stockings, baseball's first all-professional team) and his older brother, Harry (baseball's first professional manager), arranged baseball's first international tour. They brought teams from Boston and Philadelphia to England in an attempt to convince the British to abandon cricket in favor of baseball. The attempt failed, and the *London Observer* dismissed the American sport as a "rushing, helter-skelter game."

Fourteen years later, Albert Goodwill Spalding, who had been part of the 1874 series, led a tour with the Chicago White Stockings and a rival team of All-Stars. The group left Chicago by rail on October 20, 1888, and played games in Iowa, Nebraska, Colorado, and Utah. After games in San Francisco and Los Angeles, the teams boarded a boat for the Sandwich Islands (known today as Hawaii), New Zealand, Australia, Ceylon, and Egypt. The World Tour continued on to Rome, Paris, and the British Isles. As chief proprietor of baseball's biggest sporting goods business, Spalding sponsored the tour to build recognition for his brand overseas. He also was determined to convince observers that baseball was American in origin and not a descendant of the English game of rounders. "After the Civil War, organized teams became important, and baseball developed into popular show business, enjoying a prestige enhanced by American pride in having a 'national game,'" wrote baseball historian Harold Seymour. "Pride and patriotism required that the game be native, unsullied by English ancestry." Spalding believed the tour could foster this patriotic fervor.

In 1913 and 1914, the entrepreneurial New York Giants manager John McGraw and Chicago White Sox rainmaker Charles Comiskey staged an ambitious tour through Asia and Europe, with stars such as Jim Thorpe, Tris Speaker, "Wahoo" Sam Crawford, and Urban "Red" Faber. King George V attended a game played in front of 20,000 spectators at England's Stanford Bridge. This was the king's first sporting event at the stadium, and he wore a derby and dark suit. McGraw and Comiskey gave three cheers and accepted a game ball from the king when they were presented to him. After the Sox defeated the Giants, 5–4, in 11 innings, King George instructed an aide to "tell Mr. McGraw and Mr. Comiskey that I have enjoyed the game enormously."

In 1924, the two teams staged another tour with an all-star cast of future Hall of Famers, including Johnny Evers, Ed Walsh, Casey Stengel, Dave Bancroft, Sam Rice, and Travis Jackson. The teams played at Stamford Bridge in England on a cold November day, and King George again came to watch. Many games on the tour, however, were sparsely attended. Only 20 fans turned out for a game in Ireland, and lack of interest forced cancellation of other events. Finally, McGraw and Comiskey decided that America's game might not be suitable for export. (Later, in 1931, a tour featuring Lou Gehrig traveled to Japan, where interest in baseball was stronger than it was in Europe.)

One player on the 1924 tour was well prepared for a visit to the Sceptred Isle, and he wore this patriotic gray-teal pinstriped jersey manufactured by Spalding (opposite). Frank Francis Frisch, who appears in a photo with King George V and the two teams at Stamford Bridge (pages 72–73), was the son of a wealthy lace-linen manufacturer who had emigrated from Germany and raised a family in the Bronx. Frisch majored in chemistry at Fordham University, where he lettered—like Jackie Robinson a generation later—in football, basketball, track (he was nicknamed the "Fordham Flash"), and baseball. After graduation, Frisch was signed by John McGraw and the New York Giants. He went straight to the majors without the customary seasoning on a minor league team because, reportedly, Frisch's father had promised to draft him into the family business if the player did not make good from the start.

Playing second base in his debut game, Frisch, five feet seven and fearless, chased down a ball and threw the runner out in a play that convinced McGraw that "he is going to be a great ball player." In the next two years, Frisch played second, third, and shortstop. He hit .341 in 1921 and led the Giants to the World Series, where they defeated their longtime rivals, the New York Yankees.

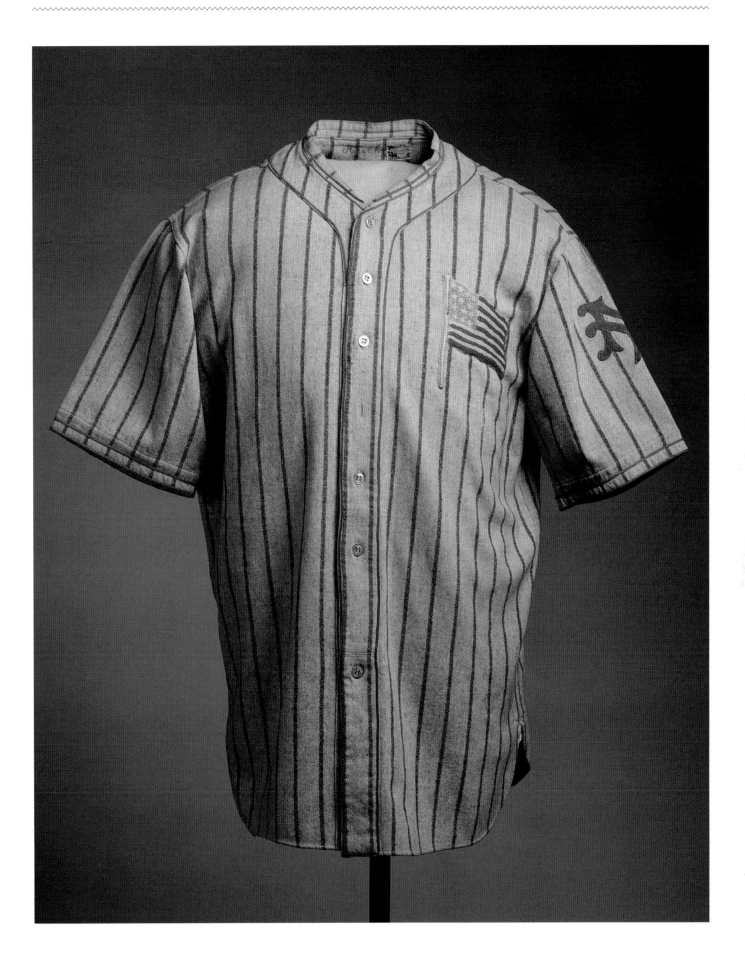

"The impudence of the Yankee knows no limits; and their baseball visit here has afforded another opportunity for the display of it."

—*London Sketch*, February 1914

A productive batter and superb fielder, Frisch was named team captain in 1922. In that position, he came under constant criticism from McGraw, who had been his champion and protector. Frisch endured the badgering for a few years, for the sake of the team. In 1927, Frisch was traded to St. Louis for another second baseman, Rogers Hornsby. As a Cardinal, Frisch set a record for assists, belted homers, and stolen bases. The Cardinals won the National League pennant in 1928 and 1930 and the World Series in 1931. Frisch was named the National League's Most Valuable Player in 1931.

In 1933, Frisch became a player-manager for the Cardinals, heading a roster that included future greats Dizzy Dean, Pepper Martin, Joe "Ducky" Medwick, and Leo Durocher. In the 1934 World Series, the Cards became known as the "Gashouse Gang" when Joe Williams of the *World-Telegram* wrote, "I picked the Tigers but the Cardinals have got me worried. They looked like a bunch of guys from the gas house district who had crossed the railroad tracks for a game of ball with the nice kids." Frisch was known as an intense manager, and Terry Moore, a rookie outfielder, saw Frisch's rough side at the Cardinals spring training camp in 1935: "I think I have had one of the toughest managers on earth. Frisch didn't like rookies, and every time I made a mistake he'd always yell, 'Who was your manager? I wish he'd taught you better than that!' Frisch was tough on you."

Frisch retired from playing in 1937. He managed the Pittsburgh Pirates from 1940 to 1946 and the Chicago Cubs from 1949 to 1951, then did color commentary on radio and television until a heart attack in September 1956 forced him to curtail his activities. He spent the remainder of his life pursuing genteel interests, which included tending his roses, reading classic literature, and listening to classical music. King George V, who preferred working with his stamp collection to appearing in public, would have approved.

World Tourists meet King George V at Stamford Bridge, England, 1924; Frisch shakes the king's hand.

THE CATCH

SAM RICE 1926–27 Washington Senators Home Uniform

Edgar Charles "Sam" Rice entered the majors in August 1915 as a 25-year-old pitcher for the Washington Senators. After moving into the outfield midway through the following season, he developed into one of the leading hitters in the American League and ended his career with a .322 lifetime average, 2,987 total hits, and six seasons with more than 200 hits. Rice, a perennial .300 hitter during his 20-year career, was a key member of the only three Washington Senators teams to win pennants, and he holds franchise records for hits, doubles, triples, and runs scored.

Rice, who adopted the nickname "Sam" in the mid-1920s, led the AL in hits in 1924, the year the Senators won their first pennant and defeated the New York Giants to claim their first and only World Series championship. The following season, Washington again won the pennant, but they lost the Fall Classic in seven games to the Pittsburgh Pirates. In that Series, Rice batted .364 with 12 hits, five runs, and three RBI. Despite tremendous success at the plate, Rice is most remembered for his exploits in right field—in particular, for one of the most controversial plays in baseball history. Twenty-nine years before Willie Mays defied baseball logic with his "miracle catch" of Vic Wertz's line drive in deep center at the Polo Grounds in Game 1 of the 1954 Fall Classic, Rice had made a catch that was just as impressive. Or did he?

It was a cold day at Griffith Stadium on October 10 for Game 3 of the 1925 World Series between the Washington Senators and Pittsburgh Pirates. Goose Goslin's homer in the sixth inning snapped the Pirates' 3–1 lead, and the Senators were ahead 4–3 going into the eighth. Reliever Firpo Marberry, the only pitcher to lead the major leagues in saves five times, took the mound for Washington in the eighth. He struck out Glenn Wright and George Grantham, and then brash Pirates backstop Earl Smith strolled to the plate. "He looked over Marberry's pitching with an arrogant

sneer," wrote the *New York Times*. "Crouched at the plate, Earl is not an easy batsman to pitch to. He worried Marberry. Then Smith caught hold of one of his pitches. His left-handed swing was deadly and true, and the ball went soaring far and straight into right field."

Rice, playing right field for Washington, charged after the ball while craning his neck to gauge what could have been the tying home run. He leaped high in the air with his left arm extended, snagged the ball, then tumbled over the right-field wall into the temporary

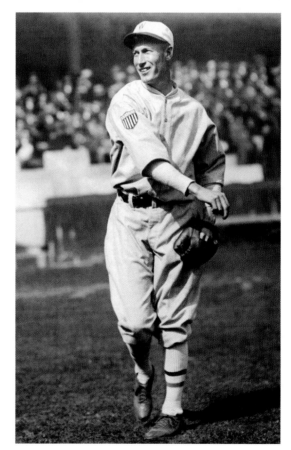

Sam Rice warming up before a game at Griffith Stadium, 1926

Monday July 26 - 1965

It was a cold and windy day the Rightfield Bleachers were crowded with people in overcoats and wrapped in Blankets, the ball was a line drive headed for the Bleachers towards right Center I turned slightly to my right and had the ball in view all the way, going at top speed and about 15 feet from Bleachers jumped as high as I could and back handed and the ball hit the center of Pocket in glove (I had a death grip on it) I hit the ground about 5 feet from a barrier about 4 feet high in front of Bleacher with all the breaks on but couldn't stop so I tried to jump it to land in the crowd but my feet hit the barrier about a foot from top and I toppled over on my stomach into first row of Bleachers, I hit my adams apple on something which sort of knocked me out for a few

"Myths which are believed in tend to become true."

—George Orwell

bleachers. Several minutes later, Rice emerged with the ball in his glove. Second-base umpire Charlie "Cy" Rigler ran over and called Smith out, explaining that as soon as the catch was made, the play was over, and so it did not matter where Rice ended up. Washington would hang onto its lead and win the game.

Pirates fans erupted. After the game, some approached Pirates manager Bill McKechnie in the visitors' clubhouse, claiming they had seen, and were prepared to sign sworn affidavits to the fact, that Rice had lost control of the ball after entering the stands. McKechnie addressed this with commissioner Kenesaw Mountain Landis and asked if it would be possible to file a protest of the umpire's decision. Landis told McKechnie that he could not appeal an umpire's decision, and the matter was officially closed. More than 1,600 Pirates fans wrote Landis to claim that Rice had dropped the ball and that a fan had probably put the ball back into his glove. Landis again refused to budge. When Landis later asked Rice whether he had caught the ball, Rice coyly replied, "Judge, the umpire said I did." Landis apparently paused briefly and said, "Sam, let's leave it that way."

"In all the future years that World Series will be played, in all the games that have been played under high nervous tension in the past, one will never see a more thrilling catch than that grand grabby by Sam Rice," Harry Cross wrote in the *New York Times*. "All Washington, and, in fact, American League fans from the Atlantic to the Pacific, who followed this afternoon's battle before the scoreboard or on the radio, raise their hats to Samuel [sic] Rice tonight." For the rest of his life, Rice refused to talk about the catch. The press offered to pay him for the story, but Rice turned down the offers, saying, "I don't need the money. The mystery is more fun." He would not even tell his wife or his daughter. When asked whether he had caught the ball, he would respond with "The umpire said I did." Finally, in 1965, Rice gave the Hall of Fame a sealed letter to be opened upon his death, which occurred in 1974. The letter (opposite) was a detailed description of the catch, and it concluded with these words:

The ball was a line drive headed for the bleachers towards right center. I turned slightly to my right and had the ball in view all the way, going at top speed and about 15 feet from bleachers jumped as high as I could and back handed and the ball hit the center of the pocket in glove (I had a death grip on it). I hit the ground about 5 feet from a barrier about 4 feet high in front of bleachers with all the breaks [sic] on but couldn't stop so I tried to jump it to land in the crowd but my feet hit the barrier about a foot from top and I toppled over on my stomach into first row of bleachers, I hit my Adam's apple on something which sort of knocked me out for a few seconds but [center-fielder Earl] McNeeley arrived about that time and grabbed me by the shirt and pulled me out. I remember trotting back towards the infield still carrying in the ball for about halfway and then tossed it towards the pitcher's mound. (How I have wished many times I had kept it.) At no time did I lose possession of the ball.

So did Rice catch the ball or not? (And did Babe Ruth really call his shot in Game 3 of the 1932 World Series?) Perhaps we'll never know. But, as George Orwell said, "Myths which are believed in tend to become true."

With their World Series victory in 1924 and an American League flag the following year, the Washington Senators decided to jazz up their uniforms. Navy blue piping adorned the sun collar and sleeve ends. Ornate, chenille-embroidered American flag shield patches were applied on both sleeves in place of the standard embroidered *W*, a patriotic tribute last seen on the left breast of the Senators' pinstriped flannel road jerseys in 1917. Sam Rice wore this Washington Senators home uniform (page 74) during the 1926 and 1927 seasons. Not only is this style rare—it was featured for only those two seasons—it is also the only known surviving example of this style of uniform outside the Walter Johnson road version housed at the National Baseball Hall of Fame and Museum.

Letter from Sam Rice to the National Baseball Hall of Fame, 1965

A LEGEND OF THE FALL

GEORGE PIPGRAS 1928 New York Yankees Road Jersey

George Pipgras stands second from the left, back row, in this New York Yankees team photograph, 1928

After Ban Johnson's American League became recognized in 1903, the New York press faced a quandary: How to distinguish the American League New York club from the Giants of the National League? Sportswriters tried Hilltoppers, Highlanders, Americans, Invaders, Greater New Yorks, and Kilties for the AL team. But none of the nicknames stuck.

In 1904, *New York Press* sports editor Jim Price coined "Yankees" or "Yanks" because it fit in headlines and perhaps also because the team played north of the Giants. Some also contend the nickname was influenced by the George M. Cohan Broadway play *Little Johnny Jones*, which featured the song "Yankee Doodle Boy." From 1927 to 1930, the Yankees displayed their nickname across the chest of their road uniforms, the only time in history the team would do so. Yankees pitcher George Pipgras wore this gray flannel road jersey (opposite) in 1928, when he shared the diamond with Earle Combs, Mark Koenig, Babe Ruth, Lou Gehrig, Bob Meusel, and Tony Lazzeri, a lineup known as Murderers' Row.

In 1928, Pipgras led the American League in wins (24), still the record for a Yankees right-handed pitcher, games started (38), and innings pitched (300.2). That year, Pipgras also threw the most memorable game of his career: a 5–0 shutout over the Athletics in September. "I guess that game was the big thrill of my career, even greater than one of our World Series games because if I had not won it, there might not have been a World Series for the Yankees that year," Pipgras recalled later in his life:

> We had a lead of 13½ games in early July 1928, but by the time we met the Athletics in mid-September, we were trailing by half a spin, and I couldn't steal or beg a winning game. I had pitched 45 consecutive innings without a run being scored for me. Anyway, we started the series with a double-header at the Stadium before a crowd that was estimated at 85,000. I don't think the Stadium ever was so packed. Huggins pitched me in the first game and Jack Quinn was my opponent. It was close up to the eighth, when Bob Meusel broke it up with a home run. I won 5–0. After that game, we all felt it was the turning point. We took the series, three games out of four, and after that never were headed.

Pipgras was 3–0 in World Series appearances with the Bronx Bombers, with a win in each of the 1927, 1928, and 1932 Series. Babe Ruth once said of Pipgras, "With his fastball he couldn't be beaten." The win streak started when Pipgras was unexpectedly substituted for Urban Shocker in Game 2 of the 1927 Series, and he beat the Pirates 6–2, pitching a seven-hitter while throwing only three curveballs. In 1928, Pipgras baffled the Cardinals with his curve, giving up just four hits in a 9–3 victory against future Hall of Famer Grover Cleveland Alexander. He then beat the Cubs 7–5 in Game 3 of the 1932 Fall Classic, the game in which Babe Ruth hit his famous "Called Shot."

"When we got to the ballpark," Pipgras said, "we knew we were going to win. That's all there was to it. We weren't cocky. I wouldn't call it confidence, either. We just knew. Like when you go to sleep you know the sun is going to come up in the morning." With such fine pitching from Pipgras, his Yankees teammates must have felt the same way.

"Never before or since has there been in the game such a coalescence of talent, such a fusion of lusty hitting and sharp pitching, and all of it torrentially consistent, dismembering the League with a meat cleaver, losing just 44 of their 154 games, setting records...with a near-homicidal attack."

—Donald Honig, on the 1927 New York Yankees

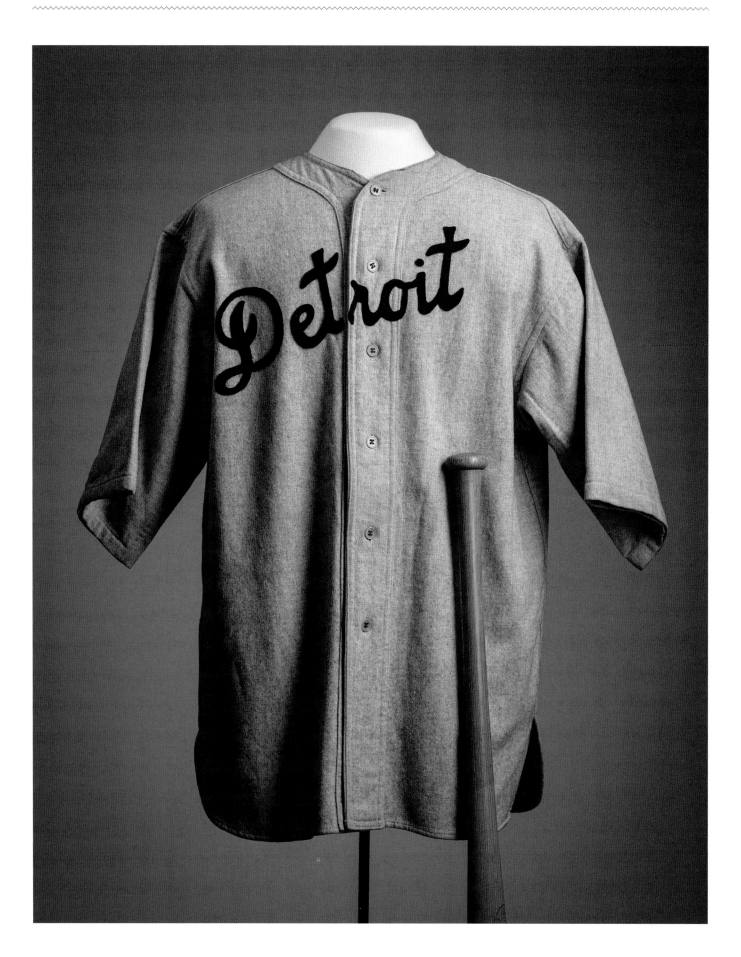

SPEAK SOFTLY, AND CARRY A BIG STICK

CHARLIE GEHRINGER 1930 Detroit Tigers Road Jersey

In a speech on September 2, 1901, then–Vice President Theodore Roosevelt Jr. described his foreign policy philosophy this way—"Speak softly, and carry a big stick"—meaning that negotiations are most effective when backed by the implicit threat of military action. His well-known words could also describe Charlie Leonard Gehringer, one of the greatest second basemen in history. Spending his entire 19-year Depression-era career with the Detroit Tigers, Gehringer was known as "the Silent Knight," one of the majors' quietest players. The limelight made him uncomfortable, praise doubly so: during a Detroit ceremony to honor him after his playing days, guest speakers showered him with adoration. When it was time for the man himself to speak, Gehringer replied, "I'm known around baseball for saying little and I'm not going to spoil my reputation." He then sat down.

Gehringer let his bat, or "big stick," do most of the talking for him, always maintaining that a batter doesn't hit with his mouth. Each year from 1926 (his first full season in the majors) to 1929, he improved his statistics in the Triple Crown categories of batting average, home runs, and RBI. During the 1930 season, when Gehringer wore this one-year-style flannel road jersey (opposite), which featured the city name for the first time in team history, he chalked up more than 200 hits (201) for the second straight year. He would eventually compile more than 200 hits in seven seasons. Gehringer led the Tigers to American League pennants in 1934, 1935, and 1940 and a World Series victory in 1935. In 1937, he won the league batting title with a .371 average and was named the league's Most Valuable Player.

Gehringer carried a big glove, too. He led American League second basemen in fielding percentage and assists seven times, and his 7,068 assists rank second in major league history for a second baseman. "He had an uncanny knack for positioning for hitters, and the hands of a magician," recalled teammate Elden Aucker. "No such thing as a bad-hop grounder in the vicinity of Gehringer. His hands would adjust so quickly, so smoothly, the bad hop was barely visible to the audience. It was just another out." Gehringer got another nickname, the "Mechanical Man," for his remarkable consistency with the bat and glove. "Charlie says 'hello' on Opening Day, 'goodbye' on closing day, and in between hits .350," observed Tigers player-manager Mickey Cochrane.

Off the diamond, Gehringer's devotion to his loved ones and sense of humility toward fans were noteworthy. A few years after his father's death in 1924, Charlie bought a house for his mom, Theresa, who was diabetic, and he lived with her until her death in 1946, declining to marry because he thought the time and attention required for her care would prevent him from being fair to a wife. On August 14, 1929, Gehringer's fans from his hometown, Fowlerville, Michigan, gathered at Navin Field, home of the Tigers, to celebrate what became known as "Charlie Gehringer Day." They presented the left-handed Gehringer with a set of golf clubs made for a right-handed player. Yet he was so touched by their thoughtfulness that he learned to play the game right-handed.

After Gehringer retired from the big leagues at the end of the 1942 season, he enlisted in the Navy Air Corps, serving as a lieutenant commander in World War II. In 1938, he had become a partner in Gehringer and Forsyth, a company that sold fabrics to automobile manufacturers. He returned to his company after the war and grew wealthy. In 1949, he married Josephine Stillen in San Jose, California, on the day that he was inducted into the Baseball Hall of Fame. Gehringer died on January 21, 1993, at 89, and his death went largely unheralded by the press and fans. "Charlie didn't know how to strut," *Washington Post* columnist Shirley Povich wrote later. "He was known as baseball's quiet man, content to let his bat and glove speak for him. With both he was an artist. His kind did not come along very often. His passing should have been better noted." Tom Stanton, who has written prolifically about the Tigers, once recalled a trip he'd taken as a youngster with his own father to Cooperstown: "It gives you a sense of the passing of time to stand beside your father, who is in his ninth decade, as he studies the mitt of the man he has admired since the days of Herbert Hoover. Charlie Gehringer's life became an allegory, its lessons implicit. Be patient. Be humble. Be loyal and loving and devoted. Above all, care for your mother."

Gehringer's game-used bat from the late 1930s with his 1930 Detroit Tigers road jersey

A CAREFUL TANTRUM THROWER

LEFTY GROVE ca. 1932-33 Philadelphia Athletics Home Jersey

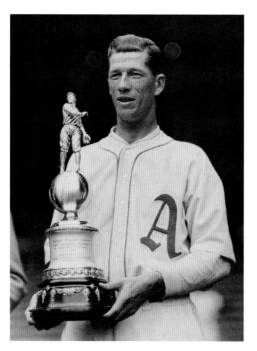

Lefty Grove
holding the 1931
American League
Most Valuable
Player award, 1932

Lonaconing Furnace, which stretches alongside a hill in the small town of Lonaconing, Maryland, commenced operations in 1839 and was the first American furnace to demonstrate that both coke and raw bituminous coal can be used as fuels in the production of iron. In 1973, it was listed on the National Register of Historic Places. Today it serves as a stark reminder of the town's proud heritage in the coal and iron trade. Down the street is another historic landmark: major league baseball's first Most Valuable Player Award, which resides in the George's Creek Library.

The award was given to Philadelphia Athletics pitcher Robert Moses "Lefty" Grove in recognition of his extraordinary achievements during the 1931 season, when he won the pitcher's Triple Crown for the second consecutive year. In addition to finishing with a 31–4 record, he led the league with 175 strikeouts, 27 complete games, four shutouts, and a 2.06 earned run average, which was more than two runs per game lower than the league average. "All things considered," said Athletics manager Connie Mack in 1931, "Grove is the best lefthander that ever walked on a pitcher's slab. He surpasses everybody I have ever seen. He has more speed than any other lefthander in the game."

Born in Lonaconing, Grove had no ambition to follow his family's path into the coal mines. When his brother sprained his ankle in 1916, Lefty covered for him in the mines for two weeks. It was enough. "Dad, I didn't put that coal in here, and I hope I don't have to take no more of her out," Grove said when his father woke him up at 5:30 a.m. on his last day of work. He found other jobs that included work as a "bobbin boy" in a silk mill, an apprentice in a glass factory, and a track layer for the railroad. In his free time, he sought solace in sandlot baseball, using a ball made of a cork stopper and an old wool sock. When Grove was 19, his pitching talent became apparent. Dick Stakem, who owned a general store in Midland, Maryland, used Grove in various town games, including one on Memorial Day 1919, when he fanned 15 batters. In a postseason game against the Baltimore & Ohio railroad team in Cumberland, Grove pitched a no-hitter, striking out 18 batters.

Grove impressed the B&O manager and the following year was hired to clean steam-engine cylinder heads and play for the B&O team in Cumberland. However, before the season started, Bill Louden, who managed the Mountaineers of Martinsburg, West Virginia, in the Class D Blue Ridge League, offered Grove $125 a month. Grove signed a contract with Martinsburg on May 5 and struck out 60 batters in 59 innings that season. Word of Grove's success reached Jack Dunn, the owner of the minor league Baltimore Orioles, who also

Philadelphia Athletics official World Series program, 1931

Grove's pitching motion was a spectacle—it has been described as "a combination St. Vitus dance and acrobatic stunt." After swinging his arms back toward center field while bowing toward home plate, Grove stretched his arms high above his head and raised his right foot in the air as he rocked backward until the knuckles of his left hand nearly brushed the mound; he then came up and over with a big stride, a fierce jerk of the wrist, and a sweeping follow-through. "Batters were confronted with a cross between a dipping oil derrick and a gyrating windmill," wrote author Jim Kaplan.

Hall of Fame shortstop Joe Sewell described Grove's fastball as "a flash of white sewing thread coming at you." Wrote sports journalist Arthur "Bugs" Baer, "Lefty Grove could throw a lamb chop past a wolf." If Grove's speed, six-foot-three frame, and intimidating glower on the mound were not unnerving enough for batters, his pitching wildness certainly would have been. "Catching him was like catching bullets from a rifleman with bad aim," batterymate Mickey Cochrane said during Grove's first year with the Athletics in 1925, when he led the American League in walks (131). "Never bothered me who was up there with the bat," Grove recalled. "I'd hit 'em in the middle of the back or hit 'em in the foot...it didn't make any difference to me."

Fortunately for batters facing Grove six years later during his hallmark 1931 season, the pitcher found his control. But his temper remained as hot as the smoldering coal in Lonaconing Furnace. As he reminisced in *Baseball When It Was a Game:*

Remember that time I was going for my seventeenth straight win, in 1931? I remember that all right. Boy, do I remember that! Would have set a new American League record if I'd have made it. Fellow named Dick Coffman with the St. Louis Browns beat me, 1–0. After I lost that game, I came back and won six or seven in a row. Would have had about 24 straight wins except for that 1–0 loss. After that game I went in and tore the clubhouse up. Wrecked the place. Tore these steel lockers off the wall and everything else. Ripped my uniform up. Threw everything I could get my hands on—bats, balls, shoes, gloves, benches, water buckets; whatever was handy. Giving [Athletics outfielder] Al Simmons hell all the while. Why Simmons? Because he was home in Milwaukee, that's why. Still gets me mad when I think about it....So now I'm tied with Joe Wood and Walter Johnson and Schoolboy Rowe at 16 straight for the American League record. But I would have had 24 if Simmons had been out there where he belonged.

discovered Babe Ruth. Dunn sent his son Jack Jr. to watch Grove pitch. As it turned out, the Martinsburg team had started the season on the road because a storm had leveled the fence that surrounded their field. So, to get Grove, Dunn agreed to pay $3,500 for a new one. "I was the only player," Grove said later, "ever traded for a fence."

From 1920 to 1924, Grove went 108–36 and struck out a minor league record 1,108 batters. In his last season with the minors, he was 26–6 with 231 strikeouts in 236 innings. In exhibition games, he even struck out Babe Ruth nine times in 11 at-bats. Dunn was able to keep Grove in the minors because the Orioles played in a league that was exempt from the major league draft, so Dunn could wait for an acceptable offer for his star pitcher. In early 1925, Dunn finally agreed to sell Grove to an old friend, Philadelphia manager Connie Mack, for $100,600, the highest sum ever paid for a player at that time.

As for the uniform Lefty tore up, we can take comfort that his legacy is enshrined with this rare surviving example (page 83), which he wore during home games at Shibe Park in his last two seasons with the Athletics (1932 and 1933). As far as his temper was concerned, Ted Williams had something to say: "He was a moody guy, a tantrum thrower like me. But when he punched a locker or something, he always did it with his right hand. He was a careful tantrum thrower."

Grove retired from baseball in 1941 when he was with the Boston Red Sox, with a career record of 300–141 and a .680 winning percentage, the highest among members of the 300-win club. He led the American League in strikeouts seven years in a row (1925 to 1931) and in wins four times (1928, 1930, 1931, and 1933), and he had the league's lowest ERA nine times (1926, 1929–32, 1935, 1936, 1938, and 1939). Though he suffered many post-retirement setbacks—a divorce, outliving his only son, and needing financial help from baseball—Grove also demonstrated a gentle side of his character that had been long suppressed. He provided baseball clothing to Philadelphia children who played in the sandlots, supported two youngsters through college, and coached children's baseball teams around Lonaconing. He was elected to the Hall of Fame in 1947, his first year of eligibility, and died at 75 on May 22, 1975. He is buried at Frostburg Memorial Park in Frostburg, Maryland, about nine miles from the Lonaconing Furnace.

"Quit now? They'll have to cut the uniform off me. I'm going out for another 300. They couldn't be any harder to get than the first 300."

—Lefty Grove

Philadelphia Athletics World Series tickets, 1931

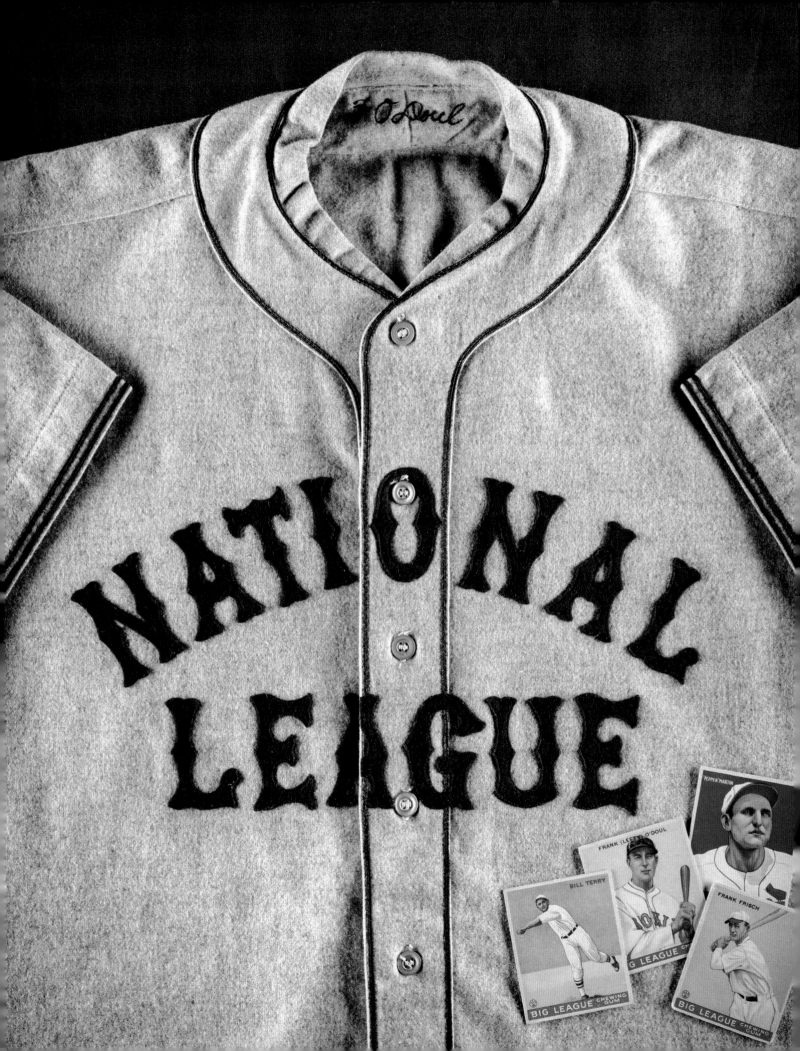

GAME OF THE CENTURY

LEFTY O'DOUL 1933 National League All-Star Game Jersey

In 1919, Enos Gordon Goudey of Barrington Passage, Nova Scotia, founded the Goudey Gum Company and opened its first factory in Boston. In 1933, chewing gum magnate William Wrigley Jr. dubbed Goudey the "penny gum king of America." That year, Goudey's company became the first to sell baseball cards with a stick of bubble gum. One card and one stick of gum were sold for a penny, giving rise to the advent of "bubble gum cards." The 1933 set is widely considered to be one of the most important baseball card sets ever produced. The set (some of which is shown opposite) is composed of 240 cards featuring striking renditions of the era's top stars, including Babe Ruth, Lou Gehrig, Jimmie Foxx, Charlie Gehringer, Al Simmons, Lefty Grove, Pepper Martin, Frankie Frisch, Bill Terry, and Lefty O'Doul. Goudey's timing was auspicious—these legends would also participate that year in Major League Baseball's first official All-Star Game.

On May 27, 1933, Chicago launched a world's fair called the Century of Progress International Exposition. The event was devised to commemorate the city's centennial while promoting a sense of hope during the nadir of the Great Depression. The theme of the event was technological innovation, and highlights included a selection of "dream cars" from all major auto manufacturers, a home-of-tomorrow exhibit, and singer Judy Garland. Mayor Edward Kelly, newly

elected and determined to make the event a success, approached Colonel Robert McCormick, owner and publisher of the *Chicago Tribune*, with the idea of hosting a major sporting event in conjunction with the Exposition. Kelly felt this would help draw more attendance to the fair. McCormick sought the help of friend and *Tribune* sports editor Arch Ward, a die-hard Chicago White Sox fan. Ward, one of the most respected sports journalists in the field, proposed a one-time exhibition game between the best players of the American and National Leagues at Chicago's Comiskey Park.

Ward dubbed his idea the "Game of the Century." As a means of generating even greater interest, fans would vote on the lineups. Initially, this vote was reserved only for *Tribune* readers, but when sports editors from other papers complained, commissioner Kenesaw Mountain Landis ordered that ballots appear in papers throughout the country. Fans nationwide were allowed to vote for as many as 18 players, and they were provided with guidelines suggesting that they choose not only their favorite players, but also players whose performances during the 1933 season warranted inclusion. Accordingly, Al Simmons of the hometown White Sox received the most votes in the American League, while the top pick in the National League was Chuck Klein of the Philadelphia Phillies, who was on his way to winning the Triple Crown that season.

Assortment of 1933 Goudey baseball cards atop O'Doul's 1933 National League All-Star Game jersey

"We wanted to see the Babe. Sure, he was old and had a big waistline, but that didn't make any difference. We were on the same field as Babe Ruth."

—"Wild" Bill Hallahan, National League
    starting pitcher in the 1933 All-Star Game

Ward was so confident the game would be a success that he told McCormick he would cover any losses with his own paycheck. With McCormick's blessing, Ward set out to secure support from the presidents of both leagues, team owners, and commissioner Landis, assuring cynics that the event would help lift baseball out of its Depression-era doldrums. By 1933, the unemployment rate had climbed from 3 percent to 25 percent, food lines were widespread, and banks were closing at an alarming rate—more than 4,000 banks closed that year alone. With league-wide attendance down from 10.1 million in 1930 to 6.3 million in 1933, a decline of more than 37 percent, and average annual players' salaries reduced from $7,500 in 1929 to $6,000 in 1933, Ward's proposal was attractive to both the owners and Landis. Furthermore, because proceeds from the event would be donated to a charity for retired players, Ward argued they could demonstrate to the country that major league baseball was not fostering a culture of profligacy when ordinary Americans were suffering from financial distress. His persistence and lobbying efforts finally won over the owners and Landis.

Tickets sold out quickly—grandstand tickets were $1.10, box seats were $1.65, and the bleacher seats, the cheapest in the park, sold for 55 cents. On July 6, 47,595 fans from throughout the country jammed Comiskey Park under bright sunshine and 90-degree heat. The *Tribune* chose Connie Mack to manage the American League team and John McGraw as the National League manager, and the opposing skippers posed for photographers before the game. The AL players wore their regular team uniforms, while the NL produced gray flannel uniforms for the event. The uniform worn by outfielder Lefty O'Doul of the Brooklyn Dodgers is featured on page 86, along with the 1933 Goudey cards of O'Doul, Frisch, Martin, and Terry. Manufactured by Spalding, the NL uniforms had "National League" in dark-navy blue felt letters across the chest and the player's number on the back to make it easier for fans

to keep score. This would be the only year in All-Star history when special uniforms were produced. Some contend the NL changed its uniform policy because fans preferred to see their heroes in the uniforms they were accustomed to, while others suggest the uniform policy may have been changed to save money.

The game lived up to its billing, and the crowd was thrilled with the star-studded lineups and exhilarating drama. In the bottom of the second inning, NL pitcher Bill Hallahan walked Jimmy Dykes and Joe Cronin before giving up a single to Lefty Gomez that drove Dykes home with the AL's first run. In the bottom of the third, Charlie Gehringer reached first base on a walk. Next up was Babe Ruth, who fittingly hit the first home run in All-Star Game history—a towering shot into the right-field upper deck—putting the AL up, 3-0. After walking the next batter, Lou Gehrig, Hallahan was replaced by Lon Warneke. In the top of the sixth, Lefty O'Doul pinch-hit for Jimmy Wilson but grounded out. Warneke followed with a triple into right field, then scored on a Pepper Martin groundout. Frankie Frisch hit a home run to bring the NL to within a run.

In the top of the sixth, with Frisch on first with two outs, Chick Hafey smashed a line drive into right field, but Ruth reached over the wall to catch it, denying the NL a chance to tie the game. Cronin led off the bottom of the sixth with a single, and he scored on Earl Averill's base hit, extending the AL lead to 4–2. Lefty Grove took the mound in the top of the seventh, while Carl Hubbell replaced Warneke in the bottom of the inning. In the ninth, Grove would take out Bill Terry, Wally Berger, and Tony Cucinello to seal the AL's 4–2 victory.

Harvey Woodruff of the *Tribune* wrote that the fans in attendance were "the most sportsmanlike crowd ever gathered for such an important event. Those familiar boos and jeers so frequently heard were at a minimum. The crowd of yesterday apparently sensed the occasion as a precursor of more such games to follow in future years and lent its best behavior." Although some owners were still lukewarm about the concept, most of the top brass in baseball shared the fans' enthusiasm for making the game an annual event. The positive feelings and publicity for major league baseball were not lost on commissioner Landis. "That's a grand show and it should be continued," he said. During the next owner's meeting, a measure was passed to make an All-Star Game an annual event to be played in a different city each year.

The Midsummer Classic would be played at the Polo Grounds the following year. It has been held every season since, except 1945, when the game was cancelled because of transportation restrictions during World War II. Two All-Star Games were played each year from 1959 to 1962 because the players wanted to raise more money for their retirement fund.

The game is now typically played on the second Tuesday in July. A campaign led by the *Sporting News* officially recognized Arch Ward for his role in pioneering the MLB All-Star Game. Beginning in 1962, the game's MVP was awarded the Arch Ward Memorial Trophy; since 2002, the honor has been called the Ted Williams Most Valuable Player Award.

The San Diego Padres and the city of San Diego hosted the 87th MLB All-Star Week at Petco Park from July 10 to 12, 2016. Events included the All-Star FanFest, home run derby, and celebrity softball game. Lefty O'Doul's National League jersey, featured here, is a poignant reminder of where the event started— with the "Game of the Century" played on a sunny afternoon in July 1933.

American League team photograph at All-Star Game, Comiskey Park, 1933

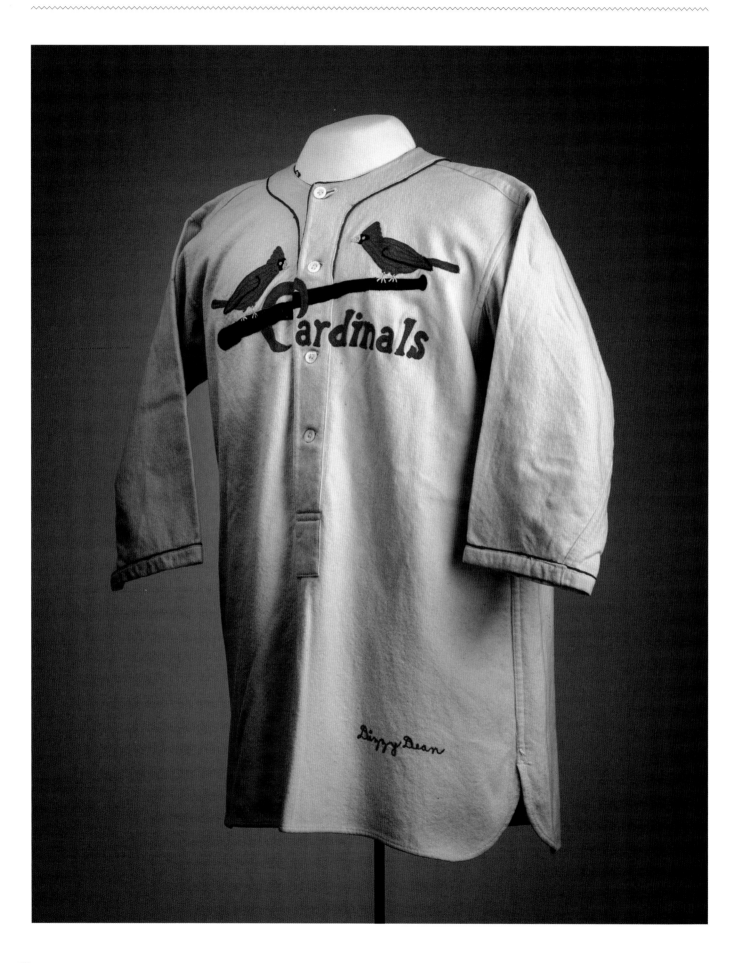

THE SPART OF ST. LOUIS

DIZZY DEAN 1933 St. Louis Cardinals Home Jersey

"A s a ballplayer, Dean was a natural phenomenon, like the Grand Canyon or the Great Barrier Reef," Red Smith wrote in the *New York Times*. "Nobody ever taught him baseball and he never had to learn. He was just doing what came naturally when a scout named Don Curtis discovered him on a Texas sandlot and gave him his first contract." Jay Hanna "Dizzy" Dean became one of the greatest pitchers in baseball history as well as a folk hero whose showmanship and coined phrases inspired audiences nationwide on radio and television broadcasts. As much as Babe Ruth had embodied the vivacious spirit and tempo of the Roaring Twenties, Dean's humble beginnings, self-confidence, and loquacious bravado appealed to a country on its knees from the devastation of the Great Depression. Fans were in awe of Ruth, but it was Dizzy Dean to whom they could relate.

Dean was born in Lucas, Arkansas, on January 16, 1910. His parents named him after Wall Street financier Jay Gould and Mark Hanna, President William McKinley's flamboyant political manager. Dean's parents had no money to give their son, but perhaps with such a name, according to author John Heidenry, "they could give him promise and personality." Dean's mother died when he was three years old, and his education ended in the second grade. His father, Monroe, was an itinerant sharecropper, drifting around the South picking cotton to make ends meet. Jay Hanna joined his father in the cotton fields when he was four, and by 10 he was picking as much as 500 pounds of cotton a day. Monroe and his three sons wandered from county to county and state to state looking for work, and the three spent many nights sleeping in a sharecropper's vacant cabin or in an open field.

Despite such circumstances, the Dean family found time for baseball. They played pick-up games with other men and boys for stakes of 50 cents or a dollar a game, the equivalent of a day's wages in the cotton fields. One day in autumn 1925, the family drove their pickup truck down a dirt road past a high wire fence with a sign that read "U.S. Government Military Reservation— Authorized Persons Only." Jay Hanna stared at the sign and recalled what his stepbrothers, Herman and Claude, had told him about the good life in the army: three meals a day, a new pair of shoes, and a salary of $19 per month. Army life seemed like an oasis compared with picking cotton 14 hours a day and driving around looking for work.

In 1927, Dean enlisted at Fort Sam Houston and discovered that army men were also permitted to play baseball. He was invited to try out for the 3rd Wagon team and quickly earned a reputation as a hard-pitching country boy. In a game against the 12th Field Artillery, Dean allowed two hits, struck out 10, hit a home run, and won 1–0. Master Sergeant James K. "Jimmie" Brought, the captain of the Artillery team, was so impressed that he arranged for Dean to be transferred to his team and promoted him to private first class. Dean returned the favor by helping Artillery win the army's championship that year.

By spring 1928, word of Dean's talent on the mound had spread. In one game, he pitched a two-hit shutout over the Medical Section team, striking out 11 and driving in two runs in a 4–0 victory. The St. Louis Cardinals happened to send a "bird dog" (a scout's scout) to see him pitch that game, where Sergeant Brought not only sang Dean's praise but inadvertently baptized him with his lifelong sobriquet. "So I told this scout—I told him you're the clumsiest kid I ever seen going into a windup, but you can throw hard and you got a good curve," Brought told Dean after the game. "I also told him you were the *dizziest* kid I ever had in my outfit."

"Me? Dizzy?" Dean asked with a smirk.

"Yeah, you," Brought replied. "Dizzy." Teammates had called Dean "Foggy" because his favorite pitch was the fogger, a fastball he claimed was so fast that batters saw only the wisp of fog it left in its path. But Brought's nickname prevailed, and Dean soon became known as Dizzy.

Dean continued to whip foggers past army batters, but he was ignored by semipro teams. Finally, in January 1929, a representative of the San Antonio Public Service Corporation visited Dean and told him that pro teams did not respect army baseball talent. To get noticed by scouts, he said, Dean should play for San Antonio Public

Official scorecard to game in which Dizzy Dean struck out 17 Chicago Cubs batters, a major league record, July 30, 1933

"The good Lord was good to me. He gave me a strong body, a good right arm, and a weak mind."

—Dizzy Dean

Service, which was part of a company team circuit, a notch below semipro. Dean quit the army, took a job as a reader of gas meters for $30 a week, and pitched for the San Antonio team in the summer. Don Curtis, a Cardinals scout, saw Dean pitch a few games and signed him on May 25, 1929. The following spring, Dizzy was sent to Missouri to join the St. Joseph Saints, a Cardinals Class A team in the Western Association.

But fate and self-confidence had more in store for Dean. One evening in the spring of 1930, after pitching a game for the Saints, the brash 20-year-old Dean met Branch Rickey, the general manager of the St. Louis Cardinals, in the lobby of the hotel where the Redbirds were staying: "Hello, Branch," Dean said while extending his hand. "I'm Dizzy Dean, the fella who's gonna win you a lot of ball games."

"Hello, Mr. Dean," Rickey replied.

"Say, Branch," Dean continued, "don't waste your time sendin' me to St. Joe. Bring me right up to the Cardinals. If I can strike 'em out here, I can strike 'em out there. I can win you a flag."

Rickey was amused by Dean's demeanor and impressed by his performance with the Saints, so, after a brief stint that summer with a Triple A team in the Texas League (a major step up from the Saints), Dean was called up by the Cardinals. He pitched his first

major league game on September 28, 1930, against the Pittsburgh Pirates, earning a 3–1 victory.

Dean's pitching genius became as lofty as his bravado. In 1933, only his second full season with the Cardinals, he won 20 games, led the National League in strikeouts (199), and struck out 17 Chicago Cubs in nine innings on July 30, setting a major league record. He wore this jersey (page 90) during Cardinals home games at Sportsman's Park throughout that extraordinary sophomore season. The jersey is a pullover garment that features four buttons along the placket. Period images of Dean show him wearing garments that have either a four- or five-button front. The dating of these images suggests that the four-button front is a 1933 uniform because the photos were taken during spring training 1934. For spring training, teams often wore uniforms from the previous season because new uniforms for the season ahead would not be ready until close to opening day.

The following year, Dean won Branch Rickey not only a National League flag but the World Series as well, which concluded with his 11–0 shutout of the Detroit Tigers in Game 7. "I always just went out there and struck out all the fellas I could," Dean quipped. "I didn't worry about winnin' this number of games or that number—and I ain't a-woofin' when I say that, either."

Dean's pitching prowess started to unwind in 1937 after he suffered a broken toe when he was struck on the left foot by a line drive while pitching in the All-Star Game in Washington. Dean returned to the mound before his injury had healed and ruined his right arm. He never regained his former glory and retired in 1941, having led both leagues in strikeouts for four consecutive years (1932–35). He remains the last NL pitcher to win 30 games in a season.

Dean's pitching days were over, but his "promise and personality" would prevail behind a microphone in the broadcast booths at Sportsman's Park (1941–46), Yankee Stadium (1950–51), and Atlanta-Fulton County Stadium (1966–68). He even got one last crack at the mound. On September 28, 1947, the perennially cash-strapped St. Louis Browns hired Dean as a radio broadcaster to drum up publicity. After broadcasting

Dizzy Dean
playing the
sousaphone
at Sportsman's
Park, 1934

several poor pitching performances in a row, he grew frustrated and said on the air, "Doggone it, I can pitch better than nine out of the ten guys on this staff!" To bolster ticket sales, Browns management took Dean up on his offer and had him pitch the last game of the season. The 37-year-old Dean pitched four scoreless innings and hit a single in his only at-bat. Rounding first base, he pulled his hamstring. He returned to the broadcast booth at the end of the game and commented, "I said I can pitch better than nine of the ten guys on the staff, and I can. But I'm done. Talking's my game now, and I'm just glad that muscle I pulled wasn't in my throat."

Dean's talking game came as naturally as his pitching. In addition to his radio and television broadcasts for the Cardinals, Browns, Yankees, and Braves, he went nationwide with Mutual (1952), ABC (1953–54), and CBS (1955–65), where he teamed first with Buddy Blattner and then with Pee Wee Reese. "Come on, Tommy, hit that old patata," he once yelped into the microphone. "This boy looks mighty hitterish to me," he observed on another occasion. "Boy, they was really scrummin' that ball over today, wasn't they?" he reported to the fans. And Dean once said on television, "The trouble with them boys is they ain't got enough spart." When pressed for an explanation, Dean replied: "Spart is pretty much the same as fight or pep or gumption. Like the *Spart of St. Louis*, that plane Lindbergh flowed to Europe in."

"That's the strangest
fella I've ever faced."

—Lou Gehrig, after Rowe
struck him out, 1934

SCHOOLBOY

SCHOOLBOY ROWE 1933 Detroit Tigers Rookie Home Jersey

The 1934 World Series was endearing because it featured two cities desperately in need of relief from the ravages of the Great Depression. Detroit and St. Louis had been hit hard, as historian Charles C. Alexander explained: "Detroit as a result of massive layoffs prompted by a plummeting automobile market [and] St. Louis because of the collapse of the Plains wheat-belt economy and the decline of the Mississippi River traffic, among other factors." In the first full year of the New Deal, many observers felt it was only appropriate that the Tigers and Cardinals made it to the Fall Classic. *New York Times* correspondent John Kieran claimed that the 1934 Series would come down to "just three men. Two Deans [Dizzy and his brother Paul] and one Rowe."

Lynwood Thomas "Schoolboy" Rowe was born on January 11, 1910, in Waco, Texas. He got his nickname while playing for a men's baseball team in his hometown, El Dorado, Arkansas, as a 15-year-old high school student. Legend has it that a heckler at a church league game yelled, "Don't let that schoolboy strike you out!" After winning 19 games for the Beaumont Exporters of the Texas League in 1932, Schoolboy joined the Detroit Tigers as a rookie in 1933, the year he wore this cream-colored pinstriped home jersey (opposite). The following year, Rowe was 24–8 and set an American League record of 16 consecutive wins, a milestone shared with only Walter Johnson, Smoky Joe Wood, and Lefty Grove.

Rowe's talent was laced with eccentricities and superstition. He always picked up his glove with his left hand and talked to the ball before his windup. During his winning streak, a reporter asked him for his secret, and Schoolboy responded that he would "just eat a lot of vittles, climb on that mound, wrap my fingers around the ball and say to it, 'Edna, honey, let's go.'" Edna Mary Skinner, a schoolteacher from El Dorado, was Rowe's fiancée. "No one else in baseball believed so much in good-luck charms," wrote author Robert Gregory:

On the day [Rowe] was trying for his seventeenth straight, his pocket contained a Canadian penny, two trinkets from China, and a copper coin from the Netherlands. Inside his shirt were four feathers plucked from the tail of a three-legged rooster. A jade elephant figure was in his glove. Beneath his hat was a rabbit's foot, taken from a rabbit said to have been shot in a graveyard at midnight. But Rowe lost the game anyway, and when he got back to the Tigers' hotel in Philadelphia, he heaved them all—like a failed witch doctor—from his sixteenth-story window. Now getting psyched up for the Series, he had begun a new collection, to which [Tigers catcher Mickey] Cochrane contributed some beads and two miniature shoes.

The press widely reported Rowe's superstitions, so Dizzy Dean wasted no time in trying to intimidate the Tigers ace. Soon after his arrival at Navin Field in Detroit before the start of Game 1, Dean passed Rowe and bantered, "If I was a four-leaf clover, you could have me, Schoolboy." Unfortunately for Rowe and the Tigers, the Dean brothers dominated the Series. Rowe was the winning pitcher in Game 2, but Paul beat him 4–3 in Game 6. The Deans each won twice, and the Cardinals beat the Tigers in seven games. This time, bravado prevailed over superstition.

Schoolboy Rowe in windup motion at Navin Field, home of the Detroit Tigers, 1933

Rowe's 1933 Detroit Tigers rookie home jersey and his game-used glove from the 1930s, plus good-luck charms (four rooster feathers and a jade elephant figure) and a pin-back button commemorating the Tigers' 1934 American League pennant

THE CATCHER WAS A SPY

MOE BERG 1934 All American Japan Tour Team Jacket

Moe Berg is seated in the front row, second from left, outside Hotel Ryokwan, Sendaishi, Japan, 1934

"Yeah, I know, and he can't hit in any of them."

—Dave Harris, Washington Senators' outfielder, when told Moe Berg spoke seven languages

The son of a pharmaceutical merchant who had emigrated from the Ukraine to America in 1894, Moe Berg was raised in Newark, New Jersey. He studied seven languages (including Sanskrit) at Princeton University and graduated with distinction in 1923. Berg was also the starting shortstop on the Princeton baseball team, and as a senior he exploited his penchant for languages by communicating in Latin with second baseman Crossan Cooper to confuse opposing base runners. After graduation, Berg signed his first major league contract and played 49 games for the Brooklyn Robins (later renamed the Dodgers). He used the money he earned playing baseball to pay for graduate study at the Sorbonne in Paris, where he enrolled in 22 classes, including Romance languages, literature, history, and medieval Latin. In 1930, Berg earned an LL.B. (an undergraduate law degree offered at the time) from Columbia Law School and tried his hand at corporate law on Wall Street. But he preferred life on the diamond. He spent the rest of the decade as a third-string catcher for the Cleveland Indians,

Washington Senators, and Boston Red Sox. As a mediocre bullpen catcher, Berg rarely played, but his time *off* the field perfectly suited a man whom author Nicholas Dawidoff describes as a "sensualist" who "was making use of baseball to plot a life of wandering curiosity."

During major league baseball's exhibition tour to Japan in 1934, Berg did some curious wandering in Tokyo. Because of a last-minute cancellation by Red Sox catcher Rick Ferrell, he was invited to make the trip along with Babe Ruth, Lou Gehrig, Jimmie Foxx, Charlie Gehringer, Lefty Gomez, and other star players. He served as the second-string catcher in a 12-city series of 22 exhibition games against Japan's first professional team, the Tokyo Giants, which was made up of the country's best former high school and college players. The tour lasted throughout the cold months of November and December, and thus, in addition to special uniforms, jackets with patriotic charm were made to keep the players warm. Berg wore the one shown (opposite) throughout this tour, including outside the Hotel Ryokwan in Sendaishi (see image above).

Official program to
U.S. All-Star Tour
of Japan exhibition
game, 1934

In Tokyo, half a million fans turned out to witness the mighty Bambino, whom the Japanese called "Babe Rusu." (Two years later, Japan would form its own professional league due to the success of this tour.) But the thunderous cheers for Ruth belied Japan's growing discontent with the United States, largely the result of American politicians' uproar over Japan's growing military presence in the Asia Pacific region. Many Japanese felt hostility, even paranoia, toward Americans. Yet the circumstances could hardly have been more inviting for an intrepid adventurer like Berg. He skipped the November 29 game in the town of Omiya, 15 miles north of Tokyo, and instead played his version of tourist. He brought along a letter from MovietoneNews, a New York City newsreel production company with which Berg had contracted to film the sights of his trip. Dressed in a black kimono and a pair of *geta* (traditional wooden sandals), Berg combed his black hair to resemble a Japanese man's hairstyle, grabbed his 16mm Bell and Howell movie camera, and quietly left his hotel. He walked southeast, and in the Ginza district he purchased a bouquet of flowers. He then proceeded north to St. Luke's International Hospital in Tsukiji, which, at seven stories, was then one of the tallest buildings in Tokyo.

At St. Luke's, he told the receptionist that he was visiting U.S. ambassador Joseph Grew's daughter, who was giving birth. Berg was told that she was on the fifth floor. He rode the elevator to her floor, dumped the flowers in a garbage can by the lift, then got back into the elevator and took it to the seventh floor. He then climbed a winding, narrow staircase to the roof of the dining area, where he found himself in a small stone tower with open windows and a panoramic view of Tokyo. He pulled the movie camera from under his kimono and began filming the city. According to author Robert K. Fitts, Berg "panned the skyline, holding the camera still on a group of factories to the west and again on the waterfront. He capped off the footage by focusing on Mount Fuji, just visible on the southwestern horizon."

Some scholars and historians maintain that Berg was acting on orders from the U.S. State Department and that his footage was used by Lieutenant Colonel Jimmy Doolittle to plan the April 18, 1942, bombing raids on Tokyo, Yokohama, Osaka, and Nagoya. Whether

either is true remains a matter of controversy, but Berg's "hospital visit" does provide a noteworthy glimpse into his adventures in espionage.

When Berg's playing career ended after the 1939 season, he accepted the Red Sox's offer to stay on as a coach. But after the Japanese bombed Pearl Harbor on December 7, 1941, Berg wanted to do his part for the war effort. On January 5, 1942, he joined Nelson Rockefeller's Office of the Coordinator of Inter-American Affairs, an agency that promoted cultural diplomacy in Latin America. During his tenure there, Berg showed his Tokyo footage to a number of U.S. intelligence officers in the Office of Strategic Services (OSS)—the forerunner to the CIA—as well as to the FBI and armed forces.

On August 2, 1943, Berg joined the Secret Intelligence branch of the OSS to learn more about Hitler's atomic bomb program. One of his assignments was to interview Italian physicists to see what they knew about Werner Heisenberg—the German physicist whom the U.S. believed was the most likely candidate to produce an atomic bomb—and team member Carl Friedrich von Weizsacker. In 1944, the OSS learned that Heisenberg would be giving a lecture in Zurich, and Berg was assigned to attend it. If Berg determined there was "indisputable evidence" that a German bomb was imminent, he was to assassinate Heisenberg. Berg concluded that the Germans trailed the United States in atomic bomb research and were not close to producing a weapon, and thus no assassination was necessary.

Berg returned to the United States on April 25, 1945, and in August he resigned from the OSS. In recognition of his civilian service during the war, he was awarded the Medal of Freedom by President Harry S. Truman on October 10. But he refused to accept it. Berg never explained why, but some historians opine that it was because he did not want to tell people about his exploits. Others claim that he was petulant about being recalled from duty in Europe and annoyed with challenges by OSS personnel to his exorbitant expenses during the war. After Berg's death, his sister, Ethel, accepted the award on his behalf.

This major league catcher was indeed a spy, though he remained a catcher at heart. He was 70 when he died on May 29, 1972, and a nurse at a hospital in Belleville, New Jersey, recorded his final words: "How did the Mets do today?"

U.S. All-Star Tour of Japan presentational pin given to the players, 1934

CURTAIN CALL

RANDY MOORE 1934–35 Boston Braves Road Jersey

Randy Moore,
1935

Apicture is worth a thousand words. But in this case, it's a picture of a rare game-worn flannel and one could write volumes about it. Not because of the ballplayer who wore it—Randy Moore, a steady outfielder for the Boston Braves. And not because the flannel was worn in a special event—it wasn't. Instead its appeal and significance derive from its design and style, which illustrate an important aesthetic trend in major league baseball uniforms during the Great Depression era. There's a little mystery, too: a subtle feature on the jersey tells the tale of the majestic yet woeful departure of the game's most celebrated home-run king, Babe Ruth.

Starting in the late 1920s, design innovations and new multicolor trim began to appear on major league uniforms, trends that continued well into the late 1930s. Perhaps no team epitomized this flowering more than the Boston Braves, whose team name was adopted in 1912 by owner James Gaffney. He was a member of New York City's political juggernaut, Tammany Hall, which used an Indian chief as its symbol. As shown on this

Boston Braves flannel worn by Moore for road games during the 1934 and 1935 seasons (opposite), nine hues were used on the "Indian head" athletic felt patch alone. The smaller version of the patch is situated in the middle of the "Braves" team lettering across the chest, and the larger form is found on the left sleeve. Along with scarlet red and navy blue trim applied to the felt team lettering on the front and the number on the back, a peach-colored soutache (see page 302 in the Compendium) decorates the sun collar area, sleeve ends, and length of the placket. No other team had incorporated such a variety of colors into its uniforms.

For Braves owner and manager Emil E. Fuchs, the team's fourth-place finish in 1935 was actually considered a banner year. His team had occupied the National League cellar, or a slot very near it, for much of the 1920s and early 1930s. In 1932, the Braves began to climb their way out. They settled at the midpoint of the National League standings in 1933 and 1934 under manager Bill McKechnie, who had previously won pennants for the Pirates and Cardinals. Fuchs was keen to maintain the team's "comeback" momentum to help pay off his debts—the impact of the Depression on the Braves franchise had caused Fuchs to fall behind on his rent for Braves Field. He was desperate to find a new drawing card that could save his club from collapse.

Down in New York, Babe Ruth was also desperate. During the 1934 season, with his best years far behind him, he had grown increasingly unhappy after absorbing a series of pay cuts as his batting average dropped. More than ever, he wanted to manage the Yankees and felt he deserved the position. "How can you manage the team," Yankees owner Jacob Ruppert asked him, "when you can't even manage yourself?" The best Ruppert was willing to do was offer Ruth the opportunity to run the Yankees' best farm team, the Newark Bears. Ruth felt that this was beneath his dignity, so he declined. Other teams had inquired about Ruth's availability for the 1935 season, but Ruppert initially opted to retain Ruth as a player for one more year. But after Ruth's mediocre performance in 1934 (.288 average, 22 homers, 84 RBI), Ruppert let the Babe go.

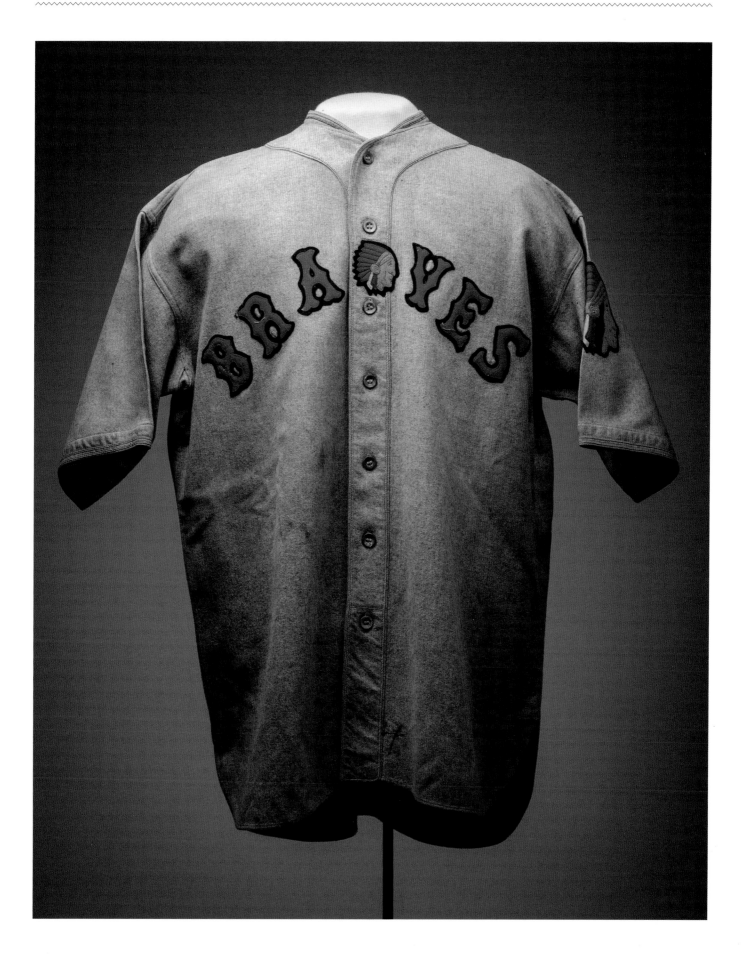

"No one hit home runs the way Babe did. They were something special. They were like homing pigeons. The ball would leave the bat, pause briefly, suddenly gain its bearings, then take off for the stands."

—Lefty Gomez

Fuchs contacted Ruth with an enticing offer: play for the Braves for a $25,000 salary plus a percentage of profits, be named vice president and assistant manager in the front office, and eventually replace McKechnie as manager. With no other offers on the table and his ego badly damaged by the Yankees—at spring training in 1935, the team reassigned his uniform number and used his locker for firewood—Ruth felt an encore in Boston was a better option than retirement. On February 25, 1935, 19 days after his 40th birthday, Ruth signed a contract with the Boston Braves. Fate had the Babe return to Beantown, where his career had started 20 years before with the Boston Red Sox.

The Braves underwent preparations for the Babe's arrival, which included the production of new sets of uniforms for him. Given Ruth's stature, he was expected to continue to wear his famed number 3. This number belonged to center fielder Wally Berger, and giving it up would cause a ripple effect through the Braves' numeric roster. Yet Berger did just that, and Randy Moore's flannel (page 101) provides the evidence. In 1934, Moore had worn number 4 for the Braves, which is identified by the 4 stitched in rust red toward the bottom of the jersey's front tail, adjacent to the soutache. On the flannel's reverse (opposite), however, a 7 appears in red and navy blue felt. If Moore's number was 4, then what is the 7 doing there? Close inspection of the jersey shows that the Braves removed the original number 4 and replaced it with number 7 sometime before the start of spring training in 1935. Number 7 was worn in 1934 by Joe Mowry and Red Worthington, but it became available for use in 1935 because neither player was on the Braves roster that year. At the time, lower numbers typically were issued to starting players (who were not pitchers), and number 7 was the only single-digit number available and the only viable option for the Braves to accommodate Ruth, Berger, and Moore. So, for the 1935 season, Ruth wore number 3, Berger wore number 4, and Moore wore number 7. Moore got two seasons of use from this weathered flannel, and while wearing it for the first six weeks of the 1935 season, he bore witness to the career climax of baseball's biggest star.

On Opening Day against the Giants at Braves Field, the Babe made Fuchs proud by clouting a 430-foot moon shot and a single off ace Carl Hubbell, helping Boston to a 4–2 victory. But the Babe's magic couldn't last. After a second home-run blast five days later, Ruth went hitless over his next 20 at-bats. "He came in with the Boston Braves to Cincinnati," recalled radio broadcaster Red Barber. "And it was very pathetic. He couldn't even get a foul ball. He was grossly overweight. There was a slanting terrace in left field to warn the players of the concrete left field fence and Ruth got tangled up on that terrace and he wound up catching line drives [by] defending himself against them....Really he shouldn't have been out there."

Ruth entered Forbes Field in Pittsburgh on May 25 eager to redeem himself. He hit three home runs that afternoon, the final one clearing the right-field roof. It was the first ball ever hit out of that park. "The Great Man unloosened his bat, took a tremendous swing and the ball traveled high and far toward the right field stands," wrote a reporter for the *Pittsburgh Press*. "Pirate players stood in their tracks to watch the flight of the ball. It was a home run all the way and when the ball disappeared behind the stands, there was a mighty roar from the crowd of 10,000."

"It was the longest cockeyed ball I ever saw in my life," said Guy Bush, who had pitched to Ruth for the last two home runs he hit that day. "That poor fellow, he'd gotten to where he could hardly hobble along. When he rounded third base, I looked over there at him and he kind of looked at me. I tipped my cap, sort of to say, 'I've seen everything now, Babe.' He looked at me and kind of saluted and smiled. We got in that gesture of good friendship. And that's the last home run he ever hit."

Ruth hit 714 career home runs in regular-season play, far more than any other player of the era. At the end of the 1935 season, Lou Gehrig was second on the career home-run list with 378, and Ruth's record would endure until 1974, when it was broken by Hank Aaron.

A week after Ruth hit his last career home run, he announced his retirement from baseball; he never got a chance to manage in the big leagues. Randy Moore shared the dugout with Ruth and played first base during that fabled game. His flannel from that season commemorates perhaps the most extraordinary curtain call in baseball history.

Back view, Moore's 1934-35 Boston Braves Road Jersey

GABBY

GABBY HARTNETT 1935 Chicago Cubs Home Jersey

It remains unclear how Chicago Cubs catcher Charles Leo Hartnett earned his nickname "Gabby." Some authors purport that teammates and the press gave him the moniker because of awkward shyness, while others claim he earned it because of his constant chatter behind the plate. Either way, what remains undisputed is that Hartnett, who caught for the Cubs from 1922 to 1941, is widely considered the greatest National League catcher of his era. At six foot one, a large man for the time, Hartnett was an intimidating presence on the field, with a

Gabby Hartnett, by photographer George Burke, autographed, 1929

Hartnett's 1935 Chicago Cubs home jersey with his 1935 National League MVP award, a 1935 Chicago Cubs regular season scorecard, and an Official National League baseball from the 1930s

remarkable throwing arm and tremendous aptitude for anticipating double steals and effectively using the pitchout. "Gabby Hartnett don't miss many fellows trying to steal second on him," wrote a reporter in the *Herald and Examiner* in 1928. "It makes no difference how fast the runner is and how much of a lead he obtains. Max Carey will attest to this. He endeavored to purloin the keystone in the fifth, but Hartnett's bullet-like heave had him [by] several feet."

Also adept with the bat, Hartnett was a six-time .300 hitter and clouted 37 home runs in 1930. He wore this Chicago Cubs home jersey (opposite) in 1935. It features a variant design of the lackadaisical bear holding a bat enclosed within a *C* found on the 1909 and 1910 Frank Chance home jersey (page 21). Hartnett batted .344, made only nine errors in 110 games, and won the National League MVP (opposite) while leading the Cubs to a 1935 World Series berth against the Tigers. Despite Hartnett's .292 average during the Series, the Cubs fell in six games. "I rated Gabby the perfect catcher," recalled Hall of Fame Cubs manager Joe McCarthy. "He was super smart and nobody could throw with him. And he also was an outstanding clutch hitter."

No wonder the Woonsocket, Rhode Island, native was behind (literally) so many iconic moments in baseball history. Hartnett was crouched behind home plate when Babe Ruth hit his "called shot" home run off Cubs pitcher Charlie Root in the 1932 World Series. He was there again when Ruth became the first man to strike out against screwball pitcher Carl Hubbell in the 1934 All-Star Game; in the same game, Hubbell fanned Lou Gehrig, Jimmie Foxx, Al Simmons, and Joe Cronin in succession, one of the most memorable feats in the Summer Classic. In the 1937 All-Star Game in Washington, Hartnett was catching when Earl Averill's line drive nailed Dizzy Dean in the left foot, an injury that forced Dean to modify his delivery and ultimately led to his premature retirement from the majors.

"I swung with everything I had, and then got that feeling, the kind of feeling you get when the blood rushes out of your head and you get dizzy. A lot of people have told me they didn't know the ball was in the bleachers. Well, I did. Maybe I was the only one in the park who did. I knew the moment I hit it....I don't think I saw third base...and I don't think I walked a step to the plate—I was carried in."

—Gabby Hartnett on hitting the Homer in the Gloamin'

Gabby was promoted to player-manager of the Cubs in 1938, and he delivered one of the greatest moments in baseball history on September 28 while *at* the plate—a ninth-inning drive into the looming darkness of Wrigley Field, the fabled "Homer in the Gloamin'" that propelled the Cubs past the Pittsburgh Pirates and into the World Series. "Most fans were unable to follow the flight of the ball in the darkness, but when it settled into the left field seats for a walk-off home run, Wrigley Field erupted with a deafening roar that could be heard for blocks," wrote author William McNeil. "Thousands of...spectators came spilling out of the stands screaming and racing toward the diamond."

But skill, statistics, and drama alone belie the essence of Hartnett, who was also affectionately referred to by fans as "Old Tomato Face" due to his florid complexion and sunny disposition. His rotund Irish face was wedged between oversize ears, and his dimpled grin often transformed into a gregarious laugh. According to one sportswriter, "There were three distinguishing characteristics associated with the likeable Irish-American—a red face, a big cigar, and a laugh in which he simply wound up and let go, laughing all over. His frame shook like a dilapidated jalopy."

"It was his winning personality that set him apart on the field," according to Hartnett's obituary upon his death on December 20, 1972. "A friendly wave to the men in the press box, a hundred handshakes with friends he made in every city in the circuit, and autographs for everyone, young and old, who asked him to sign." Gabby never turned away any fans—not even Chicago's most notorious mobster, Al Capone, as seen in this photo taken during a charity game, for Governor Louis Lincoln Emmerson's unemployment fund, between the Cubs and White Sox at Comiskey Park on September 9, 1931. Accompanied by several bodyguards, Capone had asked Hartnett to sign a baseball for his son, Al Jr., who sat to his father's right. When commissioner Judge Kenesaw Mountain Landis objected to Hartnett's fraternization with Capone, the backstop supposedly replied, "OK, but if you don't want me to have my picture taken with Al Capone, *you* tell him."

Gabby Hartnett greeting Al Capone, Comiskey Park, September 9, 1931

NUMBER 9

JOE DiMAGGIO 1936 New York Yankees Rookie Home Uniform

Yankee Stadium,
ca. 1936

May 3, 1936, was a cool, rainy day at Yankee Stadium, the indelible architectural landmark opened 13 years earlier, during the Yankees' golden years under Babe Ruth. Heavy clouds hovered over the arcade of ornate arches that encircled the interior edge of the park's roof, and within the park's cavernous interior, more than 25,000 fans (by far the largest attendance since opening day) braved the weather to witness the birth of a new era (and megastar) for the Yankees. "An astonishing portion of the crowd," wrote a *New York Post* reporter, "was composed of strangers to sport—mostly Italians—who did not even know the stadium subway station." The Bronx Bombers were batting against the St. Louis Browns in the bottom of the first. With Yankee runners on first and third, a loud cheer echoed throughout the stadium as a rookie, wearing number 9 on his pinstriped

home uniform, approached the batter's box for the first time as a Yankee. The 21-year-old sensation was already being hailed as Ruth's successor, and he wore that uniform (opposite) only during his 1936 rookie season, including the World Series. His number 9 is on the back of the jersey in athletic felt, in the collar area next to his name (in pink thread), and in the pants' waist (in red thread).

The son of Sicilian immigrants, Joseph Paul DiMaggio took the baseball world by storm that May day, igniting the Yankees' biggest offensive assault since the season's start and garnering two singles and a triple as New York trounced the Browns, 14–5. On May 10, the Yanks seized first place from Boston with a 7–2 victory over the Philadelphia Athletics in which DiMaggio belted a line drive into left off southpaw George Turbeville for his first career homer. The Yankees reeled off six wins

in DiMaggio's first seven games, and by late May, he led the league with a .411 batting average. On the last day of May, the Yankees beat the Red Sox for their fifth straight win. DiMaggio singled in the seventh to tie the game, then drove in the winning run in the twelfth with a triple. Skipper Joe McCarthy could already sniff the American League pennant, which had eluded the franchise since 1932.

The press lavished praise on the rookie, dubbing him the "Yanks' messiah" and "the Moses who is to lead their club out of the second-place wilderness." Fans turned out in droves to see DiMaggio: stadium attendance jumped by 200,000 in the first half of the season, and it was reported that the Sons of Italy populated entire sections to cheer their hero. "All the Italians in America adopted him," said teammate Lefty Gomez. "Just about every day at home and on the road there would be an invitation from some Italian-American club." These loyal fans elected DiMaggio to the All-Star Game that year with more votes than any other player, including established sluggers such as Lou Gehrig, Jimmie Foxx, Bill Dickey, Charlie

Gehringer, and Al Simmons. By mid-July, DiMaggio's appeal had reached new heights, and he appeared on the cover of *Time* (below), an honor typically reserved for world leaders.

On September 10, the Yankees clinched the pennant, then went on to finish the season 102–51, 19½ games ahead of the Tigers. In 138 games, DiMaggio collected 206 hits and batted .323 with 29 round-trippers and 125 RBI. In 669 plate appearances, he struck out just 39 times. The Rookie of the Year Award wasn't established until 1940, but had it existed in 1936, no vote would have been necessary. "The only question was whether Joe D. was the best rookie in *history*," wrote author Richard Ben Cramer. "But that debate wouldn't begin in earnest until the Yanks met the Giants for the title of titles—World Champs—in the subway series of 1936."

The 1936 Series was the Yankees' first without Babe Ruth. But the Giants were bolstered by many of the talented players who had won the 1933 Series against the Senators, and they were led by player-manager (and future Hall of Famer) Bill Terry, National League home-run leader Mel Ott, and screwball maestro (and National League MVP) "King" Carl Hubbell. The Yankees took a three-games-to-one lead before the Giants won Game 5 in 10 innings. In Game 6 at the Polo Grounds, Jake Powell hit a second-inning homer, and the Yankees led by three runs after four innings. But the Giants battled back to within one run after eight.

DiMaggio led off the ninth with a line-drive single into left field, then advanced to third on Gehrig's single. Cramer described what happened next in *Joe DiMaggio: The Hero's Life*:

> [Dickey] bounced a sharp one-hopper to first baseman Bill Terry, who made the right play—he grabbed the ball and looked across the diamond, to freeze DiMaggio on third base....But DiMaggio wasn't on third. He'd broken for home as the ball left the bat. Now he stopped in no-man's-land, while the crowd (and the Giants) screamed for Terry to gun him down. Terry fired the ball to third—but DiMaggio broke again for home. Third baseman Eddie Mayo whipped the ball past Joe to the plate, and the catcher Harry Danning blocked the baseline, crouched for collision. But DiMaggio didn't run into Danning. Joe didn't even slide. Instead, he launched himself into the air—head first, over the tag, completely over Danning...and in the air, Joe twisted his body, still falling...till he landed back of Danning, in the dirt, with his hand on the Polo Grounds plate.

Cover of Time *magazine, July 13, 1936*

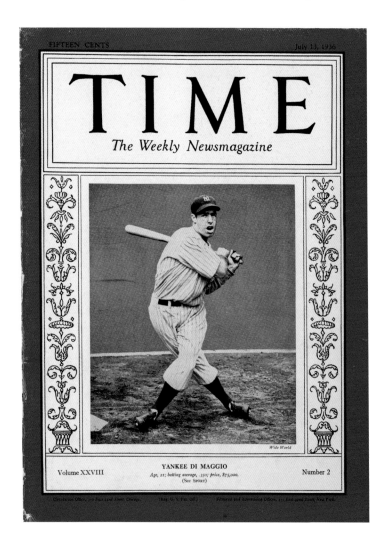

FIFTEEN CENTS   July 13, 1936

TIME
The Weekly Newsmagazine

Volume XXVIII   **YANKEE DI MAGGIO**   Number 2
Age, 21; batting average, .350; price, $75,000.
(See SPORT)

"He was in a world by himself. There was nobody who could take over a ballpark like he could....If you told me in 1938 that I would be Secretary of State, and I would be friends with DiMaggio, I would have thought the second was less likely than the first."

—Henry Kissinger, U.S. Secretary of State, 1973-77

New York Yankees pennant sold at Yankee Stadium, 1936

The Giants would unravel and the Bombers would go on to win, 13–5, to become World Champions. A second dynasty was born. "I've always heard that one player could make the difference between a losing team and a winner, and I never believed it," said Bill Terry afterward. "Now I know it's true."

With DiMaggio at the helm, the Yankees won eight more World Series titles between 1937 and 1951. Joe won three American League MVP awards (1939, 1941, 1947) and played in the All-Star Game in each of his 13 seasons. His 56-game hitting streak in 1941 became a national obsession, and in its July 14 issue, *Time* wrote, "Since it became apparent that the big Italian from San Francisco's Fisherman's Wharf was approaching a record that had eluded Ty Cobb, Babe Ruth, Lou Gehrig, and other great batsmen, Big Joe's hits have been the biggest news in U.S. sport. Radio programs were interrupted for DiMaggio bulletins." In DiMaggio's 223 at-bats during the streak, he struck out only five times and fanned only 13 times in the 1941 season. "The home run records, once hallowed, are hollow," wrote Kostya Kennedy in *56: Joe DiMaggio and the Last Magic Number in Sports*. "But Joe DiMaggio's is still there: 56 consecutive games with a hit. 'And it feels pure,' the former Giants' batting instructor Carney Lansford said to me....'You can cheat and break the home run records. You can't do that with a hitting streak.'"

As lofty as DiMaggio's feats were on the diamond, his public image was even more revered. "It is not for DiMaggio's records that we remember him," wrote Ira Berkow in the *New York Times* in 1998. "He is best remembered for the persona of Joe DiMaggio. He remains a symbol of excellence, elegance, power, and, to be sure, gentleness." He was a hero to heroes—Santiago, the resolute protagonist of Ernest Hemingway's 1952 novella *The Old Man and the Sea*, says he must be worthy of his idol, the great DiMaggio. Legendary Dodgers manager Tommy Lasorda recalled, "I knew every big leaguer when I was growing up, but Joe DiMaggio was my hero. He was everything we wanted to be." And teammate Phil Rizzuto's adoration of Joe was well known: "I used to like to just watch him shave," he once said.

On March 16, 1999, the House of Representatives passed a resolution honoring DiMaggio "for his storied baseball career; for his many contributions to the nation throughout his lifetime; and for transcending baseball and becoming a symbol for the ages of talent, commitment, and achievement." It had all started when Joe stepped into the batter's box on that showery May day in 1936. "I'm just a ballplayer with one ambition," DiMaggio said later in his life, "and that is to give all I've got to help my ball club win." Nothing could be a more fitting symbol of his extraordinary career than his rookie home uniform— after all, it was Joe who said, "I want to thank the good Lord for making me a Yankee."

THE SCHNOZZ

ERNIE LOMBARDI 1936 Cincinnati Reds Home Uniform

"Only a foolish optimist can deny the dark realities of the moment," President Franklin D. Roosevelt told an anxious crowd during his inauguration speech on March 4, 1933. The Great Depression continued to strangle the country, including baseball teams. From 1930 to 1933, the Cincinnati Reds lost approximately $600,000, forcing owner Sidney Weill to declare bankruptcy and put the franchise into the hands of a local bank. The bankers needed someone to turn things around. Branch Rickey, general manager of the St. Louis Cardinals at the time, recommended Larry MacPhail, a World War I veteran and former attorney who had recently helped Rickey rejuvenate a minor league club under the Cardinals farm system. MacPhail, whom documentary filmmaker Ken Burns described as "a born promoter" and a man "desperate to find new ways to boost attendance and rescue his club from bankruptcy in the midst of the Depression," was hired as the Reds' vice president and general manager for the 1934 season.

MacPhail persuaded Powel Crosley Jr., a Cincinnati-based tycoon who had made his fortune on electrical appliances and as the owner of a local radio station, to purchase a controlling interest in the team. MacPhail also convinced National League team owners that night games would be good for baseball and would help save the Reds franchise from plummeting attendance. The owners conceded, and at 9 p.m. on May 24, 1935,

Portrait of Ernie Lombardi, ca. 1936

President Roosevelt pressed a button in the White House that lit 632 floodlights situated on eight metal stanchions in Crosley Field, home of the Reds and recently renamed after the club's new owner. In front of 20,422 paying fans, the third-largest crowd that season, the Reds played the Philadelphia Phillies in major league baseball's first night game.

Attendance at Crosley Field more than doubled in 1935 from the previous season, and the team generated a $50,000 profit. MacPhail, who ran the Reds until 1937, seemed to have saved the club from ruin during his tenure. But another man would help bring the Reds to prosperity by the end of the decade: Ernesto Natali "Ernie" Lombardi. He was an unsung tragic hero who crouched behind home plate for the Reds from 1932 to 1941, and he wore this Cincinnati Reds home uniform (page 112) during the 1936 season, when the predominance of the color red gave way to an equal application of navy blue, which was especially evident in the chenille-embroidered "C-REDS" team logo (see page 275 in the Compendium). The overall appearance of the garment was sharp and bright, perhaps a sign of more favorable times ahead for the ball club.

Lombardi stood six foot three, weighed 230 pounds, and had hands so big he could hold seven balls in one of them. Nicknamed "Schnozz" for his enormous nose, he snored so loudly that, as Bill Rigney once said, "The entire train would shake." His base running was so inept that one opposing manager jokingly said, "Lombardi was so slow, he ran like he was carrying a piano—and the man who was tuning it." Arthur Daley of the *New York Times* once remarked that Lombardi "ran on a treadmill and couldn't outrace a snail, even with a head start." During a game against the Philadelphia Phillies at the Baker Bowl, he was thrown out at first on a line drive off the left-field wall, and he led the league in grounding into double plays four times. In Lombardi's 1,853-game career, he stole a meager eight bases.

Lombardi's hitting, on the other hand, was anything but slow. With a 42-ounce bat, he struck fear into pitchers and infielders throughout the NL, crushing line drives so hard that, as Daley wrote, it was like "a shell leaving a howitzer." Said Dodgers hurler Kirbe Higbe: "You'd see the infielders' lips moving in silent prayer when old Ernie came up." Infielders played so deep when Lombardi batted that he once said, "It took me four years to find out Pee Wee Reese was an infielder." Lombardi hit .300 or better 10 times and hit over .330 every year from 1935 to 1938. He led the NL in 1938 with a .342 average, 19 home runs, and 95 RBI en route to winning the NL MVP. His .306 career batting average ranks behind only Mickey Cochrane's and Bill Dickey's among Hall of Fame catchers. "When you look back on him and his seventeen years in the majors," wrote Daley, "you almost come to the conclusion that he was the greatest hitter of all time."

In 1939, the Reds made it to the World Series for the first time in 20 years. Although they were swept by

The Schnozz, with hands so big he could hold seven balls in one, ca. 1936

"Perhaps the most extraordinary of the Lombardi batting feats was his exploit of smashing four consecutive doubles in four consecutive innings off four different pitchers. Considering the fact that Lom always had to hit the equivalent of a triple to make a double, you can picture what sort of clouts all of them were."

—Arthur Daley, *New York Times*

the juggernaut Yankees, the Reds would get retribution the next year, when they beat the Tigers in seven games in the Fall Classic. The club was on top of the world, far from the dark days before MacPhail's arrival. As for Lombardi, life took a twisted turn. His hitting accomplishments were overshadowed by ridicule over his slow running and the "Lombardi Snooze," an incident in Game 4 of the 1939 World Series when he failed to pick up a loose ball and tag out Joe DiMaggio at home after Yankee Charlie Keller collided with him.

In 1942, the Boston Braves purchased Lombardi's contract. He became an All-Star and led the NL that season with a .330 batting average. No other catcher would win a batting title until 2006, when Joe Mauer of the Minnesota Twins won the AL title. As of 2016, Lombardi remains one of only two NL catchers to win a batting title. His made his final All-Star appearance in 1943, and the Braves traded him to the New York Giants before the 1944 season began. Lombardi's performance deteriorated over the next two seasons, and he retired from the big leagues after the 1947 season.

In 1953, the Schnozz tried to commit suicide by slashing his throat with a razor. He recovered but remained spiritually damaged, drifting around the San Francisco Bay Area for the rest of his life, working in menial jobs, including a stint as a press box attendant at Candlestick Park. When a young reporter did not recognize him, he quit. After being repeatedly rebuffed by the Hall of Fame, he said in 1974, "If they elected me, I wouldn't show up for the ceremony....All anybody wants to remember about me was that I couldn't run. They still make jokes. Let them make jokes."

On August 3, 1986, nine years after his death, the Schnozz was finally inducted into Cooperstown by the Veteran's Committee. The man who helped bring recognition to the Cincinnati Reds during the franchise's darkest chapter at last got a taste of it himself.

THE MEAL TICKET

CARL HUBBELL 1937 New York Giants Road Jersey

Jo-Jo Moore, Mel Ott, and Carl Hubbell (left to right; Hubbell is wearing jersey shown here) on dugout steps, Braves Field, 1937

Scorecard to the 1934 All-Star Game and a 1937 Wheaties cereal advertisement featuring Hubbell, along with Hubbell's New York Giants road jersey from the 1937 season

At the top of the first inning of the 1934 All-Star Game at the Polo Grounds in New York, the circumstances looked ominous for pitcher Carl Hubbell. The first two American League batters had reached base, and Babe Ruth was up next. At the mound, National League catcher Gabby Hartnett consoled his battery-mate: "We'll waste everything except the screwball. Get that over, but keep your fastball and hook inside. We can't let 'em hit in the air."

With three consecutive screwballs, Hubbell struck out the Sultan of Swat. Next up was Lou Gehrig, who took a ball and then fanned swinging through three more screwballs. Jimmie Foxx managed a foul tip before striking out on five pitches to end the inning. In the second inning, Hubbell continued the onslaught by striking out the first two batters, Al Simmons and Joe Cronin. Five Hall of Famers up and each one sent back to the dugout in succession, a feat widely regarded as one of the most astonishing in baseball history. "Here

was this frail Hubbell man," Shirley Povich of the *Washington Post* wrote, "his left arm whipping down from his shoulder in a monotonous tempo, reducing the greatest batting array ever mustered to a helpless, hapless, hitless horde of sandlotters."

Born in Carthage, Missouri, on June 22, 1903, Carl Owen Hubbell was raised on a pecan farm near the town of Meeker, Oklahoma. He attended Meeker High School and pitched for the baseball team, commanding a decent fastball and curve. After graduation and brief employment with an oil company, Hubbell began his baseball career in 1923 with Cushing of the Oklahoma State League. In 1925, the 22-year-old southpaw chalked up a 17–13 season with another semipro team, Oklahoma City of the Western League. During his time with Oklahoma City, Hubbell developed a sinker—which eventually turned into his screwball—after observing the pitching motion of former White Sox hurler Claude "Lefty" Williams. "I found out that the more I turned it over, the more I come up, and over [overhand] I could

"If I had a ballgame to be pitched, and my life hung in the balance, I'd want Carl Hubbell to pitch it."

—Red Barber, legendary radio sportscaster of the Reds, Dodgers, and Yankees, (1934–66)

get a much better break on it, you see," Hubbell recalled. "Of course, the more spin you get on the ball, the more break, and it slows it up. When I threw the screwball, I came right over the top, and I turned my arm clear over and let the ball come out of the back of my hand."

Relatively few major league pitchers have employed the screwball during their careers. "Few pitchers throw a screwball for a simple reason: it hurts," wrote author Warren Corbett. Pain is induced in the elbow by rotating the arm inward and twisting the wrist to the right (for a lefthander), the opposite of a curve. Christy Mathewson called his version the "fadeaway" when he pitched in the early 1900s, but he admitted he seldom threw it because of the strain on his arm. In his book *Pitching in a Pinch*, published back in 1912, Mathewson wrote, "Many persons have asked me why I don't use my 'fade-away' oftener when it is so effective, and the only answer is that every time I throw the 'fade-away' it takes so much out of my arm. It is a very hard ball to deliver. Pitching it ten or twelve times in a game kills my arm, so I save it for the pinches." From the beginning of Hubbell's career, managers and coaches warned him that the pitch would ruin his arm. Ty Cobb, player-manager for the Tigers, ordered Hubbell to discard the pitch during his first major league spring training, in 1926.

Hubbell abandoned the screwball for two years, and as a result his effectiveness deteriorated, his confidence was shaken, and he wallowed in the minor leagues. The Tigers sold Hubbell to Beaumont of the Texas League after the 1927 season. Beaumont manager Claude "Ug" Robertson, a former minor league catcher who appreciated the effectiveness of the screwball, had no objection to Hubbell's use of the pitch. Hubbell started the season with Beaumont and won 12 games with the screwball back in his repertoire. Dick Kinsella, a scout for the New York Giants, happened to be in Houston for the Democratic National Convention that summer and saw one of Hubbell's games. He was so impressed that he informed Giants manager John McGraw of the talented young lefty. McGraw paid Beaumont $30,000 for Hubbell's contract, and the screwballer was on his way to the big leagues in the summer of 1928.

"What made the screwball so successful was throwing it over the top with exactly the same motion as a fastball," Hubbell told a sportswriter years after his 1947 induction into the Hall of Fame. "If a hitter is

ready for a fastball, he can adjust to the breaking ball. But with a screwball, it isn't the break that fools the hitter, it's the change of speed. They couldn't time it and were out in front of it." Hubbell threw the screwball often and with pinpoint accuracy, to the bewilderment of the most prodigious sluggers of the 1930s. In 1933, he won the National League MVP by leading the league in wins (23), ERA (1.66), and shutouts (10). He also pitched a record 45 consecutive scoreless innings that season to help pave the way for the Giants' first World Series victory since 1922. Each year from 1933 to 1937, Hubbell won 21 or more games, and he helped lead the Giants to NL pennants in 1936 and 1937. From July 17, 1936, to May 27, 1937, he won a record 24 consecutive games. By the 1937 season, the year Hubbell wore this gray flannel New York Giants road jersey (page 117), with its royal-blue piping, he was at the peak of his game and was known as the Giants' "Meal Ticket."

By the end of the 1937 season, however, Hubbell's left arm was in severe pain. He later admitted that the elbow had begun to hurt in 1934 and that by 1938 the pain had become unbearable. Nevertheless, he continued to throw the screwball, to the awe of fellow players and fans. "I guess the only match in the league for [Dizzy] Dean in those years was Carl Hubbell," Chicago Cubs Hall of Famer Billy Herman recalled in *Baseball When the Grass Was Real*. "What a great pitcher and fine competitor he was. I'll tell you something about Hubbell. When he was pitching, you hardly ever saw the opposing team sitting back in the dugout; they were all up on the top step, watching him operate. He was a marvel to watch, with that screwball, fastball, curve, screwball again, changes of speed, control. He didn't have really overpowering stuff, but he was an absolute master of what he did have, and he got every last ounce out of his abilities. I never saw another pitcher who could so fascinate the opposition the way Hubbell did."

Hubbell was released by the Giants following the 1943 season, and he spent the next 35 years as the team's director of player development. Since Hubbell's day, only four prominent pitchers—Warren Spahn, Juan Marichal, Mike Marshall, and Fernando Valenzuela— have thrown the screwball. Even today, pitchers shun it for fear of its harmful consequences. According to Bruce Schoenfeld's *New York Times Magazine* article "The

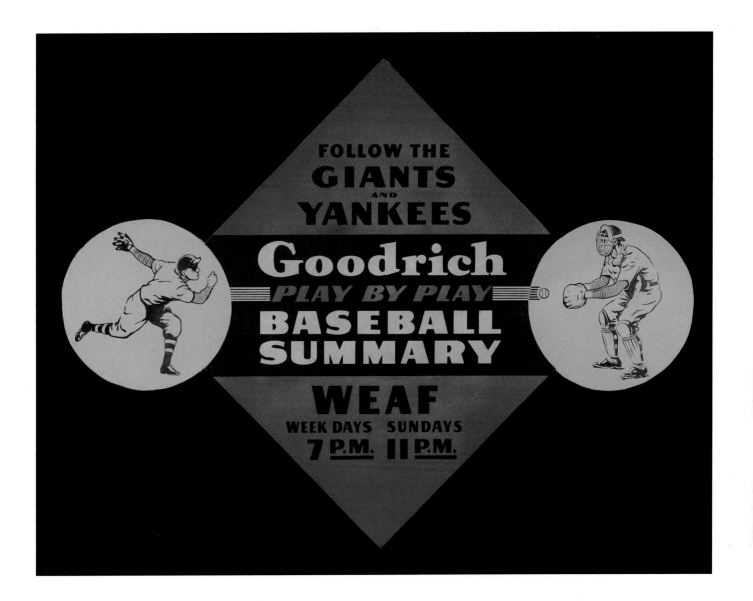

Mystery of the Vanishing Screwball": "The last great practitioner was Fernando Valenzuela, most famously a Dodger, who threw a wide assortment of pitches, none more prominent—or effective—as his screwball. Today few, if any, minor leaguers are known to employ the pitch. College coaches claim they haven't seen it in years. Youths are warned away from it because of a vague notion that it ruins arms." Schoenfeld also contended that in today's power culture, the screwball's potency has been forgotten.

Hubbell's plaque in the Hall of Fame commemorates his extraordinary records and accomplishments, but, surprisingly, it makes no mention of his screwball—an omission akin to not including "home run" on Babe Ruth's plaque. Journalist and writer George Plimpton perhaps captured the Meal Ticket best in his book *Out of My League*:

Carl Hubbell with his screwball was a particular hero. I'd read somewhere that the effect of his screwball, delivered with a violent inward snap of the wrist, put such a strain over the years on his arm that when he stood relaxed, with his arms down at his sides, the palm of his pitching hand faced out. When I stood around at the age of eleven, having read this, I did the same—faced the palm out, hoping that it would be associated with screwball pitching, and not with a malformation of the arm, which is what it looked like. One day my father finally said: "What's wrong with your arm, son? You fall out of a window?"

"Well, that's from screwball pitching," I said. *"I had hoped someone would ask."*

WEAF radio broadcast Hubbell's masterful performance in the All-Star Game at the Polo Grounds, 1934

MYTHICAL HERO

LOU GEHRIG 1937 New York Yankees Road Jersey

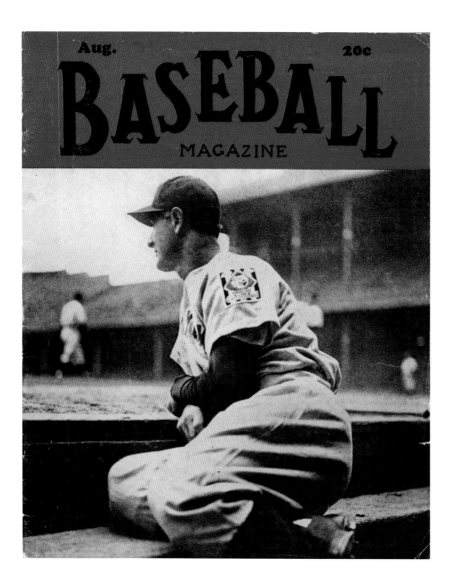

Lou Gehrig's first missed game after playing 2,130 in a row, *Baseball* magazine, August 1939

"No man or woman born, coward or brave, can shun his destiny."

—Homer, *The Illiad*

"It was commonly said at the time that Lou Gehrig lived in [Babe] Ruth's shadow," said sportswriter Fred Lieb, who covered Gehrig and the Yankees for several newspapers. "Such talk never bothered Lou. 'It's a pretty big shadow,' he said. 'It gives me lots of room to spread myself.'" Gehrig, the strong, silent type without an ounce of boast, preferred to let his bat and glove do the talking, and he was happy to cede the spotlight to Ruth. "Let's face it. I'm not a headline guy," Gehrig once said.

Gehrig achieved a lifetime batting average of .340, with 493 home runs and 1,995 RBI—including a record 185 RBI in a single year (1931) and more than 150 RBI seven times in his 17 years with the Yanks. Gehrig belted 23 career grand slams, a record that lasted until 2013, when Alex Rodriguez broke it. Gehrig is best remembered, however, for playing in 2,130 games over 14 years without taking a day off, a streak of longevity and toughness that earned him the sobriquet "the Iron Horse."

Gehrig's meteoric rise to fame, abrupt decline, and death at the age of 37 has made him somewhat of a mythical hero. His illness and how he handled himself are better remembered than all he accomplished playing 17 seasons for the New York Yankees. Gehrig seemed invincible, with no physical weaknesses, yet he withered away from a rare, incurable disease. "Don't think I am depressed or pessimistic about my condition at present," Gehrig wrote following his retirement from baseball after being diagnosed with amyotrophic lateral sclerosis (ALS), now commonly known as Lou Gehrig's disease. "I intend to hold on as long as possible and then if the inevitable comes, I will accept it philosophically and hope for the best. That's all we can do."

Born on June 19, 1903, Henry Louis Gehrig developed his work ethic as a child, partly as a result of a negative example. His father, a first-generation German immigrant, was a part-time sheet metal worker who drank too much and frequently missed work. When he interacted with his son, it was usually in a drunken rage. Gehrig's mother, also from Germany, worked as a maid, and Lou helped her do laundry and sweep stairs. He found solace in baseball and starred at Commerce High School in Manhattan, earning the attention of sportswriters, particularly after his performance in an intercity game against Chicago's Lane Tech High School on June 26, 1920. In the ninth inning of that game, Gehrig hit a grand slam, prompting the *Chicago Tribune* to write, "Gehrig's blow would have made any big leaguer proud, yet it was walloped by a boy who hasn't yet started to shave."

Lou finished high school in 1921 and entered Columbia University on a football scholarship, with plans to study engineering. Scout Arthur Irwin convinced Gehrig to try out for the Giants, and he

Lou Gehrig accepting trophy given to him by his teammates from Yankees skipper Joe McCarthy, July 4, 1939

hit six consecutive home runs in batting practice. But when Gehrig allowed a grounder to roll between his legs, Giants manager John McGraw yelled, "Get this fellow out of here! I've got enough lousy players without another one showing up." Irwin found Gehrig a spot on the Hartford Senators of the Class A Eastern League for the rest of the 1921 season.

In his sophomore year at Columbia, Gehrig set records for batting average (.444), slugging percentage (.937), and home runs (seven). His power caught the attention of Paul Krichell, a scout for the New York Yankees. The left-handed Gehrig was six feet tall and weighed 200 pounds, and he set home-run distance records on several fields. "That right field at Cornell had a high fence, then there was a road back of it, then a forest," recalled Gehrig's Columbia teammate, second baseman George Moisten. "Lou lifted his home run into the forest. I looked over at coach [Andy] Coakley, sitting near me on the bench, and he was slapping his head in wonder."

The Yankees signed Gehrig in 1923, and he played sparingly in 1923 and 1924. But in 1925, he hit 20 home runs and became the team's regular first baseman, taking over the position from 32-year-old Wally Pipp and launching his consecutive-games streak. One story suggested that Gehrig filled in for Pipp because Pipp had a headache. Pipp later conceded that Gehrig earned the position because he was simply the better ballplayer. Pipp's numbers had been in steady decline all season (.244 average), and Gehrig turned the team around, particularly in 1926, after Yankees manager Miller Huggins taught the 23-year-old Gehrig to pull pitches to the short right-field fence. Gehrig soon realized that he could pull any pitcher in the league. In 1927, sportswriters began calling the Yankees lineup (with Gehrig batting fourth after Babe Ruth) "Murderers' Row." Gehrig and the Bambino went head to head in home runs, and Gehrig finished the season with 47 to Ruth's record of 60. Gehrig was named the American League's MVP.

Gehrig enjoyed one solid season after another. In 1932, he swatted four consecutive home runs in a single game, the first time that happened in the twentieth century. Philadelphia Phillies fans, who hated the Yankees with a passion, gave Gehrig a standing ovation when he crossed home plate the fourth time. Two years later, he took home the Triple Crown, leading the league in batting average (.363), RBI (166), and home runs (49). He became the third player in baseball history to lead both the AL and NL in all three categories. When Ruth left the Yankees for the Boston Braves after the 1934 season, Gehrig became the undisputed leader of the Yankees. In 1937, Gehrig posted a team-leading .351 batting average with 37 home runs, and he helped the Bronx Bombers claim their sixth World Series

title. Gehrig wore the gray wool-flannel New York Yankees road jersey shown here (page 121) during that remarkable season.

The jersey features the 1939 Baseball Centennial Patch (see page 270 in the Compendium) on the left sleeve, which signifies that Gehrig also wore the garment in 1939, a season that would come to define his legacy. At one time, Gehrig had outfielders backing up to the fences when he stepped to the plate. But when the 1939 season started, Gehrig was so weak he could barely hit the ball out of the infield. After he missed several easy pitches that, as DiMaggio noted, he normally would have "hit into the next county," Gehrig saw the handwriting on the wall. On April 30, he played his last big league game against the Washington Senators. When the Yankees took the field in Detroit on May 2, Gehrig—his batting average down to .143— withdrew from the lineup and, for the first time in 2,130 straight games, sat on the Yankees bench. On June 19—Gehrig's 36th birthday—doctors at the Mayo Clinic in Rochester, Minnesota, diagnosed him with ALS.

Two days later, the Yankees announced Gehrig's retirement, and on July 4, the team organized Lou Gehrig Appreciation Day at Yankee Stadium. A crowd of 61,808 thundered a "hail and farewell" to baseball's Iron Horse. Mayor Fiorello La Guardia opened the ceremony by declaring Gehrig "the greatest prototype of sportsmanship and good citizenship." Members of the 1927 Yankees championship team paraded on the field. The group included Babe Ruth, Waite Hoyt, Bob Meusel, Earle Combs, Herb Pennock, Tony Lazzeri, Joe Dugan, Mark Koenig, Benny Bengough, Bob Shawkey, and George Pipgras.

Overcome by this extraordinary reception, Gehrig stepped to the microphone and kept his eyes glued to the ground as he fought to keep back the tears. Speaking steadily and calmly, he delivered one of the most celebrated speeches in American history:

> What young man wouldn't give anything to mingle with such men for a single day as I have for all these years? Fans, for the past two weeks you have been reading about the bad break I got. Yet today I consider myself the luckiest man on the face of this earth.…I've got an awful lot to live for.

Gehrig died on June 2, 1941, exactly 16 years after he replaced Wally Pipp at first base. Today, more than 77 years after Gehrig's Yankee Stadium oration, we are still moved by his embodiment of courage, humility, and strength. Here lies the armor of baseball's most mythical hero, a glorious garment worn by Henry Louis Gehrig as his life neared its tragic end.

"But suppose God is black? What if we go to Heaven and we, all our lives, have treated the Negro as an inferior, and God is there, and we look up and He is not white? What then is our response?"

—Robert Kennedy, 1966

WHAT IF?

WOODY JENSEN 1938 Pittsburgh Pirates Home Uniform

The Pittsburgh Pirates, after a third-place finish in the National League the previous season, donned uniforms for 1938 that portended a fresh start, with a script "Pirates" across the chest. The Pirates started slowly that season but rattled off consecutive wins from June 29 to July 12. By the end of July, they led the league by five games, and by September, the lead had grown to seven games. Pennant fever was in the air. The Pirates had already begun construction on a new press box atop Forbes Field, added bleacher seats for 2,000 fans, and ordered new uniforms for the Series.

Those who could not attend games listened on radios as Rosey Rowswell exclaimed that one of the Waner brothers (Lloyd and Paul) had scorched a "doozie maroonie," or extra base hit. But September proved to be the team's undoing. On September 27, the Pirates fell to the Cubs and Dizzy Dean, 2–1, in 98 minutes, and their lead over Chicago slipped to half a game. The next day, when Chicago's Gabby Hartnett launched his ninth-inning "Homer in the Gloamin,'" the Pirates slipped into second place. The Cubs clinched the pennant three days later and would go on to face the New York Yankees in the World Series. The Pirates went home for the winter.

Oh, what might have been had Pittsburgh manager Pie Traynor acted on a telegram he'd received during the winter of 1937 from Chester Washington, a writer for the *Pittsburgh Courier*, a black newspaper:

> KNOW YOUR CLUB NEEDS PLAYERS
> STOP....JOSH GIBSON CATCHER FIRST BASE
> B. LEONARD AND RAY BROWN PITCHER OF
> HOMESTEAD GRAYS AND S. PAIGE PITCHER
> COOL PAPA BELL OF PITTSBURGH CRAWFORDS
> ALL AVAILABLE....WHAT IS YOUR ATTITUDE?
> STOP WIRE ANSWER

The Pirates ignored Washington's telegram, and the game would not become integrated until 1947, when Branch Rickey brought Jackie Robinson to the Brooklyn Dodgers. But what if Traynor and the 1938 Pirates

Pittsburgh Pirates teammates, Forbes Field, 1938

had had the courage, foresight, and vision of Rickey? The players listed in Washington's telegram were the biggest stars in Negro Leagues baseball, and they played on Pittsburgh's most popular teams, the Homestead Grays and Pittsburgh Crawfords. Imagine starting the 1938 Pirates lineup with the bat control and speed of Cool Papa Bell, the greatest leadoff hitter in Negro Leagues history and reportedly so fast that, according to Satchel Paige, "He could turn out the light and jump in bed before the room got dark." Lloyd Waner could have been followed by Arky Vaughan, loading the bases for the Negro Leagues' most feared home-run slugger, Josh Gibson. Buck Leonard, who had a lifetime batting average of .320, could've been up next, before Paul Waner stepped to the plate. The first six hitters on this dream team would one day be enshrined in Cooperstown. And the Pirates pitching staff would have been equally imposing, with Cy Blanton, Russ Bauers, Jim Tobin, Bob Klinger, and relief ace Mace Brown, along with the legendary Satchel Paige and Hall of Famer Ray Brown.

It didn't happen.

The new uniforms were about the only bright spot of the 1938 Pittsburgh Pirates season. This particular uniform (opposite) was worn by outfielder Woody Jensen. How different the season—and baseball—might have been if Gibson, Leonard, Paige, or Bell had also worn Pirates uniforms that year.

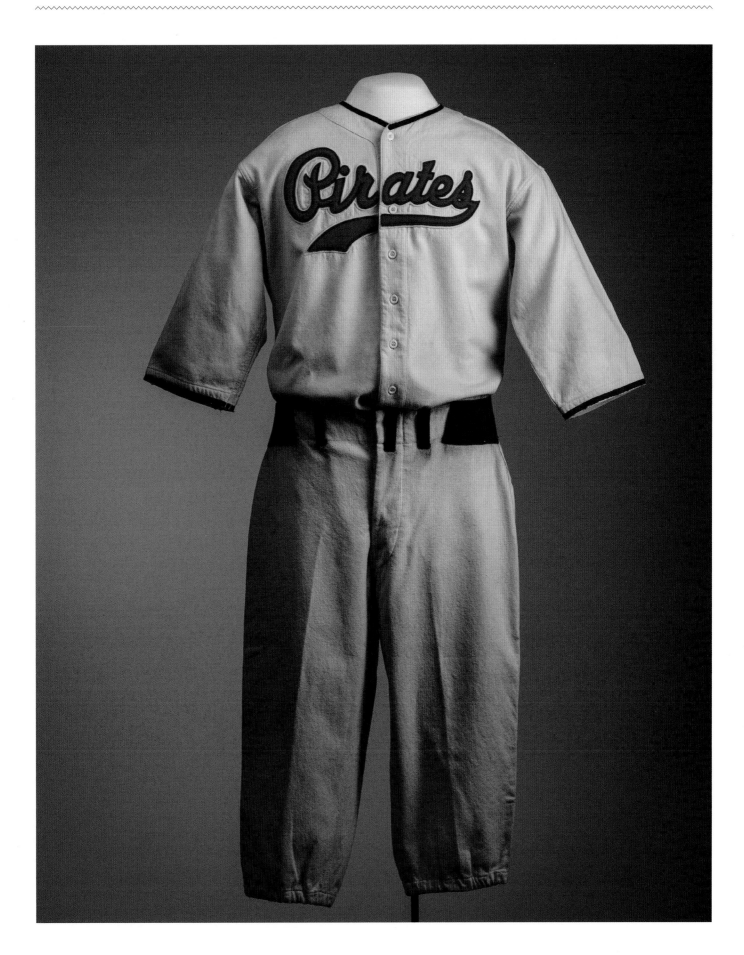

BEAUTY AND THE BEAST

JIMMIE FOXX 1938 Boston Red Sox Home Jersey and Team Jacket

On October 25, 1997, about 500 people gathered at the corner of Main and Church streets in Sudlersville, Maryland, to commemorate the unveiling of a life-size bronze statue. The celebration took place three days after the 90th anniversary of the birth of James Emory Foxx, a hometown hero in this farming community on the Eastern Shore. After Hurtt Deringer, former editor and publisher of the *Kent County News*, commenced the proceedings, John Steadman, longtime sportswriter for the *Baltimore Sun*, stepped to the microphone to deliver his speech. He told the audience that with all due respect to Hank Aaron, Willie Mays, Ralph Kiner, and others, Jimmie Foxx was the greatest right-handed slugger of all time. Soon afterward, Foxx's grandchildren pulled off the black cloth draped over the statue, and former

Maryland governor Harry Hughes read a moving tribute to the man known as "the Beast."

It's fitting that sculptor Ken Herlihy captured Foxx in his completed batting swing (left), as the Beast possessed a powerful cut that produced 534 career home runs, and the 415 he hit in the 1930s is unmatched by any other player. As lethal as his bat was to pitchers, so was his anatomy. The Beast was one of the first players to wear cut-off sleeves in the summer to show off his bulging arm muscles. Foxx's intimidation was not lost on Herlihy, a graduate of the Pennsylvania Academy of the Fine Arts, and the sculpture showcases the massive biceps that unnerved pitchers throughout Foxx's 20-year career in the big leagues. "There were a couple of men on base, and Jimmie Foxx was up," Detroit Tigers hurler Rip Sewell once recalled. "To this day I can see him standing there, his big muscled arms looking like piano legs hanging out of a churn." Yankees southpaw legend Lefty Gomez always brought Foxx into the discussion when he explained why he stopped wearing glasses on the mound: "I was pitching this particular day when my glasses clouded up on me. I took them off to clean them, glanced toward the plate, and suddenly recognized the menacing figure of Jimmie Foxx at bat. This scared me so much that I never wore the glasses again."

The Beast's physical prowess was not purely a force of nature. He had earned it on his family's farm. "I worked on a farm, and I'm glad of it," Foxx once said. "Farmer boys are stronger than city boys. When I was 12, I could cut corn all day, help in the wheat fields, swing 200-pound bags of phosphate off a platform into a wagon. We had games on the farm to test strength and grip. A fellow had to plant both feet in half a barrel of wheat and then pick up two bushels of wheat or corn and balance them on his shoulders. Another trick was to lift a 200-pound keg of nails without letting the keg touch your body. I could do that easily, but never realized it was helping me train for the big leagues." Foxx was also a fast runner and set a number of records in track events as a schoolboy. In spring 1921, as a 13-year-old, he won the junior unlimited division 80-yard dash at Sudlersville High with a time of 10 seconds. A year later, at the State Olympiad in Baltimore, Foxx set the state record in the 80-yard dash for the junior

Bronze statue of Jimmie Foxx by Ken Herlihy, Sudlersville, Maryland, 2016

Jimmie Foxx
(wearing jacket
featured here)
with Red Sox
catcher Gene
Desautels, 1938

unlimited division, clocking 8.8 seconds in the first heat and 8.6 seconds in the second.

Foxx also played catcher for the Sudlersville High baseball team and usually batted cleanup. The day after Sudlersville captured the 1923 county high school baseball pennant, Foxx, as a 15-year-old sophomore, began playing catcher for the Queen Anne's County All-Stars. In the team's season opener, Foxx smashed a triple and a homer in a 5–0 win over City College, a high school from Baltimore. He batted over .400 in the team's 30-game season. By the time Foxx was 16, scouts were turning out in droves around Sudlersville to court the burly slugger. It was said that Foxx wasn't scouted, he was trapped. "The apocryphal tale of how he was signed," according to author John Thorn, "says that he was plowing a field when a scout asked him directions to the ballpark and the youngster pointed—with his plow."

Foxx's talent was also noticed by Frank "Home Run" Baker, a future Hall of Famer and local hero from Trappe, Maryland. Baker had signed on as the player-manager for the Easton Farmers of the Class D Eastern Shore League, and he invited Foxx for a tryout in April 1924. Showing up in a pair of overalls, the high school junior told Baker he could play catcher if necessary, and he was signed for a salary estimated at between $125 and $250 a month. Foxx played for Easton through the summer, hitting .296 with 10 home runs. At the end of July, the Philadelphia Athletics purchased Foxx's contract. Foxx finished the season with a .296 batting average (three percentage points above his manager's) and then returned to Sudlersville and his senior year of high school.

The schoolboy prodigy did not finish his senior year, leaving early to attend spring training with the Athletics. Foxx made his major league debut as a 17-year-old in 1925 and saw limited playing time until the 1928 season. However, while pinch-hitting for the Athletics on May 31, 1927, Foxx belted his first major league home run off Yankees spitballer Urban Shocker in the second game of a doubleheader at Shibe Park. Foxx would go on to become the first player to challenge Babe Ruth as the home-run king. "When Babe Ruth drifts out of the home run scene, there is a young Athletic player waiting to take his place," remarked A's skipper Connie Mack. "He is Jimmie Foxx, our first baseman, who has petrified Philadelphia baseball followers in recent days with a series of home runs that carried so far as to make open-mouthed spectators believe that it was an overt violation of Ruth's well-known copyright for distance. I can never recall in my career where five straight home runs [of such distance] were made by one player. Foxx has the greatest pair of arms in America."

In every full season Ruth played from 1918 to 1931, he led the American League in home runs, reaching a career high of 60 in 1927. In 1932, Foxx hit 60 homers of his own, but rainouts washed two of them off the books. Still, his 58 that season is the most any right-handed hitter has ever smacked (he is tied with Hank Greenberg and Mark McGwire). Foxx would lead the American League in home runs three more times, in 1933, 1935, and 1939. When he retired in 1945, Foxx trailed only Ruth in all-time home runs, and he remained in second place until August 17, 1966, when Willie Mays hit career homer number 535 to surpass Foxx.

But the amazing thing about Foxx wasn't how *many* homers he hit; it was how *far* they went. "You just can't imagine how far he could hit a baseball," Red Sox teammate Ted Williams once said in an interview with author Bill Jenkinson. "As Williams told us," Jenkinson later wrote, "many of those 534 [career home runs] were hit so far that Jimmie's power now seems fictional." Tape-measure dingers seemed easy prey for the Beast, who hit 24 that cleared the 65-foot-high left-field grandstand roof at Shibe Park. Foxx's long balls landed in all sorts of peculiar spots *outside* the ballparks, striking the roofs of neighboring houses and bouncing onto streets. One left Fenway Park, passed over a factory, and dropped onto the Boston and Albany railroad tracks; another sailed over the grandstand roof of Comiskey Park in Chicago and landed in a handball court across 34th Street. According to Lynn Doyle of the *Philadelphia Evening Bulletin*, Foxx hit a homer off George Uhle of the Tigers that "was on its way to Hudson Bay when it cleared the left field roof [of Shibe Park]." Doyle later added that "an unconfirmed report says that Foxx's home run landed in an Eskimo's fish basket thirty-seven miles north of Moose Cat, Labrador." And as if that weren't enough, perhaps Foxx even hit one into outer space. When Neil Armstrong first set foot on the moon in 1969, an unidentified white object puzzled him and NASA scientists, but not Lefty Gomez. "I knew immediately what it was," he said. "That was a home run ball hit off me in 1937 by Jimmie Foxx."

After Connie Mack, the financially desperate Athletics manager, reluctantly sold Foxx to the Red Sox following the 1935 season, a 23-foot net was added atop the tin wall at Fenway Park to protect Landsdowne Street homeowners' windows from the flurry of out-of-the-park homers expected from the prolific slugger. Many of Foxx's greatest achievements certainly had come with the A's: two World Series titles (1929 and 1930), two AL MVP awards (1932 and 1933), and a Triple Crown (1933). But he enjoyed one of his finest seasons in 1938 while playing for the Red Sox and wearing this flannel home jersey and team jacket (page 126), two of only four uniform items worn by Foxx that are known to have survived. While wearing this jersey, Foxx clouted

"Jim hit many homers into that corn field. The field wasn't big enough for him."

—Mildred Smith Barracliff, cousin of Jimmie Foxx

50 home runs (a team record until David Ortiz broke it in 2006), drove in 175 runs, batted .349, and won his third MVP award. No wonder that on June 16 against the St. Louis Browns, Foxx was walked each of the six times he came to bat, establishing a modern major league record.

While Jimmie's long ball and fame soared to lofty heights, his humility and amiable disposition never strayed far from home. Teammates and peers gushed when they reminisced about Foxx, referring to him as a "perfect gentleman," "one of the nicest guys in baseball," "affable," "fun-loving," "a first-class fellow," "a man genuinely liked by everyone in baseball," and "one of the most generous men who ever lived." Perhaps Ted Williams summed it up best when he said, during his early years with the Red Sox, "I'm lucky to be working with such a real guy as Jimmie Foxx. You know, a lot of people ask me who I want to pattern myself after. Well, when it comes to hitting a baseball, Jim is the one man I want to follow, but even if he never hit a baseball, he'd still be the one I'd like to pattern myself after as a man." Jimmie Foxx may well have been known as the Beast, but behind those bulging muscles was an extraordinary man whose character was a thing of beauty.

Jimmie Foxx holding his weapons, Fenway Park, ca. 1938

THE HEATER FROM VAN METER

BOB FELLER 1939 Cleveland Indians Road Jersey

Bob Feller unleashing his heat during a no-hitter against the White Sox, Comiskey Park, April 16, 1940

"That last one sounded a little low."

—Lefty Gomez, after three pitches from Bob Feller flew by him

Official program to game played at Doubleday Field, Cooperstown, New York, June 12, 1939, shown with Feller's 1939 Cleveland Indians road jersey

In 1888, Albert Goodwill Spalding, whose sporting goods empire produced this Cleveland Indians road jersey (opposite) for use during the 1939 season (see the manufacturer's tag in the collar), led an international baseball tour with the Chicago White Stockings and a rival team of all-stars. The group left Chicago by rail on October 20 and played games in Iowa, Nebraska, Colorado, and Utah. After games in San Francisco and Los Angeles, the teams boarded a boat for the Sandwich Islands (known today as Hawaii), New Zealand, Australia, Ceylon, and Egypt. The 1888–89 World Tour continued on to Rome, Paris, and the British Isles. As chief proprietor of baseball's biggest sporting goods business, Spalding sought to use the tour to build recognition of his brand name overseas. He was also determined to prove that baseball was American in origin and not a descendent of the English game of rounders. "After the Civil War, organized teams became important, and baseball developed into popular show business, enjoying a prestige enhanced by American pride in having a 'national game,'" according to historian Harold Seymour. "Pride and patriotism required that the

game be native, unsullied by English ancestry." Spalding believed the tour could foster such patriotic fervor.

Spalding was at it again in 1905 when he used his influence to form a commission to research baseball's origins. Chaired by Abraham G. Mills, the former president of the National League, the commission found, as Spalding intended, that U.S. Civil War general Abner Doubleday had invented the game in May 1839 in the village of Cooperstown in upstate New York. Thanks to the commission's findings, baseball staged a yearlong centennial celebration in 1939 in honor of Doubleday's invention, an event that remains a milestone in the annals of our national pastime. "Baseball will throw open its doors to the fans, the sandlotters, the minor leaguers, the major leaguers, and the officials in observance of the one-hundredth anniversary of the sport next summer at Cooperstown, N.Y.," wrote the *Pittsburgh Press* on January 17, 1939. "Doubleday Field, named in honor of the 20-year-old West Point cadet—Abner Doubleday—who originated the game in 1839 will be the scene of a program starting early in May with a series of exhibition games....The major leagues will stage a Cavalcade of

York–based artist Marjori Bennett (see page 270 in the Compendium). The design of the Baseball Centennial Patch affixed to the left sleeve of the jersey (shown on page 131) was based on Bennett's winning logo. During the 1939 season, every major and minor league baseball club featured this patch on their uniforms in support of the celebration.

On June 12, 1939, the centennial program reached a high point as the National Baseball Hall of Fame and Museum in Cooperstown opened its doors for the first time. "It was a really big show," wrote historian John Thorn. "Trains full of baseball legends and dignitaries emptied into the town. The Delaware & Hudson line reopened a long-abandoned right of way and ran a special passenger service into Cooperstown." Some 10,000 visitors came to see the inaugural festivities and their heroes. Gathered on the museum's grounds at 25 Main Street that day were all 11 living inductees: Babe Ruth, Ty Cobb, Honus Wagner, Walter Johnson, Napoleon Lajoie, Tris Speaker, Grover Cleveland Alexander, Cy Young, Eddie Collins, George Sisler, and Connie Mack.

That same year, another Cooperstown legend was in the making. He was a 20-year-old farm boy from Van Meter, Iowa, who received his first career Opening Day start on the mound on April 21, 1939. He recorded 10 strikeouts and allowed only three hits in a 5–1 victory over the Detroit Tigers. By season's end, he would lead the American League in wins (24), complete games (24), and innings pitched (296.2) while wearing this Cleveland Indians road jersey (page 131). His name was Bob Feller, and in 1962 he would make his own way down Main Street to join the legends in baseball's most coveted shrine.

Feller was an early bloomer. His Cooperstown fate seemed a forgone conclusion even *before* his 1936 rookie season started, when he was just 17 years old. "This was a kid pitcher I had to get," said Cleveland Indians scout Cy Slapnicka. "I knew he was something special. His fastball was fast and fuzzy; it didn't go in a straight line; it would wiggle and shoot around. I didn't know then that he was smart and had the heart of a lion, but I knew that I was looking at an arm the likes of which you see only once in a lifetime." In his first career start on August 23, 1936, he struck out 15 St. Louis Browns, coming within one strikeout of the American League record set by Rube Waddell in 1908. Three weeks later, on September 13, he struck out 17 A's to equal Dizzy Dean's major league record, established in 1933. He finished the season with a 5–3 record and then went home to Iowa to finish his senior year at Van Meter High School. Feller's rookie performance was such a sensation that, according to journalist Richard Goldstein, he "was the best-known young person in America, with the possible exception of Shirley Temple."

United States Navy Chief Petty Officer Bob Feller as captain of a 40-mm gun crew aboard the USS *Alabama*, ca. 1943

Attack on Pearl Harbor, December 7, 1941

The *Cleveland Press*, August 15, 1945

Baseball at Cooperstown on June 12, at which time the Hall of Fame, located in the National Baseball Museum, is to be dedicated."

To organize the yearlong centennial events, major league baseball formed the National Baseball Centennial Commission in October 1938, with commissioner Kenesaw Mountain Landis serving as its chairman. Steve Hannagan, the flamboyant public relations guru who popularized Miami Beach, Sun Valley, and the Indianapolis Speedway, spearheaded publicity nationwide for the celebration, which he called the Cavalcade of Baseball. "Hannagan and the commission wanted to emphasize how baseball taught the lessons of democracy, contrasting it with what was happening across the Atlantic where Hitler and Nazi Germany were running roughshod over the European continent," according to Dennis Corcoran's *Induction Day at Cooperstown: A History of the Baseball Hall of Fame Ceremony*. "The development of the national pastime paralleled the growth and greatness of America. The Cavalcade wanted to show how baseball reached across all levels, from elementary school [to] American legion, high school, semipro, and professional." Hannagan held a nationwide contest to create the program's official insignia, and the winner was New

Feller's fastball was no rookie-year fluke. When 63-year-old umpire Bill Klem first saw him pitch in an exhibition game in the spring of 1937, he was astonished: "Feller showed me stuff the like of which I've never seen in all my life. I expected to see plenty, but I never dreamed an eighteen-year-old kid could pitch like that. His curve was as fast as most pitchers' fastballs. There's nothing compared to Feller's pitching. You can't overdo that. It was one of the thrills of all time to see that boy deliver the ball that day."

Feller's fastball even bedazzled the great Joe DiMaggio in his prime. During his epic 1941 season, when he hit in 56 consecutive games, the Yankee Clipper said, "I don't think anyone is ever going to throw a ball faster than he does. And his curveball isn't human." But following the December 7, 1941, attack on Pearl Harbor, Feller's heat was put on ice. Two days later, he joined the United States Navy, becoming the first American professional athlete to volunteer for active duty. He served four years of his prime as an antiaircraft gunner on the battleship USS *Alabama* and fought in battles at Tarawa, Iwo Jima, and the Marshall Islands. In an interview with author Donald Honig, Feller recalled:

> *Our job was to protect the carriers. We'd have those air battles, and the Japanese planes would try to get at the carriers. And sometimes they'd come after us. Torpedo bombers. They'd come in low, to get underneath our shells, sometimes so low they would fly right into a wave or a big swell. I'd be up there on the main deck with a bunch of kids, banging away with Bofors. The one that gets you you never see; that's the scary thing. You can never be sure about anything one minute to the next. Was it as scary as pitching to Jimmie Foxx? I'll say. That's for keeps, that racket. (And anyway, Jimmie couldn't hit me with a paddle.)*

Feller was decorated with six campaign ribbons and eight battle stars and later was made an honorary member of the Green Berets. He led the American League in strikeouts for seven seasons, including 1946, when he fanned 348 batters. He finished his career with 266 wins in 18 seasons with the Indians. Military service, Feller reckoned, had cost him about 100 more victories. "I know in my heart I would have ended up a lot closer to 400 than 300 if I hadn't spent four seasons in the Navy," he once said. "But don't take that as a complaint. I'm happy that I got home in one piece."

"It don't
mean a
thing
if it ain't
got that
swing...."

—Duke Ellington
lyrics, 1921

Ron Stark, *Ted Williams*, 2014, oil on canvas

SWING

TED WILLIAMS 1941 Boston Red Sox Road Uniform

For Theodore Samuel Williams, swinging a baseball bat became an obsession when he was a child. His father, Samuel Williams, a professional photographer, was rarely around and was unhappily married to May Venzor, a fanatic evangelist and lifelong street worker for the Salvation Army. Samuel and May were so neglectful of Ted and his brother, Danny, that Ted refused to visit his parents when he was older. "I was embarrassed about my home," Williams wrote, "embarrassed that I never had quite as good clothes as some of the kids, embarrassed that my mother was out in the middle of the damn street all the time. Until the day she died she did that, and it always embarrassed me."

Williams sought refuge in a playground a block and a half from his home. "The park helped provide some structure to Williams's life, given the infrequent presence of his parents," wrote Ben Bradlee Jr. in his book *The Kid: The Immortal Life of Ted Williams.* Swinging a baseball bat provided structure as well. Williams would spend his days and nights wandering the playground swinging at an imaginary ball, knocking out phantom home runs while a radio announcer in his head described the play-by-plays. He fell into all-consuming love with hitting. "Williams hit brand-new baseballs," wrote author Leigh Montville. "He hit old, scuffed-up baseballs. He hit baseballs held together with electrical tape. He hit imaginary baseballs, again and again. He walked down the street with a bat and hit flowers off their stems. He hit .583 in his junior year at Hoover High. He hit .403 in his senior year. He hit."

"When I was a kid," Williams told writer David Halberstam in 1988, "I'd see a falling star and I'd say, 'Make me the greatest hitter who ever lived.'" When Williams made his major league debut, on April 20, 1939, as a right fielder for the Boston Red Sox, he was well on his way to fulfilling his dream. He roared onto the field, announcing himself with an authority that did not quite fit with his light-hearted nickname, "the Kid," which he had earned playing minor league ball. He sought advice on hitting from legends such as Rogers Hornsby and Ty Cobb, absorbing their lessons so well that Babe Ruth dubbed him rookie of the year, even if the American League did not officially award him that designation. Ted finished his rookie season with a .327 average, 31 home runs, and 145 RBI—a harbinger of things to come and perhaps the greatest rookie batting performance in baseball history.

We know from newsreels how Williams hit, but we get an even clearer picture of his form from a popular painting by Ron Stark that captures Williams at Yankee Stadium in 1939 (page 134). His lanky upper body, to borrow the words of poet Donald Hall, "is twisted around itself, almost like a barber's pole revolving." His chiseled chin and nose are pointed straight out to follow the arc of the ball, while his lower body, loosely coiled, forms an equilateral triangle with the ground. The painting speaks to the hitter's power and grace, but also to his determination, for every inch of the man shouts that he will not be denied.

In 1941, Williams reached a career zenith. It was a fraught time in American history. The nation was still feeling the economic and psychological effects of the Great Depression. War was looming, though most Americans thought it would be fought in Europe and not in the Pacific Rim. Americans were on the lookout for heroes who could assure

Ted Williams enlisting in the United States Navy, 1942

them that America would prevail in troubled times. They found one in Ted Williams, who set a goal of hitting .400 for the 1941 season. After twisting his ankle during spring training and reinjuring it on a slide into second base, Williams opened the season as a pinch-hitter. He finally returned to the lineup in May and immediately became an opposing pitcher's worst nightmare, batting .436 his first month back in play.

On May 7, Williams clouted the longest home run ever recorded in Chicago's Comiskey Park, hitting the ball a full 600 feet. He started a 22-game hitting streak on May 15, the same day Joe DiMaggio launched his 56 game streak. While wearing the gray Boston Red Sox road uniform pictured here (page 135) as well as the other sets of uniforms he was issued that year, Williams hit a staggering .536 for the two-week period from May 17 to June 1. Hugh Duffy, who had hit .440 for the Red Sox half a century earlier, declared the 23-year-old Williams to be the best hitter he had ever seen.

By September, even fans of opposing teams were pulling for Williams to achieve a .400 season, something only five players had done in the preceding 20 years. The Red Sox closed the regular season with a doubleheader in Philadelphia. Williams entered the final games with a .39955 average—good enough, when rounded up, to give him a .400 batting average for the season. But it wasn't good enough for Williams. On the night before that September 27 match, Williams recalled, "I kept thinking about the thousands of swings I had taken to prepare myself. I had practiced and practiced. I kept saying to myself, 'You are ready.' I went to the ballpark the next day more eager to hit than I had ever been."

"I'm Ted Williams, the greatest hitter in baseball," he said into the locker room mirror. He then went out and got six hits in eight at-bats in the two games, boosting his average to .4057, which is officially rounded up to .406. No player since has broken .400— and only one has broken .390. Williams also led the American League in home runs (37), runs scored (135), and slugging percentage (.735), and he belted 185 hits that year.

Unfortunately for Williams that season, the Yankees won the American League pennant as the Red Sox failed to match their star's performance. The Yankees' Joe DiMaggio won the American League Most Valuable Player award, which some baseball scholars consider a mistake, or even a travesty. The Kid was America's hero, but Joltin' Joe stole some of his thunder.

Even more of his thunder was taken the following season. Williams was drafted into the military in January 1942, but he asked to be excused from service because he was the sole provider for his mother, and he was granted his request. Public reaction was

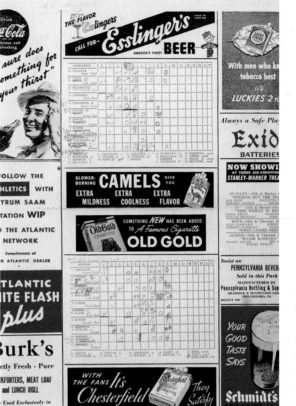

Official scorecard to game at Shibe Park when Williams went six-for-eight in two games to bring his season average to .406, September 27, 1941

extremely negative and sponsors such as Quaker Oats dropped him. Williams won the Triple Crown that season, with a .356 batting average, 36 home runs, and 137 RBI, but he finished second in MVP voting, in part because voters were angry that he had dodged military service. Williams had joined the Navy Reserve on May 22, 1942, and he went on active duty in 1943. He was commissioned a second lieutenant in the United States Marine Corps as a naval aviator on May 2, 1944.

Williams returned to baseball in 1946. He never again attained the numbers of 1941, but he remained a student and teacher of the art and science of batting, lecturing anyone who would listen on what it took to send a ball out of the park. In his case, it took hours of practice plus a scientific regard for the physics of ball and bat. Williams was also fueled by a simmering anger. Bradlee wrote in his biography that Williams carried a chip on his shoulder because he felt disquiet over his mixed ethnicity (his mother was Mexican American). It is not surprising that Williams sought to conceal his heritage in the face of Jim Crow and institutional discrimination. As a result, Williams was often self-absorbed, stubborn, scrappy, easily offended, and quick to spit out an angry remark.

Yet his personal flaws do not diminish his record. He gave America a baseball hero when it needed one the most. His name was Ted Williams, and he was the greatest hitter in baseball.

THE WAR YEARS: TRADING FLANNEL FOR KHAKI

World War II
Service All-Stars
baseball team, 1942

A 1943 Chicago
White Sox home
jersey, with a wool
Army Air Corps
utility shirt worn
by a sergeant
first class in
World War II

In the late summer and fall of 1940, England was fighting for its life in the skies over Britain while America was watching the Cincinnati Reds and Detroit Tigers slug it out in a seven-game World Series. Attendance for that Series was 281,846, while the active end strength of the U.S. Army sat at 269,022. The Marine Corps had 28,345 men under arms, as compared to the 67,468 fans who packed Cleveland's Municipal Stadium on July 17, 1941, to see Joe DiMaggio's 56-game hitting streak die in the web of Ken Keltner's glove. After a decade of struggling to climb out of the Great Depression, the nation was more than ready for baseball, but not for war.

The majority of Americans favored neutrality and had little desire to become involved in Hitler's rage over Europe and Japan's imperialism within the Pacific Rim. But as the Japanese pushed territorial ambitions in the Pacific and war clouds loomed, the United States prepared to defend itself. On September 16, 1940, President Franklin D. Roosevelt signed the

Selective Training and Service Act, which required every American male between the ages of 21 and 36 to register for 12 months of military service. By the end of 1941, nearly two million men had been drafted into the military.

Major league baseball was at its zenith in 1941. Ted Williams batted .406 that year, Joe DiMaggio hit safely in 56 consecutive games, 41-year-old Lefty Grove got his 300th career win, and Dodgers catcher Mickey Owen famously mishandled a pitch that cost Brooklyn the World Series. But the draft affected every profession, including baseball. More than 500 major league players, including Bob Feller, Joe DiMaggio, Ted Williams, and Stan Musial, would serve during the war, and two, Elmer Gedeon and Harry O'Neill, would be killed.

Still, the American people continued to watch baseball thanks to a shared belief that the sport could boost morale. On January 15, 1942, President Roosevelt sent his famous "Green Light" letter to baseball commissioner Kenesaw Mountain Landis, which concluded: "I honestly feel that it would be best for the country to keep baseball going. There will be fewer people unemployed and everyone will work longer hours and harder than ever before."

Many of these workers had churned out sporting good products before the war, but now they were turning America into the arsenal of democracy. Hillerich & Bradsby shifted production from bats to rifle stocks and nightsticks. Rawlings and Wilson began manufacturing helmets for tank crews. Baseball togs from the war years (1942 to 1945) are now among the most sought-after sports memorabilia. Two factors likely drove the scarcity of uniforms from this period: materials were redirected to wartime demands, and ball clubs extended the use of their garments to reduce costs. Many major league teams also donated uniforms for service members' use.

Shown opposite is a Chicago White Sox home jersey from the 1943 season atop an authentic wool Army Air Corps utility shirt from World War II. Such wartime uniforms still stand at proud attention, often displaying either the 1942 Hale America HEALTH patch or the stars-and-stripes patch, seen here on the jersey's left sleeve, that first appeared in 1943. Still more striking are the era's patriotic color schemes, which are not done justice by the black-and-white photography and newsreel footage of their day.

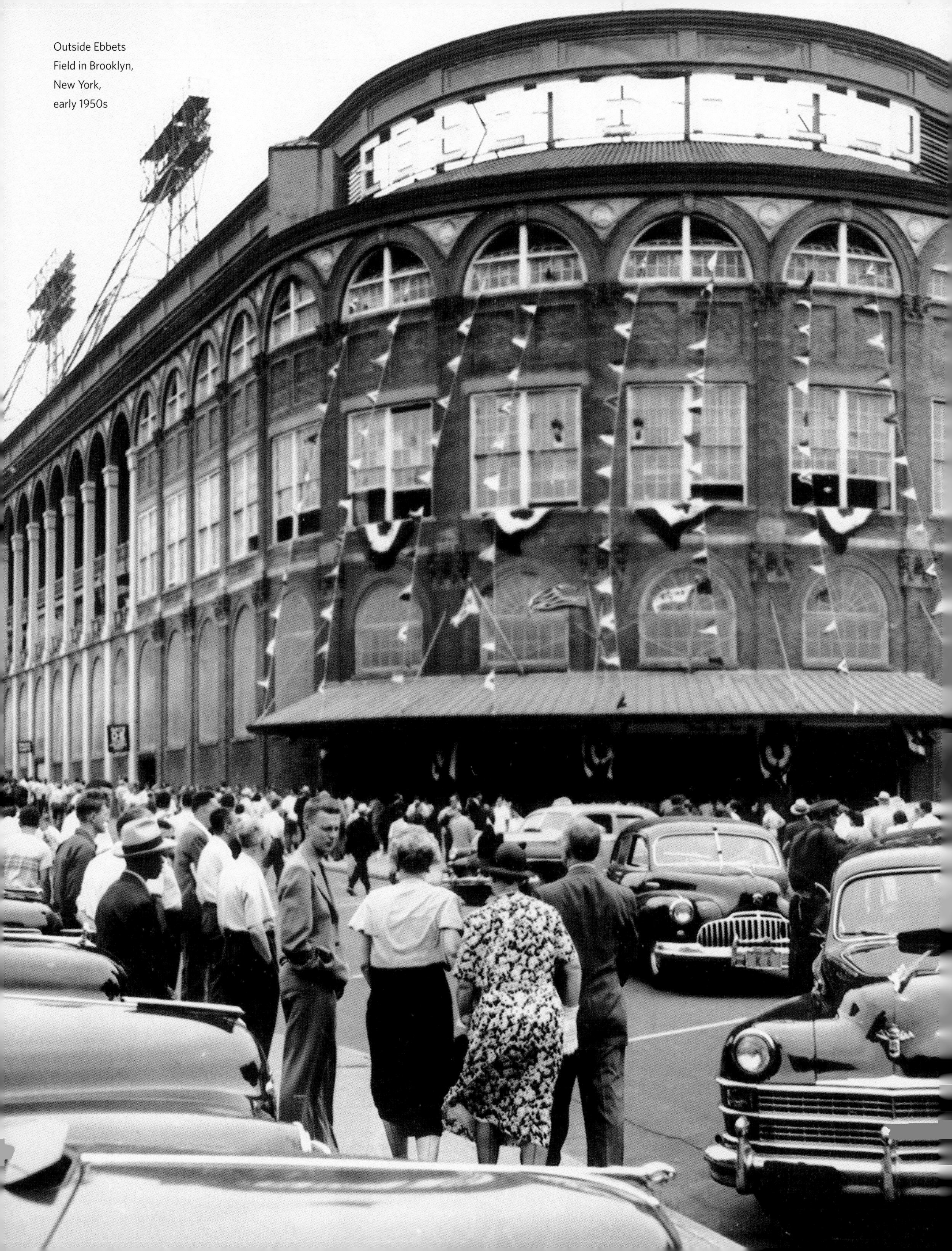

Outside Ebbets Field in Brooklyn, New York, early 1950s

THE POSTWAR YEARS

1946–1959

When World War II ended, some of baseball's greatest heroes, including Hank Greenberg, Bob Feller, Gil Hodges, and Warren Spahn, returned from the conflict to again take their place on the diamond. The nation's economy was expanding, and the population was booming, swelling the ranks of baseball fans. Television, too, established itself as a transformational medium, bringing the game to ever-increasing audiences who lived too far away to attend a ballgame. By the mid-1950s, baseball was truly America's game.

As the postwar era drew to a close, America had become a nation on the move, with affordable air travel and a growing interstate highway system. Elvis and the *Ed Sullivan Show* competed with baseball for time on television. All but one major league team was playing home games at night as well as during the day. It was a time of movement and relocation: The Giants and Dodgers moved to California, the Browns to Baltimore, the Braves to Milwaukee, and the Athletics to Kansas City. Jackie Robinson integrated baseball in 1947, and the game's new players included Larry Doby, Willie Mays, Roy Campanella, Hank Aaron, Roberto Clemente, and the ageless Satchel Paige.

A great inventory of uniforms survives from the postwar era, characterized by striking designs and durable synthetic flannel fabric that weighed half as much as the material used in the Deadball Era. National League players in Brooklyn, Boston, St. Louis, and Cincinnati even wore satin uniforms for night games. In a nod to the needs of television, teams placed player numbers on the front, back, and sometimes the sleeves of players' jerseys.

AGELESS WONDER

SATCHEL PAIGE 1948 Cleveland Indians Home Jersey

Shortly after Leroy "Satchel" Paige joined the Cleveland Indians in July 1948, a reporter asked him his age. "If someone asked you how old you were and you didn't know your age, how old would you think you were?" replied Paige. The Indians' new pitcher was not being evasive; he simply did not know when he was born. The Indians finally uncovered his birth certificate and learned that the former Negro Leagues pitcher and showboat had been born on July 7, 1906. So when he debuted with Cleveland on July 9, 1948, not only was Paige the first African American pitcher in baseball, but he also was the oldest rookie ever, at 42 years and two days.

Leroy Robert Paige grew up in Mobile, Alabama, in the heart of the Jim Crow South. As a youngster, Paige had to scramble for money to help around the house. He gathered empty bottles, delivered ice, and carried baggage at the L&N train station. When white travelers snapped their fingers, Paige shined their boots or carried luggage to their hotels for a dime a bag. After he rigged up a rope-and-broomstick contraption that allowed him to carry four satchels at a time, he quadrupled his income. He also drew jests from the other baggage boys. "You look like a walking satchel tree," one of them yelled, and forever after he bore the nickname Satchel.

After he was caught stealing suitcases, Paige was sent to the Industrial School for Negro Children at Mount Meigs, Alabama. There, his pitching skills were groomed by coach Edward Byrd, who showed Paige how to kick his foot high to black out the sky and befuddle the batter, and to reach so far forward that it seemed as if he were releasing the ball right in the batter's face. After reform school, Paige returned to Mobile and joined a semipro team. He moved to the Chattanooga White Sox in the Negro Southern League in 1926, and a year later he was traded to the Birmingham Black Barons of the Negro National League, a division of the Negro Leagues.

Records from this era and league are incomplete, but it is believed that Paige's strikeout total of 167 in 1929 is a Negro Leagues record. On April 29 of that season, he

recorded 17 strikeouts against the Cuban Stars, which exceeded what was then the major league record of 16 held by Noodles Hahn and Rube Waddell. Six days later, he struck out 18 Nashville Elite Giants, a record tied by Bob Feller in the white major leagues in 1938.

Satchel played in Cuba, barnstormed in the United States, played on loan for numerous Negro Leagues teams, and pitched for teams in Baltimore, Cleveland, Pittsburgh, California, and North Dakota. Time in the Dominican Republic, Mexico, and Puerto Rico followed before Paige rejoined the Kansas City Monarchs in 1940. No matter where he pitched, he threw fire and created a glossary of names for his repertoire of pitches: bee ball (because it hummed as it flew), jump ball, trouble ball, Long Tom, Little Tom, midnight rider, and hesitation pitch, in which he paused as his left foot hit the ground during the windup.

Satchel Paige taking a breather, 1948

Paige was too old for military service in World War II, so he spent the war years playing ball (see the program opposite), laying "the groundwork for Jackie [Robinson] the way A. Philip Randolph, W. E. B. Du Bois, and other early Civil Rights leaders did for Martin Luther King Jr," wrote Larry Tye in his book *Satchel: The Life and Times of an American Legend.* He barnstormed throughout the United States and the Caribbean with Dizzy Dean, Bob Feller, and other white big leaguers in the first games featuring black teams competing against white ones.

While pitching in the Negro World Series, East-West All-Star Games, and barnstorming events, Paige played in Comiskey Park, Wrigley Field, the Polo Grounds, Forbes Field, and other major league venues. Paige later insisted that he was the first African American player to compete in these stadiums, and in his memoir he complained that it should have been him, and not Jackie Robinson, who broke the ban on black players in the majors: "I'd been the one who'd opened up the major league parks to colored teams," he wrote, though he praised Robinson for the skill and grace of his play.

Paige was finally called up to the major leagues when the 1948 Indians needed pitching in the middle of a pennant race. Within a week, he picked up his first win, and he would rack up five more victories that season while wearing this flannel Cleveland Indians

home jersey manufactured by Wilson (page 143). His combination of overarm and sidearm pitches baffled batters and commentators alike. "When Satchel Paige wound up to pitch, he looked like a cross between Ichabod Crane and Rip Van Winkle," wrote author Al Hirshberg. "He was easy to imitate and funny to watch, unless you were the batter trying to hit against him." After one broadcaster stated that Paige's pitches may not have been strictly legal but were a pleasure to watch, Paige replied, "I never threw an illegal pitch. The trouble is, once in a while I toss one that ain't been seen by this generation."

His 2.48 ERA for the 1948 season was second best in the American League. Each game he won had fans and writers marveling over what he must have been like in his prime and which other legends of the Negro Leagues had been lost to the Jim Crow system of segregation. With a 6–1 record, he helped the Indians capture the pennant by a single game over the Red Sox. Paige played one more season with Cleveland, then spent three seasons with the St. Louis Browns. In 1952, he was 12–10 with a 3.07 ERA and was selected for the American League All-Star Team. He was released after the 1953 season and barnstormed until 1966, when he retired at age 60.

A flamboyant showman, Paige was famed in his Negro Leagues days for a fiendishly hard fastball. Though he had lost some of that heat by the time he arrived in the majors, Red Sox legend Bobby Doerr, who faced

THE GREATEST NIGHT CROWD IN BASEBALL HISTORY
78,382
INDIANS vs CHICAGO   AUGUST 20th 1948
SATCHEL PAIGE PITCHING

Satchel Paige packing stadiums in both the Negro Leagues and the big leagues

BUY U.S. WAR BONDS & STAMPS

WRIGLEY FIELD - CHICAGO

OFFICIAL SCORE CARD

"SATCHEL PAIGE DAY"

SUNDAY AFTERNOON, JULY 18, 1943

LE ROY "SATCHEL" PAIGE

BIRMINGHAM BLACK BARONS VS. CINCINNATI CLOWNS

MEMPHIS RED SOX VS. NEW YORK CUBANS

PRICE 10¢

225

"If the Yankees don't get ahead in the first six innings, the Browns bring in that damned old man, and we're sunk."

—Casey Stengel

Official scorecard, "Satchel Paige Day" Wrigley Field, July 18, 1943

Paige in 1948, said that he had "never seen a pitcher that could hit that outside corner like Satchel could." Joe DiMaggio said Paige was the best player that he had ever come across. But perhaps well beyond his brilliance on the mound was his longevity in the game. Paige was 42 when he launched his major-league career, and a record 59 years, two months, and eight days when he ended it with the Athletics in 1965. He was 33 years older than his catcher that night, yet he shut out the hard-hitting Red Sox for three innings, throwing just 28 pitches with one strikeout and no walks. The only base hit was a double by Carl Yastrzemski, an All-Star who led the league in doubles that season and had watched his father hit against Paige a generation earlier in a semi-pro game.

By Paige's own account, he pitched in more than 2,500 games on 250 teams in his 40-year career as a professional. As baseball's ageless wonder once sagely remarked, "Age is a question of mind over matter. If you don't mind, it doesn't matter."

BATTERED OLD WARRIOR

WARREN SPAHN 1949 Boston Braves Home Jersey and Cap

Warren Spahn's high kick, meant to distract the hitter's attention from the ball, 1948

Authentic World War II Purple Heart award and case, along with period newspapers covering the Battle of the Bulge, atop Spahn's 1949 Boston Braves home jersey

"He was born old," a Boston Braves teammate said of Warren Spahn. New York sportswriter Red Smith described Spahn as a "battered old warrior," while Stan Musial once remarked that he would never be enshrined in Cooperstown. It wasn't because Spahn lacked the numbers or the chops. Far from it—he was one of the best pitchers in baseball history and perhaps the best left-handed pitcher ever. But as Musial said: "He won't stop pitching."

Warren Edward Spahn was ageless, timeless, and indomitable. He entered the majors in 1942, throwing for the Boston Braves, and ended his career 23 years later, in 1965, across the continent with the San Francisco Giants. By the time he threw his last pitch, he was 44 years old, practically a Methuselah in the world of sports. In his day, it seemed that Spahn was ubiquitous, filling the sports pages with his accomplishments and earning seemingly every accolade, from the Cy Young Award in 1957, when he led the Braves to a World Series victory, to a near-record 14 appearances in All-Star Games, to election to the Hall of Fame in 1973, his first year of eligibility.

Although it may seem that Spahn was in the big leagues forever, he actually took time off in 1942. First, during an exhibition game, Braves manager Casey Stengel ordered Spahn to brush back Brooklyn Dodgers shortstop Pee Wee Reese with a fast ball. Spahn, who had pitched only four games in the majors, refused. Stengel said Spahn had "no guts" and sent him down to the minors for his insubordination. "After your shower, pick up your railroad ticket to Hartford," Stengel said.

Next, at the end of the 1942 season, Spahn joined the Army. After training as a combat engineer, he boarded the *Queen Mary* on November 9, 1944, as a staff sergeant in the 276th Engineer Combat Battalion and headed to France. He was trapped behind German lines during the Battle of the Bulge, fighting in snowy, frozen conditions, getting nicked by bullets on the abdomen and the back of his head. He and the 9th Armored Division fought their way out, then helped build the bridges used by General George S. Patton's Third Army and the Allied troops to cross the Rhine River into Germany. He narrowly escaped death when the Lundendorff bridge at Remagen collapsed, killing 28 fellow soldiers and wounding 93. Sergeant Spahn returned home with a battlefield commission and the Purple Heart.

"After what I went through overseas," Spahn said later, "I never thought of anything I was told to do in baseball as hard work. You get over feeling like that when you spend days on end sleeping in frozen tank tracks in enemy-threatened territory. The Army taught me what's important and what isn't." Spahn returned to the majors and the Boston Braves in 1946, still throwing with an odd delivery that he worked up early in his career and spent the rest of his professional life perfecting. His motion was fluid, nearly liquid, and his whole body moved with an elegant swoop punctuated by a high kick. That kick, he explained, was meant to distract the hitter's attention away from the ball. Seeing what Spahn had become, Stengel ruefully confessed, "I said 'no guts' to a kid who went on to become a war hero and one of the greatest left-handed pitchers you ever saw. You can't say I don't miss 'em when I miss 'em!"

For his part, Spahn rarely missed. He painted the corners like an artist, relying on fastballs in his early years before developing a repertoire of off-speed pitches. He joked that he really had only two pitches, one that the batter was looking for but couldn't hit and one that he wasn't looking for and couldn't hit. Spahn explained his strategy: "Home plate is 17 inches wide. I give the batter the middle 13 inches. That belongs to him. But the two outside inches on either side belong to me. That's where I throw the ball." That's certainly where he threw it in 1949, when he led the National League in wins (21) and strikeouts (151) while wearing the Boston Braves home jersey and cap shown on page 147. He continued to brush the corners of the plate in 1950 and 1951, leading the NL in strikeouts both years.

Spahn moved with the Braves to Milwaukee in 1953, where he won 20 or more games in 9 of the next 11 seasons. He pitched the most magnificent game of his career in July 1963, when Spahn faced San Francisco Giants legend Juan Marichal in a pitching duel that is still talked about by scholars of the game. Pitch after pitch the two battled, inning after shutout inning. In the 14th inning, Giants manager Alvin Dark went to the mound to take Marichal out of the game. "Do you see that man pitching for the other side?" said Marichal. "Do you know that man is forty-two years old? I'm only twenty-five. If that man is on the mound, nobody is going to take me out of here." Finally, in the 16th inning, Willie Mays hit a solo home run off Spahn to give the Giants the 1–0 victory. Marichal threw 227 pitches in the game, and Spahn threw 201. Said Hall of Famer Carl Hubbell, who attended the game: "He [Spahn] ought to will his body to medical science."

By the next year, Spahn's 43-year-old arm was starting to weaken, though he insisted he had at least one more 20-game season in him. "In a pitcher, age isn't a factor, as Satchel Paige proved," said Spahn. "Nobody knew how old he was when he helped pitch the 1948 Indians to a pennant, but he was almost certainly older than I am now. And Satch had two things going for him that I've got going for me: He was in good physical condition, and there wasn't anything wrong with his arm."

Spahn struggled in 1964, when he was 6–13 with a 5.29 ERA, and the Braves sold him to the three-year-old New York Mets, who were managed by Casey Stengel. The Mets welcomed Spahn by paying him $70,000 a year, the highest player salary in team history. After Spahn lost 11 games in a row, the Mets released him and he was signed by San Francisco, where he joined Juan Marichal in the bullpen. Spahn closed his career with three wins and four losses, then retired to a modest cattle ranch in Oklahoma. He died in 2003.

Spahn set records for games won in a career by a southpaw (363) and for winning at least 20 games in a season 13 times. He holds major league records for most times leading a league in victories (8), complete games (9), and innings pitched (5,243), and holds the National League record for lefties with 63 shutouts. He also completed 382 of 665 starts and had a career ERA of 3.09. "For the years I was watching him, Koufax was tops," Johnny Podres, famed Dodgers pitcher and later a pitching coach, once said. "But for the long haul, for year-after-year performance, Warren Spahn was the best I ever saw. He was just a master of his trade. I couldn't take my eyes off him. Watching him was an education."

United States
Army soldiers
near Ludendorff
Bridge, Remagen,
Germany, 1945

"Anybody we didn't know, we'd ask, 'Who plays second for the Bums?' If he didn't answer 'Eddie Stanky,' he was dead."

—Warren Spahn, recalling how his battalion dealt with German spies who wore American uniforms during World War II

THE NATURAL

EDDIE WAITKUS 1950 Philadelphia Phillies Home Jersey

Waitkus's 1950 Philadelphia Phillies home jersey shown with a re-creation of Ruth Ann Steinhagen's coffee table in her hotel room while she waited for Eddie Waitkus on June 14, 1949: an original Edgewater Beach Hotel room key and matchbook from the 1940s, .22-caliber bullets from the 1940s, a whiskey sour, and a photo of Waitkus

Andy Warhol. Sam Cooke. Jackie Wilson. Male public figures assaulted by women generally have been pop stars and pop artists, not baseball players. Eddie Waitkus, who played for the Chicago Cubs and Philadelphia Phillies, is a notable exception. His story faded over time, until it was revived in Bernard Malamud's 1952 book *The Natural* and a 1984 movie starring Robert Redford.

Born in Boston to Lithuanian immigrants in 1919, Edward Stephen Waitkus grew up near a baseball field in Cambridge. He developed his skills first as a pitcher but, after his father mistakenly bought him a first baseman's glove, switched positions. He was an honor student at Cambridge High and Latin School, where he batted .600. He turned down an offer to play in college and instead joined a semipro league team in Lisbon Falls, Maine. He next signed with the Chicago Cubs and played for minor league clubs in Oklahoma and Illinois. He made his major league debut on April 15, 1941, at Wrigley Field, and was drafted into the army in 1943 to fight in World War II. Waitkus survived terrible battles in New Guinea, the Solomon Islands, and the Philippines, earning four Bronze Stars for bravery in combat. Following the war, he joined the Cubs at spring training in California in 1946. He made history by hitting an inside-the-park home run immediately after another Cubs batter had done the same. He batted .304 in 441 at-bats that year.

Bookish and articulate, fluent in several European languages, a scholar of Civil War history, and an avid ballroom dancer, Waitkus cut an unlikely figure on that bruising team. In 1948, without explanation, the Cubs traded Waitkus to the Phillies after briefly moving him from first base to the outfield. As if to rebuke his former team, Waitkus played with a vengeance in Philadelphia, hitting a solid .306 in his first full month as a Phillie. He also developed into a formidable first baseman and was selected as a reserve for the 1949 All-Star Game.

On June 14, life took a strange turn for Waitkus. In perhaps the first case of what today would be called celebrity stalking, a 19-year-old woman gave a $5 tip to a bellhop at the Edgewater Beach Hotel in Chicago and asked him to deliver a note to Waitkus. The woman was a guest at the hotel, and Waitkus was staying there with the Phillies, who were in town for a game against the Cubs. Calling herself Ruth Ann Burns, the woman wrote that she had important news. Waitkus received the note late in the evening and "thought it might be someone he knew—someone from downstate or a friend of a friend," as he later told reporters. He arranged to meet the woman, whose real name was Ruth Ann Steinhagen, in her room at the Edgewater. She ordered two whiskey sours and a daiquiri from room service and sipped them while she waited for Waitkus. Her plan was to stab him with a knife when he entered the room, but he spoiled

that plan when he rushed past her and sat in a chair as soon as she opened the door. Instead, she went to a closet and pulled out a .22 hunting rifle, saying ominously to Waitkus, "I have a surprise for you." She forced him to stand and move toward the window, then told him, "For two years, you've been bothering me, and now you're going to die." Before Waitkus could react, she shot him.

Waitkus did not die. Steinhagen's bullet passed through his right lung and lodged near his spine. Doctors at Illinois Masonic Hospital later said a bullet of higher caliber would have killed him instantly. Waitkus endured four operations over the next month, then resumed play with the Phillies.

Waitkus was known for reliability and speed, both before and after he was shot. Said shortstop Granville "Granny" Hamner, "With Waitkus on first, you don't have to waste any time aiming the ball before you throw, you just let it fly. You know that if it's in the right general direction, Eddie will come up with it." The Associated Press named Waitkus the Comeback Player of the Year in 1950, the year he wore the Philadelphia Phillies home jersey, manufactured by Wilson, shown on page 151. That year, Waitkus and the "Whiz Kids" Phillies reached the World Series for the first time since 1915 but lost to the Yankees. It appeared that Waitkus was destined for a promising decade.

But something had happened to Eddie Waitkus after he was shot. Though he was affable with reporters, saying, "I would just like to know what got into that silly honey picking on a nice guy like me," he became quiet, and less outgoing. He smoked heavily. He drank heavily. He had a heavy soul, and he sank into depression. Depression led to more drinking, and more drinking led to deeper depression. Waitkus played poorly in 1953, and the Phillies let him go. He played for the Orioles for a year, but quit in September 1955, hitting a home run at his final at-bat. He was 36 and had played 1,140 professional games.

Waitkus continued to suffer after he left baseball, haunted by Steinhagen's bullet and by the bullets that had snapped around his head in the Pacific War. Today, Waitkus's condition would be diagnosed as post-traumatic stress disorder. He continued to drink, and his marriage disintegrated. He could not hold a job, and he moved from city to city. Even as Phillies fans voted him the team's best first baseman ever, he lived in flea-trap apartments, unemployed. In 1972, he entered a Veterans Administration hospital, where he died of esophageal cancer at 53.

Steinhagen, before the attack, had been so obsessed with him that she filled her small apartment with press clippings, baseball cards, and ticket stubs. When she

THE NEW YO

SS BREAKS
RY RECORD

Baseball Star Shot by Girl Rallies;
Lured by Typist He Never Knew

MRS. ROOSE\
Dinner Is Giver
of United J

ed to Hire Hall
s Graduating
st Number

I G. WEART
NEW YORK TIMES.
IA, June 15—The
nsylvania had to
Municipal Audi-
o the campus—to
ay the thousands
friends of the
g class in the 209
ounding by Ben-

sen, president of
esided at the ex-
red 2,029 degrees
omas, forty-three
our honorary de-

latter were Doc-
to Dr. Ralph J.
Nations Mediator
l director of the
ip Division; Dr.
k, president of

Mrs. Frankli
chairman of th
Commission on l
pressed confiden
there would be l
was guest of h
given by the clo
allied industries
United Jewish
New York at th
Hotel.
Mrs. Roosevel
for her "enrichr
life by noble i
noble tasks" and
that have won h
in the history o
freedom through
She then decla
to fight for a
peace, but it is
the UN are figh
think we will g
The 350 repres
ing manufacture
gamated Cloth
America, CIO, a
pledged $1,500,0
Appeal drive.

Eddie Waitkus
The New York Times

Ruth Ann Steinhagen
Associated Press Wirephoto

Continued from Page 1

Steinhagen knelt at his side and

The story as it appeared in the *New York Times,* June 15, 1949

Ruth Ann Steinhagen
in Kankakee State
Hospital, 1949,
after a jury found
her insane

was arrested, she said that she had to shoot him "to relieve the nervous tension" and that she liked Waitkus "best of anybody in the world." She was released from a psychiatric hospital three years after the attempted murder. Oddly, while in jail awaiting hospitalization, she asked to play first base on the inmate baseball squad. She never spoke of Waitkus again and lived in obscurity and seclusion in her parents' home in Chicago, dying at the age of 83 in 2013.

In 1952, the year Steinhagen was released, Bernard Malamud published his novel, which hewed closely to events in Waitkus's life, down to its title ("The Natural," the nickname bestowed on Waitkus in his first year of minor league ball). Malamud, though not a fan of baseball, captured the magic and pull of the game with his story of Roy Hobbs and his lightning-kissed, hand-carved bat. Robert Redford brought Hobbs to the screen in 1984. The book is now considered a classic of postwar American fiction and is often named among the two or three best novels about baseball ever written. What Eddie Waitkus thought of it, we do not know.

STAN THE MAN

STAN MUSIAL 1951 St. Louis Cardinals Road Uniform

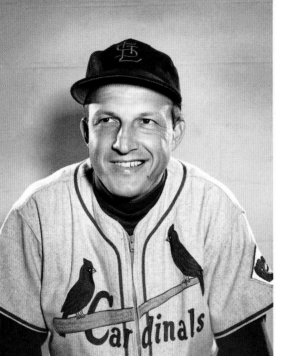

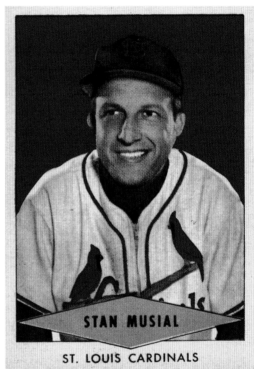

Image of Stan Musial wearing the uniform shown opposite (left) taken in 1951 and used to produce Musial's Red Heart Dog Food baseball card (right) in 1954; Red Heart produced a series of 33 cards in 1954, and among the most popular was Musial's

Musial's 1951 St. Louis Cardinals road uniform shown with an early 1950s St. Louis Cardinals equipment trunk

Braves Field, Boston, July 18, 1951. Rookie St. Louis Cardinals pitcher Joe Presko defeated Johnny Sain of the Braves, 9–6, to chalk up the Red Birds' 44th win of the season. After postgame rituals with the press and autograph seekers, the Cardinals players showered and headed to Boston's South Station, where they boarded the train to Brooklyn for a three-game series against the Dodgers. Along with confidence from their victory, the Cardinals brought to Brooklyn their equipment trunks—an original one from the early 1950s is shown opposite— which stored and protected the team's bats, gloves, gear, and, most important, road uniforms.

Before the game on July 20, longtime Cardinals equipment manager Morris Butch Yatkeman entered the visiting team's locker room at Ebbets Field, opened his players' trunks, and placed a uniform in each one. The uniform shown here (opposite) was worn in 1951

by left-fielder Stan Musial, who smacked three hits and drove in two runs against the Braves. The jersey features the National League 75th Anniversary patch on the left sleeve (see page 267 in the Compendium). Musial was eager to continue his assault against Preacher Roe and the rest of the Bums in Brooklyn.

Born in Donora, Pennsylvania, on November 21, 1920, the son of a Polish immigrant father and first-generation Czech American mother, Stanley Frank Musial took to baseball the moment he could throw one. He played in sandlot games, for his church league, and for his high school team, and he signed a contract with the St. Louis Cardinals when he was 18. The Cards thought they were acquiring a left-handed pitcher who fired fierce heat. But in 1940, while playing for a Cardinals farm team in Daytona Beach, Musial was assigned to play outfield in the absence of a regular player. He landed hard while diving to catch a ball and

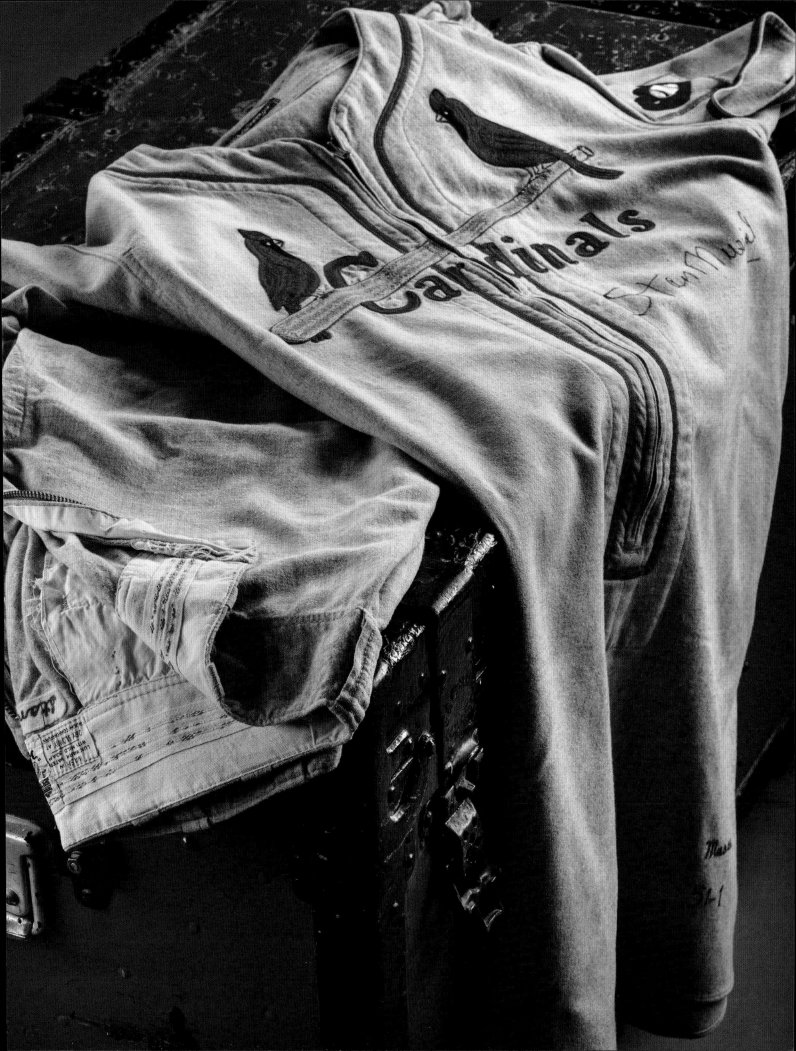

tore up his left shoulder, which forced him to stop pitching and move to the field. He played 1,896 games in left field after reaching the major leagues in 1941, and later played 1,016 games at first base, making him the first player to play more than 1,000 games in each of two different positions.

But it was as a hitter that Musial made his mark. His batting stance was so unusual that it seemed to bewitch opposing pitchers. He turned his back to the mound and contorted his body into an odd, yoga-like pose. In the words of a sportswriter in 1940: "The bent knees and the crouch give him the appearance of a coiled spring, although most pitchers think of him as a coiled rattlesnake." Author Paul Warburton was more vivid: "A lefty, he dug in with his left foot on the back line of the batter's box, and assumed a closed stance with his right foot about twelve inches in front of his left. He took three or four practice swings and followed up with a silly-looking hula wiggle to help him relax. He crouched, stirring his bat like a weapon in a low, slow-moving arc away from his body....He would then uncoil with an explosion of power. His line drives were bullets."

In 22 major league seasons, Musial batted below .300 only four times and ended with a .331 career batting average. He topped the National League in career hits (3,630, in 3,026 games) and was second in home runs (475), despite missing the 1945 season to serve in the Navy during World War II. He smacked five round-trippers in a 1954 doubleheader against the New York Giants, played in a record 24 consecutive All-Star Games (two games were played each season from 1959 to 1962), and retired in 1963 with 17 major league records.

His outstanding numbers aside, Musial was beloved by fellow players and fans—even those from opposing teams. In 1946, playing against the Brooklyn Dodgers, Musial was preparing to step up to the plate when a low, rumbling chant rose from the stands at Ebbets Field: "Here comes the man. Here comes the man." Sportswriter Bob Broeg mentioned this odd accolade in his column for the *Post-Dispatch*. Cardinal fans soon began calling Musial "the Man," later enshrined as the euphonious "Stan the Man."

Musial tolerated the nickname, but he did not act like he expected special attention. He showed up for every game ready to play, coiled himself into a snake-like stance, and bashed pitches into the stands and the parking lots. He also set an example of evenhandedness; he didn't fight, argue calls, or swear at umpires, and he was never ejected from a game. He accepted the arrival of African American players in the major leagues with a simple handshake. Jackie Robinson mentioned that Musial and Hank Greenberg of the Detroit Tigers encouraged him during Robinson's difficult year in 1947. Ty Cobb also praised Musial, contending that he and

New York Yankees shortstop Phil Rizzuto were the only players who could "be mentioned in the same breath with the old time greats." Musial demurred, saying that Cobb was in a league of his own, and that Joe DiMaggio, who played for the Yankees from 1936 to 1951, was better than he was.

Artist Norman Rockwell painted Musial for the *Saturday Evening Post*, capturing the player as he signed balls for fans in the bleachers. Tobacco brands and pet food companies also adored Musial, and the uniform shown here (page 155) was the one he wore in the photograph used to make the 1954 Red Heart Dog Food baseball card (page 154). It's not often that uniforms can be photo-matched to such an iconic image.

Musial also had ups and downs in his career. In 1959, Musial, slow and out of shape, topped 400 home runs and 3,000 hits for his career but batted just .255 for the season. Nonetheless, presidential candidate John F. Kennedy asked Musial, perhaps the most popular player at the time, to campaign for him, a request that Musial was happy to honor. As a result of his performance, the Cardinals also made a more uncomfortable request: A year earlier, Musial had become one of the first players to sign a contract that would pay him more than $100,000, but now the club asked him to take a 20 percent pay cut in consideration of his modest performance.

Musial complied, knowing that at age 40, he wasn't long for the game. Characteristically, though, Musial worked off the extra pounds and got back into shape, and his numbers improved in 1960, 1961, and 1962. His last year was 1963, when the Cardinals led their division but lost in a tight pennant race to the Dodgers, now in Los Angeles. Musial echoed his major league debut game with two base hits in his final game. The Cardinals retired his number 6, and Stan the Man was enshrined at Cooperstown in 1969, his first year of eligibility.

Musial accumulated records and accolades with modesty and with kind words for players in both dugouts. Yatkeman, who served as the Cardinals clubhouse man/equipment manager from 1924 to 1982, witnessed most of Musial's career. "We've had some great guys," Yatkeman told Dave Anderson of the *New York Times*. "But two of my favorites were Stan Musial and Roger Maris. Musial is a great guy, St. Louis loves him. He has a perfect nature. He could go four-for-four or hit five homers in a doubleheader, like he once did, or go three days without a hit, and he was the same individual. I don't remember him ever getting mad or knocking something over." Ford Frick, baseball's commissioner from 1951 to 1965, best summarized what Musial meant to the game with his inscription on the statue of Musial that stands outside Busch Stadium: "Here stands baseball's perfect warrior. Here stands baseball's perfect knight."

"A couple years ago they told me I was too young to be president and you were too old to be playing baseball. But we fooled them."

—President John F. Kennedy, to Stan Musial at the 1962 All-Star Game

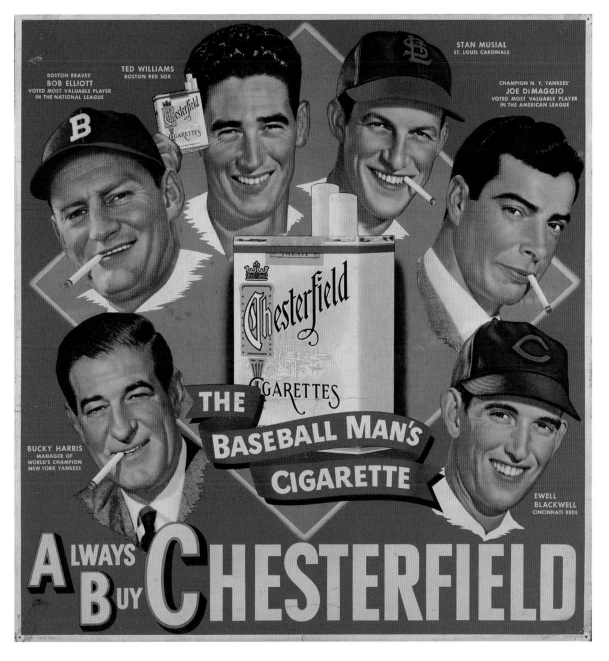

1948 National League MVP Stan Musial, an obvious choice to pitch Chesterfield Cigarettes, 1948

LAWDIE

YOGI BERRA 1951 New York Yankees Road Jersey

The outlook for 1952 seemed ominous for the New York Yankees. Joe DiMaggio's unexpected announcement that he was retiring after 13 seasons left a gaping hole to fill. The Yankees had just defeated the crosstown rival New York Giants, four games to two, in the World Series, and rookie Mickey Mantle had just completed a sterling first season. Still, the stomach of manager Casey Stengel churned at the thought of losing the team's biggest star.

Stengel need not have worried. Despite the loss of DiMaggio, the Yankees would still field a formidable squad of talent for the 1952 season, including Mantle, Phil Rizzuto, Johnny Mize, Hank Bauer, and a young Billy Martin. And the nucleus of that constellation was a homely and homespun catcher who would become one of the greatest characters—and greatest catchers—in all of baseball.

Lorenzo Pietro Berra was born on May 12, 1925, in an Italian neighborhood of St. Louis, Missouri, called the Hill. His parents were immigrants from Robecchetto, Italy, and they spoke halting English. To help their son better assimilate Berra's parents, Pietro and Paolina, anglicized their son's name to Lawrence Peter. They called him Lawdie because Paolina could not pronounce his New World name. Berra was not a good student and, against his father's wishes, he quit school after the eighth grade and found work in a coal yard and on a Pepsi Cola truck. He was fired from both jobs because he left work early to play ball and go to the movies with friends. One movie the boys attended featured a part on India and showed a yogi, a person who practices yoga. The yogi was sitting cross-legged on the floor, and when he got up he waddled. One of the friends joked that he walked like Berra, and from then on, Berra was known as Yogi.

Berra played baseball for his Catholic school and for the local American Legion team. He loved to play catcher, and it helped that he was short and sturdy, able to crouch for long stretches without cramping or tiring. He quickly became known around St. Louis for his play. Joe Garagiola, a friend who lived across the street from Berra and was also a catcher, considered Berra to be the best player in the city. The two went to a tryout with the Cardinals in 1942, and Garagiola, just 16, came away with a contract offer and a $500 bonus. A year later, he became the youngest person to play for the Columbus Red Birds, a Cardinals minor league team. Berra was offered a contract but no bonus, and in a fit of pique, he spurned it. Branch Rickey, the general manager of the Cardinals, who would become president of the Brooklyn Dodgers in 1943, hinted that he wanted to take Berra with him to Brooklyn. But Berra signed with the New York Yankees in October 1942 for a $500 bonus and a monthly salary of $90.

Berra spent the 1943 season with a minor league team in Virginia. But world history intervened, and Berra joined the Navy in 1944, volunteering to serve on

A 1951 Bowman baseball card of Berra and a 1952 New York Yankees team-signed baseball, shown on top of Berra's 1951 New York Yankees road jersey

a rocket boat—a speedy, 36-foot gunship, manned by a crew of six and armed with 24 rockets, two .30-caliber machine guns, and a twin .50-caliber machine gun. Berra and the crew trained for a top-secret operation, which turned out to be the Allied invasion of France on D-Day, June 6, 1944. Berra, a machine gunner, earned numerous commendations for bravery under fire.

After leaving the service, Berra joined the Newark Bears, a minor league team, and he was called up to the Yankees in September 1946. Berra's military service did not endear him to teammate Joe DiMaggio, in part because DiMaggio had served as a physical education instructor in California and Hawaii instead of the combat assignment he had requested. DiMaggio cut the finer figure, of course, while Berra looked like an unmade bed. One sportswriter said that the new recruit "doesn't even look like a Yankee," while a Yankees executive said Berra looked like "the bottom man on an unemployed acrobatic team." Berra ignored the critics, and soon the sportswriters began to pick on other players, especially when Berra began to deliver the goods.

In his first game as a Yankee, on September 22, 1946, Yogi went two-for-four against the Philadelphia Athletics with a home run off Jesse Flores in his second at-bat. The next day, he hit his second homer. Berra led the Yankees in RBI even though DiMaggio was held up to be the team's batting powerhouse. Berra specialized in hitting garbage pitches, and although he was just five foot seven, he could reach every corner of the strike zone with his bat. In five seasons, Berra had more home runs than strikeouts. He batted .285 for his career, and belted 358 home runs with 1,430 RBI.

As catcher, Berra was fearsome as well. He played 148 straight games from 1958 to 1959 without an error. He was lightning fast and commanded the respect of pitchers, who rarely shook him off when he called a pitch. Don Larsen, who pitched a perfect game in Game 5 of the 1956 World Series, said he did not shake off Berra once during his masterpiece. Berra led the American League in nearly every catching statistic, and set the league record with 8,723 putouts. He was the AL's most valuable player in 1951—that year he wore the gray flannel New York Yankees road jersey depicted here (page 158)—and again in 1954 and 1955. The evidence that the jersey was used in 1951 is revealed in the information printed on the gray strip tag in the collar area: "L Berra 1951–2." This stands for the player's name and year of issue, and the number 2 means the jersey was the second one manufactured by Spalding that was issued to Berra that season. The jersey also features the AL Golden Anniversary patch (see page 267 in the Compendium) that was applied to all AL uniforms in 1951.

Berra played in a record 14 World Series, and the Yankees won 10 of them, another record. Small wonder

that Stengel praised him with one of the most sideways accolades ever bestowed on an athlete: "Mr. Berra is a very strange fellow of very remarkable abilities." After the 1963 World Series, Yogi retired as a player. In 19 seasons, he was an All-Star 18 times and a 10-time World Series champ. He hinted that he might like to play golf in his retirement, but the Yankees spoiled those plans by naming him a coach. He was fired after the Yankees lost to the Cardinals in the 1964 World Series, and then hired by Stengel, who was now managing the Mets. He was named manager of the Mets in 1972, fired in 1975, and returned to the Yankees as a coach. New York won the World Series in 1977 and 1978, and Berra was named manager in 1984. Sixteen games into the 1985 season, Berra was canned by owner George Steinbrenner. He coached the Houston Astros until 1989, when he retired for good.

Berra had become a folk hero, and sportswriters and commentators loved him as much for his uncanny way of mangling the English language as for his play. He once said, "Why buy good luggage? You only use it when you travel." On another occasion: "You can observe a lot by watching." He also quipped, "When you come to a fork in the road, take it." Perhaps most famously, he said, "It ain't over till it's over," summarizing the hopes of anyone waiting for a team to pull out a victory in the last possible minute. Never mind that Garagiola, in his later career as a sportscaster, invented many of the sayings attributed to Berra. As usual, Berra had the last word on the subject: "I really didn't say everything I said."

When Berra died on September 22, 2015, obituary writers remembered those off-kilter remarks. They also honored his ability behind the plate and his years of rock-solid, steady, careful play that earned Berra the reputation of being among the best catchers, and perhaps even the very best, to ever play the game. Berra's number 8 was retired from the Yankees roster in 1972, the year he entered the Baseball Hall of Fame. A couple of months after he died, he was awarded the Presidential Medal of Freedom, and it was only then that many fans, listening to President Barack Obama's commendation, learned of Berra's heroism under fire during D-Day, 71 years earlier. "I think his military service has been a little overlooked because the men like him really didn't talk about it much," said Carmen Berra, Yogi's wife of 64 years. "He never talked about it. It wasn't a big thing to him, or to men like him. It was just what they had to do."

And as for the 1952 season? The Yankees, who signed the official American League baseball displayed with the jersey (page 158), won the AL pennant, then dusted off the Brooklyn Dodgers in seven games, in the World Series. Berra led the way, as always, to victory. Stengel may have had to eat more than his share of antacid tablets, but it wasn't over till it was over, and everything worked out just fine.

"It was like the Fourth of July out there. You couldn't stick your head up or it would get blown off."

—Yogi Berra, recalling his duties aboard a rocket boat
during the Allied invasion on D-Day, June 6, 1944

Yogi Berra diving
headlong at Carl
Furillo's flying feet
in Game 2 of the
1953 World Series

BASEBALL'S FINEST MOMENT

JACKIE ROBINSON 1952 Brooklyn Dodgers Home Jersey

Victory in Game 1 of the World Series at Ebbets Field, October 1, 1952. Clockwise from lower right: Jackie Robinson; manager Chuck Dressen; Duke Snider; Joe Black; and Pee Wee Reese

A Brooklyn Dodgers equipment trunk from the early 1950s, behind Robinson's 1952 Brooklyn Dodgers home jersey

The names of the players have been nearly forgotten, but in the earliest days of the major leagues, a few African American players took the field alongside white players. On June 21, 1879, for example, William Edward White, the son of a slave, played one game for the Providence Grays, going one for four and scoring a run in the team's 5–3 victory. Five years later, Moses Fleetwood Walker debuted for the Toledo Blue Stockings, though his calls as catcher were ignored by the white pitchers. So many white players refused to share the field with Walker and, later, with his brother Weldon that the major leagues adopted a so-called gentleman's agreement—baseball did not formally forbid African Americans from taking the field, but no team would sign a black player.

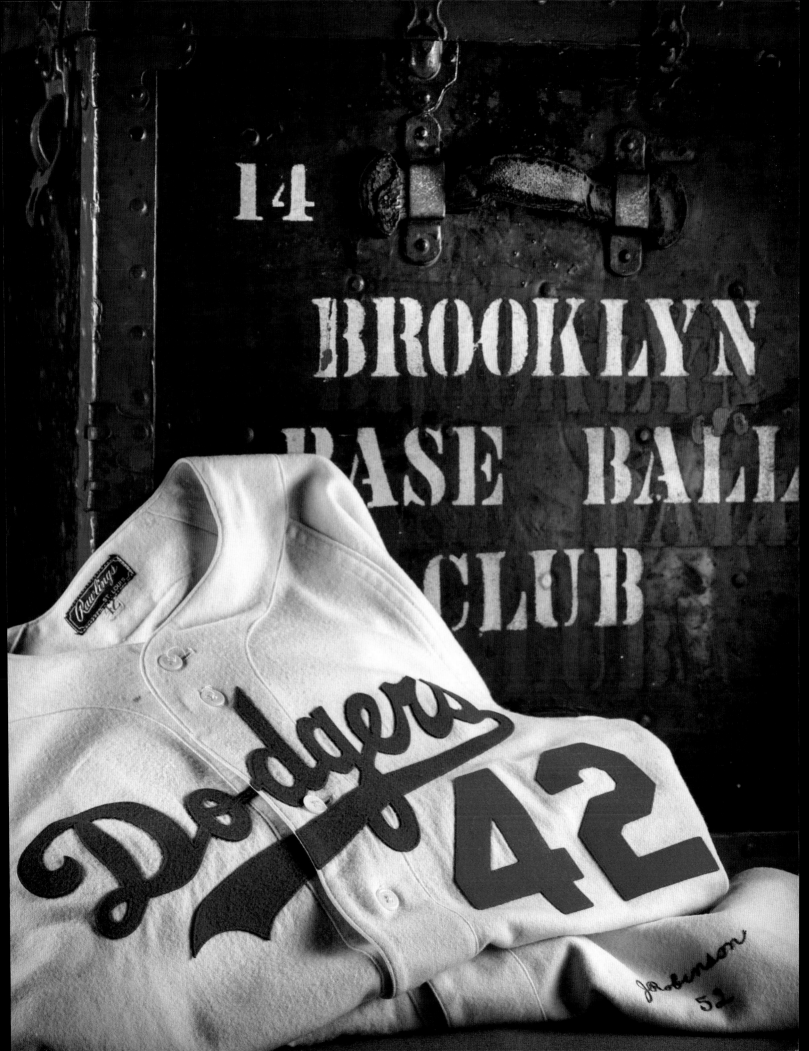

Jackie Robinson sliding into home plate, 1948

The first league for black players, called the National Colored Base Ball League, formed in 1887 and was considered a minor league. Various teams formed, played, and folded before the Negro National League was formed in 1920. Baseball remained segregated through World War II, when Branch Rickey—the president, part owner, and general manager of the Brooklyn Dodgers—divined that, since there was no formal rule against it, he could integrate the game. Rickey believed that integration would be good for America, for baseball—and for his balance sheet. "The greatest untapped reservoir of raw material in the history of the game is the black race," Rickey said. "The Negroes will make us winners for years to come, and for that I will happily bear being called a bleeding heart and a do-gooder and all that humanitarian rot." Baseball commissioner Kenesaw Mountain Landis, a steadfast opponent of integration, died of a heart attack in November 1944.

His replacement, a gregarious Kentucky politician named Albert Benjamin "Happy" Chandler, took a much more constructive view. "If a black boy can make it on Okinawa and Guadalcanal, hell, he can make it in baseball," Chandler said. Although 15 out of 16 club owners opposed integration, Rickey moved forward with his plan. In March 1945, he sent scouts to the Negro Leagues in search of a ballplayer who could put his revolutionary idea into action.

Jack Roosevelt Robinson was born on January 31, 1919, in Cairo, Georgia, the grandson of a slave and the fifth child of impoverished sharecroppers. Robinson was raised by his mother, Mallie, in a white neighborhood in Pasadena, California. White kids pelted Robinson with rocks until he and his older brother Mack pelted them back. Athletic talent came naturally to the Robinsons. Mack finished second in the 200-meter dash to Jesse Owens in the 1936 Olympics, while Jackie lettered in

"A life is not important except in the impact it has on other lives."

—Jackie Robinson

track, football, basketball, and baseball at the University of California at Los Angeles and was called the "Jim Thorpe of his race" for his multisport acumen.

After two years in the Army, Robinson signed with the Kansas City Monarchs of the Negro American League and batted .387 in the 1945 season. Dodgers scout Clyde Sukeforth saw Robinson play: "The more you talked to the guy, the more you were impressed…. The determination [was] written all over him." On August 29, 1945, Rickey invited Robinson to his office in Brooklyn and asked him whether he would react in anger if a white fan or player taunted him with a racial slur. Robinson replied, "Mr. Rickey, are you looking for a Negro who is afraid to fight back?" Answered Rickey: "Robinson, I'm looking for a ballplayer with guts enough *not* to fight back."

The Dodgers announced the signing of Robinson on October 23, 1945. He was assigned to the Montreal Royals, the Dodgers' AAA farm club, and on April 18, 1946, at Roosevelt Stadium in Jersey City, a black player took the field in organized baseball for the first time in the twentieth century. Robinson smacked four hits and scored four times to lead Montreal to a 14–1 victory over the Jersey City Giants. The headline in the *Pittsburgh Courier* the following day read, "Jackie Stole the Show." According to Joe Bostic of New York City's *Amsterdam News*, "He did everything but help the ushers seat the crowd."

A few days before the 1947 season opened, Rickey called Robinson up to the Dodgers. On opening day, 26,623 fans—more than 14,000 of them African Americans—turned up at Ebbets Field to watch a black man play in a major league game. Playing first base, Robinson failed to get a hit, but he walked and scored a run in the Dodgers' 5–3 victory. Opposing players taunted Robinson, but he quickly learned to keep his focus on baseball, answering insults, violence, and injustice with silence. "Robinson was the target of racial epithets and flying cleats, of hate letters and death threats, of pitchers throwing at his head and legs, and catchers spitting on his shoes," *Sports Illustrated's* Bill Nack later wrote.

Robinson also amassed an enviable set of statistics: In his rookie year, he hit .297 with a league-leading 29 stolen bases and finished second in the NL with 125 runs

scored. He was dazzling on the basepaths—fast, clever, and daring. He also revived the art of stealing home, making the play 19 times in his career, including a theft of home in the 1955 World Series.

His courage, resolve, and unselfish team play earned the respect of his teammates and, eventually, the opposition. Robinson was what his contemporaries called a "race man"—an African American person who dedicates his or her life to contributing to the betterment of black people. Other "race men" include Booker T. Washington, W. E. B. Du Bois, Dr. Martin Luther King Jr., and Ida B. Wells, men and women who worked tirelessly to advance African American culture and the fight for civil rights. Later, Paul Robeson, Harry Belafonte, and Muhammad Ali forfeited success in entertainment and sports to defend their political views.

In baseball, Jackie Robinson broke the color line and helped put baseball on its path to becoming America's true national pastime. "I'm not concerned with your liking or disliking me," he once said. "All I ask is that you respect me as a human being." He gained that respect through perseverance, determination, hard work, and, yes, resisting the temptation to fire back when insulted or assaulted by other players. In doing so, he helped open the door to generations of African American players. Former teammate Joe Black said, "When I look at my house, I say 'Thank God for Jackie Robinson.'" And Willie Mays once said, "Every time I look at my pocketbook, I see Jackie Robinson."

Jackie Robinson's 1952 Brooklyn Dodgers home jersey (page 163) is a reminder that baseball has often been ahead of its time. Robinson's debut came a year before President Harry Truman desegregated the military and seven years before the United States Supreme Court ruled that segregation in public schools was unconstitutional. Baseball historian John Thorn described it best when he said, "For me, baseball's finest moment is the day Jackie Robinson set foot on a major league field for the first time…I'm most proud to be an American, most proud to be a baseball fan when baseball has led America rather than followed it. It has done so several times, but this is the most transforming incident…. Jackie Robinson is my great hero among baseball heroes and he's my great hero as an American. He is an individual who shaped the crowd."

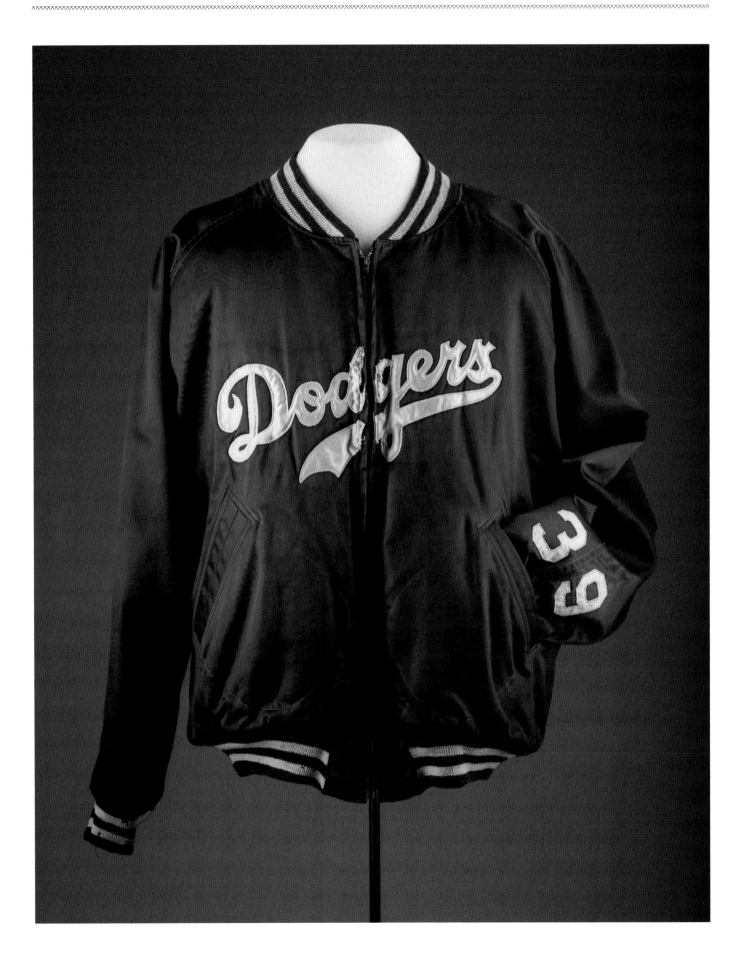

"WAIT 'TIL NEXT YEAR!"

ROY CAMPANELLA 1953 Brooklyn Dodgers Team Jacket

One of the most coveted—yet most elusive—parts of major league baseball uniforms is the team jacket. Brooklyn Dodgers catcher Roy Campanella wore the jacket featured here during the 1953 season when he picked up his second National League MVP award. He batted .312, and his 41 home runs and a league-leading 142 RBI were records for catchers, establishing Campanella as one of the best hitting backstops in the game.

After the mediocre decades of the 1920s and 1930s, the Brooklyn Dodgers were rebuilt into a contending club, first by general manager Larry MacPhail, then by Branch Rickey, also the GM. The Dodgers won pennants in 1941, 1947, 1949, 1952, and 1953, only to fall to the Yankees in all five World Series. The annual ritual of excitement followed by bitter disappointment became a common pattern for Brooklyn fans, and "Wait 'til next year!" became an unofficial Dodgers slogan. Team jackets were worn predominantly in the spring and late fall, especially during the World Series, when the weather was cold. Campanella wore this jacket in the dugout at Ebbets Field and Yankee Stadium during the 1953 World Series, suffering from cold and another loss to the Yankees. And as every Dodgers fan from this era can attest, the true meaning of "Wait 'til next year" was not learned on a sunny July afternoon; rather, it was a manifestation of the cold defeats in October.

Perhaps nobody understood this notion better than the writer Roger Kahn, who was raised in Brooklyn. Born in 1927, Kahn followed the Dodgers devoutly as a boy, then covered the team as a reporter for the *Herald Tribune*, starting in 1952. In 1972, he published *The Boys of Summer*, a poignant and evocative account of his childhood, his hometown, his work, and the 1952 and 1953 Dodgers. "You may glory in a team triumphant," wrote Kahn. "But you fall in love with a team in defeat.

Losing after great striving is the story of man, who was born to sorrow, whose sweetest songs tell of saddest thought, and who, if he is a hero, does nothing in life as becomingly as leaving it."

Campanella spent his entire career with the Dodgers, joining the team during the 1948 campaign and playing through 1957, the franchise's last season in Brooklyn. Campanella's career in the majors was limited to 10 years—the color of his skin prevented him from joining the big leagues until he was 26, and a tragic automobile accident that paralyzed him from the neck down at age 35 ended his playing days. Campanella made the fewest plate appearances of any Hall of Fame position player, but his impact was unforgettable.

The 1940s were the era of the Italian American in professional baseball. After decades of discrimination, Italian immigrants had sired a first and second generation of American children. In baseball, there was Phil Rizzuto, the Scooter, seemingly the fastest man ever to take the field. Yogi Berra, malapropisms and all, tenaciously did whatever needed to be done on the diamond. Joe DiMaggio was handsome and popular enough to marry Marilyn Monroe, the brightest star in Hollywood.

And there was Roy Campanella, who did not think of himself as particularly Italian or particularly African American, though his father was Sicilian and his mother black. His schools and sports teams in Philadelphia were integrated, and he was the leader of whatever sport he played. He insisted that baseball was supposed to be fun and said, "To play this game good, a lot of you has to be a little boy."

In 1937, the 15-year-old Campanella left high school to join the semipro Bacharach Giants as a catcher. He performed so well that the Baltimore Elite Giants, one of the best teams in the Negro National League, signed

PART IV
THE WORLD WE LIVE IN
HOW AIR WAS CREATED; STRUCTURE OF ATMOSPHERE;
WHAT MAKES WINDS BLOW; STORMS AND RAINFALL

ROY CAMPANELLA,
BASEBALL'S
GREATEST CATCHER

20 CENTS
JUNE 8, 1953

Roy Campanella's
stellar performance
immortalized
on the cover of
Life magazine,
June 8, 1953

pitch after pitch into the stands. He batted .258 as a rookie and received votes for the league's MVP award.

Brooklyn fans adored him and did not consider Campanella—Campy, as he was called—to be black. Jackie Robinson did, though, and he glowered at Campy's refusal to make an issue of race, grumbling that there was "a little Uncle Tom" inside of his beer-keg-shaped catcher. Called up in 1949 and paired with Campy as the first black pitcher/catcher duo in the majors, Don Newcombe thought more highly of his batterymate. Campanella shaped Newcombe into an extraordinary pitcher that year, and they went to the 1949 All-Star Game at Ebbets Field with Jackie Robinson and Larry Doby, making history as the first African Americans to play in the Summer Classic.

The other Dodgers loved Campanella, too. By the early 1950s, they had coalesced into one of the best-functioning teams in baseball history. Newcombe was on the mound, Robinson at second, Pee Wee Reese at shortstop, Gil Hodges at first, Duke Snider in center field. "Dem Bums," as the squad was known (see pennant, opposite), formed an anchor for the community, a team in which Brooklynites could take pride.

The Bums repaid their fans' devotion with phenomenal performances, leading the league and regularly thrashing the rival New York Giants—though not always. Every Dodgers fan of a certain age remembers the pennant race of 1951, when Dodgers relief pitcher Ralph Branca fired a fastball and the Giants' Bobby Thomson swatted it halfway to the moon, a moment later enshrined in novels by Philip Roth and Don DeLillo, to say nothing of the sporting press, as "the shot heard 'round the world." It was worse when it came to the hated American League and the Yankees. After losing to their crosstown rivals in their first five World Series appearances, the Dodgers finally beat the Yankees in seven games in 1955, the year Campy won his third MVP award. The Yankees resumed their dominance in 1956 with a seven-game triumph.

In January 1958, as the Dodgers were preparing for their first season in Los Angeles, Campanella's car skidded on ice, hit a telephone pole, and flipped. He smashed his fifth vertebra and was paralyzed from the shoulders down. Though he regained some use of his arms, Campy spent the rest of his life in a wheelchair. In 1969, the year he was inducted into the Hall of Fame, Campanella received the Bronze Medallion from the City of New York, the highest honor the city confers upon civilians. Three years later, his uniform number 39 was retired, along with Robinson's number 42 and Sandy Koufax's 32.

Campanella followed the Dodgers to Los Angeles and cheered for the team from the stands. He died in June 1993, the only black player to own three MVP trophies, the smiling optimist to the end, always assuring fans that next year would be better.

him. Although he did not categorize himself as black, the one-drop rule prevailed—one drop of African American blood classified a person as black. Campanella had received an offer to play for the Philadelphia Phillies while in high school, but the offer was rescinded when a manager took a look at his bronze skin and quickly made excuses about why he was not welcome to join the team.

Campanella played for Baltimore until 1942 and was considered the fifth-best batter in the Negro Leagues and a strong rival to Josh Gibson as its best catcher. He was playing in the Mexican League in 1946 when Branch Rickey signed him to play for the Dodgers. When Jackie Robinson crossed the color line into the majors in 1947, Campanella was playing for the minor league Montreal Royals. A year later, on April 20, 1948, the Dodgers called him up to Ebbets Field. From the beginning, he flourished. His demeanor was almost always happy, and he calmly kept his pitchers in line. Though he stood only a hair above five foot nine and weighed about 210 pounds, Campanella was so fast that one of his nicknames was "the Cat." He was also strong as a bull, slashing with an uppercut swing and sending

"'For your penance, say two Hail Marys, three our Fathers, and,' he added, with a chuckle, 'say a special prayer for the Dodgers.'"

—Priest at St. Agnes Church, Rockville Centre, New York, to seven-year-old Doris Kearns Goodwin, May 1950

Brooklyn Dodgers "Dem Bums" pennant sold at Ebbets Field, early 1950s

Young Brooklyn Dodgers fans who have shown up early for the opening game of the World Series at Yankee Stadium, September 30, 1953

MR. TIGER

AL KALINE 1954 Detroit Tigers Rookie Home Uniform

Albert William Kaline was born poor in 1934, in the middle of the Great Depression. His father, Nicholas, who worked as a broom maker while raising his family in a rundown part of Baltimore, played some minor league ball, as did other men in the family, to earn extra money and a measure of hope. Al, too, played baseball from the moment he could stand. By nine, he could throw a fastball, curveball, and changeup. Not even the loss of part of his left foot to osteomyelitis could slow him down—he ran on the side of the foot, flying from base to base—and he grew into a determined but well-liked boy, encouraged by teachers who shared his belief that he could escape the projects via the baseball diamond.

In one high school season, Kaline maintained a near-miraculous .609 batting average, and the Detroit Tigers signed him after graduation in 1953. He received a then-unusual bonus of $15,000, which he used to pay off the mortgage on his parents' house and his mother's eye surgery.

The Tigers put him in right field, where he stayed. In his first major league at-bat, on June 25, 1953, he hit a belt-high fastball to center field for an out. He got his first hit, a single, on July 8 and two weeks later earned the nickname "Baltimore Greyhound" for his base-to-base speed. And in the off-season, on the advice of Ted Williams, Kaline squeezed a baseball and swung a bat each day to strengthen his wrists and arms.

In the winter of 1953–54, he played ball in Cuba, becoming a right-field regular after Steve Souchock broke his wrist. When the 1954 season started, Souchock had yet to heal, so 19-year-old Kaline became the Tigers' starting right fielder in his first full season in the majors. Kaline wore this white flannel home uniform and stirrup socks (opposite) that season, batting .276. A year later, he accumulated 200 hits and batted .340 and, at 20, became the youngest player to win the American League batting championship.

Kaline was a consistent performer, more reliable than stellar. Over his 20 years as a Tiger, he amassed 3,007 hits, 1,622 runs, hit 399 home runs, and won 10 Gold Gloves awards—not bad for a player plagued by injuries and illness. "I'm convinced Kaline is the best player who ever played for me," said Chuck Dressen, who managed the Tigers from 1963 to 1966. "For all-around ability—I mean hitting, fielding, running, and throwing—I'll go with Al."

Kaline, called "Mr. Tiger" for his uncomplaining conquest of adversity, retired in 1974, and his number 6 became the first one retired by the Tigers. He stuck with the team, becoming a Tigers broadcaster, working in the front office, and keeping his association with the franchise for 64 years: one of the longest with the same club in major league history.

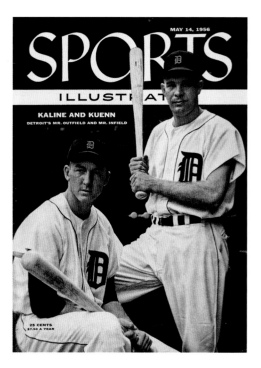

Young Detroit Tigers sluggers Al Kaline and Harvey Kuenn on the cover of *Sports Illustrated*, May 14, 1956

GIANT LEAP

HANK AARON 1954 Milwaukee Braves Rookie Road Jersey

pril 8, 1974. A crowd of 53,775 people, the largest ever assembled at Atlanta Stadium, had eyes glued on the 40-year-old batter coiled at the plate. The Los Angeles Dodgers led 3–1 in the bottom of the fourth inning, as Dodgers pitcher Al Downing wound up and hurled a fastball. Henry Louis Aaron swung, and his bat found a big piece of the ball. In the immortal words of sportscaster Milo Hamilton: "There's a drive into left-center field! That ball is gonna be...outta here! It's gone! It's 715! There's a new home run champion of all time, and it's Henry Aaron!" Said Downing later: "It was elevated, and The Hammer put the hammer on it."

With that fateful swing, Henry Aaron—Hank Aaron, familiarly, and even more familiarly, Hammerin' Hank—surpassed Babe Ruth's record for career home runs, and the moment marked the end of a long, arduous road for Aaron. Born on February 5, 1934, one of eight children, Aaron grew up in a Mobile, Alabama, neighborhood called Down the Bay during the bitterly entrenched Jim Crow era. Harsh economic conditions during the Great Depression forced every member of the Aaron family to work to make ends meet. Young Henry also found time for baseball, scavenging for gear, hitting bottle caps with broomsticks, and carving bats out of driftwood and fallen branches.

In high school, Aaron, already six feet tall but rail thin, emerged as a hitter of unusual power despite his unorthodox cross-handed batting grip in which he held the bat with his left hand over his right. In 1949, the 15-year-old Aaron—inspired by the exploits of Jackie Robinson, whom he had seen play in exhibition games as Robinson's team passed through Alabama—tried out for the Brooklyn Dodgers but did not receive a contract offer. Aaron continued to play with the Pritchitt Athletics, a local semipro team, and he joined the Mobile Black Bears, a Negro Leagues team that barnstormed along the Gulf Coast, at the end of his junior year in high school.

Before leaving high school, Henry signed a contract with another Negro Leagues team, the Indianapolis Clowns, after a scout saw him play in Mobile and telegraphed a message to team officials, saying, "This boy could be the answer." Aaron flourished with the Clowns: In 26 games, he posted a .366 batting average, hit 5 home runs, and stole 9 bases. Aaron rejected an offer from the New York Giants in favor of one from the Boston Braves that would pay him $50 more a month—enough to keep him, he later said, from being a teammate of Willie Mays.

In June 1952, Aaron reported to the Class C Eau Claire Bears team in Eau Claire, Wisconsin, and his arrival increased the town's African American population from seven to eight. The 19-year-old player took advantage of good coaching to break out of his cross-hitting posture and to work on both his power hitting and fielding. It was Aaron's first time playing against white players, and he found himself well liked in the North Woods—and so successful that the Braves promoted him to their Class A club in Jacksonville, Florida.

The Braves Jacksonville club was part of the Sally League, which, in 1953, was widely considered to be the most hostile league for blacks in the minor league system. It was a bumpy ride for Aaron, especially when the team went on the road. "Henry would have a more difficult time even than [Jackie] Robinson," wrote biographer Howard Bryant. "Where Robinson would have the benefit of going to his home in Brooklyn half of the time, the Sally League would play all of its games in the Deep South....Henry knew he might be able to win over the home fans with spirited play, but off the field, he found that Jacksonville was another southern town that was not ready to treat him with any degree of humanity." After the relative freedom he had enjoyed in the North, the ugly divisions of race were a stark reality for Aaron. For example, team officials washed the uniforms of white players between games of a doubleheader at the stadium, while Aaron's was sent to the "colored laundry" 20 blocks away. Aaron also made separate hotel and meal arrangements while his Braves teammates ate together in restaurants and hotel dining rooms. Aaron credited Jacksonville manager Ben Geraghty for his kindness in helping him deal with these slights.

It was with a great sense of relief that Aaron learned, in 1954, that he was being called up for spring training with the Milwaukee Braves. It was the team's first year in

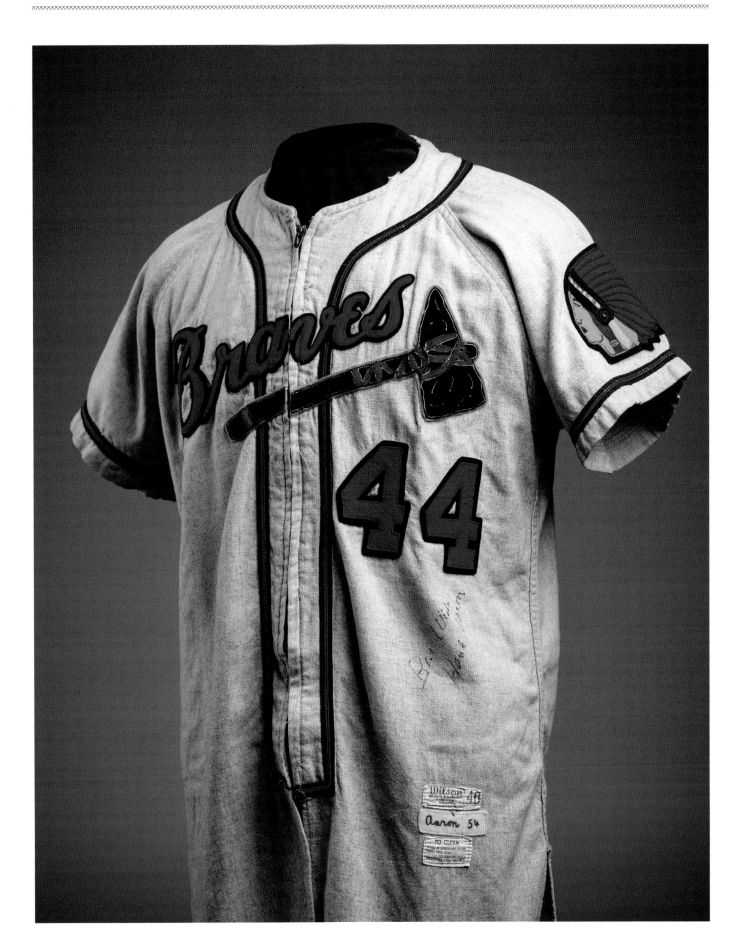

> **"When Henry arrived at the clubhouse at Braves Field that first day, Joe Taylor, the Braves clubhouse man, showed him his locker, a wooden stall with a couple of diagonal nails for his jerseys, which would be clumped in with those of the other black players. The lockers of the white players were set apart."**
>
> —Howard Bryant, *The Last Hero: A Life of Henry Aaron,* 2010

Ron Stark,
Hank Aaron,
2016, oil
on canvas

its new home, having just moved from Boston, and the coaches were approaching the game with fresh eyes. Aaron, assigned to left field, hit a home run on the first day. While playing in Puerto Rico the previous winter, Aaron, a righty hitter, had learned to hit to all fields, and not just to left and center. On April 13, wearing a Braves jersey with the number 5, he made his major league debut. He went hitless the first day but lined a double off Cardinals pitcher Vic Raschi two days later for his first big league hit. On April 23, Henry faced Raschi again and smacked his first home run. While wearing this gray road jersey manufactured by Wilson during that rookie year (page 173), Aaron batted .280 with 13 homers. After fracturing his ankle on September 5, he changed his number to 44, a serendipitous decision because he later hit 44 home runs in four different seasons.

Aaron found widespread acceptance on the field in those first years, though he still suffered indignities when traveling from stadium to stadium anywhere south of Cincinnati. He and his new wife moved to a quiet suburb of Milwaukee, where they were the only African Americans. Quiet and reserved, Aaron kept to himself when he was not playing, cooking at home and fishing in the abundant lakes of Wisconsin. He was so quiet that the Braves' management worried that he gave an impression of aloofness. As a solution, they suggested he be called "Hank," a nickname he disliked but did not protest.

In 1955, his sophomore year in the majors, Aaron set goals for himself, recalling later, "I felt that 3,000 base hits would be something I could easily achieve. All I'd have to do was play regularly, stay healthy, and do what I'm supposed to do." That season, he walloped 27 home runs and made the NL All-Star Team for the first of a record 25 times. The following year, he won the NL batting championship. In 1957, he earned his only NL MVP award on the back of 44 home runs, 132 RBI, and a .322 batting average, numbers that helped vault the Milwaukee franchise to its first and only World Series title.

To Aaron's surprise and chagrin, the Braves moved to Atlanta before the 1966 season, back into the belly of the Jim Crow beast. He later told an interviewer, "Atlanta's not bad. The only bad thing about Atlanta is that you've got Georgia coming out the other end of it." Confronting a fresh new cloud of racial discrimination,

Aaron thought of leaving baseball to join Martin Luther King Jr. in the Civil Rights Movement. King, his pastor, declined Aaron's offer, saying, "You just keep hitting. We'll take it on the other side."

So Aaron kept hitting, and he became the first black sports hero in the South. As Willie Mays would do in Harlem, he provided inspiration to young African American players. As if to harness the energy of the legendary folk hero John Henry, Aaron faced down opposing pitchers with grim determination: Hammerin' Hank he became, and pitchers trembled. When he hit home run number 500 in 1968, only three months after Dr. King's assassination, civil rights advocates sensed the depth of his fight. So, too, did segregationists, who began to write Aaron ugly letters about his presumptuousness: Who did he think he was?

When it became apparent that Aaron was chasing Babe Ruth's vaunted record of 714 career home runs, the letters poured in from all over the country. One writer sketched a diagram showing where he would be positioned, rifle in hand, to shoot Aaron if he reached the Babe's count. Another signed a death threat "KKK Forever." Aaron professed to ignore the threats, though he kept the letters as a talisman as he continued to swat away.

After ending the 1973 season with a tantalizing 713 home runs, Aaron tied the record in the first game of the 1974 season, then connected for the home run that shattered Ruth's storied 39-year-old mark on April 8. No shooter emerged, and the threatening letters slowed to a trickle after that night. Fans of every race and ethnicity cheered his victory. The great baseball veteran and broadcaster Vin Scully of the Dodgers spoke for the nation when, from the booth in Atlanta Stadium that night, he said, "What a marvelous moment for baseball; what a marvelous moment for Atlanta and the state of Georgia; what a marvelous moment for the country and the world. A black man is getting a standing ovation in the Deep South for breaking a record of an all-time baseball idol. And it is a great moment for all of us, and particularly for Henry Aaron."

Henry Aaron went on to hit 40 more home runs, then retired in October 1976, 22 years after he had debuted for the Braves. In 2007, Barry Bonds of the San Francisco Giants surpassed Aaron's count and ended his own career with 762 home runs. Aaron's 2,297 RBI and 6,856 total bases, far beyond the goal he had set for himself, remain major league records. But that night in Georgia is the one for which fans will remember him, a sublime moment of victory achieved in the face of hatred, intolerance, and injustice. With that swing of his bat, Aaron helped baseball—and the nation—take another giant leap forward, continuing the journey toward integration started by Jackie Robinson 27 years earlier.

"I remember the first time that I saw Ted in those cut-off sleeves. They were good-sized. He was a big man. A big man."

—Billy Pierce, Ted Kluszewski's former White Sox teammate

BIG KLU

TED KLUSZEWSKI 1954 Cincinnati Reds Home Uniform

New York Giants manager Leo Durocher once told a reporter that he thought Brooklyn Dodgers first baseman Gil Hodges was the strongest player in baseball. When another reporter asked him about Cincinnati Reds slugger Ted Kluszewski, Durocher replied, "I thought we were talking about human beings." This was an honest mistake because, for a brief period, the super human Kluszewski was one of the most feared hitters in the game.

Kluszewski joined the Reds in 1947, and his early seasons were hardly the stuff of legend. In the six seasons from 1947 to 1952, he topped 20 home runs in a season only once, when he belted 25 in 1950. Early in his career, Big Klu, who was six foot two and 240 pounds, cut the sleeves off his jersey to make room for his massive biceps. "At first, I did it because the sleeves were restricting me from swinging," he said. "They could never make a uniform for me that would give me enough room. So I asked them to shorten the sleeves on my uniforms, but they gave me a lot of flak. So one day, I just took a pair of scissors out and cut them off. After a while, it became kind of a symbol."

His arms unsheathed, Kluszewski destroyed National League pitching in 1953, belting 40 home runs with 108 RBI. But Kluszewski drew national attention with his performance in 1954, when he donned this size 46 home uniform manufactured by MacGregor (opposite). That season, he led the majors in home runs (49) and RBI (141), though he fell short by a dozen base hits of winning the league Triple Crown. He also lost the MVP award to Willie Mays,

who had recently returned from his stint with the U.S. Army. Needless to say, Big Klu did not miss much or often.

With his size and power numbers, it is easy to imagine Kluszewski as a free-swinging slugger who struck out often as he swung for the fences. Yet, in the history of the game, only 10 times has a player hit 40 or more home runs and struck out fewer times than he homered. Kluszewski performed the feat three times, in 1953, 1954, and 1955.

In 1956, the Cincinnati Redlegs freed the arms of all the players in the ballclub when they adopted a vest-style uniform. The results were literally out the park.

The 1956 Cincinnati team hit a total of 221 home runs, tying the Major League record set by the 1947 New York Giants. Big Klu hit 35 round-trippers that season.

Sadly, a back injury suffered during spring training in 1956 began to take its toll on Kluszewski. While his power numbers were strong that season, his days at the top of baseball's Mt. Olympus were numbered. Big Klu would never again approach his 1954 dominance. He played his final four seasons with the Pirates, White Sox, and Angels and retired after the 1961 season.

After retiring, Kluszewski returned to the Reds as hitting coach, and the Big Red Machine dominated the National League offensively during his nine years at the post. On March 29, 1988, a massive heart attack took Kluszewski's life at 63. Reds legends such as Joe Nuxhall, Pete Rose, Johnny Bench, and Tony Perez paid their respects at the funeral. During the 1988 season, the Reds wore black armbands in memory of their late teammate. There wasn't an armband large enough to do justice to Big Klu.

Big Klu, seen here in 1956, and his massive biceps striking fear into National League pitchers

Kluszewski's game-used bats from the 1950s atop his 1954 Cincinnati Reds home uniform

MR. CUB

ERNIE BANKS 1957 Chicago Cubs Home Jersey

Hank Aaron and Ernie Banks before a game at Wrigley Field, 1957

Banks's 1957 Chicago Cubs home jersey with an official scorecard (back side) for the game played between the Chicago Cubs and Milwaukee Braves, May 24, 1957

One of the great pleasures in life is having a hot dog and Coke at the ballpark. Imagine sitting in the bleachers at Wrigley Field on a sunny afternoon on May 24, 1957, before the start of a game between the Chicago Cubs and Milwaukee Braves. With the game's scorecard—like the one shown on page 181—on your lap, you bite into your frankfurter as you scan the grass in front of the ivy-covered brick outfield wall. There you see two giants of the game standing together in conversation. The first is Hank Aaron, who would

become the National League's MVP that year, wearing his gray Milwaukee Braves road uniform. Next to him is a rising NL superstar, Ernie Banks, who would hit 43 home runs that season, wearing the pinstriped flannel Chicago Cubs home jersey shown opposite. The jersey features a zipper front, which was first adopted by the Cubs in 1937. During the 1940s, 1950s, and 1960s, many teams used zippered jerseys instead of button-front jerseys, while a handful of teams wore them into the 1970s and even the 1980s (see page 311 in the Compendium).

14-1957-2-40

CUBS

HEPARD

When your taste calls for food and
...hment... you'll enjoy the choice, high quality
...erved at Wrigley Field. Add to the fun of watching
...have something good to eat and drink!

...e Ribbon Beer..."Satisfy Your Thirst For Better Beer"
...ostick...A frozen dairy food—chocolate coated
...Yellow Band Wieners...mild, tender, juicy
...trike out thirst with Coke...delicious and refreshing

Oscar Mayer

Wilson

Ernie
Banks
Mr Cub

No player in the history of baseball has been so closely identified with a single city as Ernie Banks, a favorite of Chicago fans and known for much of his career as "Mr. Cub." Less well known is that Banks, a migrant from the South, was a pioneer of civil rights in professional baseball, a living bridge between the Negro Leagues and the multiethnic but by no means postracial game of today.

Born on January 31, 1931, in Dallas, Texas, Ernest Banks attended Booker T. Washington High School and excelled in football and basketball. The school did not offer baseball, so Ernie played on a fast-pitch softball team in the church league, which fit nicely with his mother's hopes that Ernie would become a minister.

When Banks was a high school sophomore, his skill on the field became evident to anyone who saw him play. He was introduced to the owner of the Detroit Colts, a travel team from Amarillo, Texas, which served as a feeder team for the Negro Leagues. Banks tried out for the Colts and became the team's shortstop, traveling to games in Texas, New Mexico, Kansas, Nebraska, and Oklahoma. When Banks was a high school senior, the Colts played the Kansas City Stars, and Banks impressed Stars manager "Cool Papa" Bell with his demeanor and his skill on the diamond. "His conduct was almost as outstanding as his ability," said Bell, who promised Banks a job with the Kansas City Monarchs if he completed his senior year of high school. Bell recommended Banks to Buck O'Neil, the manager of the Monarchs.

The Monarchs offered Banks $300 a month, and Eddie and Essie Banks gave their consent for their son to become a professional ballplayer. In signing with the Monarchs, Banks joined one of the most storied teams in the Negro Leagues, a pillar of black baseball. "'Cool Papa' Bell was the first one who impressed me," Banks said later. "Buck O'Neil helped me in many ways. He instilled a positive influence." Banks joined the Monarchs in the middle of the 1953 season, after a two-year stint in the Army, and he played shortstop and batted .347 for the rest of the season. Banks later said that "playing for the Kansas City Monarchs was like my school, my learning, my world. It was my whole life." Banks played so well that he quickly caught the attention of the Cubs, who were making efforts to integrate. The Cubs wasted little time in signing Banks, and he made his major league debut on September 17, 1953.

> "Happiness is going eyeball-to-eyeball with those Cub fans. That's really what I appreciated most about playing in Wrigley Field."
>
> —Ernie Banks

Banks was the first African American to play for the Cubs, and Jackie Robinson advised him to keep his head down and to be prepared for insults directed at him because of his ethnicity. Banks, naturally quiet, was happy to focus on baseball, but his reluctance to speak openly in favor of the Civil Rights Movement led some activists to brand him an "Uncle Tom." It did not help when Banks said, "I look at a man as a human being; I don't care about his color. Some people feel that because you are black you will never be treated fairly, and that you should voice your opinions, be militant about them. I don't feel this way. You can't convince a fool against his will....If a man doesn't like me because I'm black, that's fine. I'll just go elsewhere, but I'm not going to let him change my life."

In 1954, his first full year and official rookie season, Banks finished second in the National League's voting for rookie of the year. He won the Most Valuable Player award in 1958 and 1959, becoming the first NL player to win the award in back-to-back seasons. As shortstop, he led the league in fielding percentage three times. In 1960, he became the first Cubs player to be awarded a Gold Glove, and he led the league in fielding percentage, double plays, put-outs, and assists. His double-play partner was Gene Baker, another Negro Leagues veteran. When Steve Bilko joined the Cubs at first base, Wrigley Field announcer Bert Wilson delighted in labeling the double-play combination "Bingo to Bango to Bilko."

A knee injury forced Banks to sit for a few games in 1961, after playing 717 consecutive games. When he returned, he was sent to left field, where he committed just one error in 23 games. In June, he moved to first base, where he played until he retired 10 years later. He played more than 1,000 games in each position—1,125 at shortstop and 1,259 at first, though he is best remembered for his years as a quick, agile shortstop.

Banks also was one of his era's most prodigious sluggers. He retired after the 1971 season, finishing his career with 512 home runs and a lifetime batting average of .274. The 277 home runs he hit as a shortstop set an MLB record later broken by Cal Ripken. He also had 1,636 RBI and 2,583 hits, and he holds Cubs records for games played (2,528) and total bases (4,706). He also played a record 2,528 games without reaching the postseason. Despite the team's failings, Chicagoans love their Cubs, and in 1969, readers of the *Chicago Sun-Times* named Banks the "Greatest Cub Ever." Banks returned the favor by repeatedly expressing his pride in having played his entire major league career with one team and for the same owners, the Wrigley family.

In his later seasons, when Banks suffered batting slumps, Cubs manager Leo Durocher complained that he couldn't remove Banks from the lineup because he was too popular: "I had to play him," Durocher said. "Had to play the man or there would have been

OFFICIAL PROGRAM 10¢

CHICAGO CUBS · WRIGLEY FIELD

Official scorecard for game played between the Chicago Cubs and Milwaukee Braves, May 24, 1957

a revolution in the street." For his part, Banks thanked Durocher profusely for his coaching. In the later years of his career, as more African American players joined the league and the Cubs, Banks became somewhat more vocal about injustice, though he always insisted he was there for baseball, not politics. He was also a lifelong Republican who supported Richard Nixon and Ronald Reagan. Heavily Democratic Chicago forgave him.

Banks was elected to the Baseball Hall of Fame in 1977, his first year of eligibility, and his number 14 was the first number retired by the Cubs. Banks was named a Library of Congress Living Legend,

a designation that recognizes those "who have made significant contributions to America's diverse cultural, scientific and social heritage." In 2013, another adopted Chicagoan, President Barack Obama, awarded him the Presidential Medal of Freedom, along with 15 other recipients, including Bill Clinton and Oprah Winfrey.

Banks died on January 23, 2015. Following a public visitation, a memorial service was held at the Fourth Presbyterian Church in downtown Chicago. After the service, a procession moved from the church to Wrigley Field, Banks's major league home from 1953 to 1971. The Friendly Confines welcomed home the franchise's greatest ambassador.

BUT THE NUMBERS DON'T LIE

EDDIE MATHEWS 1957 Milwaukee Braves Home Jersey

The Milwaukee Braves defeating the New York Yankees in the World Series, October 10, 1957

> "I know I'm a ding dong, but in my day, if you hit .330, it was OK to be a ding dong."
>
> —Eddie Mathews

Program from Game 4 of the 1957 World Series and a pin-back button sold during the Series at Milwaukee County Stadium, with Mathews's 1957 Milwaukee Braves home jersey

Born in Texarkana, Texas, on October 13, 1931, Edwin Lee Mathews Jr. grew up in a baseball household. His father played semipro ball and his mother was a knowledgeable enthusiast who, according to Mathews, "was instrumental in making me a pull hitter." Both parents coached Mathews until the day he hit a line drive that, he said, "almost took my mother's head off." Mathews became such a good hitter in high school that the Boston Braves signed him after he graduated in 1949. After three seasons in the minors, he was called up to the big time.

As a rookie in 1952, Mathews hit 25 home runs, including three in a single game. "I've only known three or four perfect swings in my time," said the legendary Ty Cobb. "This lad has one of them." The Braves relocated to Milwaukee in 1953, and that year Mathews smacked 47 round-trippers, including the first grand slam in Milwaukee Braves franchise history. That season ranks as one of baseball's best by a 21-year-old player. He then hit at least 30 home runs in each of the next 8 seasons.

Mathews threw with his right hand and batted lefty. Primarily a pull hitter, he also could punch pitches to the opposite field, into the hole between second and third base. His hitting style was both graceful and powerful, and he was as effective as Mickey Mantle, to whom he was often compared.

Good timing aided Mathews's stellar performances. One of his teammates when he joined the Braves was future Hall of Fame pitcher Warren Spahn, who taught the rookie the secrets of the pitcher's art: "Hitting is timing. Pitching is upsetting timing." Mathews was featured on the cover of *Sports Illustrated* when the first issue was published in 1954, the same year the Braves promoted Hank Aaron from the minor leagues to the Braves. In 1957, the year Mathews wore this size 44 flannel Milwaukee Braves home jersey manufactured by Wilson (opposite), the pair combined for 76 home runs.

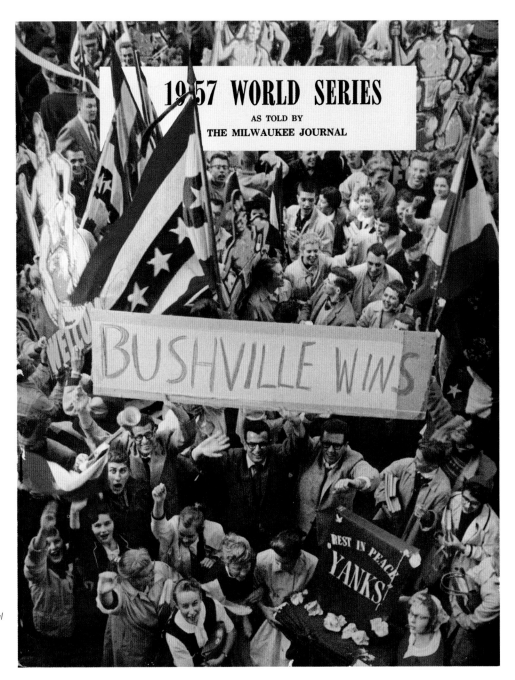

1957 WORLD SERIES

AS TOLD BY
THE MILWAUKEE JOURNAL

BUSHVILLE WINS

REST IN PEACE
YANKS

Special feature of the *Milwaukee Journal* commemorating the Braves' victory, October 1957

The two sluggers led the Braves to their first World Series victory that year, and Mathews emerged as the hero. The Yankees won two of the first three games of the Series and held a 5–4 lead in the top of the 10th inning in Game 4. A program from that game is displayed with the jersey (page 183). With the game tied in the bottom of the 10th, Mathews hit a home run over the right-field wall, giving the Braves a 7–5 victory and tying the Series. "He didn't get many hits in that Series," Hank Aaron said, "but that was the big one. That set up the whole Series for us." The next day, the Braves squeaked out a 1–0 win as Mathews scored the game's only run.

In Game 7, Mathews doubled in two runs in the third inning, then backhanded a hard grounder and stepped on third with bases loaded and two out in the ninth, sealing the Braves 5–0 win and the Series championship.

Mathews's ability as a hitter was unusual at the time, as infielders saw a lot of action because the power game was still undeveloped. As a result, third basemen were sought as fielders first and hitters second. Mathews was considered a below-average fielder when he came up, but he turned himself into a workhorse at third. Mathews's secret, he told a reporter long after retirement, was to play against the opposing third baseman, not against the whole team. "I wanted to beat him in every department: fielding, hitting, running the bases," Mathews said. "I played that game all my life, and it kept me on my toes."

In 1962, Mathews swung at a high pitch that he probably should have ignored and tore several ligaments in his right shoulder. The injury robbed him of some of his power, but he stayed with the team when it moved to Atlanta in 1966. A year later, the Braves traded Mathews to Houston, where he hit career home run number 500, an achievement matched by only six other players.

Houston traded Mathews to Detroit late in the 1967 season, and he joined a lineup that included Al Kaline. Mathews provided a shot in the arm for a team demoralized by conflicts with management, and his leadership helped the Tigers defeat the St. Louis Cardinals in the 1968 World Series. He retired at the end of that season, making him one of the rare Hall of Famers who left the game on the highest note possible.

In his career, Mathews belted 512 home runs, a record for third basemen. He also had 2,315 hits, 1,453 RBI, and a .271 career batting average. "He could hit

them just as well as I could," said Aaron. In 17 seasons, Mathews was named to the All-Star Team 12 times, though he never won the league's Most Valuable Player award. He was the only player to have played for the Braves in all three of the franchise's homes: Boston, Milwaukee, and Atlanta.

Mathews also was known to have a feisty side, and he instigated several fights and brawls. In one incident, he punched out Dodgers pitcher Don Drysdale. In another, he nearly came to blows with Jackie Robinson. Old-timers still marvel at a Mathews-led brawl against the Oakland Athletics that lasted more than 10 minutes. Despite these outbursts, Mathews was well liked by teammates and opponents.

Mathews was named coach of the Braves in 1971 and was promoted to manager in 1972, making him one of the few to play for, coach, and manage the same team. At the start of the 1974 season, Aaron needed two home runs to break Babe Ruth's all-time record of 714, one of the most coveted marks in baseball. The Braves opened the season on the road in Cincinnati, and Aaron tied the record on April 4 with his first swing of the

season. Mathews wanted to bench Aaron for the rest of the series so he could break the record in Atlanta, but he was ordered to play Aaron for at least two of the three games. Aaron played one more game in Cincinnati, then broke Ruth's record with home run number 715 on April 8 in Atlanta. Mathews's role as manager ended in July when he was fired after the team went into a slump and fell to fourth place.

The Braves retired Mathews's number 41 in 1969, and Braves players wore patches bearing the number on their uniforms after Mathews died in 2001. Mathews was inducted into the Hall of Fame in 1978 on the fifth attempt, the delay likely due to the combination of his testy relationship with the sports press and his untidy personal life. He married four times, drank, smoked, and had trouble holding down a job after leaving the game. But the numbers don't lie. Eddie Mathews may have been a flawed human being, but he holds a solid place in baseball's pantheon.

The city of Milwaukee celebrating the arrival of the Braves franchise, early 1953

President John F. Kennedy tosses out the ceremonial first ball at an All-Star Game in Washington, D.C., July 10, 1962

THE EXPANSION ERA

1960-1971

Though it lasted only about a decade, the Expansion Era saw great changes. Legendary players such as Ted Williams and Stan Musial left the game, old parks such as Ebbets Field and the Polo Grounds fell before the wrecking ball, and new stars and clubs emerged. Memories from that era include Bill Mazeroski's walk-off World Series homer, Mickey Mantle and Roger Maris battling to beat Babe Ruth's single-season home-run record, and Don Drysdale's and Sandy Koufax's daunting pitching performances.

The era opened with a flurry of activity, notably with the announcement by Branch Rickey that the formation of a Continental League would return baseball to New York and would send new teams to Atlanta, Houston, Denver, and Toronto, among other cities outside the orbit of the old 16-team system. The Continental League never materialized, but in its wake the National League returned to New York, and by 1969, major league baseball was being played in Houston, Seattle, Minneapolis, Atlanta, Oakland, San Diego, and Montreal.

The uniforms of the Expansion Era also signaled change. Baggy flannel uniforms were replaced by form-fitting cotton and synthetic blends, some with multicolored designs that required rule changes before they could be worn. Television continued to influence the game, making stars of players who wore colorful uniforms, their names clearly visible. Collectors flock to these uniforms for their variety and vitality. The uniforms are also widely available because clubs ordered as many as three home and road sets, and many of these uniforms have survived the ravages of time.

M&M BOYS

MICKEY MANTLE 1960 New York Yankees Home Uniform
ROGER MARIS 1960 New York Yankees Home Jersey

Roger Maris and Mickey Mantle (from left) at Yankee Stadium, 1961

The year 1960 was a watershed for America. In politics, Richard M. Nixon and John F. Kennedy were slugging it out, each attempting to put his stamp on a government and economy that many feared had become impersonal and soulless. The cold war grew frostier as the United States and the USSR jockeyed for influence around the world. The sexual revolution had begun. Alfred Hitchcock's *Psycho* pushed the envelope of the silver screen. And the United States sent its first troops to Vietnam.

Professional baseball underwent great changes in 1960 as well. Owners and managers squashed an effort to start a third league called the Continental League, the brainchild of New York attorney William Shea. The new league failed to play a single game, but each of the two traditional leagues agreed to expand beyond eight teams. One of those new teams was the New York Mets, and they would play in a stadium that would bear Shea's name. Across town, Ebbets Field fell before the wrecking ball, while on April 12 the former New York Giants played their first home game in San Francisco's Candlestick Park. In September, Ted Williams bid farewell to baseball, and a month later, Casey Stengel did the same to the Yankees. In 1960, players also adjusted to a season that now lasted 162 games instead of 154, which required statisticians to run a mental calculus when comparing numbers before 1960 and after.

"[Mickey Mantle was] a superstar who never acted like one. He was a humble man who was kind and friendly to all his teammates, even the rawest rookie. He was idolized by all the other players."

—Whitey Ford

"I never wanted all this hoopla. All I wanted is to be a good ballplayer and hit twenty-five or thirty homers, drive in a hundred runs, hit .280, and help my club win pennants. I just wanted to be one of the guys, an average player having a good season."

—Roger Maris

Yet one part of the game remained constant: power hitting by the Yankees. Mickey Charles Mantle entered his second decade as a Bronx Bomber. As a child growing up in the metal and mining districts of northeastern Oklahoma, he played every sport but excelled in football, for which he received a scholarship to the University of Oklahoma. That scholarship—and Mantle's baseball career— almost did not come about. He suffered an injury during football practice that resulted in the bone disease osteomyelitis. The disease was often fatal, but Mantle was cured with penicillin, then a new wonder drug. Mantle joined the Yankees in 1951 after playing shortstop in the minor leagues, and Stengel assigned him to right field, next to center fielder Joe DiMaggio. In Game 2 of the 1951 World Series, Mantle suffered the first of many career injuries when he tripped over a drainpipe in the outfield and shredded his right knee, tearing the anterior cruciate ligament. In 1952, DiMaggio retired and Mantle moved to center field, though he still hobbled from the knee injury, which was serious enough to excuse him from military service.

Mantle continued to fight on the field. By 1960, it was clear that he might be the greatest switch-hitter to ever play the game, and his stats were beginning to support the claim that he was the best center fielder of his day. He had his breakout year in 1956, in what he called his "favorite summer," with a .353 batting average, 52 home runs, and 130 RBI, earning his first league MVP award and the Triple Crown. His numbers in 1960, when he wore the pinstriped home uniform (opposite), were also compelling. That season, he led the AL in home runs (40) and runs scored (119).

Mantle's year ended strongly, though in bittersweet fashion. He batted .400 with three home runs and eleven RBI in the World Series, but the Bronx Bombers lost to the Pittsburgh Pirates when Pittsburgh's Bill Mazeroski drilled a walk-off home run in Game 7. Mantle was devastated. "There's a sick feeling in the pit of my stomach," Mantle later wrote in his autobiography. "There's an unforgettable look [on left fielder] Yogi

Mickey Mantle hitting a homer with Roger Maris on deck, 1962

Berra's face when he turns around, grim acceptance, expressed by a slow shrug of his shoulders [as the ball cleared the wall]. In the locker room, all of us are wandering around in a trance. I'm slumped on a stool, feeling so low that I can hardly peel off my uniform. In all my World Series experience, that was the only time when I really thought the better team had lost."

Despite the blow, Mantle was rewarded with a contract that would pay him $75,000 a season—then the highest salary paid to an active baseball player, though, strangely, not as much as Joe DiMaggio had

Mickey Mantle
1960 New York
Yankees Home
Uniform (opposite),
Roger Maris 1960
New York Yankees
Home Jersey (left)

Mickey Mantle (above) wearing his "Sultan of Swat Award for 1957," given to him at the Maryland Professional Baseball Players Association banquet, January 1958

Roger Maris (opposite, top) wearing his "Sultan of Swat Award for 1961," given to him at the Maryland Professional Baseball Players Association banquet, January 1962

in Kansas City and had a country boy's disdain for the big-city lights. Stengel, voluble and quick of mouth, complained, "You ask Maris a question, and he stares at you for a week before he answers." Opposing players thought him aloof, the sports press considered him a foe, and he was even curt with teammates. "I was born surly," he said, "and I'm going to stay that way. Everything in life is tough." He added, as an afterthought, "I'm miffed most of the time, regardless of how I'm doing." While wearing the pinstriped home jersey (page 191) in his first season with the Yankees, Maris belted 39 home runs and led the AL in RBI (112) and slugging percentage (.581), good enough to take home the American League MVP award. Mantle, who might have been expected to hold the newcomer at a distance, embraced Maris.

The following season, Maris, Mantle, and the rest of the Yankees started slowly. Stengel was replaced by Ralph Houk, and New York was shut out on opening day by the Minnesota Twins, the thinly disguised expansion team that had spun off from the Washington Senators and was widely considered the worst assemblage in the majors. As late as May 20, the Yankees were barely above .500, with a 16–14 record.

Finally, first Mantle, then Maris caught fire, and the two launched a friendly but meaningful competition in pursuit of Babe Ruth's record of 60 home runs in a single season. Swat after smack after smash, the sporting press made much of the presumed rivalry between the two sluggers, who were known as the "M&M Boys," but in truth Mantle and Maris were each other's biggest fans, even as fans pulled for Mantle and wished ill upon his teammate from North Dakota. Maris reacted badly: he sank into a funk, lost clumps of hair, and growled even more.

As the home runs mounted, the media coverage grew uglier, and Maris continued to suffer. "Not only was the most revered record in baseball being put in jeopardy," wrote author Bill Pruden. "but it was being done so by an outsider, the new kid from Midwest who not only sought to unseat the iconic Ruth, but was also challenging the reigning king, fan and press favorite, Mickey Mantle." Maris would never win the battle with the media, but on the diamond Maris and Mantle were steadfast teammates who were simply trying to propel the team to another World Series.

When an old shoulder injury caught up to Mantle after he hit his 54th homer, he was there to cheer for Maris when he hit number 61 into the right-field stands at Yankee Stadium on the last day of the 1961 regular season. The barbs against Maris continued even after the record fell. "Maris has no right to break Ruth's record," complained Ruth contemporary Rogers Hornsby. Baseball commissioner Ford Frick felt the same way, and he attempted to discredit the record by attaching an asterisk to it: "*Hit 61 home runs in 1961 in a 162-game season." The asterisk was intended to

earned a decade before. Even Babe Ruth earned more three decades earlier. But in the recession of 1960, Mantle was happy just to be paid to play baseball instead of working in the zinc mines back home.

Roger Eugene Maris was also happy just to have a job playing baseball, even though he was paid considerably less than Mantle. Growing up in Fargo, North Dakota, he too played football and was offered a college scholarship. He also excelled in track and basketball, but he played baseball on the sandlot and in a city league because his high school did not have a team. A scout for the Cleveland Indians offered him a chance to play in the majors—and a bonus if he made it that far. Maris spent 1954 with a minor league team in Keokuk, 1955 in Reading, and 1956 in Indianapolis before arriving in Cleveland in 1957 to play outfield for the Indians. He was traded to Kansas City in 1958, then to the New York Yankees in 1960, where he stood shoulder to shoulder with the great Mickey Mantle, who, injuries and all, was still lightning fast and ferociously strong.

Maris was a bit of a cipher. He wasn't thrilled to be going to the Yankees, since he had settled his family

acknowledge that Ruth hit sixty-one round-trippers in the 154-game season, while Maris needed 162 games to hit sixty-one. It was also Frick's way of slighting Maris's achievement.

The 1961 season was also a remarkable one for the Yankees, who finished 109–53 and beat the Cincinnati Reds in five games in the World Series. The Maris-Mantle Yankees of 1961 are considered one of the greatest baseball teams in history.

Mickey Mantle retired in 1969, with 536 home runs behind him. He did commentary on television, put his name behind a restaurant chain that failed, and attended sports memorabilia conventions, selling and signing cards and other swag. Throughout his career, he had been a heavy drinker, in part as self-medication against pain and because he thought it didn't matter: all the men in his family had died young, the seemingly inevitable fate of miners, and he figured he would do the same. When he lived beyond his expected allotment, he said, "If I'd known I was gonna live this long, I'd have taken a lot better care of myself."

Mantle entered the Betty Ford Clinic in 1993 in an attempt to stop drinking, but by then his liver was gone. A transplant forestalled death, but the cirrhosis was accompanied by liver cancer that spread elsewhere in his body. He died in 1995, at 63. Shortly before his death, he sent a rueful videotaped message to fans and fellow veterans, saying, "When I die, I wanted on my tombstone, 'A great teammate.' But I didn't think it would be this soon."

Roger Maris, meanwhile, also played through extensive injuries. If 1961 was a banner year for him, 1962 was a disappointment, as he hit just 33 home runs. The effects of old injuries worsened in 1963, and some officials in the Yankees' front office wondered whether he was faking injury so he could move to another team without penalty. Late in 1966, Maris was traded to St. Louis. The Cardinals won the World Series in 1967 and lost in 1968, and Maris retired following that season. In a dozen years in the majors, he played 1,463 games, batted 5,101 times, and clouted 275 home runs, and appeared in seven World Series. Maris retired to Florida and stayed away from baseball, avoiding nostalgia and its lucrative possibilities. He died of cancer in 1985 at 51 and was buried in his hometown of Fargo, North Dakota. Six years after his death, the asterisk was purged from his home run record.

The M&M Boys are long gone, but their might at the plate and mutual respect, even during the intense media campaign of the 1961 season, are the stuff of legend. The M&M Boys remain timeless, just like the blue pinstripes on these two glorious flannels.

"Shooting for 61 in '61" jumbo pin-back button sold at Yankee Stadium, 1961

MAZ

BILL MAZEROSKI 1960 Pittsburgh Pirates Game 7 World Series Home Uniform

Bill Mazeroski charging home after hitting one of the most storied home runs in baseball history, October 13, 1960

Front page of the *Pittsburgh Post-Gazette*, October 14, 1960, underneath Mazeroski's 1960 Game 7 World Series home uniform

ill Mazeroski was born in Wheeling, West Virginia, in 1936, the son of an alcoholic coal miner, and he grew up a few miles away in Tiltonsville, Ohio. Though good in all sports, Maz shone in baseball and was snapped up by Branch Rickey and the Pittsburgh Pirates before he left high school. He did only modestly well in his couple of seasons in the minors, but Rickey retained his faith in the young man, and in 1956, Mazeroski made the 60-mile move from Tiltonsville to Pittsburgh to make his debut in the big leagues. He was 19 years old.

Mazeroski would remain with the Pittsburgh Pirates for the duration of his 17-year career. He came to the team as a shortstop, but the coaches tried him out at several positions, and after Rickey saw him pull off an unusually graceful double play while manning second base, Maz was installed there. Over the course of his career, Mazeroski racked up statistics that sealed his reputation as one of the best defensive players ever to play the game. Yet on offense, Mazeroski was merely passable, never stellar, and he rarely hit with power. In Mazeroski's first couple of years with the Pirates, manager Bobby Bragan would pinch-hit for him as early as the second inning. In 2,163 games during his career, Maz racked up 2,016 hits but only 138 home runs.

Fans believed his defensive achievements made up for his weakness at the plate, but the voting members of the Baseball Hall of Fame did not agree. Bill Mazeroski's name came up for a vote in 1978, which was his first eligible year, but 14 long years later, he still had not been voted in. In those days, a player's name was removed from the Hall of Fame ballot 15 years after he had first become eligible, and it looked as if Mazeroski would never enjoy a berth at Cooperstown. However, the veterans' committee narrowly voted him

"[Ralph] Terry watched the ball disappear, brandished his glove hand high overhead, shook himself like a wet spaniel, and started fighting through the mobs that came boiling from the stands to use Mazeroski like a trampoline."

—Red Smith, *New York Herald Tribune*, October 14, 1960

into the hall in 2001. What made the difference? It was a moment that Pittsburgh fans still remember, a glorious instant that overshadowed Mazeroski's workmanlike years on the field.

The day was October 13, 1960. At Forbes Field, then the Pirates' home, on what is now the University of Pittsburgh campus, the mood was glum. The Pirates were facing the New York Yankees in Game 7 of the World Series, and the tide seemed to be turning in New York's favor. In the top of the sixth inning, the Yankees took a 5–4 lead on a run-scoring single by Mickey Mantle and a three-run homer by Yogi Berra. The Yankees added a couple more runs and held a 7–4 lead when the Pirates came to bat in the bottom of the eighth. Pirates center fielder Bill Virdon hit a grounder that seemed doomed for a double play, but the ball took a bad hop and struck shortstop Tony Kubek in the throat. Before the inning ended, the Pirates held a 9–7 lead. But the Yankees answered in the top of the ninth with two runs of their own.

In the bottom of the ninth, Mazeroski, who had hit only 11 home runs that season, would bat first, with the score tied 9–9. Maz was so rattled that he forgot that he was leading off the inning until Pirates coach Lenny Levy reminded him to pick up a bat. On the mound for the Yankees was reliever Ralph Terry. Berra was playing left field, and he took a few steps toward center, occupied by Mantle, and a couple of steps closer to the infield. And why not? Forbes Field had an unusually massive left field: its flagpole was 435 feet from home.

Mazeroski's batting had improved during the season, bolstered by hard work and confidence. New Pirates manager Danny Murtaugh allowed his players time to develop, and coach George Sisler had taught Mazeroski to pull the ball and to wait for curves to break. Slowly and steadily, his batting average had inched up from .237 to .273 over the summer of 1960.

Terry's first pitch to Mazeroski was high and outside, wild enough that catcher John Blanchard went to the mound to calm his pitcher. The next pitch came screaming down the middle, and Mazeroski hit it just right, sending a high fly over Berra's head. In the timeless words of radio announcer Chuck Thompson, "Here's a swing and high fly ball going deep to left....It may do it! Back to the wall goes Berra; it is over the fence! Home run! The Pirates win! 3:36 p.m., October 13, 1960." Mazeroski rounded the bases, his batting helmet jubilantly raised high in his right hand as he passed second to a hero's ovation from 36,683 screaming fans. The *Sporting News*, never known for wild praise, named Mazeroski its player of the year. The Pittsburgh Pirates home uniform Mazeroski wore on that triumphant day is pictured here (page 195).

Mazeroski would go on to play for the Pirates for another dozen years, living under the shadow cast by that hit and never again matching the moment. Oddly, he was sometimes called on to be a pinch-hitter, especially in pennant races, as if the bosses hoped lightning would strike twice. "Sometimes, yeah, I'm only known for that," he told an interviewer long after retirement. "But I always liked to play defense and that's the thing I was the best at. So, yeah, I guess the home run took away from that a bit. Still, we all want to be remembered for something, and so I'm remembered for the home run."

Mazeroski is remembered for more than that today. He was the anchor of the Pirates' infield and a model for younger players who came later. Balls stuck to his glove like Superglue sticks to skin; shortstop Gene Alley remembered that while most fielders wrapped their gloves around a ball, Mazeroski "could tilt his glove at an angle and hold his hand just so....It was a wonder the ball stayed in there." But stay in it did, and Mazeroski seldom erred. Indeed, teammate Bill Virdon, who played behind him in center field, said of Maz that "he did everything perfectly."

Mazeroski bagged the greatest number of career double plays of any second baseman in history, with 1,706, including a record 161 in one season. He led in assists in 9 of his 17 years, earned 8 Gold Gloves, and played on 7 All-Stars Teams. In that miraculous year of 1960, he led baseball with a .989 fielding percentage. He was nearly perfect in everything but power hitting— except for that one moment when a power hitter's heft was needed, and Bill Mazeroski delivered.

Official Pittsburgh Pirates Game 7 program and ticket, 1960 World Series

> ## "[The Sox needed Nellie] no more than your baby needs milk."
>
> —Bill Veeck

LITTLE NEL

NELLIE FOX 1960 Chicago White Sox Road Jersey

By 1960, 90 percent of the television-hungry U.S. public owned a set, and that year the three major networks aired more than 120 regular-season baseball games. Yet field coverage mostly consisted of a camera behind the plate and an occasional shot from a baseline. To help viewers distinguish among players, the owner of the Chicago White Sox added large numbers and names to his players' uniforms. So, if you had trouble identifying the diminutive, left-handed batter on your black-and-white Philco or Dumont set, you could look for the big number 2 on the right sleeve of his jersey and his name on its back. This player was five-foot-nine Nellie Fox, and the ingenious team owner and promotional wizard was Bill Veeck.

The 1960 "Go-Go Sox" were coming off a 1959 American League pennant and their first trip to the World Series in 40 years. Central to their success was Fox, the perennial All-Star second baseman who led the league in games played (156), plate appearances (717), and at-bats (624) while earning the league's 1959 Most Valuable Player award. The 32-year-old—aptly nicknamed Little Nel for his small frame—had already logged 13 seasons, and the key question during spring training in 1960 was how much was left in the tank of this mighty mite.

Veeck, on the other hand, was in top gear, adding baseball's first exploding scoreboard at Comiskey Park that season, which *Sports Illustrated* featured on its July 4 cover with a shot of the fireworks and the headline "Bill Veeck Baseball's Roman Candle." And Fox was his Roman charioteer. Yet, hype aside, both player and owner were firm believers in value, and both ensured that the Sox stayed in the hunt to repeat as AL champions. Fox again led the league in plate appearances (684) and triples (10), earned another trip to the All-Star Game, and added a third Gold Glove to his trophy case.

Maybe he was helped along by the new road uniforms manufactured by MacGregor, which featured, for the first time in major league history, player surnames on the back of the jersey—Fox wore the one shown here that season. Or maybe Fox and the Sox were spurred to their .662 winning percentage at Comiskey by the thrill of playing in front of their South Side followers (the White Sox led the AL in attendance, with 1,644,460 paying fans).

Alas, this was still the American League, and the Bronx Bombers were eager to end their one-season post-season drought and cash another World Series paycheck. Fox and Veeck had denied the Yankees their chance in 1959, only the second time since 1949 that the Yanks had missed the playoffs. But the Yanks prevailed in 1960, going on to play the Pirates in the Fall Classic.

Veeck left the White Sox in 1961, and two years later Fox was traded to the Houston Colt .45s, where he played in 133 games for the ninth-place team in 1964 and batted .265. In 1965, he lost the second-base job to future Hall of Famer Joe Morgan. Nellie coached with Houston (now known as the Astros) in 1966 and 1967. Morgan credited Fox with helping him maximize his potential, and the two were friends until Nellie's untimely death on December 1, 1975, at 47. When Morgan was inducted into the Baseball Hall of Fame in 1990, he said, "I wouldn't be standing here today if it wasn't for what I learned from [Fox].... Nellie impressed upon me the importance of going to the park every day bringing something to help the team....Nellie Fox was my idol."

Although, at size 40, Fox's uniform is on the small side, his impact on the White Sox and fellow players was large. In 1997, Little Nel got the recognition he deserved when the Veterans Committee voted him in to join the giants of the game in Cooperstown.

White Sox infielders Luis Aparicio and Nellie Fox, 1960

EVERYTHING ABOUT HIM LOOKED MEAN

BOB GIBSON 1964 St. Louis Cardinals Road Jersey

Gibson on the mound in Game 2 of the World Series against the New York Yankees, October 8, 1964

On October 25, 1981, in the heart of a World Series race, a Yankees relief pitcher named Rich "Goose" Gossage, known for his stern, no-nonsense demeanor, fired a fastball at home plate. The pitch, clocked at 98 mph, went wild. "I was just aiming it down the middle of the plate," Gossage said later. "But the ball got away from me." The pitch smacked Dodger third baseman Ron Cey in the side of the head and knocked him unconscious. Cey finally stood, and players from the Yankees and Dodgers helped him to the locker room.

Gossage was scary because of the wildness of his fastball. He is remembered today for beaning Cey and for striking out Pete Rose on his last at-bat in the major leagues. With a drooping Fu Manchu mustache and grim countenance, he also looked scary, though by all accounts he was a nice guy.

Bob Gibson never wanted to be known as a nice guy. He scowled. He grimaced. He growled. And that was how he treated his St. Louis Cardinals teammates. Against the enemy—and every opposing batter was the enemy—he was the Grim Reaper. He was so tough that after a line drive smashed into his leg during a 1968 game, he pitched to two more batters, unaware that his

leg was broken. "He was never pleasant," said baseball writer Roger Angell. "Everything about him looked mean." Added Gibson's longtime catcher, Tim McCarver: "Bob Gibson's demeanor was as menacing and terrifying as any athlete I've ever run across in any sport."

Gibson had no use for compliments, either. Joe Torre caught for Gibson in a 6–5 National League victory at the 1965 All-Star Game, and after the game, Torre praised Gibson on his performance. Without saying a word, Gibson showered, dressed, and left. During Game 1 of the 1968 World Series, Gibson faced Detroit's Denny McLain. When Gibson recorded his 15th strikeout to tie Sandy Koufax for the most strikeouts in a World Series game, the Busch Stadium scoreboard praised him, touching off an ovation in the stands. Gibson tipped his cap for a microsecond, and then went back to business, retiring another batter a few minutes later. He would finish with a record 17 strikeouts.

Born on November 9, 1935, in Omaha, Nebraska, Pack Robert Gibson grew up in a housing project on Omaha's north side. His father died of tuberculosis before Bob was born, and he was raised by his brother, Josh, who was 15 years older. Gibson was sickly as a child, suffering rickets, asthma, and other pulmonary

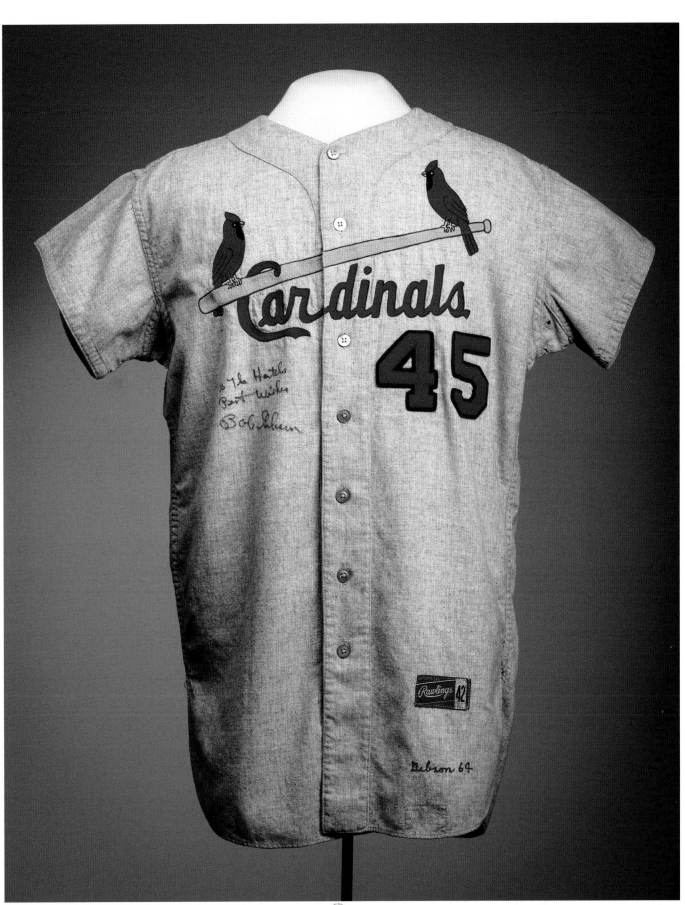

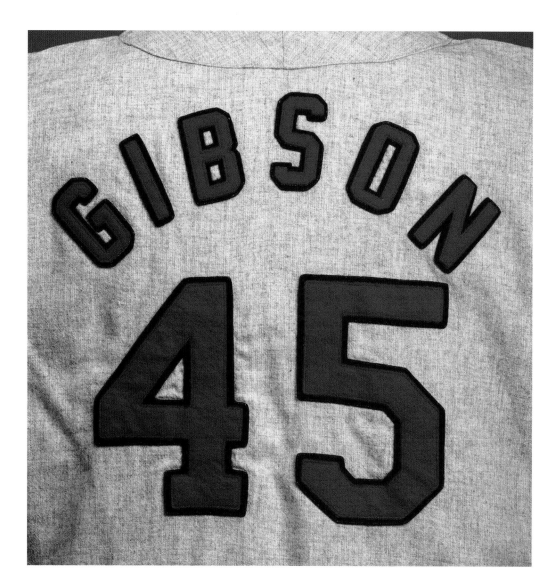

Back view of Gibson's 1964 St. Louis Cardinals Road Jersey

maladies. Josh Gibson, the program director of an Omaha community center, coached his younger brother, and Bob Gibson excelled in track and field, football, and basketball. Josh also was an excellent baseball coach, and he taught Bob to catch, play shortstop, and switch-hit. In 1951, when Bob was 16, Josh's recreation center team won the American Legion city championship. Bob was named to the All-Star Team.

Cardinals scout Runt Marr saw the 18-year-old Gibson play in 1953 and offered him a contract. Josh intervened and instead helped Bob land a basketball scholarship to Creighton University, near their home in Omaha. Gibson was the first black basketball player in the university's history, and he played so well that the university retired his number 45. In the off-season, Gibson also played baseball. He was scouted by several major league teams, including the Yankees, Dodgers, White Sox, Phillies, and Athletics, but he

held out for an offer from professional basketball. The offer never came, in part because the NBA color-barrier had fallen just a few years earlier, in 1950, and the league still had few black players. Gibson spent a year with the Harlem Globetrotters but quit because he didn't like playing a clown.

In 1956, the St. Louis Cardinals signed the 22-year-old Gibson to his first professional contract. He reported to the Omaha minor league team, where coach Johnny Keane gave Gibson a look at every position before deciding that he liked Gibson's pitching. Gibson bounced between the minors and the big time until 1959, when he earned a spot on the Cardinals roster. He was appalled to learn that Cardinals manager Solly Hemus did not like black players, but Keane replaced Hemus as manager in 1961, and Gibson's career took off. Keane may not have been completely free of the prejudices of his day, but he knew how to put together a winning team. Gibson was made a relief pitcher, then a starter, and he was joined by other black players, including center fielder Curt Flood and left fielder Lou Brock. Said Gibson: "I honestly believe that [Keane's] faith in me...supplied nourishment that I was able to feed on for years to come, especially at World Series time."

Gibson threw two pitches, a fearsome slider and perhaps the most powerful and daunting fastball of the day. He shone in the 1962 season, with 208 strikeouts in 233 innings. An injury hurt his numbers in 1963, but in 1964, he recorded 245 strikeouts in 287 innings. With two weeks left in the season, the Cardinals trailed the Phillies in the race for the National League pennant by six games. After the Phillies lost 12 of their last 15 games, the Cardinals needed a win over the lowly New York Mets on the final day of the season to capture the pennant. Gibson pitched four innings of relief to secure the victory, boosting his record to 19–12. In the World Series, he hurled complete game victories in Games 5 and 7, as the Cardinals defeated the Yankees to give St. Louis its first Fall Classic title since 1946. The game ball from Game 5 is pictured here (right) along with the Cardinals road jersey, manufactured by Rawlings, that Gibson wore throughout that extraordinary 1964 season (page 201 and opposite).

Gibson was a combined 41–24 over the next two seasons, then returned with the Cards to the World Series in 1967, where he turned in one of the greatest performances in Series history. Gibson pitched three complete games, allowed just three runs on 14 hits, and struck out nearly a batter an inning. He was even better the following season, now remembered as "the year of the pitcher," thanks to astonishing performances by Gaylord Perry, Denny McLain, Mickey Lolich, and others. Gibson outperformed even those greats of the game. He finished 1968 with a 22–9 record and a 1.12 ERA, the lowest of any pitcher since 1914. He compiled a streak of 47 scoreless innings and threw 28 complete games, with 13 shutouts. He was awarded the NL MVP and earned the Cy Young Award by unanimous vote. So ferocious was Gibson's scowling, growling, grimacing, and surgically precise work that baseball officials decided to show mercy on hitters by shrinking the strike zone and lowering the pitcher's mound for the 1969 season.

Gibson brushed back plenty of batters who dared tempt him. He reached the World Series three times and, he noted, "clicked off twenty-seven innings in each one." He pitched until 1975, when injuries and age caught up to him. During his career, he bagged an NL-record (and second overall to Walter Johnson) 3,117 strikeouts, nine Gold Gloves, and two Cy Young Awards. The St. Louis Cardinals retired the number 45 that Gibson had worn for 17 seasons, his longevity matched by his strikeout record. All in a day's ill-tempered work.

"[Gibson] pitches as though he's double-parked."

—Sportscaster Vin Scully

Two views of the ball used in Bob Gibson's World Series Game 5 win at Yankee Stadium, October 12, 1964

"Does Pete [Rose] hustle? Before the All-Star Game, he came into the clubhouse and took off his shoes and they ran another mile without him."

—Hank Aaron

CHARLIE HUSTLE

PETE ROSE 1964 Cincinnati Reds Home Jersey

On the 1964 Cincinnati Reds scorecard shown here, Mr. Red, the unofficial name of the team's mustachioed mascot in the 1950s and 1960s (see page 287 in the Compendium), is leaping over the wall in an attempt to catch a home run or foul ball. In a case of splendid serendipity, it looks as if Mr. Red is *hustling*, much like the brash young man who wore the home jersey from that same season displayed under the scorecard.

Peter Edward Rose was born in Cincinnati, Ohio, on April 14, 1941, the day before the Reds opened the season against the St. Louis Cardinals at Crosley Field. Later, on one of his many trips to Crosley, Rose became inspired by the way the Cardinals' Enos "Country" Slaughter ran out walks and raced on and off the field between innings. When he joined the Reds as a rookie in 1963, Rose replicated this style of play, for which he was given the nickname "Charlie Hustle" by Yankees pitcher Whitey Ford. In one story, Ford pinned the nickname on Rose with a derisive comment after he'd sprinted to first following a walk. Mickey Mantle told another story in Ken Burns's documentary, *Baseball*. Mantle described hitting a home run that was clearly over the wall in left field, but Rose made an all-out effort to climb the fence to catch it. Mantle said that when he got back to the dugout, Ford exclaimed, "Did you see Charlie Hustle out there?" Either way, Rose's hustle and toughness so impressed manager Fred Hutchinson that Rose replaced Don Blasingame at second base. Hutchinson's faith was rewarded when Rose earned the 1963 National League Rookie of the Year award.

By 1964, Rose had became the poster boy for the hometown kid who made good. That season, the Reds added player names to the backs of jerseys. On the back of this size 44 home jersey worn by Rose throughout the 1964 season, his name was added below the number 14. MacGregor, a Cincinnati sporting goods manufacturer, created the jerseys this way because the vest-style garment did not have enough surface area across the upper back and shoulders to display the names. Placement of the players' names below the numbers was unique to the Cincinnati club.

The Reds in 1964 were also making noise in the National League. As late as September 15, the Reds were eight and half games out of first place and had adopted the hustle style of play embodied by their young star. They scraped for every hit and every run, and they rattled off nine consecutive wins from September 20 to 27. Going into the final week of the season, Cincinnati was tied with St. Louis with four games to play, two against the Pirates and two with the Phillies, all at Crosley Field. New uniforms had been ordered, and it seemed that Rose was poised to lead the Reds to the postseason promised land. World Series tickets were printed and orders for them taken.

On September 29, Rose had a three-for-five day, spraying hits to third, left field, and center, but the Reds failed to score and the Pirates won, 2–0. Three to play and one game back. On October 1, the Reds beat the Pirates, 5–4, in a night game at Crosley, while the Cardinals had an off day. The Reds remained half a game back with two games to play.

While the Reds were hosting the Phillies for the final two contests of the season, the Cardinals were in New York, taking on the Mets in a three-game series. The Cardinals took one out of three from New York while the Reds dropped two straight to the Phillies. Rose ended up going one-for-seven in these final two contests, and the Reds came up one game short.

In spring training 1965, the Reds' uniforms from the previous year were worn by young hopefuls in the minors. Names were removed and numbers altered, a common practice when uniforms were relegated to extended organizational use. The uniform displayed here was spared the scissors and remains in original condition, a fitting reflection of Charlie Hustle, the man who wore it.

Rose's 1964 Cincinnati Reds home jersey with an official scorecard to the game played at Crosley Field between the Cincinnati Reds and Pittsburgh Pirates, May 5, 1964

DUENDE

WILLIE MAYS 1965 San Francisco Giants Home Jersey

The electrifying
Say Hey Kid on the
basepaths, 1960s

"There have been only two geniuses in the world: Willie Mays and Willie Shakespeare." So said Tallulah Bankhead, the early-twentieth-century actress, social butterfly, and rabid San Francisco Giants fan. While Shakespeare left behind a trove of plays and poems to demonstrate his genius, Willie Mays has left numbers and testimonials that attest to his exceptional abilities. "When I was in the Big Leagues, there was a tremendous amount of great ballplayers, but the guy who stood head and shoulders above them all was Willie Mays," said shortstop Ernie Banks, who played for the Cubs from 1953 to 1971. Added 1950s-era Cincinnati Reds slugger Ted Kluszewski, "I'm not sure what the

hell charisma is, but I get the feeling it's Willie Mays." Leo Durocher called Mays the best all-around player in baseball history.

Born in Westfield, Alabama, on May 6, 1931, Willie Howard Mays played all sports as a kid, but he gravitated toward baseball. After a couple of seasons playing for Negro Leagues teams in the South, he was spotted by New York Giants scout Eddie Montague. "They got a kid playing center field practically barefooted that's the best ballplayer I ever looked at," reported Montague. "You better send somebody down there with a barrelful of money and grab this kid." The Giants signed Mays, and after a couple of seasons with minor league teams, he was called up to the Giants in 1951.

Mays was happy-go-lucky on and off the field, and he learned to negotiate ethnic landmines in the segregated South, disarming hostility with friendliness. He arrived in Manhattan smiling pleasantly to everyone, including opposing pitchers. When he had trouble remembering the names of teammates, he called out, "Say hey over there" to get their attention. He quickly earned a nickname: The Say Hey Kid.

The Giants' rookie failed to get a hit the first dozen times he stepped to the plate, but on his 13th at-bat, facing Braves southpaw Warren Spahn, Mays sent the ball sailing over the left-field stands of the Polo Grounds. Spahn later said in jest that he blamed himself for Mays's success: "I'll never forgive myself. We might have gotten rid of Willie forever if I'd only struck him out." Mays won the National League Rookie of the Year award in 1951 as the Giants reached the World Series, losing to the New York Yankees. Mays played center field alongside two fellow African Americans, Hank Thompson and Monte Irvin, and gained considerable attention from the press and from African American fans in nearby Harlem.

Mays could play nearly any position, and teammate Orlando Cepeda once remarked, "Mays could do everything. There's lots of us who think he's the best ever." After two seasons of military service, Mays returned to New York in 1954, and the Giants coaches put him in center field for good. He flourished under the guidance of manager Leo Durocher, who had a tremendous fondness for his young star, saying, "If he could cook, I'd marry him."

In addition to winning the batting title with a .345 average in 1954, Mays hit 41 home runs, drove in 110 runs, and led the league in triples (13) and slugging percentage (.667). In the 62 seasons from 1931 through 1992, only two other National League hitters bested Mays's slugging percentage: Stan Musial (.702 in 1948) and Henry Aaron (.669 in 1971). Sportswriters named 23-year-old Mays the 1954 league MVP.

Willie Mays making one of the most celebrated catches in baseball history, Game 1, 1954 World Series, Polo Grounds

The Giants swept the Cleveland Indians in the 1954 World Series, and in Game 1, Mays made his iconic over-the-shoulder catch in deep center field off Vic Wertz's line drive at the Polo Grounds. Biographer James S. Hirsch described Mays's catch in his book *Willie Mays: The Life, The Legend:*

[Don] Liddle threw his fastball but aimed it poorly. The ball stayed over the plate, almost at the shoulders. Wertz extended his thick arms, rotated his wrists, and hit the ball squarely….The ball's distance wasn't the only problem. Mays had no angle on it. The ball was winging directly over his head, which is one of the toughest catches in baseball…. Mays, barreling toward the bleacher wall, looked over his left shoulder, slowing a bit, then continued with his head straight, arms thrashing, legs churning….At the last moment, he looked up, extended his arms like a wide receiver, and opened his Rawlings Model HH glove. The ball fell gently inside. He had ten feet to spare." Connoisseurs consider it one of the greatest fielding plays in baseball history, though Mays thought it was a routine catch. "I had the ball all the way," he said in postgame interviews.

In 1957, he won the first of a dozen consecutive Gold Glove awards. Stealing bases, catching fly balls, hitting: Whatever Mays did, he did to perfection, often leading the league. He was the first player to hit 300 home runs and steal 300 bases in a career. And he's one of the few major league players to hit four home runs in a single game, which he did against the Milwaukee Braves. In 1965, the year he wore the flannel San Francisco Giants home jersey manufactured by Wilson shown on page 206, the 34-year-old Mays hit 52 home runs and was again the NL's MVP, 10 years after he had won his first MVP in 1954. In his career, Mays belted 660 home runs, and it's been said that he should have hit 760, but the Giants moved to San Francisco after the 1957 season and Mays never got the hang of the winds at Candlestick Park.

Mays played for the Giants for more than 20 years. He was traded to the New York Mets in 1972, a move that turned out to have some generosity hidden behind it. The Giants were on the verge of bankruptcy, and the Mets included an option for Mays to coach following his retirement. Mays returned to New York and swatted his 660th home run on August 16, 1973. He retired at the end of that season at 42, the oldest player then on the field, with 3,283 hits, 1,903 RBI, a .302 batting average, and a record 24 All-Star Game appearances. He coached for six years, finally leaving the game in 1979, the year he was elected to Cooperstown in his first year of eligibility.

Willie Mays is considered one of the few great five-tool players—outstanding at hitting for power, hitting for average, running bases, throwing, and fielding. He deserved Tallulah Bankhead's accolade, but Mays is revered not only for what he did but for how he did it. He scored more than 2,000 runs in his career, and he is remembered for his cap flying off his head as he rounded third base. His more than 7,000 putouts are regarded as exciting, spectacular, and sometimes breathtaking. "As a fan, Mays commanded all of your attention, whether he was trotting to the outfield, making a basket catch or standing in the batter's box," said Hall of Famer Joe Morgan. "I could not take my eyes off Mays."

George Frazier, the late journalist for the *Boston Globe,* called this irresistible quality *duende.* He remembered sensing it first when he saw Joe DiMaggio grace an outfield. In 1963, Frazier wrote a series of essays in which he tried to explain the meaning of the word. *Duende* essentially means a special force that makes someone or something irresistibly attractive. "So difficult to define, but when it is there it is unmistakable, inspiring our awe, quickening our memory," wrote Frazier. Frazier added that *duende* is a power that transmits a profound feeling from the heart of the artist to his audience "with the minimum of fuss and the maximum of restraint."

Willie Mays was a baseball genius, and he also had *duende.* Frazier paid Mays the ultimate compliment when he wrote that the only way to describe an athlete's combination of talent and star power was to say, "That guy has some Willie Mays in him, the same way you used to say this singer or that had some Elvis in him."

"If somebody came up and hit .450, stole 100 bases and performed a miracle in the field every day I'd still look you in the eye and say Willie was better. He could do the five things you have to do to be a superstar: hit, hit with power, run, throw, and field. And he had that other magic ingredient that turns a superstar into a super superstar. He lit up the room. He was a joy to be around."

—Leo Durocher, manager of the
 New York Giants (1948–55)

"THE CLUB KNOWS I DON'T WORK THAT DAY"

SANDY KOUFAX 1966 Los Angeles Dodgers Road Jersey

Sandy Koufax winding up in Game 7 of the World Series, 1965

In baseball's earliest years, many municipalities banned games on Sunday, the day of rest in the Judeo-Christian tradition and, at the time, a day when shops were shuttered, restaurants were locked, and streets were empty. Although those "blue laws" and the days off they mandated are largely a thing of the past, some players and places still observe the Sunday-off rule. In 2006, a mostly Mormon team from Utah forfeited a game in the Little League World Series that was to be played on Sunday. Said a harried official, rejecting the team's request for a schedule change, "We weren't going to change the schedule for their sake. If we did that, then we'd have to do it for the Seventh-Day Adventists, for the Jewish [players].... Pretty soon, we wouldn't be able to put on a tournament."

If that official had been sensitive to history, he might have heard in his comment echoes of what major league officials said in the 1960s with respect to a young pitcher named Sanford Koufax, who wrestled with a choice befitting Job: Should he throw a baseball on the High Holy Day of Yom Kippur?

Sandy Koufax was born Sanford Braun on December 30, 1935, in Brooklyn, New York, to parents who were Sephardic Jews of Hungarian descent. They divorced, and, when Sandy was nine, his mother, Evelyn, married a lawyer named Irving Koufax. Like the Williamsburg boys in Chaim Potok's great novel *The Chosen*, Koufax—raised a few miles from Williamsburg in the Jewish neighborhood of Borough Park—was infatuated by baseball. Yet young Sandy was more often

found on the basketball court because the game had a longer playing season and there were more courts than diamonds in urban Brooklyn. Koufax also played sandlot baseball, and a coach asked him to pitch for a team in the Coney Island Sports League.

Following graduation from Lafayette High School, Koufax headed to the University of Cincinnati, where he planned to study architecture. He made the basketball team as a freshman, and in spring made the varsity baseball team. Koufax quickly developed as a solid pitcher, striking out 51 batters in 31 innings in his first season. Manager Branch Rickey of the Pittsburgh Pirates watched Koufax pitch during a tryout and said he had "the greatest arm I have ever seen." A Brooklyn Dodgers scout said Koufax's fastball made the hair on his arms stand on end, and the Dodgers signed him for a $6,000 salary and $14,000 bonus. Koufax returned to his home borough of Brooklyn.

He debuted for the Brooklyn Dodgers on June 24, 1955, taking the mound at the start of the fifth inning against a Milwaukee Braves lineup that included Johnny Logan, Eddie Mathews, and Hank Aaron. Koufax pitched two scoreless innings and struck out two. Two months later, on August 27, he pitched a complete game shutout against the Cincinnati Reds, giving up two hits and five walks. He picked up his second win, also a shutout, on September 3. Despite this early success, Koufax did not see much playing time his first few seasons with the Dodgers. Sure, he had a supernatural fastball, but his other pitches needed work, he was wild, and he was injury-prone. The Dodgers moved to Los Angeles in 1958, and in 1960, Koufax begged management to release him from his contract so he could go to another team and get more playing time. He also became increasingly frustrated with his performance—from 1955 through 1960, his ERA was 4.10 and he won 36 games while losing 40, with 405 walks in 691⅔ innings.

The Dodgers' wisely declined his request to be traded, and in 1961 the team began helping Koufax refine his pitching mechanics. One coach located a flaw in his windup, while second-string catcher Norm Sherry told Koufax that he could throw without so much force and still strike out opposing batters. "Why not have some fun out there, Sandy?" Sherry said. "Don't try to throw so hard and use more curveballs and changeups." Koufax listened. That season, he won 18 games and led the National League with 269 strikeouts. Said fellow Dodgers pitcher Don Sutton of Koufax, "A foul ball was a moral victory."

"I'm going to ask the Pope to see what he can do about rain."

—Walter O'Malley, owner of the Los Angeles Dodgers, when Sandy Koufax announced his decision not to pitch in Game 1 of the 1965 World Series because it fell on Yom Kippur

The next season was even better, and 1963 was better still. Koufax led the National League with 25 wins (with 5 losses), a 1.88 ERA, 11 shutouts, and 306 strikeouts. The Dodgers then beat the New York Yankees in the World Series, and Koufax earned the Cy Young and NL Most Valuable Player awards. Marveled Yankees catcher Yogi Berra, "I can see how he won twenty-five games. What I don't understand is how he lost five." People began talking of Sandy Koufax in the hushed, awed tones that they would of a departed legend, even though he was just coming into his own.

In 1965, despite constant pain in his pitching elbow from arthritis, Koufax pitched 335⅔ innings and led the Dodgers to another pennant. On September 9 that year, he pitched a perfect game against the Chicago Cubs at Dodgers Stadium, and he finished the year by winning his second pitchers' Triple Crown, leading the league in wins (26), ERA (2.04), and strikeouts (382, the modern-day record until Nolan Ryan struck out 383 batters in 1973). Koufax captured his second unanimous Cy Young Award. Trying to hit one of Koufax's fastballs, said Pirates batting phenomenon Willie Stargell, was "trying to drink coffee with a fork." Said Cubs legend Ernie Banks, "Sandy's curve had a lot more spin than anybody else's. It spun like a fastball coming out of his hand. And he had the fastball of a pure strikeout pitcher—it jumped at the end. The batter would swing half a foot under it. Most of the time we knew what was coming, because he held his hands closer to his head when he threw a curveball. But it didn't matter."

On October 6 of that year, the Dodgers faced the Minnesota Twins for Game 1 of the World Series. It was also the first day of Yom Kippur, the Jewish feast of atonement, and Koufax told Dodgers management that he could not pitch. "There was never any decision to make," he later wrote in his autobiography, *Sandy Koufax: A Lefty's Legacy*, "because there was never any possibility that I would pitch. Yom Kippur is the holiest day of the Jewish religion. The club knows I don't work that day."

That decision was controversial then, and it remains somewhat controversial today. Baseball historians have wondered why Koufax, secular and not openly observant, decided to sit out a game when he had played on other high holidays earlier in his career. Regardless of Koufax's reason, his decision provided a poignant message and example to other Jewish people, and to people of religious faith everywhere. Recalled rabbi Elliot Strom, then a teenager in Toronto, "For kids growing up then, there was a sense of, 'Here is someone on the world stage.' You could think of a million good arguments why he should go and pitch that day. But if not pitching was that important and the right thing to do, that ought to tell the rest of us something." Strom

adds that his father chided him when he asked to stay home and watch the game instead of going to services, saying, "The star pitcher for the Dodgers is not going to pitch in the game. This is the kind of commitment he's showing. Where is your commitment?"

Future Hall of Famer Don Drysdale replaced Koufax on the mound for Game 1 of the Series, and he gave up seven runs in the first three innings before being yanked. The Dodgers lost the game, 8–2. Said Drysdale to his coach when he was removed, "I bet right now you wish I was Jewish, too." The Dodgers went on to win the Series in seven games. Drysdale came back to win Game 4, while Koufax lost Game 2, then shut out the Twins to win Games 5 and 7.

Sandy Koufax played professional baseball for only a dozen seasons before the arthritis in his pitching elbow forced him from the game. "In those days there was no surgery," he later recalled. "The wisdom was if you went in there, it would only make things worse and your career would be over, anyway. Now you go in, fix it, and you're okay for next spring." The 30-year-old Koufax

retired in November 1966, a few months after another amazing season in which he led the NL in wins (27), ERA (1.73), innings pitched (323), and strikeouts (317). He led the Dodgers to the NL pennant and won his third Cy Young Award, though the Baltimore Orioles swept the Dodgers in the World Series. Pictured on page 211 is the Los Angeles Dodgers road jersey manufactured by Rawlings that was worn by Koufax during that superb final season. He was inducted into the Baseball Hall of Fame in 1972. At 36, he was the youngest player—and the second Jewish player after Hank Greenberg—to be inducted into the Hall.

High praise came from the legendarily tough Casey Stengel, who once said of Koufax, "Forget the other fellow," referring to Walter Johnson, whom Stengel had played against. "The Jewish kid is probably the best of them." Said Steve Stone, the only Jewish pitcher besides Koufax to win a Cy Young Award, "Teams come and go, players come and go, I don't believe your religious beliefs come and go." That is the lesson that Sandy Koufax taught the world.

Sandy Koufax concentrating before windup, 1966

THE GREAT ONE

ROBERTO CLEMENTE 1966 Pittsburgh Pirates Home Jersey and Helmet

Roberto Clemente
at the plate,
early 1960s

> "Any time you have an opportunity to make a difference in this world and you don't, then you are wasting your time on Earth."
>
> —Roberto Clemente

Prior to the integration of the major leagues in 1947, stars from the Negro Leagues played in the Caribbean during the off-season. The level of play became so good that white major league players wanted to participate as well. In 1947, for example, the New York Yankees traveled to Puerto Rico and were beaten by the Ponce Leones team in an exhibition game. Major league scouts scoured the Caribbean Leagues for low-cost, high-impact talent. Two Puerto Rican players reached the big leagues in the early 1940s, but the doors flew open in the 1950s. Baseball fever in Puerto Rico reached unprecedented heights, and the island's greatest star was Roberto Clemente.

Roberto Clemente Walker was born on August 18, 1934, to Melchor Clemente and Luisa Walker de Clemente in Carolina, a municipality east of the Puerto Rican capital of San Juan. Roberto was the youngest of Luisa's seven children. Although Puerto Rico suffered from the ravages of the Great Depression—farms and banks failed, unemployment was high, and many Puerto Ricans had no food—Melchor retained a job as a foreman in the sugar cane fields. Moral discipline and religion were important to Roberto's parents, and these values remained influential to Roberto throughout his life as he navigated segregation, the challenges of a career in baseball, and efforts to Americanize his personality and identity.

Clemente played all sports, but baseball was his favorite. "I loved the game so much that even though our playing field was muddy and we had many trees on it, I used to play many hours every day," he wrote in his journal. "One day I hit ten home runs in a game we started about 11 a.m. and finished about 6:30 p.m." He helped his father load and unload sugar trucks and threw the javelin at Vizcarrondo High School. He signed to play in the Puerto Rican league while still in high school, and he hit .356 the year he graduated. Al Campanis, a scout for the Brooklyn Dodgers, heard tales of Clemente's skills before he ever saw him, and on February 19, 1954, the Dodgers signed the 19-year-old outfielder to a $10,000 bonus and $5,000 salary. The Dodgers already had a full roster, so they sent Clemente to the Montreal Royals, a minor league team, for the 1954 season. According to prevailing rules, playing for the Royals made Clemente eligible for the rookie major league draft. The Dodgers tried to keep Clemente out of the spotlight, but Pittsburgh coach Clyde Sukeforth, who had a sixth sense for talent, snatched Clemente when the draft was conducted in November 1954.

Clemente debuted for the Pittsburgh Pirates on April 17, 1955. Branch Rickey, the Pirates manager, was not impressed with his new player, though he trusted Sukeforth's judgment. He criticized Clemente's running ("bad, definitely bad") and his lack of power as a hitter. He praised Clemente's "beautiful throwing arm" but concluded that he needed work—"He can run, throw, and hit," Rickey said. "He needs much polishing, though, because he is a rough diamond." Clemente sought coaching to improve his game, and after batting .255 as a rookie, he boosted his average to .311 in his second season. His numbers went up and down the next couple of years, but by 1960 he had become reliably consistent in everything he did on the field.

Off the field, Clemente faced other types of challenges. In making that 1955 debut, Clemente crossed a double color line: black and Latino. Although Jackie Robinson had integrated baseball eight years earlier, black players were still not common in MLB. Clemente also was the first Latino to play at Forbes Field, and although he insisted, "I don't see color," it bothered him that others did. And Clemente did not recuse himself from questions of racial justice. Unlike Jackie Robinson, Clemente wore his anger on his sleeve. "They have an open preference for North Americans," he said of the sports press. "Mediocre players receive immense publicity while true stars are not highlighted as they deserve."

Clemente was a star whose significance went well beyond the numbers. He carried himself with grace, even nobility, and he impressed others as much with his personality as with his athletic prowess. Bowie Kuhn, then the commissioner of baseball, said, "He gave the term 'complete' a new meaning. He made the word 'superstar' seem inadequate. He had about him the touch of royalty." Clemente played "a kind of baseball that none of us had ever seen before," wrote sportswriter Roger Angell, "throwing and running and hitting at something close to the level of absolute perfection, playing to win but also playing the game almost as if it were a form of punishment for everyone else on the field." In the 1971 World Series, he was a one-man team—hitting, catching fly balls, firing monstrous heat from the outfield so his infielders could tag runners

Tragic death of Roberto Clemente, as reported by *Pittsburgh Post-Gazette*, January 2, 1973

out—and won the Series MVP. As he told Angell, "I want everybody in the world to know that this is the way I play all the time. All season, every season. I gave everything I had to this game."

Clemente's World Series play showed how true that was. The Pirates transformed from a struggling franchise into a championship organization after Clemente joined the team. In 1960, he hit .314 with 16 home runs, leading the Pirates to face the Mickey Mantle/Roger Maris–era New York Yankees in the World Series. Pirates second baseman Bill Mazeroski was the star of the Series because he hit the game-winning home run in the bottom of the ninth inning in Game 7. But Clemente was impressive, too. He batted .310 with nine hits in the Series, and in the eighth inning of Game 7, his bat and hustle kept the Pirates' momentum alive. Yankees reliever Jim Coates got two quick strikes on Clemente, and he was one strike away from getting the Yankees out of their most serious trouble of the afternoon when Clemente eventually hit a blooper toward first. First baseman Bill Skowron and Coates raced for the ball, and Skowron reached it at at the edge of the infield grass. Clemente's speed forced Skowron to hold the ball when Coates failed to reach first base in time to cover. The high chopper allowed Bill Virdon to score from third, cutting the Yankees' lead to 7–6. Hal Smith followed with a three-run home run to give the Pirates a 9–7 lead.

Clemente played for the Pirates for another dozen seasons. In 1966, he achieved career highs in home runs (29) and RBI (119) while wearing the flannel Pittsburgh Pirates home jersey and batting helmet shown on page 215. That year Clemente won his first and only National League MVP award.

On his last at-bat in 1972, Clemente collected his 3,000th base hit, making him the 11th player to reach that milestone. Clemente and Mazeroski were the only Pirates remaining from the 1960 team, and Clemente was preparing for retirement. At season's end, he left baseball and threw himself into his charity work. On December 31, he boarded a plane to fly to Managua, Nicaragua, to ensure that relief supplies for victims of a devastating earthquake did not wind up in the hands of black marketers. The overloaded cargo plane crashed into the sea off Puerto Rico immediately after takeoff. Clemente's body was never found.

Roberto Clemente gave everything to the game of baseball. In Pittsburgh, he is still referred to as "the Great One." His honors speak for themselves, among them four National League batting titles and 12 Golden Glove awards. In 1973, Clemente became the first player from Latin America to be inducted into the Hall of Fame. Normally, a player may not be inducted until at least five years after retirement, but an exception was made for Clemente because of the circumstances surrounding his death.

Clemente was a constant advocate for equality and fair treatment for African American and Latino players, a profound contribution to the game not noted in the record books. His fierce ethnic pride and capacity to bear a much larger identity—not just for Puerto Rico but for all of Latin America—was a responsibility he embraced and carried with dignity and grace. He didn't see himself as merely a representative of Latin America. He saw his career in baseball as a means to help Latin Americans—especially underprivileged Puerto Ricans— make their lives better. Said his old friend Luis Mayoral, a prominent Spanish-language broadcaster, "Roberto Clemente was to Latinos what Jackie Robinson was to black baseball players. He spoke up for Latinos; he was the first one to speak out."

The Great One at bat in Forbes Field, early 1960s

A LOT TO SMILE ABOUT

TOM SEAVER 1967 New York Mets Rookie Home Jersey

Tom Seaver and his wife, Nancy, celebrating his National League Rookie of the Year award, 1967

Tom Seaver and his wife, Nancy, had a lot to smile about when this photo was taken at their home in Manhattan Beach, California, on November 20, 1967. The 23-year-old pitcher for the New York Mets had just heard about his selection as National League Rookie of the Year, becoming the first Met in history to earn that honor. The couple was joined in the photo by their black poodle, whose name, Slider, also happened to be Seaver's go-to pitch. While wearing the pinstriped flannel home jersey shown opposite, Seaver rewrote the Mets' pitching record book that season, with 16 victories, 18 complete games, 170 strikeouts, and a 2.76 ERA. "You've got a nice pitch, kid," the normally restrained Hank Aaron said to Seaver. "Good fastball, nice curve."

But Seaver brought to the Mets much more than just a devastating repertoire of heat. He gave the team

hope. The 1967 Mets went 61–101 and finished 10th in the National League, 40½ games behind the St. Louis Cardinals, who went on to win the World Series. As Mets broadcaster Howie Rose later said to author Bruce Markusen, Seaver brought a sense of optimism. Before he joined the Mets, Rose said, "There was this inescapable culture of losing, and at least among their fans, a growing sense of losing was going to be something permanent. People who watched [Seaver] as a rookie got the sense that they had finally developed a player who was capable of doing special things, and therefore capable of helping the Mets achieve some pretty good things of their own along the way."

Born on November 17, 1944, George Thomas Seaver joined the North Rotary team in the Fresno Little League as a nine-year-old pitcher and outfielder. Early on, he was recognized as a mature and thoughtful hurler.

"Kid, I know who you are, and before your career is over, I guarantee you everyone in this stadium will, too."

—Hank Aaron

"Even...in high school, Tom was a thinking pitcher," said Dick Selma, Seaver's teammate in high school and on the Mets. "He knew how to set up a hitter by working the corners of the plate and the batter would usually pop the ball."

After graduating from high school in 1962, Seaver played one year at Fresno City College and then was recruited to play for Rod Dedeaux at the University of Southern California. After posting a 10–2 record as a sophomore, Seaver was drafted in the 10th round of the 1965 MLB draft by the Los Angeles Dodgers, but Seaver and the Dodgers could not agree on the terms of a contract. He signed with the Atlanta Braves, but that contract was voided on a technicality. Seaver's contract went into a lottery, and the Mets won. He spent one season in the minor leagues, and then joined the Mets in 1967.

After Seaver's phenomenal rookie season, he pitched superbly in 1968, and his performances seemed to ignite his teammates. In 1969, the hitherto hapless Mets found themselves climbing from the cellar and into contention. On May 21 in Atlanta, Seaver shut out the Braves to improve to 6–2, and the team evened its record at 18–18. Seaver was still not satisfied. That .500 mark was "neither here nor there," Seaver said, adding that his teammates' embrace of mediocrity "isn't going to get us very close to a pennant." As Mets broadcaster Ralph Kiner wrote in his 2005 memoir, "Tom Seaver was the driving force behind the players, always pushing the team to be better than they were, never letting them settle."

Seaver continued to pitch steadily, reliably, and well in 1969. He struck out 25 Chicago Cubs batters and just missed a perfect game when outfielder Jim Qualls hit a ninth-inning single. Mets lore would refer to it as the "imperfect game." The Mets went on to win the NL pennant with a 100–62 record, then faced the much-favored Baltimore Orioles in the World Series. Seaver led the "Miracle Mets" to victory in four games, though it didn't hurt that the Mets had Nolan Ryan and Tug McGraw in the bullpen. Seaver earned the Cy Young Award that year, and the ticker-tape parade that followed the win was described by the *Wall Street Journal* as a more colossal celebration than those held for V-E Day, Charles Lindbergh's flight, and the return of the Apollo astronauts, rolled into one.

Seaver insisted, however, that 1971 was his single best year, and he led the league in strikeouts with 289. He finished second in voting for the Cy Young that year to the Cubs' Ferguson Jenkins. Seaver's career ended less remarkably than it began. In 1977, following a long contract dispute with the Mets, he was traded to the Cincinnati Reds. He gained a bit of payback when he defeated the Mets, 5–1, on his first trip back to Shea Stadium. Seaver was traded back to the Mets in 1982, then pitched for the Chicago White Sox for two seasons, chalking up his 300th victory in 1985. He was sent to the Boston Red Sox in 1986 and was sidelined with an injury when Boston lost to the Mets in the World Series.

Seaver knew it was time to leave the game. He had amassed all the numbers he needed, rising to the top of the pitching aristocracy, where his peer group was limited to Nolan Ryan and Randy Johnson. Yet the Mets called him up unexpectedly in 1987, and he pitched poorly in three starts. "I've used up all the competitive pitches in my arm," he said. The following season, the Mets retired his number, the 41 portrayed on the jersey shown on page 219. It is the only player number the franchise has ever retired.

In the end, Seaver won 311 games and struck out more than 200 batters in 10 seasons, including an NL record nine in a row. He won three Cy Young Awards (1969, 1973, and 1975) and played in a dozen All-Star Games. Hank Aaron claimed Seaver was "the toughest pitcher I've ever faced," and in an ESPN poll, Hall of Famers Bob Gibson, Juan Marichal, Jim Palmer, Nolan Ryan, Steve Carlton, Bert Blyleven, and Don Sutton all said Seaver was the best pitcher of their generation. On January 7, 1992, he was voted into the National Baseball Hall of Fame by a higher percentage (98.8) than any other player in history.

After retirement, Seaver provided color commentary for the Mets and, perhaps incongruously, the Yankees. He scouted for the Mets for a bit, then returned to his native California, where he has since occupied his time growing wine grapes with Nancy on a 3.5-acre vineyard in Calistoga. Seaver Family Vineyards produced its first vintage in 2005 with two cabernets, "Nancy's Fancy" and "GTS."

Forty-nine years after they smiled for that photo in their Manhattan Beach home, "Tom Terrific" and his wife still have a lot to smile about.

Official scorecard for Tom Seaver's major league debut, Shea Stadium, April 13, 1967

1967 OFFICIAL PROGRAM AND SCORECARD 25 CENTS

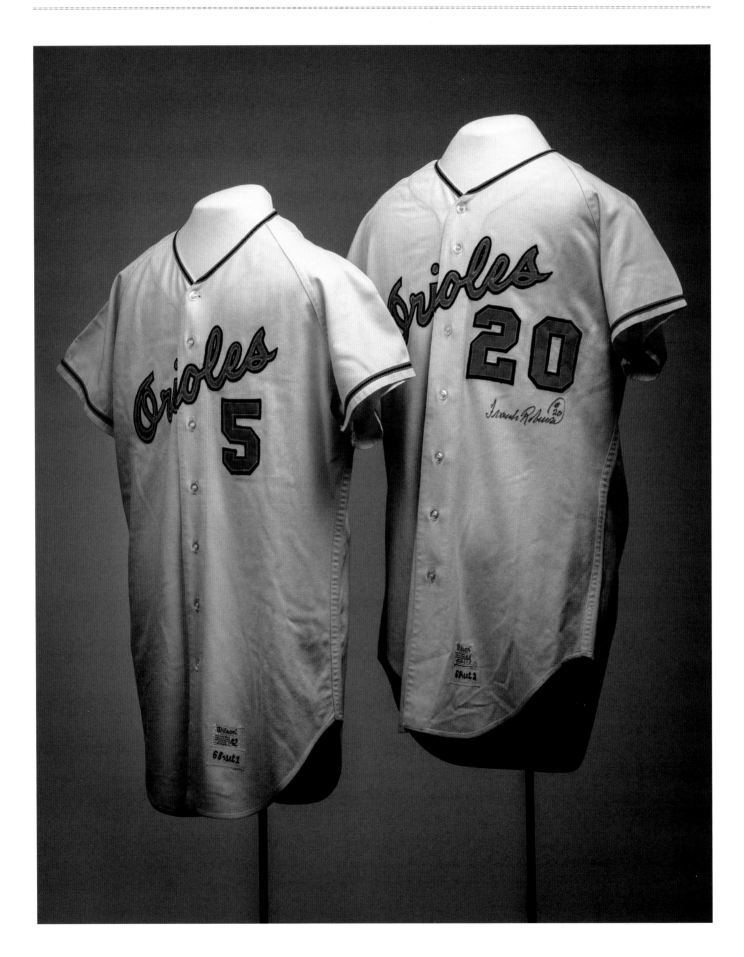

A MAJOR LEAGUE FRIENDSHIP

BROOKS ROBINSON 1968 Baltimore Orioles Home Jersey
FRANK ROBINSON 1968 Baltimore Orioles Home Jersey

When Brooklyn Dodgers players heard on October 23, 1945, that the team was bringing Jackie Robinson aboard, many of them signed a petition to say they would rather be traded than play alongside a black man. Shortstop Pee Wee Reese, a southerner from Kentucky who would become team captain in 1950, refused to sign the petition, which effectively nullified the effort. Later, when Robinson took infield practice during a game in Cincinnati, fans and opposing players taunted and threatened him. After hearing the catcalls, as reported by author Roger Kahn, "Reese walked across the field from his shortstop position, put his arm around Robinson and faced the crowd and the opposing bench, sending a courageous message of respect in an era stained by racial intolerance. Robinson, who endured insults and threats throughout his career, later said he never again felt alone on the ballfield after that day."

Two decades later, Brooks Robinson, another white ballplayer, defied his upbringing in the Jim Crow South to befriend Frank Robinson, an African American player who joined Brooks on the Baltimore Orioles in 1966. Brooks and Frank struck up a lifelong friendship, much as Reese and Jackie Robinson had done two decades earlier. Brooks Calbert Robinson was born in Little Rock, Arkansas, in 1937. His father was a firefighter and played semipro baseball. Robinson inherited his father's fair-minded attitude

and love of baseball, and he honed his throwing skills on his childhood newspaper route, imagining that the papers he threw to customers' porches were baseballs.

After graduating from Central High School in 1955, Robinson signed with the Baltimore Orioles for $4,000. Baltimore was not a strong franchise, and team officials convinced Robinson that "with us, you have the chance to move up faster than with probably any other club." He made his major league debut on September 17, 1955, against the Washington Senators, and got two hits in four at-bats.

Robinson would spend his entire 23-year career with the Orioles, and he was always somewhat erratic on offense. He had a good season in 1959 and a better one in 1960, when the Orioles finished second to the New York Yankees in the race for the American League pennant. Still, one season he would hit .251 with 11 home runs (1963), and the next he would hit .317 with 28 homers and 118 RBI, earning the AL Most Valuable Player award.

On defense, however, Robinson distinguished himself at third base the moment he joined the Orioles. He won the Gold Glove 16 consecutive seasons, led the American League in fielding percentages a still-unmatched 11 times, and appeared in the World Series 4 times. In the 1970 Fall Classic, Brooks batted .429 with two home runs and six RBI, and he was named MVP. He also made several jaw-dropping plays to rob the Reds of apparent base hits. So extraordinary was

"I don't see why you reporters keep confusing Brooks [Robinson] and me. Can't you see that we wear different numbers."

—Frank Robinson

his performance that after the series, Cincinnati Reds manager Sparky Anderson quipped, "I'm beginning to see Brooks in my sleep. If I dropped this paper plate, he'd pick it up on one hop and throw me out at first." By the time he retired after the 1977 season, Robinson held almost every major fielding record for third basemen, including games (2,870), fielding average (.971), putouts (2,697), assists (6,205), and double plays (618). It was largely because of his brilliant work that ESPN named the 1969 and 1973 Orioles the best defensive teams in baseball history.

But even beyond his defensive prowess, Brooks Robinson deserves to be remembered for his friendship with Frank Robinson, who was traded to the Orioles in 1966 after 10 seasons with the Cincinnati Reds. Frank Robinson was raised in Oakland, California, on August 31, 1935. One of his teammates on the basketball team at McClymonds High was Bill Russell, and his baseball teammates included future greats Vada Pinson and Curt Flood. As a rookie with the Reds in 1956, Frank hit a rookie-record 38 home runs. He won the league MVP in 1961 and had an even better season in 1962, when he hit .342 with 39 home runs and 136 RBI. He was traded to the Orioles before the start of the 1966 season for three unheralded players in a deal still considered one of the most lopsided in baseball history.

Brooks Robinson could easily have felt threatened when Frank joined the Orioles, because Frank was also a born leader and had posted great numbers as an out-fielder for the Reds. But Brooks welcomed Frank, telling the press that Frank was "exactly what we need." In his first year with the Orioles, Frank led the American League in RBI (122), batting average (.316), and home runs (49) to win the Triple Crown. He also blasted the first home run out of Memorial Stadium and into the parking lot. The 1966 Baltimore Orioles reached the World Series for the first time in franchise history and swept the heavily favored Los Angeles Dodgers. Frank was named AL MVP that season, becoming the first player to win the award in both the American and National Leagues.

Although Brooks welcomed Frank to the Orioles, the still southern city of Baltimore was not so kindly disposed. In his first year, Frank could not find suitable housing. He threatened to quit the Orioles and even moved his family back to his native California until he

was able to buy a house in a mixed-race development. Later, thanks primarily to his experiences in Baltimore, Robinson became an outspoken advocate on the issue of civil rights for African Americans. Frank and Brooks hit back-to-back home runs in the first inning of Game 1 of the 1966 Series, steamed to another World Series in 1969, losing to the Mets in a dramatic upset, then returned in 1970 to crush the Cincinnati Reds for a bit of revenge for Frank—and the MVP for Brooks. In 1971, the Orioles lost the World Series to the Pittsburgh Pirates.

It came as a surprise to both Robinsons when, in 1972, the Orioles traded Frank to the Los Angeles Dodgers. Frank was traded again in 1974, to Cleveland, and a year later he was named player-manager of the Indians. The move made Frank the first African American manager in baseball, and he remained the Indians' manager after retiring as a player in 1976. Frank then coached the Orioles from 1979 to 1980 and again from 1985 to 1987, for a total of 16 seasons with the team as player, coach, and manager.

Frank also became the first African American manager of a National League team in 1981, when he took over the San Francisco Giants. He later managed the Montreal Expos, moving with the team to Washington, D.C. in 2005 to manage the transplanted and renamed Washington Nationals. He retired in 2006 with 1,065 wins and 1,176 losses as a manager. As a player, he batted .294 for his career and hit 586 home runs, at the time the fourth-highest total in history.

After his retirement in 1977, Brooks became a color commentator for the Orioles. The pair entered the Orioles Hall of Fame in 1977, and the team retired Brooks's number 5 and Frank's number 20. Both players were inducted into Cooperstown, Frank in 1982 and Brooks the following year. In 2012, the Orioles erected a statue of Frank near one of Babe Ruth outside Camden Yards. At the inauguration, Frank paused to thank Brooks, calling him "my brother" and lauding him as "one of the nicest individuals that I have ever come across in life or in this game." In honor of their friendship, the Wilson-manufactured flannel Baltimore Orioles home jerseys that were worn by Brooks and Frank throughout the 1968 season are shown together (page 222), a fitting tribute to greatness achieved through friendship in a tumultous year of the Civil Rights Movement.

Frank Robinson (left) and Brooks Robinson taking a break from batting practice, late 1960s

THE FINEST IN THE FIELD

JOHNNY BENCH 1968 Cincinnati Reds Home Uniform

When the Crosley Field faithful poured through the turnstiles at Findley and Western on April 10, 1968, they were greeted with several changes. Noticeably absent from the cover of the team yearbook was the mustachioed Mr. Red, who had been the team's mascot since 1955. He was replaced by a montage of baseballs. Gone, too, were the pinstripes, which had adorned home uniforms since 1958 and had been supplied by MacGregor, a local company. The Reds' new uniforms were crisp and clean and suited the family-friendly image sought by the team's new general manager Bob Howsam. The new garments were produced by St. Louis–based Rawlings Sporting Goods, which had long advertised that its products were "the Finest in the Field."

The Reds also introduced in 1968 a new player who would quickly develop into another version of "the Finest in the Field." The player was a 20-year-old rookie catcher from Binger, Oklahoma, named Johnny Lee Bench. While wearing the flannel Cincinnati Reds 1968 home uniform shown here, Bench launched his meteoric rise to stardom. He got his first start on April 17 and stayed in the lineup for 81 straight games. In all, he caught 154 games that year, a record for a rookie catcher, and hit .275, with 15 home runs and 82 RBI. These numbers were particularly commendable because 1968 is remembered as "the year of the pitcher," when the league batting average was only .243. Bench earned the National League's Rookie of the Year award and his first of 10 Gold Glove awards. He would eventually also win a pair of National League MVP Awards (1970 and 1972), earn two World Series rings (1975 and 1976), and appear in 13 All-Star Games.

Bench was a powerful hitter who would become even more fabled for his defense. His throwing arm, which kept would-be base-stealers on their toes throughout his career, was described by writer Roy Blount Jr. as "about the size of a good healthy leg, and it works like a recoilless rifle." At six foot one and 200 pounds, Bench seemed both larger and more agile than his peers behind the plate. He had massive hands that

> "When Johnny Bench was born, I believe God came down and touched his mother on the forehead and said, 'I'm going to give you a son who will be one of the greatest baseball players ever seen.'"
>
> —Cincinnati Reds manager Sparky Anderson to the press after his Reds swept the Yankees in the 1976 World Series

could hold seven baseballs. He was one of the first to catch one-handed, with his right hand resting behind his back to protect it from foul tips. He used a hinged catcher's mitt, rather than the prevalent circular "pillow" style, allowing him to more easily field bunts and make plays at the plate. After the rookie Bench took a high throw and tagged out a Chicago runner, Cubs manager Leo Durocher said, "I still don't believe it. I have never seen that play executed so precisely." Giants manager Herman Franks saw Bench make a similar play against his club and said later that Bench was the "best catcher I've seen in 20 years."

Bench's bat was most lethal when it counted. He retired after the 1983 season with 389 career home runs, the most by any catcher. Four of those round-trippers are still remembered by baseball fans. First was his game-tying blast in the bottom of the ninth inning off Pirates pitcher Dave Giusti in the 1972 National League Championship Series. Second and third, his pair of homers in Game 4 of the 1976 World Series delivered the title to Cincinnati and completed the Reds' postseason sweep of the Phillies and the Yankees. This dramatic win over the resurgent Bronx Bombers solidified the reputation of the Big Red Machine. Finally, Bench hit the last home run of his career on September 17, 1983—on "Johnny Bench Night" at Riverfront Stadium. During the pregame ceremonies, Bench thanked the people of Cincinnati and then vowed, "I'm gonna try like hell to play good for you tonight."

For 17 seasons, Bench did that. And much more.

THE KNIT ERA

1972–1999

By the end of the 1960s, more Americans were watching football on television than were watching baseball on the screen or in ballparks. Instead of baseball stadiums, cities were building multipurpose parks capable of hosting a baseball team, a football squad, or a rock concert. Astroturf, domes, and exploding scoreboards became commonplace. Free agency, the designated hitter, and relief pitching came of age. Players had agents, facial hair, and money, while their clubs looked forward to postseason playoffs and interleague play.

It was the time of Oakland's Mustache Gang and of Cincinnati's Big Red Machine. The Yankee-Dodger World Series rivalry was reborn. Hank Aaron eclipsed Babe Ruth, Carlton Fisk smacked the most famous homer in Red Sox history, Reggie Jackson got his candy bar, Pete Rose surpassed Ty Cobb, and Cal Ripken showed that great things can happen to those who come to work each day prepared to give their best. It was a time of modern heroes—and a few villains as well.

All of this was done in knit uniforms that briefly used a cotton-polyester blend and then quickly morphed into all-synthetic products. Form-fitting pullovers of the 1970s and 1980s gave way to baggy uniforms by the end of the century. Stirrups became a thing of the past. Nostalgia crept in with returns to popular styles and logos from times past. New manufacturers, some from outside the United States, as well as licensed "official suppliers," became the norm. A new, more broadly scaled baseball equipment industry was born, centered on the greats of the games and the uniforms they wore.

Photograph of the National
League team in knit uniforms before
the start of the All-Star Game,
Milwaukee County Stadium, 1975

RED SOX ROOKIES

CARLTON FISK 1972 Boston Red Sox Rookie Road Jersey

In 1972, the Topps Company issued its 787-card set in series form, releasing a new group of cards every few months. Card number 79, described simply as "Red Sox Rookies" on the first series checklist, featured the faces of Mike Garman, Cecil Cooper, and Carlton Fisk. Garman was a pitcher of dubious promise who had seen action in Fenway in 1969 and 1971. Cooper had hit .310 in his 14 games with the Sox in 1971. Fisk had logged a pair of games with Boston in 1969, and, despite his decent performance toward the end of the 1971 season where he played 14 games (.313 with two home runs in 14 games), he was tagged as the Red Sox third-string catcher for 1972. Fans, collectors, and kids pulling the card from a 10-cent wax pack likely wondered why they hadn't instead pulled number 37 (Carl Yastrzemski) or 49 (Willie Mays). Card number 79 may have been destined for the spokes of a Schwinn Stingray or packaged with number 80 (Tony Perez) in hopes of trading for number 130 (Bob Gibson). But while Perez and Gibson eventually ended up in Cooperstown, neither started his career as Rookie of the Year, as Carlton Ernest Fisk did.

The 24-year-old rookie got off to a fast start in 1972. By June 13, Fisk had amassed 32 hits, including 20 for extra bases, and he was batting .278, with a .574 slugging percentage. By July 12, his slugging percentage had jumped to .629. "Fisk is rapidly gaining the reputation of being the Johnny Bench of the American League," said *Boston Herald American* sportswriter Larry Claflin. For the season, Fisk caught 131 games, batted .293 with 22 home runs, led the AL in triples (9), and became the first player to be selected as the league's Rookie of the Year by a unanimous vote. He also won the Gold Glove and finished fourth in balloting for the league's Most Valuable Player.

But Fisk brought much more to the Red Sox than a remarkable rookie season. He fostered a new kind of game, one quite different from that of Yastrzemski. In 1961, Yaz had taken on the burden of leading the team after Ted Williams retired at the end of the 1960 season. Red Sox first baseman George Scott recalled Yaz's feats during the 1967 season: "Yaz hit forty-four homers that year, and forty-three of them meant something big for the team. It seemed like every time we needed a big play, the man stepped up and got it done." Yaz would move past Williams to become the all-time Red Sox base hit leader in 1977 and two years later would become the first AL player to accumulate both 400 home runs and 3,000 lifetime hits.

While Yaz inspired teammates through his extraordinary accomplishments, Fisk inspired with hustle and grit. His approach to the game was steeped in an intense work ethic, tenacity, and a relentless determination to win, traits he adopted from his parents and honed playing baseball and basketball while growing up in Charlestown, New Hampshire. Fisk's father, Cecil, adhered to a simple philosophy in raising his four sons and two daughters: "I expected them to do as well as they could, whatever they did." Competition was personal combat for Carlton, and victory was the source of inspiration and satisfaction; he found losing unacceptable and humiliating. Biographer Doug Wilson wrote that Fisk had a "perfectionist's drive to excel and a single-minded devotion to duty." He "tolerated nothing less than maximum effort, from himself or his teammates." Fisk often would yell at his own pitchers to motivate them, and he encouraged them to throw inside to opposing batters, increasing the pitchers' effectiveness. "If you play against him you hate him," said manager Eddie Kasko, "but if you play with him and want to win, you love him. He plays as if he were on the Crusades."

The Red Sox switched to new knit pullover uniforms in 1972, following the trend away from wool flannel uniforms. However, the Sox opened the season wearing their wool flannel uniforms from the previous season, because of either a late order or delayed delivery from the manufacturer, Stall & Dean, or the supplier, McAuliffe. The Sox didn't debut their new knit uniforms until the 1972 All-Star Game in Atlanta on July 25. The jersey shown here (opposite), a V-neck pullover knit design, may have been worn by Fisk at that game—the first of his 11 Summer Classic appearances. He definitely wore this jersey during road games the balance of his extraordinary rookie season.

The Red Sox came out of the 1972 All-Star break five games out of first place, after finishing 1971 in third place and 18 games out of first. The 1972 Red Sox kept pushing and punching while their catcher kept swinging. Behind Fisk's bat, Boston took a half-game lead into Detroit for the final three-game series that would decide the American League Eastern Division title. Although Fisk called and caught masterful games on October 1 and 2, he was hitless at the plate, and the Sox dropped the pair. Fisk then sat out the final game of the season, with the division race settled in favor of the Tigers.

Fisk's 1972 Boston Red Sox rookie road jersey, his 1972 Topps rookie baseball card, and two unopened 1972 Topps baseball-card wax packs

As history would have it, Fisk's opportunity for redemption came three years later on the biggest stage a player could hope for, a do-or-die moment in Game 6 of the 1975 World Series. The Red Sox were down three games to two against the Cincinnati Reds. Fred Lynn's three-run homer in the first inning gave the Sox a 3–0 lead. The Reds led 6–3 going into the bottom of the eighth, but Boston's Bernie Carbo hit a pinch-hit, three-run homer to tie the game. In the ninth inning, the Red Sox failed to score despite loading the bases with no outs, and the game headed into extra innings with the score tied 6–6.

> "And all of a sudden the ball was there, like the Mystic River Bridge, suspended out in the black of the morning."
>
> —Peter Gammons, *Boston Globe* staff writer, on Carlton Fisk's game-winning home run in the 12th inning of Game 6 of the 1975 World Series

It was 12:33 a.m. when Fisk stepped to the plate to lead off the bottom of the 12th against Pat Darcy, the eighth Reds pitcher of the night. Before stepping into the batter's box, Fisk tugged and pulled at the synthetic fabric of his form-fitting knit jersey (similar to the one he wore in the latter half of his rookie season), as if to announce he needed room for his body to do something big. On Darcy's second pitch, Fisk lofted a high shot down the left-field line. His eyes glued to the ball's flight, he took a few steps toward first base, then waved his arms wildly, willing the ball to stay fair. When it bounced off the foul pole for a home run, giving the Red Sox a 7–6 victory, John Kiley, the Fenway Park organist, launched into Handel's "Hallelujah Chorus" as Fisk circled the bases in front of 35,205 hysterical fans. Fisk's game-winning blast is considered by many to be the zenith of baseball drama and an exclamation point on the greatest game ever played. In Game 7, however, Boston's Bill Lee failed to hold onto another 3–0 lead, and the Reds took the Series with a 4–3 victory. The Red Sox were again denied their first World Series championship since 1918.

Carlton Fisk may have shared Topps card number 79 with two other players, but he holds for himself a plaque in Cooperstown that reads:

> *A commanding figure behind the plate for a record 24 seasons, he caught more games (2,229) and hit more home runs (351) than any catcher before him. His gritty resolve and competitive fire earned him the respect of teammates and opposing players alike. A staunch training regimen extended his durability and enhanced his productivity—as evidenced by a record 72 home runs after age 40. His dramatic home run to win game six for the 1975 World Series is one of baseball's unforgettable moments. Was the 1972 American League Rookie of the Year and an 11-time All Star.*

Carlton Fisk willing his game-winning home run to stay fair in Game 6 of the World Series, 1975

THE STUFF OF LEGEND

NOLAN RYAN 1972 California Angels Home Jersey

Nolan Ryan's fastball broke so many bats during games that fans complained the ball had razor blades attached to it. The sound of this pitch smacking into a catcher's mitt was described as a "muffled rifle shot." It ripped holes in mitts and numbed the fingers of catchers. In short, the pitch was frightening, for both catcher and batter. "No matter how much padding I put in my glove, as each game wore on, I had fewer fingers on my left hand capable of gripping a bat," recalled Jerry Spinks, Ryan's batterymate at Alvin High School near Houston, Texas. Major league slugger Reggie Jackson once said, "I love to bat against Nolan Ryan and I hate to bat against Nolan Ryan. It's like ice cream. You may love it, but you don't want it shoveled down your throat by the gallon. I've never been afraid at the plate but Mr. Ryan makes me uncomfortable. He's the only pitcher who's ever made me consider wearing a helmet with an ear flap."

From 1963, when Ryan was a high school junior—and already attracting major league scouts by averaging two strikeouts per inning, including 21 in one game—until 1993, when he retired from the majors at 46, his overpowering fastball and longevity of throwing it so effectively have been the stuff of legend. Ryan accumulated more strikeouts (5,714) and no-hitters (7) than any other pitcher in major league history. He wore this Rawlings ribbed-collar, button-down knit home jersey in 1972, his first season with the California Angels.

Lynn Nolan Ryan broke into the major leagues as a New York Met on September 11, 1966, an undersize right-handed pitcher with an oversize future. He pitched three innings that season, missed 1967 with an elbow injury, then returned to the majors for good in 1968. After four seasons with the Mets, Ryan had a World Series ring but little else. His 1971 salary of $20,000 was above the league minimum but about a third less than the average major league salary. He had accomplished his early career goal of pitching long enough in the majors to qualify for a pension, but inconsistent control prevented him from fulfilling predictions of greatness. In his first four seasons, his career record stood at 29–38. In 500 innings, he struck out nearly a batter an inning, though he also averaged six walks per game. His mediocre performance was largely due to three factors. First, his commitment to the Army Reserve disrupted his schedule, often forcing him to go more than a week between starts; second, despite having the fastest fastball in the National League, Ryan was largely ignored by Mets manager Gil Hodges, in part because Hodges had an effective pitching rotation in Tom Seaver, Jerry Koosman, and Gary Gentry; and third, the only advice Ryan received from pitching coach Rube Walker was "to throw as hard as [you] can for as long as [you] can." Following the 1971 season, Ryan told his wife, Ruth, that he would quit the game if the Mets failed to trade him that winter.

Ryan got his wish. On December 10, 1971, the pitcher was packaged with Frank Estrada, Don Rose, and Leroy Stanton and shipped to the California Angels in exchange for Jim Fregosi. Mets manager Hodges told Joseph Durso of the *New York Times*, "You always hate to give up on an arm like Ryan's. He could put things together overnight, but he hasn't done it for us and the Angels wanted him. I would not hesitate making a trade for somebody who might help us right now, and Fregosi is such a guy." Coming off a third-place finish and 14 games back in 1971, Hodges was looking for an impact player for 1972. Hodges, however, would not live long enough to see how the trade panned out. He died of a heart attack on April 2, 1972, while the club was in spring training.

Fregosi, a six-time All-Star with the Angels, hit .232 for the 1972 Mets and would be traded to the Texas Rangers in the middle of the 1973 season. As for Nolan Ryan, his 1972 campaign was nothing short of extraordinary. He led the American League in strikeouts (329), shutouts (9), and fewest hits allowed over nine innings (5.3). To paraphrase "Nuke" LaLoosh from the 1988 baseball classic *Bull Durham*, the kid from Alvin, Texas, was here to announce his presence with authority.

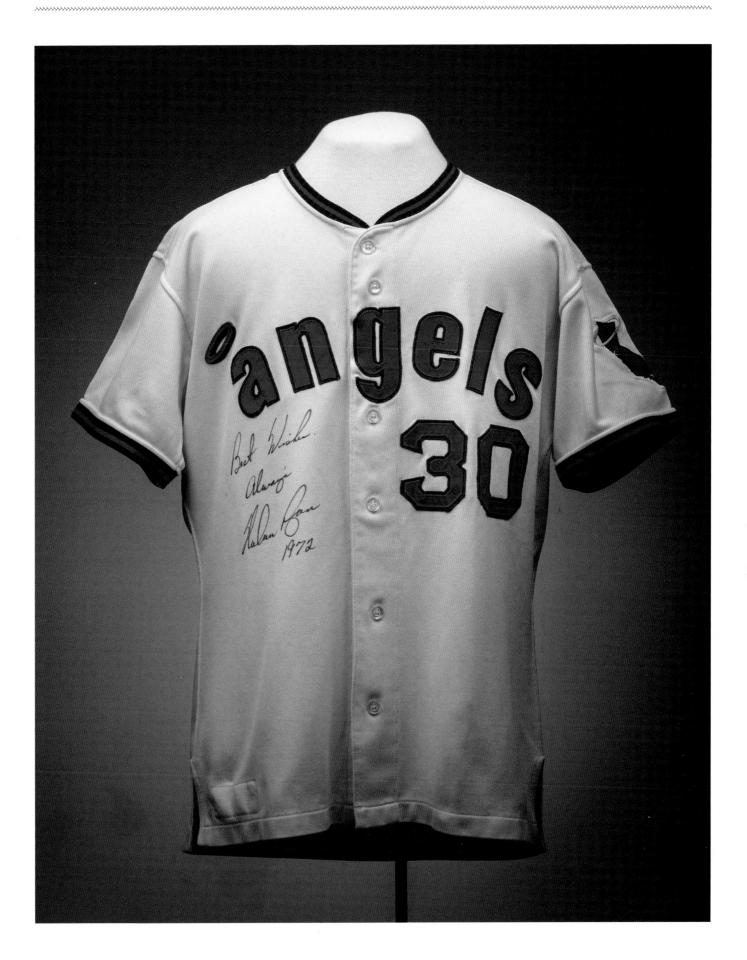

The Ryan Express
at work, ca. 1972

"He is the only pitcher you start thinking about two days before you face him."

—Dale Murphy, two-time National League MVP

Angels fans were not accustomed to seeing a pitcher like Ryan. Andy Messersmith and Clyde Wright had been the mainstays of the Angels pitching staff in 1971, and between them they struck out 314 batters, 15 fewer than Ryan whiffed by himself in 1972. Free of the issues that had constrained him with the Mets, Ryan had the most productive eight seasons of his career with the Angels. His Army Reserve duty was completed, so he could develop a better rhythm by pitching every four days. Angels pitching coach Tom Morgan reconstructed Ryan's delivery, taught him how to throw a sharp-breaking curveball, and provided moral support. Ryan also underwent a comprehensive weight-training program to build strength. Before 1972, baseball authorities believed weight training made a player brawny, limiting the flexibility needed by a pitcher to generate arm speed and by a hitter to develop bat speed. Ryan became the first big-league pitcher to lift weights to enhance his performance.

As an Angel, Ryan threw four no-hitters to tie Sandy Koufax's career record, struck out 383 hitters in 1973 to break Koufax's single-season mark of 382, produced four other 300-strikeout seasons, and led the American League in strikeouts in all but one season with the team. He twice won 20 or more games in a season and won 19 in two other seasons, and his fastball was clocked at a record 100.9 miles per hour. Although Ryan never won the Cy Young Award as an Angel, his performance during the 1972, 1973, 1974, and 1977 seasons would seem to merit the honor. But Ryan was hampered by the Angels' inability to score runs, which denied him the lofty win-lose record needed to win the award. In Ryan's first five years with the Angels, the team finished last in the American League in runs scored four times and next to last the other year. Detroit Tigers and Texas Rangers manager Billy Martin said of those Angels teams, "They could take batting practice in a hotel lobby and never break anything." Ryan echoed the challenge of pitching for the weak-hitting Angels: "I feel like I have to pitch a shutout every night or lose. If I throw one bad pitch, I'll be beaten." Six times in 1972, he allowed two or fewer runs and lost because the Angels could not score a single run.

Ryan played eight seasons in California, then moved to the Houston Astros in 1980, where he became the first athlete on a professional sports team to earn $1 million per year. His performance was as impressive as his pay. He struck out hitter number 3,000 on July 4, 1980; broke Walter Johnson's 76-year-old record of 3,509 career strikeouts on April 27, 1983, at 36; and notched strikeout number 4,000 on July 11, 1985. In 1987 and again in 1988, Ryan was the oldest pitcher to lead his league in strikeouts. "At the age of forty-one, Nolan Ryan is the top power pitcher in the league," said Pete Rose during Ryan's final season (1988) with Houston. "You can talk about Dwight Gooden, you can talk about Mike Scott, you can talk about whoever you want, but none of them throw as consistently hard as Ryan does."

Although his time was up with Houston, Ryan's fastball would continue to sizzle 230 miles north in Arlington when the Texas Rangers signed him on December 7, 1988. From 1989 to 1991, Ryan compiled a record of 41–25 and fanned more batters than anyone else in the American League (736). On August 22, 1989, he earned strikeout number 5,000, and that same year, at 42, he posted his sixth 300-strikeout season. If that wasn't enough, on June 11 the following year, Ryan pitched his sixth no-hitter (beating the World Series champion Oakland Athletics), despite chronic pain in his lower back. He then recorded win number 300 on July 31 that year against the Milwaukee Brewers. Finally, on May 1, 1991, Ryan shut down the Toronto Blue Jays, the AL's best-hitting team, to earn his seventh and final no-hitter.

On June 16, 1992, the California Angels retired Ryan's number 30. The team that gave birth to his legend somehow foreshadowed the end. While throwing a fastball in the first inning of a game against the Seattle Mariners on September 22 the following year, the 46-year-old Ryan tore the ulnar collateral ligament in his right elbow. His career was over. In 1996, the Rangers and Astros retired his number 34, making him one of only nine players to have their numbers retired by more than one major league team. Ryan was a first-ballot inductee into the Hall of Fame in 1999, with 98.79 percent of the votes. Throughout his career, Ryan's strikeout victims included 1,176 different players, and, equaling a twentieth-century record held by Jim Kaat, he pitched during the administrations of seven U.S. Presidents—Lyndon B. Johnson, Richard M. Nixon, Gerald Ford, Jimmy Carter, Ronald Reagan, George H. W. Bush, and Bill Clinton.

"There's always one guy who defies the odds," said Toronto's Joe Carter, hero of the 1993 World Series. "In baseball, Nolan Ryan is that guy." All great American tales have a beginning, and the Nolan Ryan story began in a California Angels jersey in 1972.

"I have
no problem
with Bruce
Springsteen."

—Dave Winfield, when
asked by the *New York
Daily News* why he had
such a problematic
relationship with "the
Boss" (a nickname shared
by Springsteen and New
York Yankees owner
George Steinbrenner)

ONCE A PADRE, ALWAYS A PADRE

DAVE WINFIELD 1975 San Diego Padres Home Uniform

It's certainly nice to be wanted. It's even better when you are wanted by teams representing major league baseball (San Diego Padres), the National Basketball Association (Atlanta Hawks), the American Basketball Association (Utah Stars), and the National Football League (Minnesota Vikings). Such was the lot of David Mark Winfield when he came out of the University of Minnesota in 1973.

The Padres selected Winfield as a pitcher in the first round of the 1973 draft (fourth pick overall, just behind shortstop Robin Yount). It did not take the Padres long to realize that Winfield possessed an arm and a bat that needed to be in the lineup every day. By 1974, Winfield was a fixture in the Padres outfield. The same year, the team was purchased by Ray Kroc, the retired CEO of McDonald's. Kroc not only quieted relocation rumors by keeping the team in San Diego; he also kept Winfield and the Padres in mustard and brown uniforms, though he toned down the look slightly, as is the case with this 1975 home uniform manufactured by Wilson. Winfield would wear this style of uniform for the bulk of his tenure in San Diego.

Winfield was a perennial All-Star for the Padres from 1977 to 1980, earning two Gold Gloves (out of a career total of seven). But on December 15, 1980, Winfield inked a record 10-year, $23 million contract with George Steinbrenner and the New York Yankees.

Winfield's time in pinstripes was as productive as it was acrimonious. In nine seasons (1981 through a portion of 1990), Big Dave racked up eight All-Star appearances, five Gold Gloves, and 205 home runs. From 1981 through 1984, Winfield was the most effective run producer in major league baseball. In 1985, however, things turned sour. Following Winfield's poor performance in an important September series, Steinbrenner ridiculed him and declared that Winfield wasn't worth the money he was being paid. Steinbrenner also tried to trade him, but rules prevented him from doing so without Winfield's consent.

Winfield finally agreed to a trade to the California Angels in 1990. He would go on to play for the Blue Jays (where he won a World Series ring in 1992), Twins (where he collected career hit number 3,000), and Indians before retiring in 1995. As for Steinbrenner, commissioner Fay Vincent suspended him for two years in 1990 for paying gambler Howie Spira $40,000 to dig up "dirt" on Winfield after the player sued the Yankees for reneging on an agreement to donate $300,000 to his charity.

Winfield's philanthropy was as impressive as his baseball career. In 1973, his first year with the Padres, he began buying blocks of tickets for families who couldn't afford to go to Padres games. Winfield then partnered with San Diego's Scripps Clinic, which brought a mobile clinic to the stadium parking lot for health check-ups. He was the first active athlete to establish a charitable foundation, the David M. Winfield Foundation. Winfield's charitable work has earned him the YMCA's Brian Piccolo Award for Humanitarian Service, baseball's first-ever Branch Rickey Community Service Award, and major league baseball's Roberto Clemente Award.

In 2001, Winfield was elected to the Hall of Fame on the first ballot, and he was enshrined with teammate Kirby Puckett. Winfield was the first person to enter the Hall as a Padre.

Dave Winfield at bat, 1975

GO WHEN IT SEEMS RIGHT TO GO

LOU BROCK 1977 St. Louis Cardinals Home Jersey

Lou Brock diving back to first base to beat the throw over to Expos first baseman Tony Perez, 1977

"I don't want to be in your goddamn movies, Brock."

—Pitcher Don Drysdale, when he asked Lou Brock what he was doing with his camera in the dugout and Brock replied that he was taking home movies

Base stealing is an art that requires speed, intuition, and cunning. A good stealer will be on the next base before a befuddled pitcher knows what's happened. Lou Brock, in 19 years with the Chicago Cubs and St. Louis Cardinals, baffled scores of National League pitchers by stealing more bases than any player before him.

Brock grew up in the Mississippi Delta and long pondered how he would make his mark in baseball. After hitting .500 in his sophomore year at Southern University, a historically black college in Baton Rouge, Louisiana, Brock tried out for the Chicago Cubs and was signed as an amateur free agent. He played part of the 1961 season in the minor leagues and was promoted to the major leagues in September.

In 1964, Brock was traded to St. Louis, a deal still considered a textbook example of atrocious front office judgment. Playing left field, he had a sterling inaugural season with the Cards, batting .348, and he was the catalyst in the team's World Series triumph over the New York Yankees, going 9-for-30 (.300), with two doubles, a home run, and five RBI.

Cardinals coach Johnny Keane suggested that Brock develop his base-stealing skills. "Go when it seems

Brock's 1977 St. Louis Cardinals home jersey with his cleats from the 1970s

right to go," Keane advised. To learn where an opposing pitcher was vulnerable, Brock studied film that he shot with an 8mm camera. He led baseball in steals eight times, and he swiped an astonishing seven bases in the 1967 World Series, as the Cardinals beat the Red Sox in seven games. In 1974, he stole a single-season record 118 bases. Three years later, in 1977, while wearing these spikes and this St. Louis Cardinals knit home jersey made by Rawlings, he topped Ty Cobb's career record of 892 steals. Brock retired after the 1979 season with a career total of 938 steals. His records have since been broken by Rickey Henderson, who stole 130 bases in 1982 and 1,406 in his career, but Brock remains second all-time in both categories.

Because of his integrity and character, Brock was named winner of the Roberto Clemente Award in March 1975 and the Lou Gehrig Memorial Award in 1977. A year later, the National League announced that its annual stolen-base leader would receive the Lou Brock Award, making Brock the first active player to have an award named after him. The Cardinals retired his number 20 the following year, and in 1985 he was enshrined in Cooperstown.

JOURNEY FROM GATÚN TO COOPERSTOWN

ROD CAREW 1978 Minnesota Twins Road Jersey

Players from the first half of the twentieth century recall, with varying degrees of fondness, their memories of traveling from city to city aboard a train. Yet if ever a player was uniquely qualified to speak about riding the rails, it would be Rodney Cline Carew. He may be the only Hall of Famer born on one. Carew was named in honor of Dr. Rodney Cline, the man who delivered him when Carew's Panamanian mother went into labor aboard a segregated train passing through the Panama Canal Zone town of Gatún on October 1, 1945.

Carew's journey to Cooperstown began when, at 14, he moved with his mother and brother to New York. Carew attended George Washington High School and worked as a stock clerk in a grocery store. In 1964, he joined the New York Cavaliers, a sandlot baseball team from the Bronx Federation League. Monroe Katz, whose son Steve also played for the Cavaliers, was a bird-dog scout (a scout's scout) for the Minnesota Twins. After watching Carew spray a series of line drives, he passed word of the young talent to Herb Stein, a New York–area scout for the Twins. "Stein told me that I had a pair of wrists that exploded with the pitch," Carew said. "He said he liked the way I could hit an inside pitch to left field. Unusual for a left-handed batter." After three seasons in the minors (1964–66), Carew reached the show in 1967, and he was an All-Star every year but his last, 1985.

The uniforms of the 1970s, the heart of Carew's career, were sleek, form-fitting double knits in myriad colors that had more in common with the polyester leisure suits of the day than with their wool flannel predecessors. Powder blue was in full swing, as with this double-knit product from Wilson, a 1978 Minnesota Twins road jersey worn by Carew. During the 1970s, Carew scratched out base hits in record numbers, winning American League batting titles from 1972 to 1975 and in 1977 and 1978. He also batted above .330 in the four years of the decade that he failed to lead the league in hitting. With his 1972–75 title streak, Carew became only the second player (the first was Ty Cobb) to lead the major leagues in batting average for three consecutive seasons. Carew's .388 batting average in 1977 was the highest since Ted Williams had hit .388 in 1957. In tribute to their star's performance, the Minnesota Twins placed a statue of Carew, in a comfortable crouch, his bat barrel held parallel to the ground, outside Gate 29 at Target Field.

At the end of the decade, Carew was traded to the California Angels. The Yankees had expressed early interest, but that deal fell apart. Yankees owner George Steinbrenner said that Carew "doesn't understand the privilege of playing for the New York Yankees in the greatest city in the world and has stated that New York would not be his first choice and that he'd be more comfortable somewhere else."

Carew closed his career with the Angels in 1985. At 40, he retired after failing to receive any acceptable offers as a free agent. Unbeknownst to Carew and his peers, major league owners were in collusion to reduce or eliminate offers to free agents in order to drive down the prices that players could command. Nine years later, Carew would be awarded $782,000 in damages for lost income.

Carew ended his playing career with 3,053 hits and a .328 batting average. Although best known for his feats on the baseball diamond, Carew was also a force in the community. In 1975, he received the Order of Vasco Núñez de Balboa, which is given to an individual who best displays distinguished diplomatic services and contributions to international relations with other states. Established in Panama in 1941, it is that country's highest award, and Carew was the first athlete to receive it. In 1977, he was the recipient of the Roberto Clemente Award, which is bestowed annually on the player who best exemplifies the game on and off the field. "Fans everywhere are aware of Rod Carew's magic with a baseball bat," said commissioner Bowie Kuhn when he made the presentation. "Carew's magic, however, doesn't stop with his excellence on the diamond. His many charitable activities in the Minneapolis–St. Paul area, especially with youngsters, make him an outstanding choice."

In 1991, the long voyage from the Canal Zone ran its course when Carew sailed into the Hall of Fame, the first player from Panama to be enshrined there.

"If God had him no balls and two strikes, he'd still get a hit."

—Steve Palermo, American League umpire (1977–91)

MIDWEST ROYALTY

GEORGE BRETT 1980 Kansas City Royals Road Uniform

George Brett watching a hit fly during his .390 season, 1980

stocker and feeder market, and the nationally known American Royal parade and pageant," Porte wrote. The American Royal is a festive event featuring livestock shows, horse shows, rodeos, and a championship barbeque competition held annually in Kansas City since 1899. In 1971, the Royals produced their first winning season, with a second-place finish under manager Bob Lemon. Two seasons later, the Royals adopted their iconic "powder blue" road uniforms and moved from Municipal Stadium to the brand-new Royals Stadium (now known as Kauffman Stadium). The franchise had great momentum. All they needed was a poster child. They finally found their man in George Brett.

Born in Glen Dale, West Virginia, on May 15, 1953, George Howard Brett was the youngest of four sons in a baseball-enthralled family. One brother, Ken, pitched in the 1967 World Series for the Boston Red Sox, while brothers John and Bobby played in the minor leagues. George hoped to follow in the path of his three older brothers, and, after he graduated in 1971 from El Segundo High School, outside Los Angeles, the Kansas City Royals selected him in the second round of the MLB draft.

After spending 1972 and most of the 1973 season in the minors, Brett made his big-league debut on August 2, 1973, and he finished the season with five hits in 40 at-bats in 13 games. He became the Royals' starting third baseman in 1974 but struggled at the plate until Charlie Lau, the Royals' batting coach, straightened him out. Lau taught Brett to protect the entire plate and fixed weaknesses in Brett's swing that pitchers were exploiting. Brett finished the year with a .282 batting average in 113 games.

D espite its regal-sounding name, the Royals were not named after any king, queen or monarchial cause. In 1968 the team held a public contest to name the team, which received more than 17,000 entries. The winner was Sanford Porte, a bridge engineer from the suburb of Overland Park. "Kansas City's new baseball team should be called the Royals because of Missouri's billion-dollar livestock income, Kansas City's position as the nation's leading

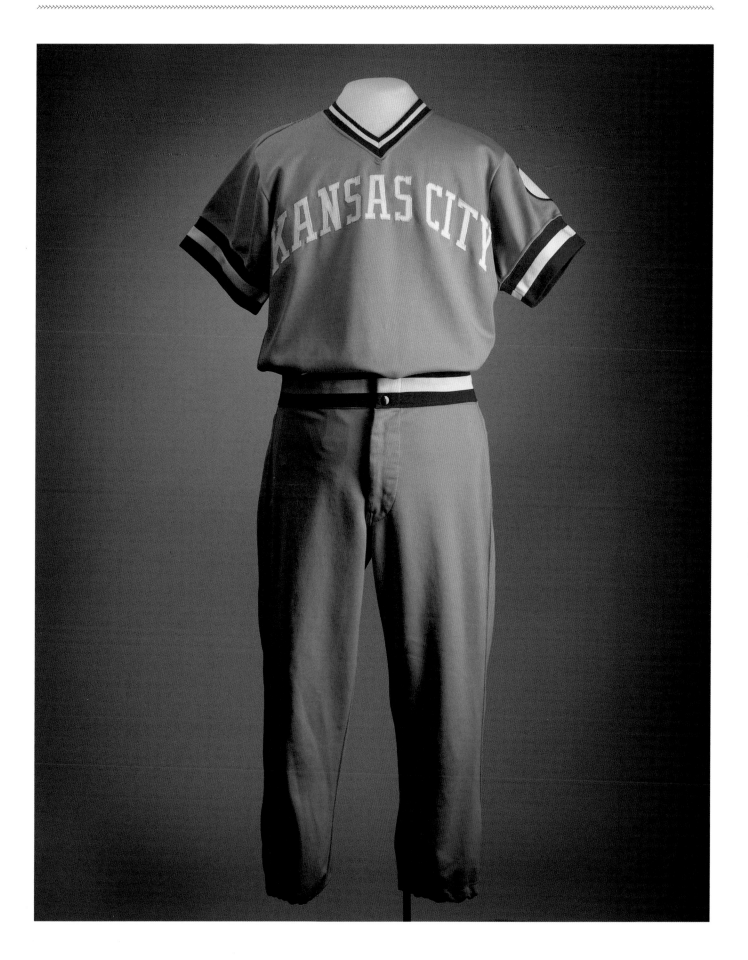

Brett surpassed the .300 mark for the first time in 1975, hitting .308 and leading the American League in hits and triples. The following year, he won his first batting title with a .333 average. In 1979, he finished third in AL MVP voting and became the sixth player in league history to have at least 20 doubles, triples, and homers in one season (42, 20, and 23). He batted .329, with an on-base percentage of .376 and a slugging percentage of .563.

King George thrilled Royals fans for 21 seasons, from 1973 to 1993. He retired as one of only four players (the others are Hank Aaron, Willie Mays, and Stan Musial) in major league history with a career batting average higher than .300 (.305), more than 300 home runs (317), and more than 3,000 base hits (3,154). While Brett is famous for his "pine tar" bat tirade in 1983, it was his performance during the 1980 season that solidified his position as one of the greatest hitters in the game.

"Greatness," as defined for a major league hitter, is something of a statistical oddity in professional sports. If an NBA player makes 30 percent of his shots, he won't be in the league for long. An NFL quarterback who completes 30 percent of his passes better have a solid running attack. But the major league batter who hits safely in 30 percent of plate appearances is a candidate for Cooperstown. In 1980, George Brett flirted with hitting .400 for the season, an accomplishment the major leagues had not seen since Ted Williams hit .406 in 1941.

Yet Brett was slow out of the gate in 1980. He went zero for six against the Oakland Athletics on May 21, and his average for the season was a subpar .247. The Elias Sports Bureau calculated that the odds of a lifetime .300 hitter ending the season with a .400 average were one quadrillion, nine hundred trillion to one. Hitters tend to cool off at the plate as temperatures heat up in July and August, but not George Brett. After missing a month, from June 10 to July 10, because of injuries, he hit .494 (42 for 85) in 21 games in July, lifting his average for the season to .390. The month of August came and went and Brett was sitting at .403 with five weeks to go. Even on the road, fans turned out in droves to catch a glimpse of what they hoped was history in the making. When they did, they saw Brett in this royal blue V-neck pullover uniform manufactured by Wilson (page 245 and opposite).

In early September, Brett suffered a wrist injury and missed nine games. On September 19, his average was an even .400, but a 4-for-27 slump lowered his average to .384 by month's end. Brett ended the 1980 regular season with a major league–leading .390 average—third behind Tony Gwynn's .394 in 1994 and Ted Williams's all-time record of .406 in 1941—but his season was far from over. As if the regular season had been a harbinger, Brett led the Royals to their first

"KC's Caught World Series Fever '80" pin-back button, 1980

AL pennant. They swept the Yankees in the three-game playoffs, which was sweet revenge because the Yankees had knocked Kansas City out of the postseason in 1976, 1977, and 1978. In Game 3, Brett crushed a home run into the third deck of Yankee Stadium off Yankees closer Goose Gossage.

For the first time in franchise history, the Kansas City Royals were in the World Series, where they would face the Philadelphia Phillies, a team that had not appeared in the Fall Classic since 1950. A buzz filled the air. Neither ball club had won a World Series—the last time two clubs with no Fall Classic victories met for the title was in 1920, when the Cleveland Indians beat the Brooklyn Dodgers in seven games. This was also the first time that baseball's championship was played entirely on Astroturf. During the Series, Brett made headlines when he left Game 2 in the sixth inning because of hemorrhoid pain. After minor surgery, he returned and hit a home run in Game 3 as the Royals won in 10 innings, 4–3. After the game, Brett famously quipped, "My problems are all behind me." Although he hit .375 for the Series, the Phillies won in six games. Brett was crowned the 1980 American League Most Valuable Player.

In 1999, Brett was elected to the Hall of Fame with what was then the fourth-highest voting percentage in baseball history (98.2 percent), trailing only Tom Seaver, Nolan Ryan, and Ty Cobb. In 2007, Cal Ripken Jr. passed Brett with 98.5 percent of the vote. The Royals retired Brett's number 5 on April 7, 1994, only the second number retired in team history. In 2006, Brett was voted Kansas City's "Hometown Hero" by fans, one of the few players to receive more than 400,000 votes. "King" George Brett was not only one of the greatest hitters in baseball history—he was true-blue Midwest royalty.

Back view, Brett's 1980 Kansas City Royals road uniform

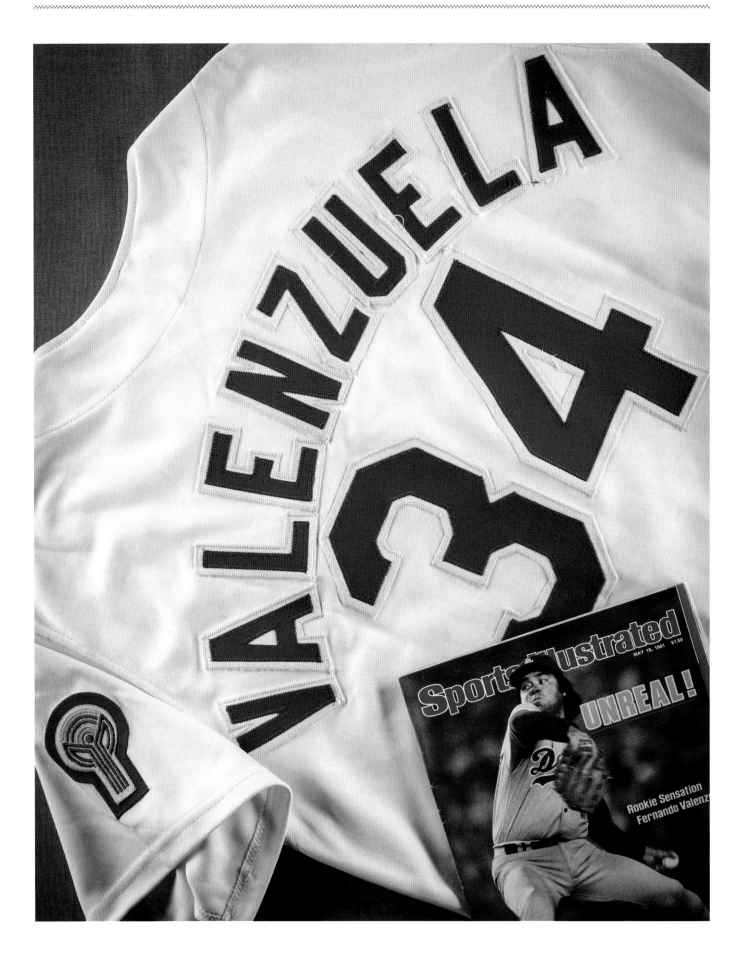

FERNANDOMANIA!

FERNANDO VALENZUELA 1981 Los Angeles Dodgers Home Jersey

Recall *Bull Durham*. The irreverent 1988 film about minor league ball? Carolina League femme fatale Annie Savoy instructs pitcher Ebby Calvin "Nuke" LaLoosh to "breathe through your eyelids," so he starts looking at the sky as he winds up. His skyward windup inevitably drew comparisons to that of real-life Dodgers pitcher Fernando Valenzuela, another sensation of the 1980s.

The Dodgers were already a solid ball club when they called up the genial and portly rookie from Navojoa, Mexico, in September 1980, and little did anyone realize that the team now had a blockbuster in the making. At the start of the 1981 season, Valenzuela was slated to be the Dodgers' number-three starter, but he was given the ball on Opening Day after scheduled starter Jerry Reuss was injured. With Valenzuela's five-hit shutout of the defending division champion Houston Astros, "Fernandomania" was launched.

In his first eight starts, he bagged eight victories (seven complete games and five shutouts) and allowed a miserly four earned runs in 72 innings. At season's end, he became the first player to win Rookie of the Year and Cy Young Awards in the same season. In Cy Young voting, he topped the great Tom Seaver, 70 votes to 67. Valenzuela also outpitched Seaver in almost every category, including innings pitched (192–166), complete games (11–6), shutouts (8–1), strikeouts (180–87), and ERA (2.48–2.54). To round it out, Valenzuela took home the Silver Slugger award as the best hitter at his position. Postseason, he won games in the Division and League Championship Series, and, in Game 3 of the World Series against the Yankees, he threw a gut-wrenching 147 pitches to eke out a 5–4 victory. That win launched the Dodgers' four-game winning streak to the World Series championship.

Valenzuela became a focus of national fascination. Fans came out in droves to Dodgers games at home and on the road. Eleven of his twelve starts at Dodger Stadium in 1981 were sellouts. On the road, he drew 13,000 more fans than other Dodgers starters did in his first two years. "I truly believe that there is no other player in major league history who created more new fans than Fernando Valenzuela," said Jaime Jarrín, the Dodgers Hall of Fame Spanish-language broadcaster. "Fernando turned so many people from Mexico, Central America, [and] South America into fans. He created interest in baseball among people who did not care about baseball." Latino fans from all parts of California and throughout the world had found a new hero.

Los Angeles celebrated its bicentennial in 1981, and the Dodgers marked the event with a commemorative patch on the left sleeve of their jerseys—Valenzuela wore the one featured here (opposite) throughout the 1981 season. The patch depicts an angel, arms extended, with various colors radiating from it, representing the diverse cultural heritage of the City of Angels. Although similar to the Dodgers jersey that debuted in Brooklyn in 1952, the 1981 version was manufactured by the Mizuno Corporation of Osaka, Japan, and supplied by the West Coast firm W. A. Goodman & Sons.

Baseball, always a game of nicknames, labeled Valenzuela as "El Toro" (the Bull). It was well deserved. Dodgers manager Tommy Lasorda said, "He never got rattled and he never looked at the bullpen. When I went out to get him,...he never wanted to come out." The 1986 season was the Bull's apex, his first and only 20-win season. Released by the Dodgers after the 1990 season, he bounced around professional ball until 1997, when he finished with five winless games for the St. Louis Cardinals.

Dodgers owner Walter O'Malley had once longed to tap Southern California's growing Latino market by finding a Mexican Sandy Koufax. He never pulled it off, and he died a year before Valenzuela joined the Dodgers. Yet El Toro, with his eyes to the sky, would've exceeded even O'Malley's wildest dreams.

A copy of the May 18, 1981 *Sports Illustrated* issue atop Valenzuela's 1981 Los Angeles Dodgers home jersey

HEART, SOUL, AND MIND

MIKE SCHMIDT 1981 Philadelphia Phillies Road Jersey

If ever a ballplayer put his heart and soul into the game with the passion that Van Gogh devoted to his art, that player would be Philadelphia Phillies third baseman Mike Schmidt. Fortunately, unlike Van Gogh, Schmidt never lost his mind.

In the 13 seasons from 1974 to 1986, Schmidt led the National League in home runs eight times and won 10 Gold Gloves, demonstrating a rare combination of power at the plate and strong defense. And, like many great artists, he often saved his best performances for when they counted most. On October 3, 1980, the Phillies went into Montreal tied with the Expos for first place in the NL East. With a sacrifice fly in the first inning and a solo home run in the sixth, Schmidt led the Phillies to a 2–1 victory and the division lead. A day later, again against the Expos, he hit his 48th home run of the season in the 11th inning, giving the Phillies a 6–4 victory and the division crown. His home-run total that year topped the National League by 13 and set a team record (breaking his own mark of 45 from a year earlier) that would stand until 2006, when first baseman and NL MVP Ryan Howard hit 58. Coupled with a league-leading 121 RBI, Schmidt was the clear choice for that season's NL Most Valuable Player award. In the 1980 World Series, Schmidt hit two homers and drove in seven runs as the Phillies beat the Kansas City Royals in six games, delivering Philadelphia its first Fall Classic triumph in franchise history.

But Schmidt's greatest season may have been the strike-shortened 1981 campaign, when he led the NL in home runs, runs scored, RBI, total bases, and walks. In addition, he posted career highs for batting average (.316), on-base percentage (.435), and slugging average (.644) and earned the NL's MVP award for the second consecutive year. Not only did Schmidt's play set him head and shoulders above his peers, but his Adonis-like torso was perfectly captured by the tapered, powder-blue, zipper-front, size 46 Wilson road jersey featured here. Phillies teammate Pete Rose once said, "To have his body, I'd trade him mine, my wife's, and I'd throw in some cash."

> "I put my heart and my soul into my work, and have lost my mind in the process"
>
> —Vincent van Gogh

Batting and fielding prowess aside, Schmidt also possessed an intimate sense of himself, his skills, and what he owed the fans and the game. On May 29, 1989, after 18 seasons with the Phillies, Schmidt called a press conference to announce he was leaving the game. Fighting back tears, Schmidt said, "Over the years of my career, I've set high standards for myself as a player. I've always said that when I don't feel I can perform to those standards, that's when it would be time to retire." He walked away from more than $500,000 in salary that year because he felt he no longer was the Mike Schmidt whom fans were paying to see. He never lost his respect for the game—his mind was always in it. Fans across the country replied in kind, voting Schmidt to the National League All-Star Team for the 12th time. The Phillies retired his number the following year, and in its January 29, 1990, issue, the *Sporting News* named Schmidt the "Player of the Decade" for the 1980s.

"If you could equate the amount of time and effort put mentally and physically into succeeding on the baseball field and measured it by the dirt on your uniform, mine would have been black," Schmidt once said. In the 35 years since he wore this blue knit jersey, the dirt has faded. But Mike Schmidt's passionate approach to the game has remained eternal.

Mike Schmidt connecting against the Pittsburgh Pirates at Three Rivers Stadium, May 1981

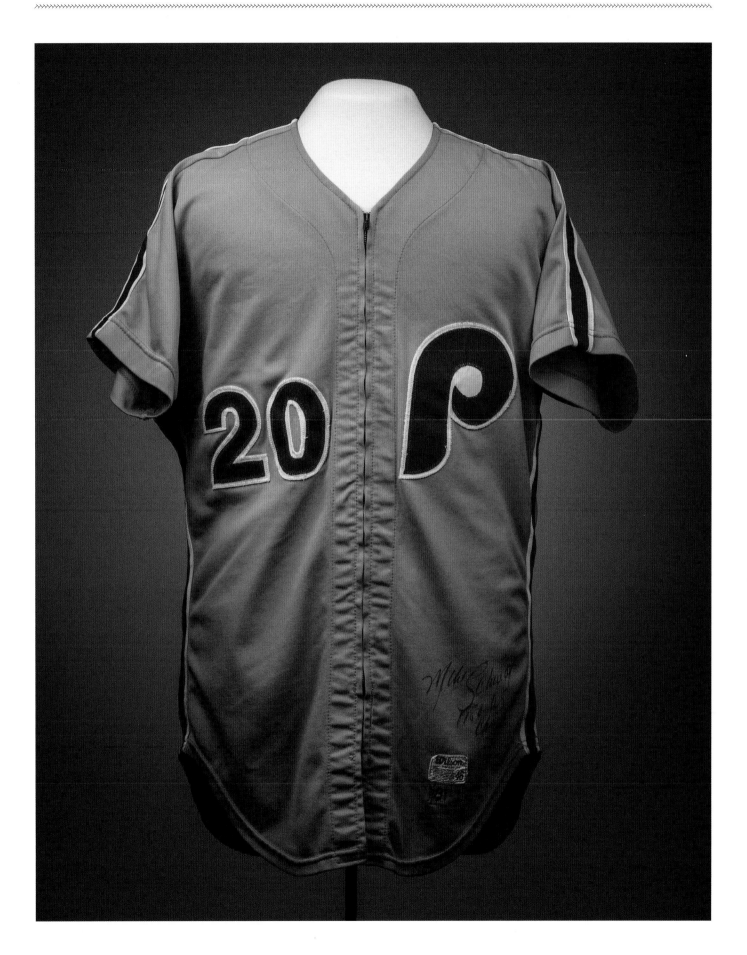

THE IRON MAN

CAL RIPKEN JR. 1984 Baltimore Orioles Road Jersey

Cal Ripken celebrating with Baltimore fans after playing his 2,131st consecutive game, breaking Lou Gehrig's record, September 6, 1995

Anyone who plays baseball long enough is almost certain to enter that dark period known as "the slump," when the bat fails to connect with the ball and numbers slide. Back at the turn of the twentieth century, playing for the Cincinnati Reds and the Brooklyn Dodgers, catcher Bill Bergen went to bat 46 times before he got a hit. His lifetime batting average: .170. Frank Robinson, now enshrined in the Hall of Fame, had one of the greatest rookie seasons in baseball history with the Cincinnati Reds. But an 0-for-20 slump in his second season left Robinson wondering whether he would ever hit a baseball again. And Mark Reynolds struck out more than 200 times in each of three seasons (2008 to 2010) with the Arizona Diamondbacks. After his mother chided him for whiffing so often, Reynolds said, "Mom, it's not that easy."

Calvin Edwin "Cal" Ripken Jr. would sympathize with all these players. He was drafted out of high school in 1978 in the second round by the Baltimore Orioles. He played shortstop and third base in the minors, was a utility infielder when he was called to the Orioles in 1981, and was named Baltimore's starting third basemen in 1982. That year was key for several reasons. He suffered a slump to start the season and was batting just .118 on May 1. He broke out of the slump after receiving advice from Reggie Jackson: "Just know what you know you can do, not what everybody else tells you to do." Next, he sat out the second game of a doubleheader on May 29. That was the last game he would miss until 1998, a 16-year streak that would extend to 2,632 consecutive games, a major league baseball record that may never be topped. And on July 1, Ripken moved to shortstop, where he remained until the final five years of his career.

Ripken was an unlikely shortstop. While most who play the position are small, lithe, and lightning-fast, Ripken was six foot four, weighed 225 pounds, and lacked speed. But he possessed authority and nothing got by him. After earning American League Rookie of the Year honors in 1982, he was named MVP in 1983, hitting .318 with 27 home runs. He led the Orioles with 211 hits and led the league with 121 runs scored. He also was named to the All-Star Team for the first of 19 times, and he led the Orioles past the Philadelphia Phillies in what was known as the I-95 World Series, so called for the interstate that runs the 100-odd miles between the two cities.

The next year, Ripken donned the knit Orioles road jersey pictured here (page 253), the shoulder patch commemorating the team's 30th year in Baltimore (the team had been franchised as the St. Louis Browns). Ripken signed a $1 million contract that year, his salary matching that of Houston Astros pitcher Nolan Ryan, who had hit the $1 million mark four years earlier. Ripken earned his pay by belting 27 home runs, scoring 103 runs, and batting .304. He also made 583 assists, a league record.

And so it went. Ripken played every inning of every game in 1985 and again in 1986. In 1987, Ripken's father, Cal Ripken Sr., replaced Earl Weaver as the Orioles' manager. On September 14, with the Orioles trailing Toronto, 17–3, Ripken sat out half the eighth and ninth innings, ending his streak of consecutive innings at 8,243. The previous longest run of 5,152 consecutive innings had been set from 1885 to 1890.

With the exception of the 1989 season, when the Orioles battled the Toronto Blue Jays for the AL East title, Baltimore suffered a steady decline from 1984 to 1991. When the 1990 season opened, Ripken had played 1,271 consecutive games. Early on, he was stellar in the field but struggled with the bat. Hitting just .200 for the year when he stepped to the plate during a game on June 12, Ripken was booed by fans at Baltimore's Memorial Stadium. That game was number 1,308 in a row for Ripken, and only Lou Gehrig, who played 2,130 consecutive games from 1925 to 1939, played more without a day off.

To snap his slump, Ripken tried positive thinking. He tried visualizing success. He listened to well-meaning advisors. He thought about sitting out a few games, telling *Philadelphia Inquirer* writer Dave Caldwell, "I've actually considered more rest from time to time." Ripken finally snapped his hitting slump in 1992 and later realized that he had been thinking so hard that he psyched himself out.

Ripken emerged from his troubles at the plate just as the Orioles moved into their new ballpark. Appropriately, it was Ripken who batted last at Memorial Stadium in 1991 and first at the new Camden Yards to start the 1992 season. The Orioles finished third in the AL East in 1992 and 1993 before the players' strike of 1994 and early 1995 pushed the pause button on Ripken's effort. Baseball resumed play in April 1995, and on September 6, Ripken played in his 2,131st game in a row to break Gehrig's all-time record. Fans who had booed him a few years before now cheered for 22 minutes as Ripken circled the ballpark, stopping to shake hands with fans up and down the rails. It was a stunning, astonishing, utterly satisfying moment for baseball fans everywhere. With characteristic modesty, Ripken put his accomplishment in the larger context of history: "It wasn't me, personally, that people were celebrating," he said. "It was an attachment to a feeling about baseball that goes back to its history." The game was broadcast by ESPN, and it ranks as one of baseball's most-watched games. President Bill Clinton and Vice President Al Gore attended, and Clinton sat with ESPN commentators and called Ripken's fourth-inning home run. A poll of fans by MLB.com ranked the game the "Most Memorable Moment" in MLB history, topping Gehrig's farewell speech in 1939 and the 1947 game in which Jackie Robinson broke baseball's color barrier. One of the balls from the game, signed by the four umpires, is shown opposite.

The Orioles fell to the New York Yankees in the American League Championship Series in 1996, and a year later lost to Cleveland in the AL Championship Series. On September 20, 1998, after playing 2,632 games in a row stretching 16 seasons, Ripken sat out against the New York Yankees. Three years later, following the 2001 season, Ripken played his final game at Camden Yards and retired. Inducted into the Baseball Hall of Fame in 2007, Cal Ripken's name has become a byword for a work ethic that consists of showing up and doing your best. Former Secretary of State Condoleezza Rice appointed Ripken to the position of special envoy for sport, praising him as one who symbolized the ideals of "hard work and diligence and the willingness to really put it all on the line every day." Ripken has reflected on this theme in many of the 30 or so books he has written, including *Parenting Young Athletes the Ripken Way*, in which he encourages adults to allow their children to enjoy playing what is, after all, a game.

Above all, Ripken demonstrated how the game was meant to be played. Joe Torre summed it up best when he said, "Cal is a bridge, maybe the last bridge, back to the way the game was played. Hitting home runs and all that other good stuff is not enough. It's how you handle yourself in all the good times and bad times that matters....Being a star is not enough. He showed us how to be more."

"Lou [Gehrig] has monstrous numbers and was like Babe Ruth. How was it possible to compare him to me?"

—Cal Ripken Jr.

Official American League ball used in Cal Ripken's 2,131st consecutive game

BO KNOWS

BO JACKSON 1993 Chicago White Sox Home Jersey

Bo Jackson rounding the bases against the New York Yankees, April 9, 1993

A fox knows many things, but a hedgehog one important thing." So wrote the Greek poet Archilochus some 2,700 years ago. By that philosophy, Bo Jackson is clearly a fox, one that draws from a variety of experiences. Jackson's talents were displayed not only in football and baseball, but also in the Nike "Bo Knows" advertising campaign that aired in 1989 and 1990. "Bo knows cricket!" the campaign extolled. "Bo knows surfing!" "Bo knows guitar!" Though, as a fellow Bo—Bo Diddley— admonished, he really didn't know guitar, at least not until he taught himself to play.

Born in 1962 in Bessemer, Alabama, Vincent Edward "Bo" Jackson grew up to become a multisport athlete who was big, strong, and exceptionally fast. In 1982, he was selected by the New York Yankees in the second round of the draft but chose to go to Auburn University, where he starred as an outfielder in baseball

and a running back on the football team. He won the Heisman Trophy in 1985 as the best college football player in the country. In 1986, he was drafted by the NFL's Tampa Bay Buccaneers but decided to play baseball for the Kansas City Royals, which had drafted him in the fourth round. That team had defeated the St. Louis Cardinals in the World Series the year before and was full of top-rate players. Jackson was sent to the farm club, the Memphis Chicks, for seasoning.

Jackson was called up to the major league team in September 1986, after 53 games in Memphis. In his fifth game with the Royals, he borrowed a bat from fellow Alabaman Willie Wilson and smacked a pitch 475 feet to left-center field, then the longest home run ever hit at Royals Stadium. He spent the first five years in the majors with the Royals (1986–90), racking up four 20-home-run seasons. The 1989 season was Jackson's career high point. He belted 32 homers and had 105

RBI and he was named the Most Valuable Player in the All-Star Game, where he became only the second player to hit a home run and steal a base in the same game (the first was Willie Mays). In 1990, Jackson crushed home runs in four consecutive at-bats and performed his "wall run," when he chased down a fly ball and snagged it near the wall. Rather than smack into the wall, Jackson ran up it at full speed, took a few steps parallel to the ground, then pushed off and landed upright on the ground, ball in glove.

Jackson had also reached a four-year agreement with the NFL's Oakland Raiders in 1987 to join the team at the end of the baseball season. That year, he played in 116 games for the Royals and seven for the Raiders, becoming the first athlete to play games in the same year in two professional sports. He was also the first two-sport All-Star. At six foot one and 230 pounds, Jackson was not only big but also fast enough to qualify for the NCAA championships as a sprinter. His time of 4.13 seconds in the 40-yard dash for scouts before the 1986 NFL draft remains controversial because it is almost too fast to be believed.

In 1991, at the height of the "Bo Knows" campaign, events caught up with Jackson. The hip injury that he suffered in football in a January 1991 playoff game limited his playing time in baseball. The Royals put him on the disabled list but balked at paying his salary, which was roughly the equivalent of $4 million in today's dollars. The Royals released Jackson in 1991, and he quickly signed with the Chicago White Sox. He played 23 games in Chicago in 1991 and sat out the 1992 season after doctors replaced his hip with an artificial joint. While wearing this size 48 knit home jersey manufactured by Russell Athletic (page 257), he played most of the 1993 season and was awarded Comeback Player of the Year. The White Sox lost in the American League Championship Series that season to the Toronto Blue Jays in six games.

Jackson played baseball for only eight seasons, and he sat out many games because of injuries. He had a career batting average of .250 and hit 141 home runs. He played so well during one game against the New York Yankees in 1989 that the Big Apple crowd gave him a standing ovation. The 1989 season was also his best on

Chicago White Sox after their World Series win, October 26, 2005

"Baseball and football are very different games. In a way, both of them are easy. Football is easy if you're crazy as hell. Baseball is easy if you've got patience. They'd both be easier for me if I were a little more crazy and a little more patient."

—Bo Jackson

Bo Jackson throwing out the ceremonial first pitch before the White Sox take on the Houston Astros in Game 2 of the World Series at U.S. Cellular Field, October 23, 2005

the football field, as he rushed for 950 yards and scored four touchdowns. Jackson played 38 games in four seasons with the Raiders, rushing for 2,782 yards and averaging 5.6 yards per carry.

Even at the height of his career and the "Bo Knows" campaign, Jackson carried himself modestly. "I'm just another player, you know?" he protested before a press corps eager to make him a legend. Meanwhile, Jackson continued to pull off magnificent feats, hitting home runs, stealing bases, and showing off his arm by throwing out runners at home from the warning track in left field. In 1995, one year after he retired from baseball, he returned to Auburn and earned his Bachelor of Science

degree, carrying out a promise to his mother. Said George Brett, Jackson's fellow Royal: "This is not a normal guy."

In his day, Bo Jackson was ranked with basketball legend Michael Jordan as the greatest athlete in the world. The marketing industry maintains that the "Bo Knows" campaign remains one of the most successful advertising drives in history. And it may have been a matter of luck that Bo Jackson's magic rubbed off on the White Sox when they chose him to throw the first pitch before Game 2 of the 2005 World Series. The Sox routed the Houston Astros that day, then swept the Fall Classic, breaking a nine-decade-long dry spell. Yes, Bo knows baseball.

THE BIG UNIT

RANDY JOHNSON 1997 Seattle Mariners Road Jersey

Randy Johnson on the mound in 1997, where his six-foot-ten frame made him an intimidating sight

"[Johnson] was so tall, it looked like he was delivering the ball from Little League distance. It was very uncomfortable, especially for a left-handed hitter. You never looked forward to facing him."

—George Brett

Ever since childhood, Randall David Johnson was destined to throw heat. He hurled fastballs against the side of his family's house until the nails came loose, and as a senior in high school he pitched a perfect game. He later pitched three seasons at the University of Southern California before he was drafted by the Montreal Expos in 1985. The 6-foot-10 southpaw made his big league debut on September 15, 1988, and during batting practice that year, the 5-foot-8 Tim Raines ran into Johnson and said, "You're a big unit." The nickname stuck.

Johnson was traded to the Seattle Mariners in 1989 and a year later threw the Mariners' first no-hitter, blanking Detroit 2–0. Johnson struggled with control early in his career and led the American League in walks in 1990, 1991, and 1992. But his approach to the game changed after his father, Bud Johnson, died on Christmas Day 1992. "From that day on, I got a lot more strength and determination to be the best player I could be," said Johnson. "What my dad went through [as a police officer and security guard] was pressure. That was life and death. This is a game."

Johnson's performance took off. He led the American League in strikeouts all four years from 1992 through 1995. In 1993, he fanned 308 batters, the first of six seasons that he topped 300 strikeouts in a season. He won his first Cy Young Award in 1995, had back surgery in 1996, and made a full comeback in 1997 while wearing the Seattle Mariners knit road jersey shown here. The jersey features a patch commemorating the Mariners' 20th anniversary in the American League and a patch celebrating the 50th anniversary of Jackie Robinson breaking the color barrier in 1947 (see page 284 in the Compendium).

In 1997, Johnson posted a 20–4 record, 2.28 ERA, and 291 strikeouts, including two 19-strikeout games. Johnson was traded to the Houston Astros in 1998, then was taken by the Arizona Diamondbacks expansion team in 1999, and he again won the Cy Young Award. On May 18, 2004, the 40-year-old Johnson became the oldest pitcher to notch a perfect game when he beat the Atlanta Braves, 2–0.

Johnson retired after the 2009 season. In 22-major-league seasons, his record was 303–166 with a 3.29 ERA. He struck out 4,875 batters, second all-time to Nolan Ryan's 5,714, and threw 37 shutouts. In 2015, Johnson was elected to the National Baseball Hall of Fame in his first year of eligibility.

"The last three innings, that's when you really think about it. You can't help feel the emotion of the crowd. I can feel my heart thumping through my uniform."

—David Cone

PERFECT

DAVID CONE 1999 New York Yankees Home Jersey

Only two sports make reference to the "perfect game": bowling and baseball. To achieve a perfect game in bowling, the bowler must knock down all 10 pins each time he rolls the ball. In baseball, the perfect game is one of minimums. A pitcher must face the minimum number of batters (27) without allowing a single batter to reach base. In 135 years of major league baseball history, only 23 pitchers have thrown a perfect game. And only one time, in Game 6 of the 1956 World Series, was a perfecto thrown in the postseason. In that game, Yankees right-hander Don Larsen set down 27 consecutive Brooklyn Dodgers en route to etching his name into the annals of baseball lore.

July 18, 1999: Before an interleague game against the Montreal Expos at Yankee Stadium, the Yankees staged Yogi Berra Day to honor their legendary catcher. During the ceremony, Larsen was called to the field to join Berra, his perfect-game batterymate from 43 years earlier. Larsen threw out the ceremonial first pitch to Berra, and this was expected to be the day's highlight. The Expos were 22½ games out of first place, and only 42,000 fans had turned out to watch the game under cloudy skies and temperatures approaching 100 degrees.

At 1:35 p.m., 36-year-old right-hander David Cone took the bump for the Yankees and proceeded to retire Wilton Guerrero, Terry Jones, and Rondell White, in order. In the bottom of the second, the Yankees pushed five runs across the plate. Through three innings, Cone did not allow an Expo to reach base. During a 35-minute rain delay in the bottom of the third, Cone played catch in the bowels of the stadium with Yankee batboy

Luis "Squeegee" Castillo to stay loose. When the game resumed, Cone continued to send Expo batters back to the dugout, one after the other.

By the middle innings, fans were locked on the plate appearance of every Expo batter, and "no-hitter traditions" began to surface in the dugout. With the exception of teammate Chili Davis, Yankee players and personnel stopped talking to Cone. When Cone went to the clubhouse after the sixth inning to change his undershirt (a midgame ritual), even the clubhouse boys vacated the area.

Cone was in the zone. Yankee radio announcer Michael Kay said, "His stuff was almost like Wiffle-ball stuff." But as the game entered the late innings, Cone was hardly cool on the inside. "I keep using this expression, 'I could feel my hair growing,'" Cone said. "My head was on fire. You're so anxious to get it done, but at the same time you're fighting just to contain yourself to keep a sense of rhythm and tempo going. But you're still so anxious just to make the one pitch that's gonna get this thing over with."

In the ninth inning, Cone struck out Chris Widger, and Ryan McGuire hit a fly ball to left field that Ricky Ledee caught in blinding sunlight. The game ended with an Orlando Cabrera pop foul to third baseman Scott Brosius. As if at center court at Wimbledon, Cone dropped to his knees like Roger Federer in exhaustion and exaltation. He had done it, an 88-pitch, 10-strikeout gem, which the Yankees won, 6–0. David Cone's perfection in pinstripes is reflected here in the 1999 New York Yankees home jersey that he wore, along with one of the balls that he used, on that special day.

Official American League baseball and home jersey from Cone's perfect game on July 18, 1999

WASH IN
WARM WATER
MILD SOAP

SET
I
1956

SLOWLY AT
M TEMPERATURE

WASH IN LUKEWARM WATER,
100°F. WITH MILD SOAP,
DO NOT USE BLEACH. DO
NOT TUMBLE OR USE
AUTOMATIC DRYER.

MacGregor
SET
I
1964
MADE IN U.S.A.

son
42

STRUCTIONS
KE WARM WATER
H NEUTRAL SOAP
USE BLEACHING

T DRY IN AUTOMATIC

WILSON SPORTING GOODS CO

MADE IN U.S.A.

1965

COMPENDIUM

In late April 2016, a three-page handwritten manuscript went up for auction. It sold, and quickly, for $3.26 million, one of the highest sums ever paid for a piece of sports memorabilia. Those three pages, dating to 1857, mark the gathering of representatives from 14 teams in New York, and they enshrine from that meeting the first formal rules of the game we now call baseball, establishing such conventions as nine players to a side, nine innings to a game, and 90 feet from base to base.

Baseball is a game of people, of course: although most of the tens of millions who have played it over the centuries have not risen to the fame of Babe Ruth, Stan Musial, Roberto Clemente, Jackie Robinson, and other heroes of the field, they have all become part of a great river that traverses our nation's history—for baseball is a game that is much more than a game, as every aficionado knows. It is a game of rules and conventions, as those three pages and the inches-thick modern rulebook illustrate. It is a game of nuance and trivia, rewarding encyclopedic study of its history. And it is emphatically a game of things: balls, bats, cleats, caps, jerseys.

The compendium that follows summarizes these manifold components: people, times, and things. Its entries, from "3D" to "Zig-Zag Stitch," give special pride of place to the uniforms that players have worn over the years, from the heavy outfits of the Deadball Era of the modern game's early years to the ultralightweight fabrics sported by players taking the field in our own time. From wool to flannel and satin to space-age synthetics, those uniforms, more than any other artifact of baseball, chart the evolution of America's pastime.

With changing styles and fabrics came changes to the laundry and care instructions for uniforms.

3D lettering for the 1970 Indians, 1940 Browns, and 1956 Senators (top to bottom)

3D: *Short for* three-dimensional; *descriptive term applied to alphanumeric font style employed by various major league clubs over the years. The combination of layering and offsetting of fabrics creates the 3D effect.* Such uniforms are certainly attention getters, and memorable 3D-lettered jerseys are worn by the St. Louis Browns in their only appearance in the World Series (1944), by the Washington Senators in the movie and stage productions of *Damn Yankees* (1958), and by Cleveland Indians catcher Ray Fosse when he had his iconic collision with Cincinnati Reds hometown hero Pete Rose at the plate to end the 1970 All-Star Game in Cincinnati, Ohio.

1925: *Year in which the National League celebrated its 50th anniversary.* To mark the event, National League teams wore a five-inch chenille embroidered patch in the shape of a baseball. This was the first time an entire league had worn a common commemorative patch. Even in black-and-white photos, it is possible to discern that this patch was produced with at least two variations: blue background with yellow lettering and yellow background with blue lettering. The Pittsburgh Pirates regular season uniforms featured this patch worn on the sleeve, but images from the 1925 World Series show National League Pirate players with the patch on the chest of their home

1969 anniversary patch

1925 National League Golden Jubilee patch

uniforms, confirming that the Pirates ordered new uniforms for the 1925 World Series. This patch design was so popular that it made a reappearance in the 1990s with the advent of Turn Back the Clock games. **(SEE TURN BACK THE CLOCK UNIFORM)**

1951: *Year of formally recognized league anniversaries: the 75th anniversary of the National League and the 50th anniversary of the American League.* To commemorate these anniversaries, special patches were produced and worn by each league during the regular season. The patches were not present on the 1951 World Series uniforms of either the New York Giants or the New York Yankees. In some instances, images of major league clubs from spring training 1952 continue to show these patches. Finding the National League version presents far more of a challenge to collectors than locating one of the American League offerings, perhaps due to the nondescript design of the National League offering. Once the patch was removed from the jersey, there was almost nothing about it that would indicate what the patch was or how it had been worn. As a result, there may have been a higher chance of someone discarding the patch as time passed. **(SEE PAGE 158)**

1969: *Year in which major league baseball celebrated its 100th anniversary.* To mark this occasion, uniforms of a majority of major league teams featured a rectangular tricolor patch showing the silhouette of a player prepared to swing. Notable exceptions included the Pittsburgh Pirates home and road vests, the Seattle Pilots home uniforms, and the Padres road uniforms, which instead featured a patch commemorating the 200th anniversary of the founding of the City of San Diego.

1973: *Year by which all major league teams had transitioned to knit uniforms.* For much of the twentieth century, baseball uniforms were made of wool flannel or a wool-cotton blend. The Pittsburgh Pirates were the first team to

DID YOU KNOW...

The uniforms worn in the 1934 All-Star Game featured cloth numbers on the back that corresponded to a player's position in the batting order. The numbers were added after fans complained that the 1933 All-Star Game was confusing to follow because American League players wore their own uniforms while the National League squad donned an event-specific ensemble.

Patches worn by various Major League Baseball teams in 1976

switch to synthetic knit uniforms, in 1970, while the Montreal Expos, Kansas City Royals, and New York Yankees were the final teams to change to cooler, lighter, more durable knits. This year was also the first year that a stadium was celebrated on a uniform. Although the Astrodome had been displayed on patches worn by the 1966 Houston Astros, the 1973 Yankees marked the 50th anniversary of Yankee Stadium with a commemorative sleeve patch.

1976: *Year that featured the simultaneous celebrations of the American Bicentennial, the 100th anniversary of the National League, the Massachusetts Bicentennial, and the Summer Olympics in Montreal.* For those with an affinity for uniform patches, 1976 is your year. All National League teams except the Montreal Expos wore a patch to commemorate the centennial of the National League. Because Montreal was also hosting the Olympics, Expos uniforms featured a

patch with the five interlocking Olympic rings and an upward extension forming a letter *M* for Montreal. Several teams adopted a second element. For example, the Chicago Cubs wore an additional patch to celebrate their 1876 National League membership (they were called the White Stockings at the time) and the fact that the National League was founded in Chicago. The Philadelphia Phillies opted for a local touch with a patch of the Liberty Bell. And the New York Mets wore an armband to mark the passing of original team owner Joan Payson and manager Casey Stengel. In the American League, the Oakland Athletics wore their own version of the Liberty Bell patch. The Cleveland Indians wore a "Spirit of '76" patch, and the Detroit Tigers wore a patch to celebrate the 200th anniversary of the founding of Detroit. The Boston Red Sox carried over their Massachusetts Bicentennial patch from 1975 for portions of the 1976 season. They also

wore an armband to honor club owner Tom Yawkey, who died July 9, 1976. The Texas Rangers wore a state patch with "1776–1976" on it. They would keep the state patch a few more years but drop the bicentennial dates.

All-Star Game Uniform: *Uniform specifically ordered for or altered for use in the All-Star Game.* The inaugural 1933 game saw the National League outfitted in special road uniforms manufactured by Spalding with the words "National League" across the chest in athletic felt. Following this event, teams would wear their respective home or road uniforms depending on the league affiliation of the hosting city. In 1976, the National League All-Stars posed for pregame shots wearing special nineteenth-century-style pillbox caps, but the players wore their regular season caps during the game. In 1978, the San Diego Padres wore a patch to showcase their city's hosting of the event, but the patches were not worn by other National League players during the game. This trend held true with the teams hosting All-Star Games in 1979 (Seattle), 1980 (Los Angeles), 1982 (Montreal), 1983 (Chicago, AL), 1984 (San Francisco), 1986 (Houston), and 1987 (Oakland). Not until the 1988 game, hosted by the Cincinnati Reds, were patches worn by all players participating in the midsummer classic.

Alteration: *Change made to a uniform post-manufacturer that serves a functional purpose. Such changes include cutting sleeves, removing portions of a collar, shortening the tail, or taking in the garment for sizing. Alterations also may include adding items such as patches or armbands or changing a number during the season.* Uniforms are work garments worn by skilled artisans plying their trade. Players and teams have long altered uniforms either to make them more practical or to prolong their use and wear. This practice was more common during the flannel era because teams were more frugal and because later knit uniforms were designed to be more form fitting. These alterations frequently involved the sleeves or the area around the neck. Upon moving from New York to the windswept outfields of San Francisco's Candlestick Park, Giants Hall of Fame outfielder Willie Mays had his loose-fitting flannel pants tapered from the knee to the ankle.

Athletic Felt: *Fabric used for lettering and numbering during much of the flannel era.* Typically made from a wool-blend fabric, athletic felt can be found with or without a thin layer of backing material, depending on the vintage. When this fabric is affixed to a garment with a straight or "in-line"/"running" stitch, the backing material can be observed. In older uniforms with this style of stitching, the backing should show signs of aging, such as discoloration or cracking. The absence of such signs may indicate a modern restoration.

Willie Mays running the bases in altered form-fitting flannel pants

Athletic felt

Aged and cracked athletic felt backing

founding of the game, as determined by the Mills Commission. This was the first common patch worn by American and National League teams in the same season. The patch was based on the design of the official centennial insignia developed in 1938 by Marjori Bennett of New York. The patch featured the image of a player completing his swing set against a field of four red and three white alternating stripes, which signified balls and strikes. Superimposed on this field of stripes was the outline of a baseball diamond and a baseball. The patch was produced with a number of variations, the most notable being the orientation of the batter.

Batboy: *Generic term used to describe team personnel tasked with the job of organizing and maintaining a team's uniforms, bats, and equipment.* Over the years, batboys have worn uniforms ranging from discarded players' uniforms to ones ordered and annotated with tagging or lettering/numbering to reflect issuance and use by a batboy. During the 1940s, the St. Louis Cardinals and Browns shared the use of Sportsman Park and the services of batboy Robert Scanlon. When both St. Louis teams ended up in the 1944 World Series, Scanlon had more than a full-time job on his hands. To fulfill his requirements to both clubs, Scanlon worked for the "designated" home team for each contest.

Batting-Practice/Warm-Up Jersey: *Garment worn by players during pregame activities.* The Chicago White Sox introduced the use of a warm-up jersey in 1972 when the team switched to knit jerseys. Other clubs wore them sparingly during the 1970s, but by the mid-1980s, batting-practice jerseys had become a

Batboy

Barnstorming Uniform: *Uniform worn during postseason exhibition series, often called barnstorming tours. In many instances, this was the major league uniform that a player wore during a previous season. In other cases, special uniforms were supplied for the events.* The word *barnstorming* appears to have originated during the time when barns served as places to gather for political or theatrical events. The term also applied to pilots in the post–World War I era, because barns were located in rural areas where planes could land and paying passengers could be taken up for flights. With respect to baseball uniforms, the

most widely recognized examples are probably the uniforms donned by players during the 1927–28 exhibition series between Babe Ruth's "Bustin' Babes" and Lou Gehrig's "Larrupin' Lou's." While "Bustin'" likely refers to Ruth's prodigious home runs, "Larrupin'" likely derives from the Dutch word *larpen*, which means "to slap or thrash," or from a colloquial definition of *larrupin*, which means "exceedingly good to the taste."

Baseball Centennial Patch: *Patch worn at various levels of organized baseball (major, minor, Negro Leagues) in 1939 to commemorate the 100th anniversary of the*

DID YOU KNOW...

In 1914, the Base Ball Players Fraternity reached an agreement with the owners so that "every club shall furnish each player with two complete uniforms, exclusive of shoes. The player shall make a deposit of $30 therefore, which shall be returned to him at the end of the season or the termination of his contract, upon the surrender of the uniforms by him to the club. The words 'complete uniforms' shall be construed to mean two pairs of trousers, two shirts, two belts, two caps, stockings as required, and a coat or sweater." The players were still responsible for uniform cleaning and upkeep.

mainstay for most teams. From 1977 to 1983, the Pittsburgh Pirates wore yellow-and-black warm-ups to complement their multicolored uniforms. In rare cases, batting-practice jerseys found their way onto the field of play, most pointedly when Pete Rose wore his pregame warm-up during the 1979 All-Star Game. In 1982, Majestic Athletic began producing batting-practice/warm-up jerseys for the major leagues.

Birds on the Bat: *Popular name of the historic and decorative design on the jerseys of St. Louis Cardinals uniforms.* The design was the brainchild of Cardinals general manager Branch Rickey, who was inspired by red paper cutouts of cardinals used as decorations on white tablecloths at a church dinner. The cutouts were designed by Allie May Schmidt, and Rickey hired her father, commercial artist Edward H. Schmidt, to create the first generation of the logo that appeared on the front of Cardinals jerseys in 1922. Since that time, the design has undergone many modifications, ranging from the size and orientation of the bird to the color of the bat on which it rests to more subtle details, such as moving the tail feathers from the front of the bat to behind it. In 1956, the Cardinals donned home and road versions of a uniform that featured the name "Cardinals" in script font cut from wool-blend athletic felt instead of an embroidered logo. This uniform's left sleeve featured an embroidered bird that was swinging a bat with all the authority of Stan "the Man" Musial. Frank Lane, the team's new general manager, justified the design change by stating, "We took the bird insignia off to make the Cardinals' uniforms lighter; those insignias were backed up by canvas. I wanted a light uniform because of the hot summers we have in St. Louis."

Bleeding/Color Transfer: *Stains on a uniform from the transfer of color from one fabric to another.* These stains are often found on the inside collar or gusset where the jersey comes into contact with a colored undergarment. Stains may also surround lettering and numbering if laundry instructions were not followed.

St. Louis Cardinals jerseys from 1943, 1951, and 1965 (left to right)

Bob Sullivan's patch

For example, colors may have bled when garments with wool-blend felt were laundered instead of dry cleaned, or when early knit uniforms were laundered in warm or hot water instead of the recommended cold water.

Bob "Sully" Sullivan: *Milwaukee Brewers equipment manager from 1971 to 1985.* Although the New York Yankees marked the passing of legendary clubhouse man Pete Sheehy in 1985 with the traditional sleeve armband, the 1986 Milwaukee Brewers wore the first named patch in honor of a clubhouse person. The patch featured the name "Sully" and was worn on home and road uniforms.

Brooks Robinson Sporting Goods Company: *Business enterprise of the Baltimore Orioles Hall of Fame third baseman Brooks Robinson.* Located at 122–124 South Howard Street in Baltimore, the company had a brief but memorable foray as a supplier of major league baseball uniforms, including the burnt-orange uniforms worn sparingly by the Baltimore Orioles in 1971 and 1972. These uniforms may not have been a hit with players or fans, but they are among the rarest style of knit uniforms from the 1970s, with less than a handful of surviving examples known. The Orioles were told to wear these orange outfits for the first time on September 16, 1971; Boog Powell skipped batting practice and Frank Robinson stayed off the field for as long as possible to avoid being seen in them. But Robinson could not hide long, and later that day, wearing the new orange uniform, he hit home run no. 501. However, not every Orioles player disliked the new uniforms. Infielder Chico Salmon told the Associated Press, "It brings out the blackness in me." Other surviving examples of uniforms provided by the company include those donned for Old-Timers' Games in the 1970s.

Brownie the Elf: *Nickname of the mascot adopted by the St. Louis Browns prior to the 1952 season.* The name "Brownie" appears to have its origins in Scottish/English lore and refers to a mythical creature that inhabits homes and performs small tasks to earn its keep. The St. Louis Brownie is one of the more decorative uniform and jacket patches of the 1950s, but the mascot's run was brief. In 1954, the team moved to Baltimore and became the Orioles.

Bumble Bee Uniform: *Nickname given to the striped Pittsburgh Pirates uniforms worn from 1977 to 1979.* Introduced in 1977, the Bumble Bee uniforms were the first major league outfits provided by a foreign manufacturer. Descente, a French-Japanese company known primarily for ski apparel, created the striking jersey and pants, which consisted of a white body with alternating vertical black and yellow stripes. The team also had black uniforms and yellow uniforms, and mixing jerseys and pants gave the team nine possible combinations before cap variations were included. The 1977 Bumble Bee uniforms did not feature players' names on the backs, but the 1978 and 1979 offerings did, possibly because they were sometimes worn on the road. Descente provided the Bumble Bee and black uniforms, while the American company Rawlings, which had supplied the Pirates knits since 1970, furnished the yellow uniforms. It's interesting to note that, at $80, the Descente uniforms were more expensive than the Rawlings offerings. In 1980, the Pirates returned to traditional-looking home uniforms from Rawlings. Wilson manufactured the yellow uniforms, while Descente continued to supply the black uniforms through 1983. Though its seven-year association with major league baseball was brief, Descente left a lasting impression on the fabric of the game.

Cadet Collar: *Also known as a "military collar." Common from 1909 to 1920, it featured a band of fabric sewn to display in an upright or standing manner with a slight gap at the front.* (SEE PAGE 23)

Carry-Over: *Term that describes a uniform used by a major league club during a subsequent season(s); also used to describe the continued use of a manufacturer's tag after a different one has been introduced.* Before baseball uniforms became collectibles, they were essentially a business expense for a major league club. To maximize their

Brownie the Elf

Orange Baltimore Orioles uniforms supplied by Brooks
Robinson Sporting Goods Company

Brooks Robinson

Bumble Bee uniforms

Chain-stitch embroidery

return on investment, clubs commonly kept uniforms in their inventory for multiple seasons. Images from early in the twentieth century show players wearing a mix of uniform styles spanning several seasons, as clubs typically ordered a single home and road uniform for each player. General manager Branch Rickey, in an attempt to keep costs to a minimum for the 1920 St. Louis Cardinals season, is said to have had uniforms from the previous season cleaned and mended instead of ordering new ones. While some teams sold or distributed major league uniforms to minor league teams, others used uniforms from previous seasons to outfit a large number of players for spring training. Still others carried over uniforms from one year to the next at the major league level, a practice that continued well into the 1970s. When Roger Maris broke Babe Ruth's single-season home run record on October 1, 1961, he wore the carry-over Spalding home uniform that he had worn during the 1960 season. This is one of the most significant uniforms in major league history.

Chain-Stitch Embroidery: *Manner of embroidery typically associated with supplemental information, such as player, year, set, or size, that is done with a series of interlocking stitches.* Often one of the most important physical aspects of a uniform is the supplemental information chain-stitched into the garment. This is the primary basis for attributing a jersey to a particular player and season. The stitching requires significant study to ensure that it is original to the jersey. Examination of the jersey using a digital microscope facilitates the evaluation of use and wear. If the chain stitch is period to the garment, we expect to see a difference in the fade of the thread where it enters and exits the protective barrier of the body of the garment. In the top example at left, it appears that the thread used in the chain-stitch embroidery is a salmon color, but examination with a digital microscope reveals the thread's original dark red color.

Charles O. Finley: *Owner of the Kansas City and Oakland Athletics from 1960 through 1980.* Ever the showman and promoter, Charles O. Finley locked horns with the baseball establishment on more than one occasion. Prior to the 1963 season, the rules called for home uniforms to be white and road uniforms to be gray. After Charlie Finley petitioned major league baseball and had the rule changed, he ushered in a gold-and-green look that has been synonymous with the Athletics ever since. Not only were these Wilson-supplied uniforms atypical in color, they were also constructed of heavier durene-cotton fabric. Other innovations in apparel during the Finley era included nicknames on the backs of jerseys and the introduction of white cleats in 1967. Although the color of

the uniforms became a topic of mild conversation, Cleveland Indians manager Joe Adcock objected to the use of white shoes by A's pitchers because he felt they might distract the batter. Adcock filed a protest with then–American League president Joe Cronin on April 11, 1967, but Cronin rejected Adcock's appeal, thus opening the door to other shoe colors.

Chenille Embroidery: *A unique type of embroidery that is not at all similar to traditional embroidery.* Chenille embroidery uses a machine that feeds yarn from the bottom to create a textured surface similar to a carpet. This embroidery does not take place directly on the garment. The designs are instead put onto a background fabric, and the embroidered fabric is then cut and sewn onto the garment. This step is quite similar to the application of a patch.

Chenille embroidery

Cleveland Indians jersey patches from 1975, 1964, and 1947 (left to right)

Connie Mack won nine American League pennants and five World Series titles, was inducted into the Hall of Fame in 1939 while still an active skipper, and lost 3,814 games along the way. Although A's uniforms during Mack's tenure remained consistent and nondescript, the 1950 team commemorated his golden anniversary with appropriately trimmed and colored uniforms that sported a patch to celebrate his longevity in the game.

Contrived: *Term used to describe physical characteristics of a uniform that are intended to convey false impressions of the piece. Examples can include contrived player attribution or contrived use and wear.*

Convex Button: *Button whose surface curves outward. These buttons are typically associated with Cincinnati uniform manufacturer P. Goldsmith & Sons, later MacGregor-Goldsmith and later MacGregor.* Because of their unique style, convex buttons, in particular the two-hole variant, can be used to identify a jersey's manufacturer in period images.

Convex button

Cotton Twill: *Fabric used for lettering and numbering that has an almost "light canvas" look and feel.*

Cotton Whipcord: *Worsted (compactly twisted cotton yarn made from long-staple fibers) fabric with a distinct diagonal rib.*

Danny Thompson: *Major league baseball infielder (1970–76) who played for the Texas Rangers in 1976 and died December 10, 1976, of leukemia.* Players had long commemorated the passing

Chief Wahoo: *Name of the caricature Indian mascot that first appeared as a logo on Cleveland Indians uniforms in 1947.* The image of a Native American first appeared on a Cleveland uniform around 1928. The mascot that became known as Chief Wahoo was designed in 1947; this logo featured a toothy Indian with a large nose, which some collectors refer to as the "hook nose" style. This design was also found on jackets and team promotional material. In 1951, the design was changed to give Chief Wahoo a less prominent nose. This design is similar to the one in use today. From 1954 to 1957, Cleveland's caps featured a smaller version of the chief inside the wishbone C. In 1972, Chief Wahoo was removed from Indians knits, but the chief returned from 1973 to 1978, appearing on a circular sleeve patch, swinging a bat from the right side of the plate. In 1979, the patch reverted to the style introduced in 1951.

Coach's Uniform: *Term used to describe a uniform manufactured for a manager or coach who appeared on the roster for a major league club.* The term is worth mentioning because it has a direct and material bearing on the value of uniforms that may have been worn by a player after his playing days ended. The term also

provides clarification on uniforms that may be identified as "coaches' uniforms" but may actually have been worn by spring training instructors.

Concave Button: *Button whose surface curves inward. These typically have a raised lip or rim.* Button style is always worth noting because different manufacturers used different styles. Collectors should check that buttons on a particular uniform are consistent with period images and with the buttons from a particular manufacturer.

Concave button

Connie Mack: *Manager of the Philadelphia Athletics from 1901 through 1950.* During his 50 years at the helm,

Doc Ellis's 1977 Texas Rangers home jersey with Danny Thompson no. 4 armband

of teammates or team personnel by wearing black armbands. In 1972, teams also began wearing patches bearing a player's number. In tribute to Thompson, the 1977 Rangers combined an armband and a patch bearing Thompson's number (4) on a single piece of fabric. The Thompson tribute is unique in major league history and is a key tool in helping collectors spot fakes of this style.

Deion Sanders: *One of the few athletes to play professional baseball and football at the same time. On October 11, 1992, Sanders played for both the Atlanta Falcons (NFL) and the Atlanta Braves (MLB), becoming the only athlete to play in a professional football and baseball game on the same day.* In 1997, major league baseball commemorated the 50th anniversary of Jackie Robinson's integration of the national pastime with a patch worn on all major league uniforms. Sanders decided to make his tribute to Robinson more personal by wearing his pants cuffed high to display

his stirrups and by trimming his sleeves to make his jersey look like a vest. He said he was inspired to cut the sleeves by an image of Robinson on a recently released Wheaties box. Baseball officials informed Sanders and the Cincinnati Reds that the alterations to the jersey violated league policy on "uniform uniformity." As a sign of team unity, and with the full support of team captain Barry Larkin, the rest of the Cincinnati Reds players altered their uniforms accordingly.

Durene: *Often used as a fabric descriptor, a type of fabric, but probably better used to describe a process of chemically treating cotton-nylon to enhance durability. For a fabric descriptor, consider using durene cotton, durene nylon, or durene cotton-nylon.* Durene's use as a major league fabric was spotty and short-lived. The Chicago Cubs experimented with a rayon-based knit fabric in the 1940s but discarded the idea because of player discomfort and cost. The *Sporting News* reported in 1944 that the change from

flannel to durene cost the Cubs an additional $2,000 per year. In 1956, the Cincinnati Redlegs wore home and road uniforms made of material described as durene, and they continued to use the material in side panels through 1960. The last attempt to incorporate the fabric into a major league uniform was in the 1963 season by Charlie Finley of the Kansas City Athletics. Tests on the 1956 Redlegs and 1963 A's uniforms showed that durene was almost 30 percent heavier and retained 25 percent more heat than flannel.

Extended Organizational Use: *Term used to describe the policy of retaining uniforms for subsequent use at the major*

DID YOU KNOW...

During a road trip to Milwaukee in 1977, thieves stole the Kansas City Royals road uniforms from the clubhouse, so Kansas City wore the Brewers road uniforms during the June 12 game at County Stadium.

Durene fabric (top); traditional wool-blend flannel fabric (bottom)

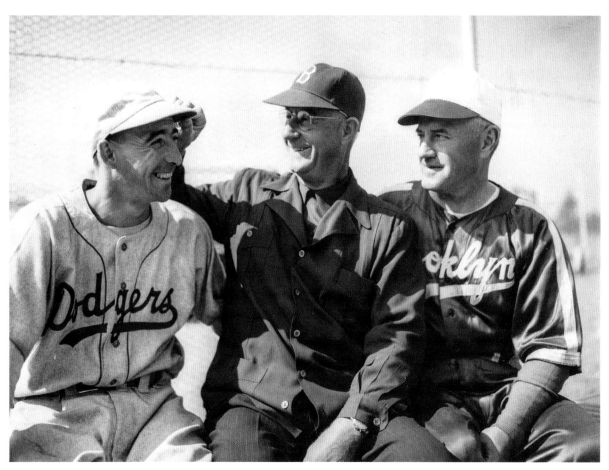

Extended Organizational Use: Dodgers coaching staff wearing night satin uniforms, last worn in 1945, during 1949 spring training

league level or during spring training when demand for on-hand uniforms would exceed availability. Many player number changes, name changes, and other alterations were performed to help teams meet the demand for uniforms. Contrary to what has been stated for years, these changes were not always signs that a uniform had been "sent down to the minors." Often the additional uniforms were needed for spring training because those rosters were larger than regular season rosters. Period photos confirm that players in spring training were outfitted with an amalgamation of uniforms from seasons past. At no time was this practice more obvious than in the years immediately following World War II. Consider the number of players on the Cincinnati Reds spring training roster during and after the war:

1941: *38 rostered players*
1942: *35 rostered players*
1943: *31 rostered players*
1944: *29 rostered players*

1945: *31 rostered players*
1946: *68 rostered players*

Extra Length: *Term used to describe material added to extend the torso length of the jersey in the tail.* The tagged size of a uniform refers to the measurement across the chest. But, as we know, all ball players were not created equal. Although not tagged as such, extra length (greater than that found on a regularly sized product of a manufacturer) can be seen in examples of flannels going back to the 1950s and 1960s. But it is not until the 1980s that we begin to see supplemental tagging in uniforms to denote extra length. Collectors have often taken the presence of these tags on uniforms from the 1980s and 1990s as a sign of authenticity because the tags don't appear in retail offerings. The presence of an extra length tag should not be considered an automatic qualifier because these tags can be found on blank jerseys or added post-manufacturer. When looking at

a jersey with an extra length tag, it is important to verify that extra length is a player characteristic and that the jersey is longer than a similarly sized garment with a standard torso measurement by the same manufacturer.

Eyechart: *Nickname given to San Diego Padres catcher Doug Gwosdz.* If you're reading this book, then there's a high probability you've been asked to read the Snellen Eye Chart at some point in your life. If, from the prescribed distance, you can correctly recite the letters on line 5, PECFD, then you can be said to have at least 20/40 vision. Now, imagine a visiting manager or umpire being handed a lineup card with GWOSDZ written on it. Though Doug Gwosdz was not a player whose power at the plate during his brief major league career (1981–84) would have earned him a slot at number five in the batting order, his name certainly could have earned him that distinction in an ophthalmologist's office.

Supplemental tagging for extra length in both the tail and sleeves

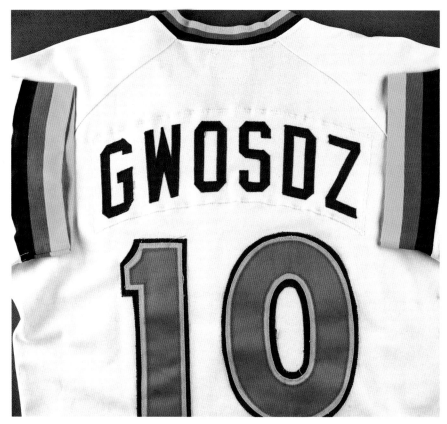

Doug "Eyechart" Gwosdz's San Diego Padres home jersey

Fabric Sample Catalog: *Sample booklet produced by manufacturers for use by their sales force to help potential clients make decisions about product ordering and pricing.* These catalogs are rare and provide insight into the styles, pricing, and fabrics of uniforms. When used to support research and evaluation, they facilitate the assessment of the quality or grade of the garment through comparative analysis of the fabric used for a major league garment and the material of the jersey being offered.

Finishing: *Term used to describe the work performed on the inside of the jersey after the embroidery is complete. This work may include trimming loose threads and cutting or tearing away excess backing.*

Flag Tag: *Small rectangular supplemental tag typically used to denote year of issuance or set number for a particular uniform; provides a reference for inventory control and tracking.* These tags appear to have been introduced by manufacturer

1934 Goldsmith catalog showing top-of-the-line Major League Baseball fabrics

Interior of a 1948 St. Louis Cardinals home jersey

MacGregor-Goldsmith around 1949. They soon became a staple of major league products produced by Rawlings and Spalding as well. The tags have also been used to denote size in a garment.

Flannel: *Generic term used to describe a fabric and type of uniform worn until the early 1970s, when flannel was replaced by knit.*

Flannel Fabric Weight: *Numerical reference to the weight of one yard of an uncut fabric used to manufacture a uniform; typically expressed as eight-ounce, six-ounce, or four-ounce.* It is not uncommon to hear flannel uniforms described as being made from eight-ounce wool flannel. Though partially true, the statement lacks context with respect to time and period. Early in the twentieth century, uniforms were

made of wool and the fabric weight would have been eight ounces. A jersey of this material may have weighed more than 1.5 pounds. Eight-ounce fabric was the standard until the mid-1930s, when some manufacturers offered six-ounce fabric as an option. By the 1940s, six-ounce wool or wool-blend fabric had become common. Following World War II, the use of synthetic fabrics became more prevalent, and in 1952, Rawlings introduced its "Hall of Fame" flannel, a blend of 45 percent wool and 55 percent Dacron. That material broke the six-ounce barrier, coming in at 5.71 ounces per yard. The race was on. By 1956, Wilson was making a 4.5-ounce jersey that was 75 percent wool and 25 percent nylon. During this period, Wilson's made-to-order uniforms still featured pants made from six-ounce fabric, though pants could be made from the lighter fabric if specified. By 1958, Rawlings was back in the lead with four-ounce and six-ounce products. By the early 1960s, MacGregor and Spalding also offered uniform material in these weights, featuring a blend of 60 percent wool and 40 percent nylon. This proportion may have been too light and less durable than

desired. By 1966, Rawlings had crept back up to a five-ounce fabric that was 65 percent acrylic and 35 percent wool. This appears, by weight and composition, to be the fabric used until the end of the 1972 season, when the flannel era ended.

Font: *Term used to describe the type style used for the lettering and/or numbering on a uniform.* Font styles, either alpha or numeric, are often manufacturer or period specific and should be verified with period images when performing imagery analysis on a uniform. Consider the use of McAuliffe products by the New York Yankees in the 1950s. Though McAuliffe was an atypical supplier of uniforms to the team during this period, the 1953 Yankees World Series uniforms featured both diamond point numeric font and a unique logo design for the interlocking *NY*. Period images combined with database examples confirm that these characteristics are not associated with Wilson or Spalding products. The button style excludes MacGregor as the supplier. Yet period uniforms supplied by McAuliffe feature these characteristics. In this instance, font style can be used to verify the accuracy of assigning the uniform to an atypical manufacturer during a specific period of time.

Foxing: *Term used to describe a type of staining that appears as rust-like spots. Fungus or mildew spores growing on or in the fabric typically cause foxing.*

Gusset: *The separate section of fabric in the underarm where the sleeves are joined to the body of the uniform. Gussets strengthen the area, enhance freedom of movement, and provide ventilation; they*

Gusset

can also be found in the crotch area of pants. The 1913 Spalding uniform fabric sample catalog boasts that ventilated gussets would be introduced in all of its major league uniforms that season. Vented gussets remained common until the 1930s, when a cotton-elastic fabric was frequently used. This type of gusset was found intermittently into the 1950s, predominantly in Spalding and Wilson products.

HEALTH Patch: *Worn in 1942 to express support for the Hale America Physical Fitness Program.* According to an article in the February 12, 1942, edition of the *Sporting News*, "Hale America HEALTH shields will be worn on the uniform sleeves of all players and umpires in the major and minor leagues this season in cooperation with the wartime physical fitness program, directed by John B. Kelly, head of the Physical Fitness Division of the Office of Civil Defense, it was announced February 7, by J. G. Taylor Spink, coordinator. Originally, the National League had adopted the Minute Man insignia for uniforms, but in order that the senior major might join the Hale America program, president Ford Frick has instructed all clubs to affix the HEALTH shield to players' uniforms. As their part of the program, manufacturers

have agreed to place the insignia on the uniforms without cost." The HEALTH shield patch was also worn in the Negro Leagues and by some school programs. Although the patch can be found on uniforms after 1942, those uniforms should be considered garments carried over from the 1942 season.

Heat Press-On: *Twill that has glue backing on it so it can be heat pressed onto a garment.*

Houston Colts: *Original name of the 1962 National League expansion team.* To select the name, the team held a contest and fans submitted suggestions. "Houston Colts" was submitted by William F. Neder, a Houston insurance salesman. Neder's proposal was accepted, but the team questioned whether to emblazon its jerseys with a pony or a pistol. The problem was solved when, before the start of the 1962 season, the team changed its name to the Houston Colt .45s, which led to the creation of one of the most striking and prized flannel baseball uniforms in history. Club vice president George Kirksey described the name change in a November 27, 1961, statement: "We felt the combined name made it clear we're talking about guns and not a young horse."

The name and logo would not last long. The Colt .45, the pistol said to have "made all men equal," was manufactured by Colt Firearms, and the company objected to the uncompensated use of its logo and name on team merchandise. In 1965, the team changed its name to the Houston Astros. Prior to the start of the 1965 season, team owner Judge Roy Hofheinz is reported to have ordered all items bearing the Colt .45s logo taken to a local dump and thrown away. Whether or not this story is true, Colt .45s uniforms, caps, and jackets are among the rarest and most desirable collectibles from the 1960s. Collectors should be cautious when buying Colt .45s home jerseys because the design is the same as the design of the jerseys worn by the Moultrie Colt .22s of the Class D Georgia-Florida League. The differences between the uniforms involve the manufacturer, the sleeve style, and the font style of the numbers on the back of the jersey.

In-Line Embroidery: *Appliqué done with a continuous line of single stitches and typically associated with supplemental information such as player, year, set, and size.*

In-line embroidery

1942 Hale America HEALTH patches

Houston Colt .45s collectibles

Ernie Lombardi's 1936 Cincinnati Reds jacket, one-year style

Jacket: *Generic term used to describe the outer garment of a uniform set.* Of all the uniform items (jersey, pants, cap), jackets were issued in the fewest numbers. In the early twentieth century, jacket orders were a mix of sweaters, coats, and traditional jackets. By the 1930s, as sweaters began to fall out of fashion, teams began to order both heavy and light coats. These ranged from thin windbreaker-type garments often worn under the jersey to traditional bench jackets to what are commonly referred to as "bullpen parkas." Images and surviving examples suggest that teams ordered jackets with names and numbers for specific players, and unlabeled jackets for general team use. Surviving examples and period images also strongly suggest that new jackets may not have been ordered each year, likely due to the increasing cost and durability of jackets.

Jackie Robinson: *First African American to play in the major leagues during the modern era.* In 1997, major league baseball honored the 50th anniversary of Jackie Robinson's integration of the modern game with a commemorative patch worn by players in all clubs. In addition, Robinson's no. 42 was retired, though players already wearing the number were permitted to continue wearing it. Below are the last players to wear no. 42 for each club:

Yankees: *Mariano Rivera* (1995–2013)
Mets: *Mo Vaughn* (2002–03)
Twins: *Michael Jackson* (2002)
Tigers: *Jose Lima* (2001–02)
Astros: *Jose Lima* (1997–2001)
Angels: *Mo Vaughn* (1999–2000)
Mariners: *Butch Huskey* (1999)
Indians: *Michael Jackson* (1997–99)
Orioles: *Lenny Webster* (1997–99)
Brewers: *Scott Karl* (1995–99)
Marlins: *Dennis Cook* (1997)
Rangers: *Marc Sagmoen* (1997)

Athletics: *Buddy Groom* (1996–97)
Giants: *Kirk Rueter* (1996–97)
Pirates: *Jason Schmidt* (1996–97)
Royals: *Tom Goodwin* (1995–97)
Reds: *Roger Salkeld* (1996)
White Sox: *Scott Ruffcorn* (1996)
Phillies: *Toby Borland* (1994–96)
Expos: *Kirk Rueter* (1993–96)
Rockies: *Armando Reynoso* (1993–96)
Cardinals: *Jose Olivo* (1995)
Padres: *Pedro Martinez* (1993–94)
Braves: *Armando Reynoso* (1991–92)
Cubs: *Dave Smith* (1991–92)
Blue Jays: *Xavier Hernandez* (1989)
Dodgers: *Ray Lamb* (1969)

Jackie Robinson patch, 1997

Knit: *Also referred to as "double-knit." Generic term used to describe uniforms first manufactured in 1970. The fabric initially contained a blend of cotton and nylon before transitioning to 100 percent synthetic.* The first knit uniforms were produced by Rawlings for the Pittsburgh Pirates when they transitioned from Forbes Field to Three Rivers Stadium in July 1970. The jerseys were a pullover design with a square-cut tail and were made of 60 percent nylon and 40 percent cotton. By 1974, the dominant knit fabric blend was 95 percent polyester and 5 percent nylon. Use of knit fabrics opened the door for form-fitting uniforms and an explosion of color. The use of color became even more important after 1972, when color TV sales first outpaced sales of black-and-white sets in the United States.

Laundry Instructions: *Information found either on a separate tag or as part of a manufacturer's tag that indicates how the garment is to be cleaned and cared for. Because instructions have evolved with the fabric and often vary from manufacturer to manufacturer, laundry tags can help confirm dating and manufacturer attribution during the evaluation process.*

Laundry Pen/Marker: *Ink writing implement used to make handwritten annotations on a uniform. Not in widespread use until the 1950s.* In the case of teams such as the New York Yankees of the 1950s and 1960s, laundry pens and markers were used to denote either the original year of issuance or the year for which the jersey was to be carried forward. In other cases, as with the Cincinnati Reds road uniforms of the early to mid-1970s, annotations on the Wilson tag denote the set of the uniform.

Lon Keller: *Graphic design artist credited with creating the famous New York Yankees bat and top hat logo in 1946.* In baseball circles, certain symbols and logos achieved almost instant and universal recognition. One such example is the interlocking *NY* displayed on the

Laundry instructions

Examples of the iconic Yankees logo by Lon Keller

front of Yankees uniforms since 1936. Another is the "Bronx Bombers" bat and top hat logo created by Lon Keller. This design never appeared on a Yankees jersey, but it was featured on a sleeve patch worn to commemorate the team's 50th anniversary in 1952, and as a sleeve patch for team jackets starting in the 1960s.

Louis IX of France: *Also known as St. Louis the Crusader King; ruled France from AD 1226 to 1270.* In conjunction with the 1904 World's Fair, a large plaster model was created of the Crusader King. Following the event, the model was recast in bronze and presented to the city of St. Louis. This statue would symbolize the city until 1965, when the Gateway Arch was completed. A sleeve patch bearing the image of Louis IX was worn by the St. Louis Browns from 1937 to 1940, the only time in history that a canonized saint, as well as a European

monarch, was featured on a major league uniform. For collectors, finding one of these patches, let alone a jersey with the patch still intact, is nothing short of a royal miracle.

Louis IX jersey patch, ca. 1940

Manufacturer: *Term used to identify the business entity that produced a uniform. The manufacturer is typically confirmed by a label or unique manufacturer's characteristic.*

Manufacturer's Characteristic: *Unique aspect of a uniform that allows it to be associated with a specific manufacturer.*

Manufacturer's Tag: *The label sewn into a uniform that identifies the manufacturer; often confused with supplier or distributor tags.*

DID YOU KNOW...

Brooklyn Dodgers pitcher Dazzy Vance bleached the right sleeve of his undershirt to make it more difficult for batters to pick up the flight of the ball as it left his hand.

Mr. Red: *Unofficial name of the mustachioed mascot of the Cincinnati Reds in the 1950s and 1960s.* While Ted Kluszewski, Wally Post, Gus Bell, and Ed Bailey had the attention of National League pitchers in the mid-1950s, many in America were focused on the "Red Scare," or the threat of communism. In 1954, millions of people watched live TV coverage of the House Un-American Activities Committee's investigation of communist organizations. Due to political concerns, the Reds changed the team nickname to Red Stockings for the 1953 and 1954 seasons and to Redlegs from 1955 to 1958, and then changed back to Reds in 1959. Mr. Red first appeared in the team's yearbook in 1953, was featured as a sleeve patch on the 1955 uniforms, and appeared on road jerseys and jackets in 1956. Mr. Red would make his 15th appearance in the 1967 season, but the logo was replaced in 1968 with a clean-cut, crisply attired version more in keeping with the vision of the team's new general manager, Bob Howsam.

Name in Collar (NIC): *Term or abbreviation often used when a uniform is for sale; refers to the attachment of supplemental player identification in the collar area.* When the name of the player is affixed in the collar area, it is typically done in one of two ways. Each presents its own challenges when a uniform is examined for originality and player attribution.

1. *Direct embroidery:* The player's name is sewn directly into the garment, typically through the front panel or section of fabric in the collar. It must have been done prior to the closure of the collar area, which is when the front and rear panels are sewn together. When looking for signs of contrived application, make sure the stitch line that closes the collar has not been opened and then resewn.

2. *Embroidery on a swatch:* The embroidery is sewn onto a fabric swatch and the swatch is either sewn onto the collar fabric or affixed just below the

collar on the rear panel. When the swatch is sewn directly into the jersey below the collar, the stitch line can be seen when the garment is viewed from the back. When dealing with a jersey constructed in this manner, it is best to confirm this method of appliqué through imagery analysis.

Name in Tail (NIT): *Term or abbreviation often used when a uniform is for sale; refers to the attachment of supplemental player identification to the tail area.* A player's name may be added to the tail through either direct embroidery or embroidery on a swatch that is fastened to the garment.

Collectibles showing Mr. Red, beloved unofficial mayor of Crosley Field in the 1950s and 1960s

Elmer Riddle's 1941 Cincinnati Reds road jersey, with name in collar

George Earnshaw's 1936 St. Louis Cardinals road jersey, with name in tail

Name on Back Removed (NOBR): *Term or abbreviation often used when a uniform is for sale; refers to the identifiable removal of a player's name from the back of the jersey. May have been accomplished either by removal of individual letters or by removal of the material plate to which the letters were attached.* Removing players' names was a common occurrence because uniforms were a consumable business expense for a ball club. Removal of the name allowed the jersey to be reissued to another player. In some instances, as with the Montreal Expos of the late 1970s, teams placed a nameplate over the original lettering instead of removing the name. "Over-plating" was also employed by the Glenn Falls White Sox (Chicago AA affiliate) on the front of the softball-style jerseys they inherited from their parent club in the early 1980s.

Negligee Collar: *Also referred to as a "Western collar"; a wide collar intended to lie flat against the upper portion of the shoulder or neckline.* Common in the late nineteenth and early twentieth centuries and featured briefly on uniforms worn by the Chicago White Sox from 1976 to 1981. (SEE PAGE 15)

New York Mets: *Name given to the New York National League expansion team of 1962; shortened version of the name Metropolitans.* After a four-year drought, the senior circuit returned to Gotham in 1962 in the form of the New York Mets. The team's home uniforms drew heavily on the past, with physical and visual linkages (Dodger blue, Giant orange, Yankee pinstripes) to a time when New York was the Capital of Baseball, as filmmaker Ken Burns described it. Although the Mets did not set the league on fire with stellar play, they still outdrew the more powerful Yankees at the box office during the 1960s. In 1965, the Mets were the only New York team to don a patch commerating the New York World's Fair, unlike in 1938, when all three New York clubs (Dodgers, Giants, and Yankees) wore a World's Fair patch.

Old-Timers' Day/Reunion Uniform: *Phrase used to describe a uniform manufactured for use at a specific commemorative event; examples include Old-Timers' Games and reunions associated with past events of prominence, such as the 20th anniversary of a World Championship.* For the earliest of these

1962 New York Mets home jersey reused through 1965 by evidence of the World's Fair patch on the left sleeve

events, players often wore uniforms from their playing days or contemporary uniforms provided by the clubs. By the late 1950s, teams such as the St. Louis Cardinals had begun outfitting players with replica uniforms. In 1959 and 1964, the Cardinals ordered uniforms from Rawlings in period style to commemorate the 25th and 30th anniversaries of the 1934 World Championship team. Around 1977, the Yankees began ordering uniforms for these events instead of having players wear uniforms retained from their playing days. Debbie Tymon, Yankees vice president of marketing and organizer of events for 10 years, told the *New York Times* on July 9, 2004, that each player "is asked for his clothing size, so that a new uniform is in his locker when he arrives at the Stadium. All players get to keep their spiffy new pinstriped togs, which means that perennial invitees like Whitey Ford and Moose Skowron may be harboring years'

worth of golden years uniforms. Why a new one each year? I don't want to hear at 12:30 that day that someone has forgotten their uniforms....Marty Appel ran the Old-Timers' Days for the Yankees from 1968 to 1977. They were not sponsored, and the Yankees always played another team. I remember calling the Braves and saying, 'We're having Lew Burdette, can we borrow a No. 33 uniform?'"

During the 1970s and 1980s, there were two Old-Timers' series of note: the Equitable Old-Timers' series and the Cracker Jack Old-Timers' series. In the Equitable events, players wore period knits or uniforms of a knit fabric reminiscent of a design from their playing days. In some instances, players in the Equitable wore flannels from their own career or flannels that had been provided to them for similar events after their playing careers had ended. The Cracker Jack Old-Timers'

series was held from 1982 to 1986 in Washington, D.C. National League greats wore road gray and blue, while American League players wore home white and red.

Type I Old-Timers' Uniform: *Uniform produced in the contemporary style and fabric of the team for the event*

Type II Old-Timers' Uniform: *Uniform produced in an older style, in keeping with the event it commemorates*

Type III Old-Timers' Uniform: *Uniform produced for the event without reference to the uniform worn by the player during his playing days*

Cincinnati Reds Old-Timers' Game uniforms, August 17, 1959

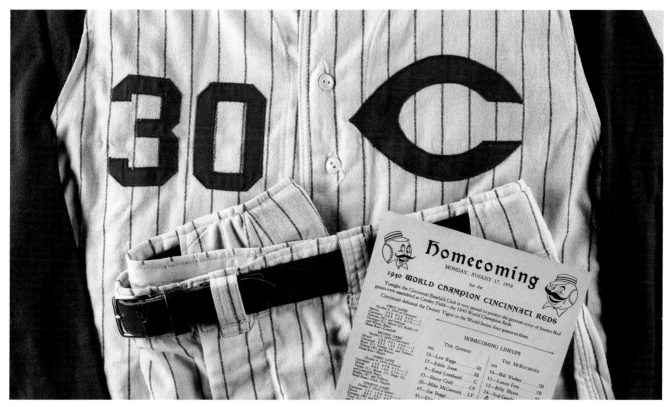

Paul Derringer's Old-Timers' Game uniform and game program, August 17, 1959

Palm Beach: *Trade name used originally by P. Goldsmith & Sons in 1936 to describe a new, lighter fabric with a more open weave. Later used to describe a series of lighter fabrics used for the manufacture of uniforms on a limited basis.* The fact that these uniforms did not catch on was not for lack of trying on the part of the manufacturer. Goldsmith took out advertisements in the *Sporting News* to tout the fabric as a "revolutionary, yet practical improvement." The manufacturer claimed the breathable uniforms would "preserve the vitality of the player during the hot weather months of July, August and September, when every game counts." Palm Beach was used in uniforms worn by the Cincinnati Reds in 1936 and by both the Reds and the Chicago Cubs in 1937. In 1938, both the Reds and the Cubs discarded the material, but Palm Beach headed to New York. According to a newspaper report, the "Dodgers are letting themselves in for it this year; executive Leland Stanford ['Larry'] MacPhail has ordained uniforms of crinkly Palm Beach material for extra hot days...and for the second games of double bills." P. Goldsmith & Sons transitioned into MacGregor-Goldsmith and continued to provide this product line as an alternative. Palm Beach was used to outfit select players of the Brooklyn Dodgers and Cleveland Indians in the late 1940s.

Paul "Daffy" Dean's St. Louis Cardinals Palm Beach jersey, ca. 1935

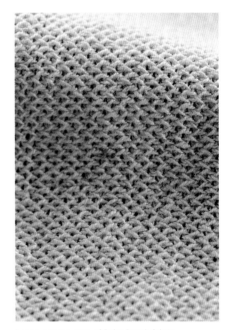

Loose, open weave of Palm Beach fabric

Pinstripes

Placket

Pinstripe: *Decorative striping woven into the fabric of the uniform.* The pinstripe is both an attractive addition and a valuable research and evaluation tool. Over the years, and within years, the width of pinstripes and the space between them have changed. When this size and distance are known, they provide a confirmed scale by which other facets of the jersey may be assessed. The pinstripes also provide a visual grid that can be used to assess the alignment and positioning of lettering and numbering. Because the pinstripe is an integral part of the fabric, it can be evaluated with respect to how it runs, breaks, and aligns at points where various sections of fabric are sewn together, which can help to differentiate uniforms worn by a particular player during a particular season.

Placket: *The opening between fabric sections on the front of a jersey that facilitates ease in donning or removal; also referred to as the "button line."*

Powell Crosley Jr.: *Owner of the Cincinnati Reds from 1934 to 1961.* Powell Crosley Jr. was a successful Cincinnati businessman who, at the urging of Reds general manager Larry MacPhail, purchased the Reds in 1934. The following season, Crosley helped bring night baseball to the major leagues. Crosley's contributions to baseball uniforms did not come until after his death on March 28, 1961. The Reds had adopted a vest-style uniform in 1956 and planned to introduce a new style of vest

DID YOU KNOW...

The Brooklyn Dodgers were the first team to add numbers to the front of their uniform, in 1952. Numbers have since been placed either to the left or the right of the center of the jersey. The lone exception was the 1972 Chicago Cubs road uniform, a pullover jersey on which the number was placed in the center of the chest.

uniform in 1961. When Crosley died a few weeks before the season opener, the Reds opted instead to add a conventional armband to the left side of the vest. Because there are no sleeves on a vest, the Reds attached the armband around the vest's left armhole, a first for major league uniforms. In 1962, the Reds retained the armband on the left side and added an identical band to the right side. This style remained the standard for Reds home and road uniforms through the 1966 season.

Prototype: *Uniform design or product developed to provide a physical reference to guide potential changes in design or manufacturer.* The uniform that a baseball fan sees on the field is the end result of what is often a long process of trial and error. The 1972 Atlanta Braves, for example, considered 16 prototypes when they made the transition from flannels to knits. The Braves worked with Sand-Knit and solicited the opinions of Braves star Hank Aaron and former player Eddie Mathews, who suggested a pullover design with an open, two-button collar for comfort. Prototyping includes both design and materials. In 1952, when Rawlings introduced its lightweight "Hall of Fame" flannel fabric, the company produced four sets of uniforms for local St. Louis Cardinals (Enos Slaughter and Gerald Staley) and Browns (Jim Rivera and Clint Courtney) to evaluate. *Prototype* and *salesman's sample*, though often used interchangeably, have different meanings. (SEE SALESMAN'S SAMPLE)

Pullover: *Term used to describe a jersey that is donned and removed over the head; most prevalent before 1935 and following the introduction of knits in the 1970s.*

Prototype of a 1950 Washington Nationals road jersey

Prototype of a 1961 Cincinnati Reds home jersey

Prototype of a 1956 St. Louis Cardinals road jersey

1954 Chicago White Sox home jersey with raglan sleeves

Ray Kroc's initials on San Diego Padres jerseys

Raglan Sleeve: *Sleeve style constructed in one piece that is joined to and extends outward from the collar of the jersey.* The raglan sleeve is named for Lord Raglan, First Baron Raglan, whose left arm was amputated due to an injury suffered in the 1815 Battle of Waterloo. Raglan's tailor looked for ways to allow Raglan to dress himself and move with ease and comfort. The raglan sleeve provides mobility and flexibility in the arm and shoulder and has remained popular in baseball jerseys.

Ray Kroc: *Owner of the San Diego Padres from 1974 to 1984.* Ray Kroc's name is more commonly associated with the golden arches of McDonalds than with the gold-and-brown uniforms of the Padres. Kroc kept the Padres in San Diego in 1974 when many believed the team was moving to Washington D.C. The passing of numerous club owners had been honored with armbands, but the 1984 Padres became the first major league club to feature a departed owner's initials on uniforms. In another rarity, the Padres continued to wear Kroc's initials (RAK) on their jerseys for the 1985 and 1986 seasons.

Repair: *Most commonly used in its noun form to denote work done to correct damage or condition.* Repairs to uniforms are common. What distinguishes repair from restoration or conservation is time. If the work was performed while the jersey was in use, it is considered a repair. If the work was done after the jersey left team circulation, it is considered a restoration.

Replica: *Uniform or portion of a uniform originally manufactured as a copy or reproduction.* In the early 1980s, Peter Capolino came across approximately 12,000 yards of vintage flannel baseball uniform fabric and the idea of creating replicas of vintage uniforms was born, in the form of the Mitchell & Ness product line. In the early 1990s, hot on the heels of the retro craze, Willabee & Ward teamed with major league baseball to produce a collection of 40 patches and logos that spanned 125 years of professional baseball history. Even though both product lines are of high quality, there are obvious differences between replicas and the originals on which they were modeled.

Restoration: *Effort or work undertaken to restore a uniform, as much as possible, to its original condition or appearance.* Finding pre-1980s uniforms in original condition can be nearly impossible, thanks in large part to the economics of reuse. The older the uniform, the greater the chance it has been altered or damaged. The visual appeal of jerseys means almost everything to some collectors, thus the desire to have them restored. In some cases, the restoration may be as simple as replacing a patch that was removed. In other instances, lettering, logos, and player numbers may be removed before the restoration. Still other restorations may involve conservation work to improve appearance or to stabilize portions of the jersey.

Restorations can be accomplished using either period or contemporary items or fabrics. The latter is most common because of the limited supply of surviving period items. Although uniforms restored with contemporary materials may be an affordable alternative, this type of restoration can have a negative impact on the value of the jersey for some collectors. It is essential that a collector know what to look for to determine whether a jersey has been restored, because this information is not always known or acknowledged at the time of sale or auction.

1. *Know what right looks like:* To know what is correct, you need to reference an original offering. This can come from information garnered from period photographs or comparison to on-hand examples. A study of alphanumeric font styles for the jersey in question is a great place to start. When dealing with patches, collectors should realize that a number of them have been commercially reproduced over the years. Some reproductions are more accurate than others.

2. *Understand the element of time:* If a jersey is said to be "all original," then all aspects of lettering, numbering, patches, and so forth are assumed to have been on the garment for the same length of time, and all areas should show commensurate use and wear.

3. *Look for trace evidence of a previous application:* By and large, this refers to thread remnants found on the patch or jersey. If the patch is a period original offering that has been restored, it is possible that some portion of the thread originally used to affix it to the jersey remains.

Roberto Clemente: *Pittsburgh Pirates Hall of Fame outfielder who died in a plane crash on December 31, 1972, while delivering humanitarian aid to earthquake victims in Nicaragua.* The loss of Roberto

Roberto Clemente no. 21 patch, 1973

Roberto Clemente 25th anniversary patch, 1997

Assorted salesman's sample tags with supplemental tagging denoting fabric content and/or product number

Clemente devastated the Pirate family. When the team turned out for spring training in 1973, players wore a small black ribbon (approximately four inches long and one and a half inches wide) attached loosely to their left sleeves. On March 20, 1973, the Pirates announced that they would honor Clemente in the upcoming season by wearing a circular patch bearing the player's no. 21 on their left sleeves. This was the first time that

a team wore a memorial patch with a player's number. This tribute was worn only at the major league level, so the number of patches issued was limited. It is arguably the rarest patch of the 1970s and one of the rarest overall. In 1997, the Pirates marked the 25th anniversary of Clemente's passing with a patch that featured a silhouette of the player walking away and tipping his cap. This was the first major league patch to feature a player's likeness. The Clemente patch was worn on home uniforms, while road uniforms bore a patch commemorating the 50th anniversary of Jackie Robinson's integration of major league baseball.

Salesman's Sample: *Term used to describe a uniform or uniform-related product issued to create awareness of a manufacturer's uniform line.* One of the more obvious and defining characteristics of a salesman's sample is the information contained on supplemental tagging on the garment. This tagging typically features information related to product number and/or fabric content. Salesman's samples also were frequently produced with the names and numbers of prominent players on them. As a result, a number of these samples have made their way into collections because supplemental tagging was removed and use and wear were added to the garment to deceive collectors into thinking they were acquiring a game-worn jersey of the player in question. Salesman's samples, when properly identified, are helpful in identifying fabric content and price changes over the years.

Satin: *Fabric and term used to describe the special uniforms worn by the Brooklyn Dodgers, Boston Braves, St. Louis Cardinals, and Cincinnati Reds during the 1940s and 1950s.* In 1944, the Brooklyn Dodgers wore uniforms made of "shiny white satin trimmed in royal blue" for 14 home night games and uniforms of a "light shade of

Satin: 1948 Boston Braves home jersey, 1945 Brooklyn Dodgers road jersey, and 1948 Cincinnati Reds cap

1948 Cincinnati Reds satin uniforms

blue with white piping" on the road. The fabric was described at the time as jockey satin, and the team thought it would be more reflective, thus enhancing the experience of night baseball. The Dodgers would keep the home whites through the 1950 season, but the road blues were discarded after 1945, relegated largely to use by coaches in spring training. The Boston Braves joined this fabric fray on May 11, 1946, when they unveiled home white satins in conjunction with their first night game, and they continued

DID YOU KNOW...

During the 1960s, major league clubs commonly sent uniforms to their minor league affiliates for their use. In June 1967, Oneonta Yankees general manager Nick Lambros displayed Mickey Mantle's 1966 Yankees home uniform for local Little Leaguers.

to use the uniforms at home through 1948. That year, the St. Louis Cardinals and Cincinnati Reds also donned satin uniforms, which means that half of the eight-team National League wore satin that season. The problem with satin, from the players' perspective, was that it was too hot.

Saturday Night Specials: *Name given to the maroon uniforms ordered by the Philadelphia Phillies from Rawlings in 1979.* Uniforms often are described as a "rare one-year style," but what can be said about the rarity and value of a "one-game style" uniform? On May 19, 1979, the Philadelphia Phillies were slaughtered 10–5 by the Montreal Expos while wearing their blood-red uniforms for the first time. The response to the togs from players, fans, and photographers was overwhelmingly negative. The next day, team publicity director Larry Shenk announced that the team would continue to wear the "Saturday Night Specials" until it lost two in a row in them. The Phillies then changed their mind and decided not to wait for a second showcase. On May 25, Shenk announced

that the team would discontinue use of the uniforms because they "caused problems for the photographers" and "they ran a bit big, they did not fit the players too well."

Seattle Pilots: *Name of the American League expansion team that played in Seattle for one year (1969); it relocated to Milwaukee and was renamed the Brewers in 1970.* The year 1969 was one for moves: man moved to the moon, the New York Mets moved to a place of prominence in World Series history, and baseball moved to Seattle. The Pilots' name and uniform design were nested in the city's connection with the aviation and maritime industries. During spring training, the Pilots wore generic white and steel-gray Wilson uniforms with the word "Pilots" across the chest in blue. The home (Wilson) and road (Spalding) uniforms created for the regular season featured shades of blue, red, and yellow and were among the most colorful in history. In addition, though most clubs sported the major league baseball 100th anniversary patch, the Pilots wore it only on road uniforms. The team's

transfer to Milwaukee in 1970 was not finalized until just before the start of the season, so the Brewers played their early games in Milwaukee in uniforms designed to be worn in Seattle, as evidenced by the captain's braid on the sleeve ends.

Serged Seam: *An overlocking stitch sewn over the edge of one or two pieces of cloth for edging; commonly used on nameplates on the back of knit jerseys or to attach the lining to the interior collar or placket of a jersey.*

Serged seam

1969 regular season Seattle Pilots cap

1969 regular season Seattle Pilots road jersey

DID YOU KNOW...

On August 31, 1972, the Texas Rangers sold Frank Howard to the Detroit Tigers. He traveled to Oakland the next day for a game against the Athletics. Because his new uniform was not ready, Howard played his first game as a Tiger wearing one of Mickey Lolich's road uniforms, with no. 29 and "Lolich" on the back.

Set Identification: *Physical annotation or tagging on a uniform that identifies a jersey as one particular offering from a uniform order.* Set identification or set tagging has a practical purpose as it relates to inventory control. The first set tags appear to have been introduced by MacGregor-Goldsmith around 1949. They are common on later products from Rawlings and Spalding but rarely are found on Wilson or McAuliffe pieces. These small "flag tags" featured a set number (1 or 2) and a year of issuance. A SET 1 uniform does not necessarily denote an early season issuance or that a SET 2 uniform was one issued later in the season. These numbers refer to the designation within a particular order. If a team obtained its uniforms from more than one manufacturer (and there is evidence of multiple suppliers within the same year), then both uniforms could be identified as Set 1 products by the manufacturers. Additionally, with the increase in the number of uniforms ordered in the late 1960s and 1970s, it is possible to see more than one Set 1 or Set 2 jersey of a particular player during a single season from the same manufacturer. In some instances, handwritten annotations on a manufacturer's label denote set number as well.

Certain manufacturers, including W. A. Goodman & Sons, identified products using alphabetic references, such as Set A, Set B, Set C, or Set P for postseason order.

Set identification for other manufacturers, most notably Wilson, was either incorporated into a swatch or sewn directly into the garment.

As a cautionary note, these year/set tags also can be found in jerseys ordered for use by minor league clubs, so the presence of one in a jersey is not a definitive sign that the garment is a major league offering.

Set-In Sleeve: *Sleeve that is constructed of a separate portion of fabric and "set into" the body of the garment at the shoulder.*

Side Panel: *Separate section of fabric used to join the front and rear panels of a jersey.* This manner of construction made its debut in 1958 with the Cincinnati Reds uniforms provided by MacGregor. The Reds would later abandon the design, but a less pronounced version from Rawlings was incorporated into the vest worn by the Cleveland Indians in the mid- to late 1960s.

Sleeve Extension: *Detachable portion of the jersey that allowed the sleeve to be extended from the elbow down to the wrist; typically associated with uniforms from the early twentieth century.*

Sleeve Length: *Distance in inches from the point where the sleeve meets the gusset to the end of the sleeve cuff.* Sleeve length has changed over time and should be considered a player characteristic. Early in the twentieth century, sleeves commonly ran the length of the arm or featured extra material that could be buttoned onto the sleeve to extend its length. Well into the 1930s, a sleeve length of eight to nine inches that extended to the elbow was common. By the 1940s, sleeve lengths were commonly in the five- to six-inch range. By the 1950s, sleeve lengths showed more variation and, in some instances, were annotated as part of the supplemental tagging on the uniform itself.

Sluggers such as Ted Kluszewski, Ralph Kiner, and Gil Hodges preferred nearly sleeveless jerseys that did not interfere with their swing. If the length of a sleeve is purported to be original, then it should be considered a physical characteristic that is supported by contemporary images.

DID YOU KNOW...

In 1987, the Rawlings Sporting Goods Company was named the official supplier of major league baseball uniforms. While this was the first time in history that a manufacturer had been granted such a marketing concession, it did not mean that all major league teams were required to wear Rawlings uniforms. Both the Yankees and the Red Sox continued to wear Wilson uniforms.

Sleeve extensions. Notice the buttons in the elbow area that enable the extensions to be added or removed from the jersey.

Sleeve length

Soutache: *A narrow or flat decorative braid used on a uniform; most commonly found at the collar, sleeve ends, or running the length of the placket.*

Spikes: *Term used to describe footwear worn by baseball players.* One of the most obvious changes in footwear took place in 1967 when the Kansas City Athletics began wearing white shoes instead of black. In the 1970s, when artificial surfaces began to appear in outdoor stadiums, players modified traditional spikes to accommodate higher surface temperatures and wore plastic-tipped, soccer-style cleats to improve traction. In addition, to complement their new knit uniforms, teams began wearing shoes in a variety of colors: red in St. Louis, blue in Kansas City and Los Angeles, maroon in Philadelphia. The holdout remained the Cincinnati Reds, who were mandated by owner Bob Howsam to continue to wear black shoes. Reds players were even forced to use shoe polish to cover logos from manufacturers such as Adidas and Puma. The only exception for Cincinnati players was footwear worn during All-Star Games. Cincinnati would continue its fashion edict until around 1984, which happened to coincide with the return of Pete Rose and may have been linked to Rose's endorsement contract with Mizuno Sporting Goods.

Spring Training Uniform: *Uniform produced specifically for use and wear during spring training.* Teams routinely wore uniforms from previous seasons in spring training, but some organizations ordered additional uniforms for the preseason workups. Though extra uniforms were necessary because of the larger number of players at the spring sessions, they also served practical purposes. One of the better examples was seen at Dodgertown in Vero Beach,

Blue-and-red collar soutache on a 1947 Philadelphia Phillies home jersey

Spring training uniform

Florida, from the late 1940s through the 1960s. In 1949, for example, the Dodgers ordered three different caps for spring training. Players wore the traditional royal-blue offering with a white *B* for Brooklyn; scouts wore a blue-billed, white-domed cap with no lettering, and injured and incapacitated players sported a solid gray cap.

By 1960, the Dodgers had started issuing separate uniforms for minor league players. The jersey featured a single letter on the left breast (where a number is typically found) to indicate the level and location of the player's current assignment:

A: *Montreal:* AAA, International League
B: *Spokane:* AAA, Pacific Coast League
C: *St. Paul:* AA, American Association
E: *Atlanta:* AA, Southern Association
H: *Macon:* A, South Atlantic League
N: *Green Bay:* B, Indiana-Illinois-Iowa League
S: *Great Falls:* C, Pioneer League
T: *Reno:* C, California League
W: *Kokomo, Panama City, Orlando, and Odessa:* D, various leagues

Stars and Stripes Patch: *Also sometimes referred to as the "War Patch." First appeared in 1943 and was worn through 1945, though not by all clubs in all years;*

continued limited use by the Chicago White Sox and Detroit Tigers in 1946, and last worn at the major league level by the Washington Nationals in 1947.

Stars and Stripes patch

Straight stitch

Straight Stitch: *Also known as an "in-line" or "running" stitch; used to attach letters, numbers, logos, and patches to a jersey; often does not completely close the end of the applied fabric to the jersey.*

Sun Collar: *Style of collar formed by the addition of a small section of fabric that gradually increases in height from the throat to the rear of the jersey; the name is said to come from the protection the collar offered the player from the sun.* The sun collar is associated with the period prior to the early and mid-1930s, but it remained a preference of some older players well past that time. Surviving examples and period photographs document that players frequently cut away these collars as a matter of personal preference.

Supplemental Player Identification (SPI): *Phrase used to describe features added to a jersey that enable attribution to a particular individual.* The most obvious form of SPI is the player number, first added to major league jerseys in 1916 by the Cleveland Indians. The jerseys were used for portions of the 1916 and 1917 campaigns. The St. Louis Cardinals added player numbers in 1923, but this was short-lived. By the mid-1930s, numbers had become a staple at the major league level. In 1937, the Philadelphia Athletics became the last team to add numbers.

As a function of tagging, SPI may consist of the player's name embroidered directly into the garment or embroidered into a fabric swatch that was then sewn to the garment. **(SEE NAME IN COLLAR AND NAME IN TAIL)**

In other instances, SPI is conveyed through a numeric code that includes data elements such as size, year of issuance, and set number.

Sun collar on a St. Louis Browns road jersey, ca. 1926

Various supplemental tags denoting suppliers and distributors

Supplier/Distributor: *Business entity that facilitates the outfitting of a major league club as part of a direct or collaborative production or sales effort; not considered a full-time uniform manufacturer.* Manufacturing a baseball uniform is a significant undertaking and often involves multiple suppliers. For example, the shell may be produced by a major manufacturer while lettering and numbering are provided by a smaller outfit. This arrangement is best seen when the uniforms feature tagging from both entities (M-manufacturer/S-supplier):

1920s St. Louis Cardinals: *Rawlings (M)/ Leacock (S)*

1940s Boston Red Sox: *Spalding (M)/ McAuliffe (S)*

1940s Boston Red Sox: *Wilson (M)/ McAuliffe (S)*

1940s Chicago Cubs: *Wilson (M)/ Halas Sporting Goods (S)*

1940s Detroit Tigers: *Wilson (M)/ Lowe & Campbell (S)*

1940s–1950s Philadelphia Athletics: *MacGregor-Goldsmith (M)/ Mitchell & Ness (S)*

1950s Philadelphia Athletics: *MacGregor (M)/Pearson (S)*

Uniforms provided by McAuliffe to various major league clubs in the 1960s and 1970s followed a different process. Tim McAuliffe did not have capacity to produce product, so he outsourced production to companies such as Stall & Dean of Brockton, Massachusetts, then added his label to the finished product.

Swatch: *Term used to describe a small section of fabric on which supplemental information was sewn prior to being attached to a jersey.*

Swatch

Swiss Embroidery: *Manner of appliqué typically associated with supplemental information such as player, year, set, and size; done with a series of closely placed back-and-forth stitches.*

Tackle Twill: *Generic term denoting a nylon-polyester fabric used for lettering and numbering on uniforms.*

Tail Strap: *Also referred to as a "fat strap." Combination of two elongated sections of fabric and additional openings*

Tail strap

on the button line that enabled the jersey to be secured and prevented it from becoming untucked from the pants. As a common facet of construction, the fat strap was on the way out by the 1930s. In most instances, surviving uniforms show that these straps were cut away by the players as a matter of personal comfort. This is typically seen on a jersey with a section of fabric removed from the lower rear center. Though material was also cut away from the rear tail of the jersey and used to patch pants, a garment originally outfitted with a fat strap would feature, at the bottom of the placket, buttonholes through both layers of the placket.

Team Number Change: *Phrase used to describe a period alteration involving the change of a uniform number after a jersey was issued to a different player than originally intended; also may involve an alteration made when a player changed his assigned roster number.*

DID YOU KNOW...
Road uniforms of the flannel era were almost always gray, though teams could specify the shade of gray when they placed their orders. Predominant shades of gray were as follows:

Yale Gray: Light brown hue
Steel Gray: Neutral hue
Pearl Gray: Light blue hue

CUT SHOWS
Style of sleeve, ½ length.
Style of cap, any style.
Style of Stockings, calf stripe. No. 3, footless.
Style of shirt No. 6EC, New York, with silk edging cord.

Sample Shows Color No. A3P

Also Furnished in The Following Colors:

No. A1Y
Plain Yale Grey

No. A2P
Pearl Grey with Broad Navy Stripe

No. A3X
Plain Steel Grey

Ted Turner: *Flamboyant owner of the Atlanta Braves in the late 1970s.* Turner looked to make a big splash when he came to the helm in 1976, so he took a page from the Charlie Finley playbook and added player nicknames to the backs of jerseys. Memorable monikers included:

Cannon: *Jimmy Wynn* (previously nicknamed the Toy Cannon)

Channel: *Andy Messersmith,* because he wore no. 17 and Channel 17 was Turner's WTCG TV station

Chopper: *Dave May*

Gallo: *Roger Moret*

Heavy: *Earl Williams*

Howdy: *Darrell Evans,* because he was said to resemble the TV character Howdy Doody

J. Bird: *Jerry Royster*

Knucksie: *Phil Neikro*

Nort: *Darrel Chaney,* because he was said to resemble Ed Norton of *The Honeymooners*

Poco: *Biff Pocoroba*

Row: *Roland Office*

Taco: *Marty Perez*

Tequila Sunrise: *One of the many colloquial names used to describe the multicolored knit jerseys first worn by the Houston Astros in 1975.* When the Houston Astros decided to order knit uniforms for the 1975 season, they dropped Wilson and placed their order with Sand-Knit. The Rainbow Wonders, as the uniforms were also known, were so unique that the same design was worn at home and on the road. Not only was the design revolutionary, but the uniforms also could have been considered the "coolest" of the day because the jerseys were manufactured from a knit fabric that weighed about 30 percent less than the Wilson knits of years past. Initial reaction to the uniforms was mixed. Dodgers relief pitcher Charlie Hough said they resembled "Hawaiian softball uniforms," while others felt the Astros looked like "something that has dropped off a rainbow."

Touring Uniform: *Uniform worn during special exhibition games; term is often associated with uniforms manufactured to be worn during a publicized event.* Without a doubt, these are some of the more attractive and rare uniforms that exist. Examples include those produced for:

1913: *World Tour* (New York and Chicago)

1927–28: *Ruth's Bustin' Babes and Gehrig's Larrupin' Lous*

1931: *Tour of Japan*

1934: *Tour of Japan*

Wayne Granger's 1975 Houston Astros jersey, one-year style for rear numbering

Ted Turner's creative naming conventions

Turn Back the Clock (TBC) uniforms

Turn Back the Clock (TBC) Uniform:

Uniform designed to commemorate a vintage style or a point in a team's or city's baseball history; also referred to as "throwback" or "nostalgia night" uniforms. The concept of wearing retro uniforms during major league play began with the Chicago White Sox on July 11, 1990, to commemorate the team's final season in Comiskey Park. For this game against the Milwaukee Brewers, the White Sox wore uniforms designed to look like their 1917 home apparel. Other clubs embraced the idea during the decade, and both teams donned vintage apparel

in many games. Major league clubs also wore replica uniforms of Negro Leagues or minor league teams. For their 1992 TBC game, the San Francisco Giants donned replicas of their 1942 uniforms, complete with the Hale America HEALTH patch. This event also featured the use of a mechanical scoreboard in right field and a pregame parade of 1940s automobiles. Stadium employees wore 1940s clothing, and fans who came dressed in period attire were invited to take part in the pregame parade. Major league teams now consider uniforms worn by their teams in the 1970s and 1980s to be vintage or nostalgic. Illustrative examples of the first-generation 1990s offerings include:

1990: *Chicago White Sox*
(1917 home uniforms)

1991: *Baltimore Orioles*
(1966 home uniforms)

1991: *Cincinnati Reds*
(1957 road uniforms)

1991: *Philadelphia Phillies*
(1957 home uniforms)

1991: *San Francisco Giants*
(1925 home uniforms)

1992: *Chicago Cubs*
(1948 road uniforms)

1992: *Cincinnati Reds*
(1962 road uniforms)

1992: *New York Mets*
(1962 home uniforms)

1992: *Philadelphia Phillies*
(1942 road uniforms)

1992: *Philadelphia Phillies*
(1948 home uniforms)

1992: *Pittsburgh Pirates*
(1939 home uniforms)

1992: *San Francisco Giants*
(1939 San Francisco Seals road uniforms)

Vest-style uniforms: 1956 Cincinnati Reds home, 1965 Cleveland Indians road, and 1968 Oakland A's home (left to right)

1992: *San Francisco Giants*
(1942 home uniforms)

1993: *Cincinnati Reds*
(1925 road uniforms)

1993: *Milwaukee Brewers*
(1920s road uniforms)

1993: *Philadelphia Phillies*
(1933 home uniforms)

1993: *Pittsburgh Pirates*
(1925 home uniforms)

1993: *Pittsburgh Pirates*
(1933 road uniforms)

1994: *Oakland Athletics*
(1925 Oakland Oaks home uniforms)

1994: *San Francisco Giants*
(1925 San Francisco Seals road uniforms)

1995: *Kansas City Royals*
(1947 Kansas City Monarchs road
uniforms)

1995: *Seattle Mariners*
(1947 Seattle Steelhead home uniforms)

1996: *Baltimore Orioles*
(1930s International League home
uniforms)

1996: *Milwaukee Brewers*
(1946 home uniforms)

1996: *Seattle Mariners*
(1946 Seattle Rainiers road uniforms)

1997: *Atlanta Braves*
(1912 road uniforms)

1997: *Atlanta Braves*
(1938 Atlanta Crackers home uniforms)

1997: *Boston Red Sox*
(1908 home uniforms)

1997: *Kansas City Royals*
(1977 road jerseys)

1997: *Philadelphia Phillies*
(1938 Philadelphia Stars road uniforms)

In 1998 and 1999, major league clubs
introduced "Turn Ahead the Clock
Uniforms," which featured futuristic
designs not yet envisioned or worn.

Vest: *Jersey designed without sleeves.*
Vests were introduced by the Chicago
Cubs in 1940, but the look was short-
lived. When the Cubs met the White
Sox in the 1941 postseason, the team
switched from vests to a "robin's egg blue"
road uniform of a durene-cotton-type
fabric. Cost was apparently a key factor.
According to an article in the February
11, 1943, issue of the *Sporting News*, the
vest-style uniforms "cost about $2,000

DID YOU KNOW...

The retail price for a Rawlings major league
uniform was $20 in 1936. In 1966, the price
was $56.95 and a vest-style uniform cost
$53.50. By comparison, Mickey Cochrane
was the highest-paid major league player in
1936, at $36,000, while Sandy Koufax was
baseball's top earner in 1966, at $130,000.

more per wardrobe than the orthodox uniforms." Players and fans reacted poorly to the vests as well. The Cincinnati Redlegs resurrected vests in 1956 and would wear them in some form through the 1966 season. The Pittsburgh Pirates jumped on the sleeveless bandwagon in 1957 and continued wearing them until they introduced knit uniforms in July 1970, giving the Pirates the longest reign in the shortest of sleeves (14 years). The Cleveland Indians made a run at the vest style from 1963 to 1969, incorporating a zipper closure. The Athletics (Kansas City and Oakland) wore vests from 1962 to 1971 and take home the prize for the most vest styles and colors. Baltimore

also sported a vest during portions of the 1968 and 1969 seasons. The vest returned to major league baseball in 1993, this time worn by the Cincinnati Reds (home) and the Florida Marlins (home).

Whipcord: *A worsted (compactly twisted woolen yarn made from long-staple fibers) fabric with a distinct diagonal rib.*

White Elephant: *Term used in 1902 by New York Giants manager John McGraw to describe the wild spending by Connie Mack's Philadelphia Athletics. McGraw's comment to a reporter was meant to be derogatory, but the A's defiantly adopted the term as a mascot.* By at least 1911, the A's featured the "white elephant" design on team sweaters. It appeared as a sleeve patch for the 1918–19 seasons and migrated to the left breast of the jerseys from 1920 to 1927. The design made a historic comeback on the jersey sleeves when the Philadelphia franchise relocated to Kansas City in 1955. The Kansas City A's featured it as a colorful connection to their Philadelphia lineage for the 1955 and 1960 seasons.

DID YOU KNOW...

Prior to 1907, Pittsburgh Pirates players transported their own uniforms while on the road. For the 1907 season, Pirates manager Fred Clarke ordered special trunks and had the uniforms transported from the railroad station to the clubhouse.

World Series Uniform: *Separate uniform or set of uniforms ordered for the World Series.* The New York Giants took the field for the 1905 World Series in specially ordered black uniforms. Ordering new uniforms for the World Series remained a common practice throughout the twentieth century. Because of the amount of time it takes to produce uniforms, teams often placed their orders before they knew the outcome of the pennant race. Some World Series uniforms are year-tagged to the season in question while others bear the year-tagging of the upcoming season. The Cincinnati Reds uniforms worn during the 1970 World Series are a classic example of uniforms year-tagged for the following season.

DID YOU KNOW...

The iconic interlocking *NY* that has graced the front of Yankees jerseys since 1936 was taken from an 1877 design by Tiffany & Co. for a medal given by the New York City Police Department to Officer John McDowell, one of the first NYC policemen shot in the line of duty.

"White elephant": 1960 Kansas City A's home jersey shoulder patch

"White elephant": 1950 Philadelphia A's home jersey shoulder patch

1970 Cincinnati Reds regular road uniform (top); 1971 Cincinnati Reds World Series road uniform (bottom)

Examples of supplemental tagging for year identification

The 1970 Reds regular road uniforms (Wilson products) featured "Cincinnati" arched across the chest in red-over-white twill fabric. For the World Series, the team's road uniforms featured "Cincinnati" arched across the chest in solid red fabric. This style carried over to the 1971 season, the team's last in flannel uniforms. For the 1987 World Series, the St. Louis Cardinals wore a patch to denote their participation in the World Series. The Cardinals' opponent, the Minnesota Twins, wore no such patch. The following year, both Fall Classic teams, the Los Angeles Dodgers and Oakland Athletics, sported World Series patches, a tradition that continues today.

Year Identification: *Physical annotation or tagging that identifies the year of intended issue of the jersey.* The annotation of year of issuance, either tagged or sewn, did not become common until well into the 1930s. Year annotations may be included on the set tag, embroidered into the garment, or embroidered on a swatch and affixed to the jersey. Beginning around 1959, McAuliffe began using small box tags to denote the year of issuance, a practice also employed by Spalding in the 1960s and 1970s. On a functional level, year identification is similar and complementary to the set tag or set identification. On emotional and financial levels, the impact of year identification can be significant because it can be used to place a jersey in a hallmark season for a player or team.

Zig-zag stitch

YKK: *Initials of the Japanese company that is the world's largest manufacturer of zippers.* Though not noteworthy with respect to baseball uniforms, it is important to know that the initials YKK did not appear on uniforms until the early 1960s. This chronology is key because a number of major league uniforms from the 1940s and 1950s featured zippers (Cardinals, Giants, White Sox, Dodgers, Pirates, Cubs, Nationals, Browns, Red Sox, and Braves), and these zippers were manufactured by Talon. Finding a YKK zipper in a jersey of this vintage is a sign that the original zipper has been replaced.

Zig-Zag Stitch: *Manner of application used to attach letters, numbers, logos, and patches to a jersey; the resulting stitch pattern closes the ends of the fabric being attached to the body of the jersey.*

■■■■■■■■■■■■■■■■■■■■■■■■■■■■■■■■■■

ACKNOWLEDGMENTS

Henry David Thoreau once said, "If you have built castles in the air, your work need not be lost; that is where they should be. Now put the foundations under them." This book project certainly felt like it was high in the clouds when we started building it in 2013. And we want to thank many special people for serving as the foundations of this endeavor.

First and foremost, we owe a world of gratitude to the fellow collectors and venerable institutions that have graciously allowed us access to their extraordinary collections of twentieth-century game-worn Major League Baseball uniforms. Every one of them shares our passion and devotion to these treasured relics, and without them this book would not have been possible. We are deeply grateful to Thomas Tull; the Bill DeWitt family; Paula Homan and the St. Louis Cardinals Hall of Fame and Museum; Dan Scheinman; Gary Cypres; and Jeff Idelson, Erik Strohl, Tom Shieber, and Sue Mackay at the National Baseball Hall of Fame and Museum. Their friendship and support at the genesis of this project were critical to turning dream into reality. Their kindness, hospitality, and patience during our long photo shoots are also greatly appreciated.

After securing access to this treasure trove of game-worn baseball uniforms, we needed a publisher who would help articulate our admiration for these glorious garments. More important, we wanted a team of professionals who, like Lou Gehrig and Cal Ripken, would give their all to help create and shape this book project. We found that team at Smithsonian Books. We want to thank Carolyn Gleason for believing in this project from day one and going to bat for us to procure approval to publish this book. Her friendship, guidance, and patience over the past two and a half years have been invaluable. This has been a massive project-management undertaking, and we thank Christina Wiginton, Jaime Schwender, and, in the early days of the project, Raychel Rapazza for their exceptional dedication and tireless efforts throughout the process. The editorial team of Steve Malley, Laura Harger, and Greg McNamee were exceptional, and their fine-tuning and trimming of the edges, where necessary, were impeccably done.

Finding the right images to help tell our story was not an easy task, especially since there is a Grand Canyon of images associated with baseball history. Amy Pastan came to our rescue with her seasoned eagle eye for the perfect photos. The man who helped bring all of this together so beautifully was our book designer, Stuart Rogers. And to top this all off, we are very thankful to the marketing team of Matt Litts and Leah Enser, who gave us excellent advice and guidance throughout the later stages of the project.

To do proper justice to these beautiful uniforms, we also needed a genius behind the camera lens. The challenge was to maintain visual splendor and integrity from cover to cover—after all, there are only so many ways to shoot a uniform. Photographer Francesco Sapienza magically delivered vitality, flair, and beauty to all the uniforms and complementary artifacts featured in this book. Our journey with Francesco started in July 2015 and ended, more than 350 shots later, in May 2016.

Authors are always in search of inspiration, and renowned baseball historian and writer John Thorn has been just that. His research and prose on baseball history and its artifacts have moved us in many ways. To have John write our foreword, in his typically erudite fashion, is a great honor for us, and we are deeply thankful to him.

We would also like to thank Troy Kinunen, Aaron Vold, and the MEARS Museum staff for their unfailing support throughout this project. We thank Colonel (Ret.) Lee Wimbish for his willingness to talk uniforms at the drop of a hat. And, of course, we tip our hat to Marc Okkonen for his ongoing and inspirational work on baseball uniforms.

A number of special people kindly provided help, support, and assistance during photo shoots. In particular, we want to thank Marissa Kiersch, Ted Greenberg, Sarah Brandt, Elise Yvonne Rousseau, and Eden Man of 4D Studios, and José, who graciously stayed late with us on a Saturday shoot at the Sports Museum of Los Angeles.

Last but certainly not least, we thank Jessica Friedman for all her help and support with the contractual and documentation work associated with this project.

SELECTED BIBLIOGRAPHY

Alexander, Charles C. *Breaking the Slump: Baseball in the Depression Era.* New York: Columbia University Press, 2002.

——. *John McGraw.* Lincoln: University of Nebraska Press, 1995.

Angell, Roger. *Game Time: A Baseball Companion.* Orlando, FL: Harcourt, 2003.

——. "Sprezzatura." *New Yorker*, March 3, 2015.

——. *The Summer Game.* New York: Viking, 1972.

Anton, Todd, and Bill Nowlin, eds. *When Baseball Went to War.* Chicago: Triumph Books, 2008.

Appel, Marty. *Pinstripe Empire: The New York Yankees from Before the Babe to After the Boss.* New York: Bloomsbury USA, 2012.

——. *Yesterday's Heroes: Revisiting the Old-Time Baseball Stars.* New York: William Morrow, 1988.

Bak, Richard. *Lou Gehrig: An American Classic.* New York: Taylor Trade, 1995.

Barra, Allen. *Yogi Berra: Eternal Yankee.* New York: W. W. Norton, 2010.

Baseball Magazine, 1908–1920.

Baumgarten, Linda. *What Clothes Reveal: The Language of Clothing in Colonial and Federal America.* Williamsburg, VA: Colonial Williamsburg Foundation, 2002.

Benson, Michael. *Ballparks of North America: A Comprehensive Historical Reference to Baseball Grounds, Yards and Stadiums, 1845 to Present.* Jefferson, NC: McFarland, 1989.

Bjarkman, Peter C. *Warren Spahn.* New York: Chelsea House, 1994.

Blaisdell, Lowell L. *Carl Hubbell: A Biography of the Screwball King.* Jefferson, NC: McFarland, 2010.

Bolt, Robert. *A Man for All Seasons.* London: H. M. Tennent, 1960.

Boston, Talmage. *1939: Baseball's Pivotal Year.* Fort Worth, TX: Summit Group, 1994.

Bradlee, Ben Jr. *The Kid: The Immortal Life of Ted Williams.* New York: Little, Brown, 2013.

Broeg, Bob. "The Mystery of Stan Musial." *Saturday Evening Post*, August 28, 1954.

Bryant, Howard. *The Last Hero: A Life of Henry Aaron.* New York: Pantheon Books, 2010.

Buckallew, Fritz A. *A Pitcher's Moment: Carl Hubbell and the Quest for Baseball Immortality.* Oklahoma City: Forty-Sixth Star Press, 2010.

Carroll, Jeff. *Sam Rice: A Biography of the Washington Senators Hall of Famer.* Jefferson, NC: McFarland, 2007.

Cassidy, David. *Uncertainty: The Life and Science of Werner Heisenberg.* New York: V. H. Freeman, 1991.

Clavin, Tom, and Danny Peary. *Roger Maris: Baseball's Reluctant Hero.* New York: Touchstone, 2011.

Colbert, David, ed. *Baseball: The National Pastime in Art and Literature.* Richmond: Time Life Books, 2001.

Condon, Dave. *The Go-Go Chicago White Sox.* New York: Coward-McCann, 1960.

Cook, William A. *Big Klu: The Baseball Life of Ted Kluszewski.* Jefferson, NC: McFarland, 2012.

Cramer, Richard Ben. *Joe DiMaggio: The Hero's Life.* New York: Simon & Schuster, 2000.

Creamer, Robert W. *Babe: The Legend Comes to Life.* New York: Fireside, 1974. Reprint, New York: Simon & Schuster, 1992.

——. *Baseball and Other Matters in 1941.* Lincoln, NE: Bison Books, 1991.

Dawidoff, Nicholas. *The Catcher Was a Spy: The Mysterious Life of Moe Berg.* New York: Vintage Books, 1994.

——, ed. *Baseball: A Literary Anthology.* New York: Library of America, 2002.

Deford, Frank. *The Old Ball Game: How John McGraw, Christy Mathewson and the New York Giants Created Modern Baseball.* New York: Grove Press, 2006.

Dempsey, Jack. "Why Bob Feller Is a Champion." *Liberty Magazine*, August 9, 1941.

Deveaux, Tom. *Washington Senators, 1901–1971.* Jefferson, NC: McFarland, 2005.

DeVito, Carlo. *Yogi: The Life & Times of an American Original.* Chicago: Triumph Books, 2008.

Drebinger, John. "61,808 Fans Roar Tribute to Gehrig." *New York Times*, July 5, 1939.

Ehrgott, Roberts. *Mr. Wrigley's Ball Club: Chicago and the Cubs during the Jazz Age.* Lincoln: University of Nebraska Press, 2013.

Eig, Jonathan. *Luckiest Man: The Life and Death of Lou Gehrig.* New York: Simon & Schuster, 2005.

Einstein, Charles. *Willie's Time: A Memoir.* Carbondale: Southern Illinois University Press, 2004.

Eisenberg, John. *From 33rd Street to Camden Yards: An Oral History of the Baltimore Orioles.* New York: McGraw-Hill, 2000.

Elfers, James E. *The Tour to End All Tours: The Story of Major League Baseball's 1913–1914 World Tour.* Lincoln: University of Nebraska Press, 2003.

Enders, Eric. *100 Years of the World Series*. New York: Barnes & Noble Books, 2003.

Feeney, Charley. "Roberto Collects 3,000th Hit, Dedicates It to Pirates Fans." *The Sporting News*, October 14, 1972.

Feldmann, Doug. *Dizzy and the Gashouse Gang: The 1934 St. Louis Cardinals and Depression Era Baseball*. Jefferson, NC: McFarland, 2000.

Feller, Bob, and Burton Rocks. *Bob Feller's Little Black Book of Baseball Wisdom*. New York: McGraw-Hill, 2001.

——. *Bob Feller's Little Blue Book of Baseball Wisdom*. Chicago: Triumph Books, 2009.

Fitts, Robert K. *Banzai Babe Ruth: Baseball, Espionage, & Assassination during the 1934 Tour of Japan*. Lincoln: University of Nebraska Press, 2012.

Fountain, Charles. *The Betrayal: The 1919 World Series and the Birth of Modern Baseball*. New York: Oxford University Press, 2016.

——. "George Frazier's duende." *Boston Globe*, June 12, 2011.

Freedman, Lew. *The Day All the Stars Came Out: Major League Baseball's First All-Star Game, 1933*. Jefferson, NC: McFarland, 2010.

——. *Game of My Life: Chicago Cubs: Memorable Stories of Cubs Baseball*. Champaign, IL: Sports Publishing, 2007.

Frommer, Harvey. *Rickey & Robinson: The Men Who Broke Baseball's Color Barrier*. New York: Macmillan, 1982.

Gaines, Bob. *Christy Mathewson, the Christian Gentleman: How One Man's Faith and Fastball Forever Changed Baseball*. Lanham, MD: Rowman & Littlefield, 2014.

Gazel, Neil R., "Nellie Does Right by White Sox." *Baseball Digest*, August 1951.

Gentile, Derek. *The Complete Chicago Cubs: The Total Encyclopedia of the Team*. New York: Black Dog & Leventhal, 2002.

Gershman, Michael. *Diamonds: The Evolution of the Ballpark*. New York: Houghton Mifflin, 1993.

Gibson, Bob, and Lonnie Wheeler. *Pitch by Pitch: My View of One Unforgettable Game*. New York: Flatiron Books, 2015.

——. *Stranger to the Game: The Autobiography of Bob Gibson*. New York: Penguin Books, 1994.

Goldman, Rob, and Reid Ryan. *Nolan Ryan: The Making of a Pitcher*. Chicago: Triumph Books, 2014.

Golenbock, Peter. *The Spirit of St. Louis: A History of the St. Louis Cardinals and Browns*. New York: HarperCollins, 2000.

——. *Wrigleyville: A Magical History Tour of the Chicago Cubs*. New York: St. Martin's Press, 1996.

Goodwin, Doris Kearns. *Wait Till Next Year: A Memoir*. New York: Touchstone, 1997.

Gough, David, and Jim Bard. *Little Nel: The Nellie Fox Story*. Alexandria, VA: D. L. Megbec, 2000.

Greenberg, Eric Rolfe. *The Celebrant*. Lincoln: University of Nebraska Press, 1983.

Halberstam, David. *Summer of '49*. New York: Perennial Classics, 1989.

——. *The Teammates*. New York: Hyperion, 2003.

Hawkins, Jim. *Al Kaline: The Biography of a Tigers Icon*. Chicago: Triumph Books, 2013.

Hawkins, Joel, and Terry Bertolino. *The House of David Baseball Team*. Chicago: Arcadia, 2000.

Heidenry, John. *The Gashouse Gang*. New York: Public Affairs, 2007.

Hirsch, James S. *Willie Mays: The Life, the Legend*. New York: Scribner, 2009.

Hogan, Lawrence D. *Shades of Glory: The Negro Leagues and the Story of African-American Baseball*. Washington, DC: National Geographic Society, 2006.

Honig, Donald. *Baseball When the Grass Was Real: Baseball from the Twenties to the Forties Told by the Men Who Played It*. Lincoln: University of Nebraska Press, 1975.

Hornbaker, Tim. *War on the Basepaths: The Definitive Biography of Ty Cobb*. New York: Sports Publishing, 2015.

Hyslop, Don. "Fred Lake." Society for American Baseball Research, http://sabr.org/bioproj/person/803bfe71.

Jackson, Bo. *Bo Knows Bo*. New York: Doubleday, 1990.

James, Bill. *The Bill James Historical Baseball Abstract*. New York: Villard Books, 1986.

Kahn, Roger. *The Boys of Summer*. New York: Harper & Row, 1972.

——. *The Era: 1947–1957, When the Yankees, the Giants and the Dodgers Ruled the World*. New York: Ticknor & Fields, 1993.

——. *The Head Game: Baseball Seen from the Pitcher's Mound*. San Diego: Harcourt Press, 2000.

Kansas City Star. George Brett: A Royal Hero. New York: Sports Publishing LLC, 1999.

Kaplan, Jim. *The Greatest Game Ever Pitched: Juan Marichal, Warren Spahn, and the Pitching Duel of the Century*. New York: Triumph Books, 2013.

——. *Lefty Grove: American Original*. Cleveland: Society for American Baseball Research, 2000.

Kaufman, Louis, Barbara Fitzgerald, and Tom Sewell. *Moe Berg: Athlete, Scholar, Spy*. Boston: Little, Brown, 1974.

Kennedy, Kostya. *56: Joe DiMaggio and the Last Magic Number in Sports*. New York: Sports Illustrated Books, 2012.

——. *Pete Rose: An American Dilemma*. New York: Sports Illustrated Books, 2014.

Klima, John. *Bushville Wins!: The Wild Saga of the 1957 Milwaukee Braves and the Screwballs, Sluggers, and Beer Swiggers Who Canned the New York Yankees and Changed Baseball*. New York: St. Martin's Press, 2015.

Lanctot, Neil. *The Two Lives of Roy Campanella*. New York: Simon & Schuster, 2011.

Lane, F. C. "At Coffeyville with Walter Johnson." *Baseball Magazine*, April 1915.

Lang, Jack, and Peter Simon. *The New York Mets: Twenty-Five Years of Baseball Magic*. New York: Henry Holt, 1986.

Leavy, Jane. *The Last Boy: Mickey Mantle and the End of America's Childhood*. New York: Harper Perennial, 2010.

——. *Sandy Koufax: A Lefty's Legacy*. New York: First Perennial, 2003.

Leerhsen, Charles. *Ty Cobb: A Terrible Beauty*. New York: Simon & Schuster, 2015.

Lowenfish, Lee. *Branch Rickey: Baseball's Ferocious Gentleman*. Lincoln: University of Nebraska Press, 2007.

Maaddi, Rob. *Mike Schmidt: The Phillies' Legendary Slugger*. Chicago: Triumph Books, 2010.

Mansch, Larry. "Hitting Bob Feller." *The National Pastime* 17. Cleveland: Society for American Baseball Research, 1997.

———. *Rube Marquard: The Life and Times of a Baseball Hall of Famer*. Jefferson, NC: McFarland, 1998.

Maraniss, David. *Clemente: The Passion and Grace of Baseball's Last Hero*. New York: Simon & Schuster Paperbacks, 2006.

Markusen, Bruce. *Roberto Clemente: The Great One*. Champaign, IL: Sports Publishing, 1998.

McCabe, Neal, and Constance McCabe. *Baseball's Golden Age: The Photographs of Charles M. Conlon*. New York: Harry N. Abrams, 1993.

———. *The Big Show: Charles M. Conlon's Golden Age Baseball Photographs*. New York: Harry N. Abrams, 2011.

McGee, Bob. *The Greatest Ballpark Ever: Ebbets Field and the Story of the Brooklyn Dodgers*. New York: Rivergate Books, 2005.

McNeil, William F. *Gabby Hartnett: The Life and Times of the Cubs' Greatest Catcher*. Jefferson, NC: McFarland, 2004.

Mead, William. *Low and Outside: Baseball in the Depression, 1930–1939*. Alexandria, VA: Redefinition Books, 1990.

Millikin, Mark R. *Jimmie Foxx: The Pride of Sudlersville*. Lanham, MD: Scarecrow Press, 1998.

Montville, Leigh. *The Big Bam: The Life and Times of Babe Ruth*. New York: Anchor, 2007.

———. *Ted Williams: The Biography of an American Hero*. New York: Doubleday, 2004.

Murphy, Cait. *Crazy '08: How a Cast of Cranks, Rogues, Boneheads, and Magnates Created the Greatest Year in Baseball History*. New York: Smithsonian Books, 2007.

Myers, Doug. *Essential Cubs: Chicago Cubs Facts, Feats, and Firsts—From the Batter's Box to the Bullpen to the Bleachers*. New York: McGraw-Hill, 1999.

National Baseball Hall of Fame and Museum. *Baseball as America: Seeing Ourselves through Our National Game*. Washington, DC: National Geographic Society, 2002.

Newhall, Beaumont. *The History of Photography: From 1839 to the Present*. New York: Museum of Modern Art, 1982.

New York Times. "75,000 Expected at the Stadium for Lou Gehrig Appreciation Day." July 4, 1939.

———. "Best Player Award Goes to Lou Gehrig." October 11, 1927.

Neyer, Rob, and Eddie Epstein. *Baseball Dynasties: The Greatest Teams of All Time*. New York: W. W. Norton, 2000.

Okkonen, Marc. *Baseball Uniforms of the 20th Century: The Official Major League Baseball Guide*. New York: Sterling, 1991.

Okrent, Daniel, and Harris Lewine, eds. *The Ultimate Baseball Book*. Boston: Houghton Mifflin, 1979.

Okrent, Daniel, and Steve Wulf. *Baseball Anecdotes*. New York: Harper Perennial, 1989.

Pepe, Phil. *1961*: The Inside Story of the Maris-Mantle Home Run Chase (Rough Cut)*. Chicago: Triumph Books, 2011.

Pietrusza, David, Matthew Silverman, and Michael Gershman, eds. *Baseball: The Biographical Encyclopedia*. New York: Total Sports Illustrated, 2000.

Polner, Murray. *Branch Rickey: A Biography*. New York: Atheneum, 1982.

Rader, Benjamin. *Baseball: A History of America's Game*. Chicago: University of Illinois Press, 1993.

Rains, Bob. *Cardinal Nation*. 2nd ed. St. Louis: Sporting News, 2003.

Rainy, Chris. "Earl Yingling." Society for American Baseball Research, http://sabr.org/bioproj/person/ccd1aa36.

Rampersad, Arnold. *Jackie Robinson: A Biography*. New York: Ballantine Books, 1998.

Rebello, Stephen, and Richard Allen. *Reel Art: Great Posters from the Golden Age of the Silver Screen*. New York: Artabras, 1988.

Reidenbaugh, Lowell. *The Sporting News: Take Me Out to the Ballpark*. St. Louis: The Sporting News, 1983.

Reischauer, Edwin O. "What Went Wrong?" In *Dilemmas of Growth*, edited by James William Morely. Princeton, NJ: Princeton University Press, 1971.

Ribowsky, Mark. *The Complete History of the Home Run*. New York: Citadel Press, 2003.

———. *A Complete History of the Negro Leagues 1884–1955*. New York: Birch Lane Press, 1995.

———. *Don't Look Back: Satchel Paige in the Shadows of Baseball*. New York: Simon & Schuster, 1994.

Riley, James A. *The Biographical Encyclopedia of the Negro Baseball Leagues*. New York: Carroll & Graf, 1994.

Ripken, Cal Jr., and Donald Phillips. *Get in the Game*. New York: Gotham Books, 2007.

Ritter, Lawrence. *The Glory of Their Times: The Story of the Early Days of Baseball Told by the Men Who Played It*. New York: Macmillan, 1966.

———. *Lost Ballparks: A Celebration of Baseball's Legendary Fields*. New York: Viking Press, 1992.

Robinson, Frank, and Al Silverman. *My Life Is Baseball*, 2nd ed. Garden City, NY: Doubleday, 1975.

Robinson, Frank, and Berry Stainback. *Extra Innings: The Grand Slam Response to Al Campanis's Controversial Remarks about Blacks in Baseball*. New York: McGraw-Hill, 1988.

Robinson, Ray. *Iron Horse: Lou Gehrig in His Time*. New York: W. W. Norton, 2006.

Robson, Kenneth S., ed. *A Great and Glorious Game: Baseball Writings of A. Bartlett Giamatti*. Chapel Hill, NC: Algonquin Books, 1998.

Rogers, C. Paul. "Jack Coombs." Society for American Baseball Research, http://sabr.org/bioproj/person/f64fded8.

Rogers, Phil. *Ernie Banks: Mr. Cub and the Summer of '69*. Chicago: Triumph Books, 2011.

Rosenfeld, Harvey. *Iron Man: The Cal Ripken Story*. New York: St. Martin's Press, 1995.

Rubin, Louis D. Jr., ed. *The Quotable Baseball Fanatic*. New York: Lyons Press, 2000.

Rucker, Mark. *The Brooklyn Dodgers: Images of Sports*. New York: Arcadia, 2002.

Ryhal, Gregory. "Frank Chance." Society for American Baseball Research, http://sabr.org/bioproj/person/21604876.

Schoor, Gene. *Seaver*. Chicago: Contemporary Books, 1986.

Seymour, Harold. *Baseball: The Early Years*. New York: Oxford University Press, 1960.

——. *Baseball: The Golden Age*. New York: Oxford University Press, 1971.

Shiner, David. "Johnny Evers." Society for American Baseball Research, http://sabr.org/bioproj/person/efe76f7c.

Shlaes, Amity. *The Forgotten Man: A New History of the Great Depression*. New York: Harper Perennial, 2007.

Sickles, John. *Bob Feller: Ace of the Greatest Generation*. Lincoln, NE: Potomac Books, 2005.

Silverman, Al. *Warren Spahn: Immortal Southpaw*. Sport Magazine Library 9. New York: Bartholomew House, 1961.

Simon, Tom, ed. *Deadball Stars of the National League*. Washington, DC: Brassey's, 2004.

Skipper, John C. *Charlie Gehringer: A Biography of the Hall of Fame Tigers Second Baseman*. Jefferson, NC: McFarland, 2008.

——. *Frank Robinson: A Baseball Biography*. Jefferson, NC: McFarland, 2014

Smith, Ron. *61*: The Story of Roger Maris, Mickey Mantle and One Magical Summer*. New York: McGraw-Hill/Contemporary, 2001.

——. *Baseball's 25 Greatest Moments*. St. Louis: Sporting News, 2002.

——. *Heroes of the Hall: Baseball's Greatest Players*. St. Louis: Sporting News, 2002.

Snelling, Dennis. *Johnny Evers: A Baseball Life*. Jefferson, NC: McFarland, 2014.

Sporting Life, 1900–1917.

Stang, Mark. *Baseball by the Numbers*. Lanham, MD: Scarecrow Press, 1996.

——. *Cubs Collection: 100 Years of Chicago Cubs Images*. Wilmington, OH: Orange Frazer Press, 2001.

Stevens, Bob. "Little Things Add Up to Big Plunge for Snoozing Giants." *The Sporting News*, August 17, 1960.

Stockton, J. Roy. *The Gashouse Gang and a Couple of Other Guys*. New York: A. S. Barnes, 1945.

Stout, Glenn. *Fenway 1912: The Birth of a Ballpark, a Championship Season, and Fenway's Remarkable First Year*. New York: Houghton Mifflin Harcourt, 2011.

Stout, Glenn, and Richard A. Johnson. *Yankees Century: 100 Years of New York Yankees Baseball*. New York: Houghton Mifflin, 2002.

Sullivan, Neil J. *The Diamond in the Bronx: Yankee Stadium and the Politics of New York*. New York: Oxford University Press, 2001.

Theodore, John. *Baseball's Natural: The Story of Eddie Waitkus*. Lincoln, NE: Bison Books, 2006.

Thomas, Henry W. *Walter Johnson: Baseball's Big Train*. Lincoln, NE: Bison Books, 1998.

Thorn, John. *Treasures of the Baseball Hall of Fame: The Official Companion to the Collection at Cooperstown*. New York: Villard, 1998.

——, ed. *The Armchair Book of Baseball*. New York: Galahad Books, 1985.

Thorn, John, et al. *Total Baseball: The Official Encyclopedia of Major League Baseball*. 7th ed. Kingston, NY: Total Sports, 2001.

Tierney, John P. *Jack Coombs: A Life in Baseball*. Jefferson, NC: McFarland, 2008.

Travers, Steven. *The Last Icon: Tom Seaver and His Times*. New York: Taylor Trade, 2011.

Tye, Larry. *Satchel: The Life and Times of an American Legend*. New York: Random House, 2009.

Tygiel, Jules. *Baseball's Great Experiment: Jackie Robinson and His Legacy*. New York: Oxford University Press, 1997.

Vaccaro, Mike. *The First Fall Classic: The Red Sox, the Giants, and the Cast of Players, Pugs, and Politicos Who Reinvented the World Series in 1912*. New York: Anchor Books, 2009.

Vacchianno, Ralph. "David Cone Throws a Perfect Game for Yankees on Yogi Berra Day at the Stadium in 1999." *Daily News*, July 19, 1999.

Vecchione, Joseph J., ed. *The New York Times Book of Sports Legends*. New York: Times Books, 1991.

Vecsey, George. *Baseball: A History of America's Favorite Game*. New York: Modern Library Chronicles, 2006.

——. *Stan Musial: An American Life*. New York: Ballantine Books, 2011.

Veeck, Bill, and Ed Linn. *Veeck as in Wreck: The Autobiography of Bill Veeck*. Chicago: University of Chicago Press, 1962.

Voigt, David Quentin. *Baseball: An Illustrated History*. University Park: Pennsylvania State University Press, 1987.

Wallace, Joseph, ed. *The Baseball Anthology*. New York: Harry N. Abrams, 1994.

Wancho, Joseph. "Ernie Lombardi." Society for American Baseball Research, http://sabr.org/bioproj/person/23f3d8e3.

——. "Randy Johnson." Society for American Baseball Research, http://sabr.org/bioproj/person/e905e1ef.

Ward, Geoffrey C., and Ken Burns. *Baseball: An Illustrated History*. New York: Alfred A. Knopf, 1994.

Weintraub, Robert. *The House That Ruth Built*. New York: Back Bay Books, 2011.

——. *The Victory Season: The End of World War II and the Birth of Baseball's Golden Age*. New York: Back Bay Books, 2014.

Will, George. *A Nice Little Place on the North Side: A History of Triumph, Mostly Defeat, and Incurable Hope at Wrigley Field*. New York: Three Rivers Press, 2015.

Wilson, Doug. *Brooks: The Biography of Brooks Robinson*. New York: Thomas Dunne Books, 2014.

——. *Pudge: The Biography of Carlton Fisk*. New York: Thomas Dunne Books, 2015.

Winfield, Dave. *Winfield: A Player's Life*. New York: W. W. Norton, 1988.

Zingg, Paul J. *Harry Hooper: An American Baseball Life*. Chicago: University of Illinois Press, 1993.

This book may be purchased for educational, business, or sales promotional use. For information, please write: Special Markets Department, Smithsonian Books, P.O. Box 37012, MRC 513, Washington, DC 20013

Published by Smithsonian Books
Director: Carolyn Gleason
Managing Editor: Christina Wiginton
Assistant Editor: Laura Harger
Editorial Assistant: Jaime Schwender
Art direction by Nancy Bratton and Jody Billert

Edited by Steve Malley
Designed by Rogers Eckersley Design

Library of Congress Cataloging-in-Publication Data
Wong, Stephen, author. | Grob, Dave, author. | Smithsonian Institution, issuing body.
Game worn : treasures of baseball's greatest heroes and moments / Stephen Wong and Dave Grob.
Description: Washington, DC : Smithsonian Books, 2016.
Identifiers: LCCN 2016015599 (print) | LCCN 2016025269 (ebook) | ISBN 9781588345714 (hardback) | ISBN 9781588345721
Subjects: LCSH: Baseball uniforms—United States—History. | Baseball uniforms—United States—History—Pictorial works. | Baseball—Collectibles—United States. | Baseball—Collectibles—United States—Pictorial works. | Smithsonian Institution. | BISAC: SPORTS & RECREATION / Baseball / History. | ANTIQUES & COLLECTIBLES / Sports Cards / Baseball. | SPORTS & RECREATION / Baseball / General.
Classification: LCC GV879.7 .W66 2016 (print) | LCC GV879.7 (ebook) | DDC 796.357028/4—dc23
LC record available at https://lccn.loc.gov/2016015599

Manufactured in China, not at government expense.
20 19 18 17 16   5 4 3 2 1

Unless otherwise noted below, all images were provided by Francesco Sapienza.

Key: top (*t*), bottom (*b*), left (*l*), right (*r*)

John Andreozzi: 45, 134, 175. **Atlanta Braves**: 306 *l*. **Boston Public Library**: 128: Courtesy of the Boston Public Library, Leslie Jones Collection. **Getty**: 54, 124, 130: Photos by Mark Rucker/Transcendental Graphics, Getty Images; 93, 115, 146, 169 *b*, 178, 188, 232–33: Bettman/Getty Images; 95, 100: Photos by Sporting News and Rogers Photo Archive via Getty Images; 106–7: AFP/Getty Images; 113, 207: Photos by Rogers Photo Archive/Getty Images; 140–41: *NY Daily News* Archive via Getty Images; 154: Kidwiler Collection/Diamond Images/Getty Images; 161: Photo by Leroy Jakob/*NY Daily News* Archive via Getty Images; 162, 225: Photos by Stanley Weston/Getty Images; 189, 200: Photos by Walter Iooss Jr./*Sports Illustrated*/Getty Images; 210, 217, 236, 240, 252: Photos by Focus on Sport/Getty Images; 244, 259: Photos by Rich Pilling/MLB Photos via Getty Images; 250: Photo by George Gojkovich/Getty Images; 256: Photo by Tom G. Lynn/Time Life Pictures/Getty Images; 258: G. N. Lowrance/Getty Images; 260: Doug Pensinger/Allsport/Getty Images; 273 *bl*: Photo by John Iacono/*Sports Illustrated*/Getty Images. **John F. Kennedy Presidential Library and Museum**: 186–87: Robert Knudsen. White House Photographs. John F. Kennedy Presidential Library and Museum, Boston. **Library of Congress**: 20, 32, 64, 301 *t*: Bain News Services, Library of Congress; 269: Photo by Marvin E. Newman, *Look Magazine*, Library of Congress. **Eden Man, 4D Studios**: 12–13, 26–27, 49, 119, 157, 181, 184. **National Archives**: 133 *t*: National Archives photo no. 12009098, Department of Defense, Department of the Army, Office of the Deputy Chief of Staff for Operations, U.S. Army Audiovisual Center, ca. 1974–5/15/1984. **National Baseball Hall of Fame Library, Cooperstown, NY**: 37, 75, 136, 138, 142, 176, 182, 199, 228, 273 *br*. **News Syndication**: 72–73. **Thomas Ng:** 7. **Jaime Schwender**: 127.

For permission to reproduce illustrations appearing in this book, please correspond directly with the owners of the works, as seen above. Smithsonian Books does not retain reproduction rights for these images individually or maintain a file of addresses for sources.